MASTERING
THE ART
OF
PSYCHOTHERAPY

MASTERING
THE ART
OF
PSYCHOTHERAPY

The Principles
of Effective Psychological Change:
Challenging the Boundaries of Self-Expression

WILLIAM F. SYMES,
MDIV, LPC

GREEN WRITERS PRESS *Brattleboro, Vermont*

Printed in the United States

10 9 8 7 6 5 4 3 2 1

Green Writers Press is a Vermont-based publisher whose mission is to spread
a message of hope and renewal through the words and images we publish.
Throughout we will adhere to our commitment to preserving and protecting
the natural resources of the earth. To that end, a percentage of our proceeds
will be donated to environmental activist groups like 350.org. Green Writers
Press gratefully acknowledges support from individual donors, friends, and
readers to help support the environment and our publishing initiative.

Giving Voice to Writers & Artists Who Will Make the World a Better Place
Green Writers Press | Brattleboro, Vermont
www.greenwriterspress.com

ISBN: 978-09961357-5-7

The Mandala was created by Donna Van Renselaar.

For more information and resources, visit the author's website:

www.emotionalinsight.com.

Typeset by Dede Cummings in Dante.

PRINTED ON PAPER WITH PULP THAT COMES FROM FSC-CERTIFIED FORESTS, MANAGED FORESTS
THAT GUARANTEE RESPONSIBLE ENVIRONMENTAL, SOCIAL, AND ECONOMIC PRACTICES BY
LIGHTNING SOURCE ALL WOOD PRODUCT COMPONENTS USED IN BLACK & WHITE, STANDARD
COLOR, OR SELECT COLOR PAPERBACK BOOKS, UTILIZING EITHER CREAM OR WHITE BOOKBLOCK
PAPER, THAT ARE MANUFACTURED IN THE LAVERGNE, TENNESSEE PRODUCTION CENTER
ARE SUSTAINABLE FORESTRY INITIATIVE® (SFI®) CERTIFIED SOURCING.

CONTENTS

CONTENTS

DETAILED TABLE OF CONTENTS

CONTENTS

PREFACE:
A Psychological Super-System:
Expressive Psychodynamics

MOST SCIENTIFIC disciplines develop their own version of the grand unified theory as part of a structured super-system to explain all of the dynamics and phenomena of their field. As a science still in its infancy, psychology has yet to develop such a super-system, although some of the significant elements of such a theory currently exist. Our challenge as clinicians, and perhaps as students of awareness, is to differentiate between those theories and methods that make up the elements of the periodic table of psychology and those theories and methods that are simply the bricks and mortar that house that periodic table. This book is an attempt to assemble a super-system of psychological principles that will enable anyone to understand and apply effective methods for psychological evolution.

The fundamental obstacle to psychological health is self-expression: psychological suffering is an expressive disorder. Our personality, or perhaps more specifically, our personality structure, restricts and shapes self-expression in our quest for social approval and social safety, and as a result, we all suffer the consequences of blunted self-expression. However, the difference between mild, moderate, and severe pathology (a fixed point of view and fixed self-expression) is the percentage of the psyche that is being restricted by the personality structure. This varies from person to person, with some people suffering from small distortions in perception and small obstructions in self-expression to those with extreme perceptual and expressive challenges, enduring the corresponding symptomology.

Most of our psychological suffering is the result of an adversarial approach to our own unconscious, the contents of which are crucial for an accurate view of the world, an appropriate response to the world, and our overall energy levels.

Regarding our engagement with our unconscious, I am reminded of a well-worn joke: A man walking down a darkened street comes upon a stranger furiously searching for something under a street lamp. Upon inquiry, it becomes clear that the fellow has lost his keys. The man decides to help, and after a stretch of futile searching, asks the stranger where he remembers last having the keys. The stranger points down a darkened alley nearby and says, "Oh, I lost them down that dark alley over there, but the light is so much better here."

Of course, the answer to this dilemma, as well as our own, is not to search in the dark, but to illuminate the darkness.

We tend to resist exploring the shadowy territory of our unconscious either as a result of unfamiliarity with the psychological geography or a denial of, and dissociation from, what we are seeing. In truth, it's not really dark. We have our eyes closed.

In either case, the psychological symptoms that irritate us and are fueled by the restricted contents of the unconscious point to a dynamism within the unconscious that seems intent on making unconscious contents conscious.

It is difficult to determine if this drive to integrate consciousness is somehow a feature of the physics of the material world or the physics of awareness itself. The material world does not always seem to work for the benefit of the human organism, as it provides advantages to other organic life who compete with our viability. Given this, I would conclude that the drive to achieve integration, wholeness, and individuation (mastering one's psychological design) is an aspect of awareness, which then applies its will to the material world. In this scenario, awareness would function as an independent, or perhaps, interdependent and *interconnected* agent, potentially the source of all life in the universe.

What evidence exists to indicate that we are psychically connected to each other? I would argue that the illusion of separateness is an aspect of the physical world, and once one identifies the activities of the "ocean of awareness" (to use Buddhist vocabulary), it is difficult not to recognize its influence. Dr. Leonard Shlain, in his marvelous book, *Art and Physics: Parallel Visions in Time, Space, and Light*, observed that the disciplines of art and physics share a marvelous synchronicity. As cutting-edge physicists challenged longstanding assumptions about the cosmos, cutting-edge artists were simultaneously and independently illustrating those new realizations. How could Picasso be inspired to illustrate the unfolding of the universe as one approached the speed of light? Or how is it that physics suddenly provides a theory and a language to understand Picasso's works? The shared simultaneity within these unique disciplines suggests that these challenging new insights were "forcing" themselves into the collective consciousness. It is as if, at the level of awareness, there is one thought and two responses: physics and art. In truth, if consciousness is actually *shared*, then this pulse from the unconscious should eventually be registered in every discipline and in every culture. It is simply a matter of identifying the way in which this "quantum" consciousness manifests. This relationship between art and physics is simply a template for examining how the unconscious exerts its will universally.

These influences, some to our benefit and some to our destruction, affect everything that is aware. Whereas subtle or complex ideas are only shared by a few, the baser attitudes are shared by many. We see the spectrum throughout human history, from the think-tank experiments in which a few brilliant, dedicated people open their minds to consider potentials greater than that which any one of them could consider independently, to the horrifying group dynamics of the Nazis in which the lowest common denominator of morality ruled the judgment of the masses. Awareness is interconnected with all that is alive, and humanity is affected by the rising and falling of these emotional tides. Awareness is not passive. In fact, it is the force behind evolution.

The dynamics of awareness are certainly essential elements in a psychological periodic table, as is the mechanism (personality) that serves as an interface between awareness and the physical universe. Step by step, psychological thinkers, researchers, and clinicians are building a body of knowledge that will eventually lead to a psychological super-system in which the structure and dynamics of the psyche (awareness, physical body, personality, and the unconscious) will be as clearly understood as auto-mechanics (or at least quantum physics).

This book is my attempt to narrow the complexity of human behavior into those key components that define the fundamental dynamics of consciousness and psychological evolution.

*Structural secret: There are more than twenty-five pages of italicized paragraphs sprinkled throughout this book. Each one of these paragraphs presents a core idea intimately associated the specific chapter, as well as with the broader view of this book. For a super-quick read, the italicized paragraphs represent the fundamental architecture and content of this psychological system.

ACKNOWLEDGMENTS

I WANT to thank my life partner and wife, Dr. Patsy Watkins, for her love, unfailing support, enthusiasm, and conviction that I was capable of producing this book.

I wish to thank my editor, Gabrielle Idlet, who conspired with me to think boldly, and whose skill in editing clarified my intent. It was my privilege to work with such a talented professional.

I am extremely grateful to my book agent and publisher, Dede Cummings, for taking a leap of faith and believing in my book. (And thanks to my dear friend Crescent Dragonwagon, for the introduction.)

I want to thank my "crew," those significant mental health professionals who demanded that I produce this book and who were willing to read and give feedback during the process: Yolanda Nally, Stacey Bailey, Josh Newman, and Holly Knox. In particular, I would like to doubly thank Yolanda Nally, LCSW, for documenting our conversations, for her insightful interviews, and for insisting that this book be written—without her there would be no book.

I would like to thank Ed White, M.D., my psychiatric partner and college roommate, for all of the think-tank moments in our shared practice. There is no greater practitioner of "crazy wisdom" than the good doctor and I cherish those memories of our discussions on the nature of consciousness and spiritual awareness.

I would like to thank my dear friends and spiritual conspirators, Dr. Charles and Ramona McNeal. Their generosity, kindness, love, and brilliance have helped nurture and sustain me these past three decades.

I would like to thank Conrad Sommer, MD, my supervisor at the Gestalt Institute of St. Louis, who exploded the boundaries of the therapeutic relationship. Conrad brilliantly conveyed sanity to all who shared his space.

I wish to thank my father, William Finley Symes Sr., for the profound gift of curiosity, and my mother, Gene Dickson Symes, for the gift of music.

I would like to show my greatest appreciation to Rev. Robert D. Mutton, my first and most significant clinical supervisor. Bob's vision of community, service, and compassion are without peer in my experience. I am proud to call him mentor, colleague, and friend.

And finally, I would like to thank my clients, who taught me everything. I offer my deepest gratitude to those loving and wonderful people who have shared their lives and life journeys with me over the years, amazing me with their suffering, honesty, humor, and courage.

Dedicated to:

REV. ROBERT D. MUTTON

Without whom this would not be possible

Section One:

THE FUNDAMENTALS

The View

Structure of the Psyche

Personality Structure

Trauma Dynamics

Psychodynamics

The Architecture of Attitude

The Rules

CHAPTER ONE
THE VIEW

WHAT IF?

What if every aspect of who you are and who you are designed to be is actually built into your psychological structure at birth and waiting for activation? What if self-image and self-worth are directly linked to self-expression? What if the most joyous moment of your life is actually your normal state of mind?

Jungian psychology proposes that everyone has access to a deeper level of psychological completion within the unconscious, called the Self, which acts as an organizational structure for the collective unconscious. Jung proposes two levels of the unconscious: the personal unconscious, which compensates for the excesses of personality, and the collective unconscious, which contains the psychological potential of humanity. The Self is the structural organization of the collective unconscious. Personality is essentially a distorted mirror of the Self.

- The Self organizes the full psychological potential of a human being.

- The Self responds to reality accurately and directly without distortion or delay.
- The Self is the energetic resource for the human psyche.
- The Self brings the excesses of personality into balance.
- The Self is the author of our psychological growth.
- The Self is the interconnection between all forms of awareness.

The stages of development that every child experiences either activate or repress the influence of the Self. The parts of our psyche that work well (creativity, expression, insight) need only natural growth and expansion to reach their design potential. These parts of the psyche have been encouraged and nurtured as a child matures, and as such, serve as bridges to the Self: brilliance without editing. The parts of the psyche that are dysfunctional and symptomatic (anxiety, tension, stress, guilt, shame, fear, resentment) result from inconsistent parenting and cultural rigidity at best and gross physical discipline and psychological and emotional abuse at worst. As the child experiments with the world, gathering data, interpreting experience, and practicing emotional responses (building an inventory of experiences), the personality structure is born out of the conditioning by the environment. It is our personalities that regulate access to and expression of this deeper psychological capacity. Personality is the guardian at the gates of perception and self-expression.

When personality is too rigid, it is a brutal dictator that distorts our perception of reality, inhibits self-expression, and produces massive symptomatic shifts of self-image, self-worth, and energy levels.

Many in the medical community today, as well as the founding psychoanalysts, believe that the human being is purely a biological system. They contend that awareness itself is created as the byproduct of a complex biological system. In this theory, the personality structure either helps or hinders the optimal functioning that the body requires and all psychological symptoms are the expressions of distress when the body's functions are limited or blocked from timely expression: the stronger the block, the more significant the symptoms.

In the early 1900s, Carl Jung, the noted Swiss psychiatrist and colleague of Sigmund Freud, proposed that there are two systems at play in human beings: the biological system and the psychological system, each with its own expressive goal. Jung accepted Freud's description of the biological system but not his perception of the origination of awareness. For Jung, the psychological system is as complicated as the biological system and has expressive and evolutionary goals of its own. Jung outlined the *psychodynamic* structure of the personality as having three contributing components: the influencing neural-emotional complexes, compensatory function of the unconscious, and deeper wells of the collective wisdom available through the Self. The Jungian perspective posits two separate and interdependent systems influencing the experience of life and living; the same rules and consequences of expression and repression that apply to the body apply to the psyche as well.

The psyche, like the body, is not a passive system that tolerates restriction without consequences. In the biological system, holding your breath causes painful symptoms to arise fairly quickly. In the psychological system, holding back anger or sadness or sexual expression can immediately create a variety of symptoms that cause suffering and inappropriate or even self-destructive behavior.

The personality is the psychological mechanism that determines one's level of expression and the amount of sublimation, repression, or dissociation. As such, the personality is not only a guardian designed to protect the individual against punishment, but it is also a censor that restricts self-expression in order to meet the moral and ethical rules of social conformity. That restriction substitutes suffering for emotional expression.

The fundamental idea shared by many cultures throughout the world is that human beings are flawed, with corrupt desires, feelings, and thoughts that must be continually guarded against lest they lead to immoral or unethical behavior. Thus we begin the first part of our psychological journey in the quest for perfection, usually based on the approval and training of others. But what if human beings are not inherently corrupt, and it is actually this attempt to correct the "flaws" of humanity by family, society, and religious institutions that does the damage to our self-image and self-expression? What if the problem is that we perceive flaws where there is perfection?

So here we have the child, freshly entered into the world and spontaneously interacting with all the characters of his universe. The immediate lesson the child learns is that certain emotional expressions produce pleasurable experiences, and other emotional expressions produce painful experiences. His personality and nervous system are quick to adopt the expressions that produce pleasure and begin the systematic repression/restriction/avoidance of expressions that trigger pain. He learns the rules of inhibiting emotional expression from the significant people and circumstances in his life with the mother or primary caretaker having the most significance in the development of personality structure.

The emotional expression or repression that we learn ultimately has energetic consequences. Limiting ourselves to behaviors that seek the approval of the people around us produces a highly symptomatic personality structure. Seeking approval is simply using one's ability to meet the needs of others in order to play it safe, but this occurs at the expense of living a full life. Approval-seeking behavior, in most cases, requires strategic repression of specific emotions, and repressing emotions creates psychological and psychosomatic symptoms. Ego/personality is simply the mechanism that redirects self-expression into the other behaviors or symptoms that the people around us find more acceptable to their own self-concerned agendas.

Throughout childhood we learn to tolerate the stress this compromise produces. We come to believe that stress is normal, and although unfortunate, stress is better than the punitive consequences a more genuine response would trigger. In simpler terms, who wants to get punished for saying what he or she really feels or thinks? So we keep our responses to ourselves and tolerate the tension and stress resulting from that repression.

OUR NATURAL ALLY

But what if nature herself wants us to be conscious and provides opportunities to correct this blunted expression? Could it be that our "designer" (however one wishes to interpret that concept) intended for us to be conscious in order to fulfill our design destiny or purpose? And might each moment simply be an opportunity for genuine, authentic, and honest self-expression?

Instead of settling for a personality structure that mitigates and redirects emotional expression into symptoms, we can begin to build bridges to the Self, accessing the deeper psychological gifts of spontaneity, wisdom, energetic motivation, creativity, insight, and service.

Throughout our lives, we build an inventory of experiences that remain in our memories as significant. Falling in love, spiritual transformations, stunning encounters with nature, amazing conversations, powerful dreams, sacred places, significant coincidences, drug experiences, insights, and meetings with remarkable people all contain a shared aspect: these events *feel* energetic. They have an energetic impact and leave their fingerprints on our nervous system in the form of strong emotion, a sense of place and purpose, a timeless quality, and interconnectedness. Our descriptions of these charged experiences may vary; terms like *amazing, stunning, beautiful, spiritual, connected, loving, timeless, acceptance, forgiveness, presence of God, purpose, mercy, startling, thrilling, peaceful, clear,* and *insight* are widely shared. The single most common element of each of these encounters is their energetic sensation.

What if these high-energy experiences are not those rare moments—few and far between in our lives where we feel most alive— but rather, our normal state of mind? Practical experience, however, points out that these are not everyday experiences, and that they are, unfortunately, rare for many people. But what if the problem is that we have come to expect less of our lives, that we actually defend our suffering as normal and accept disappointment and frustration? What if we have been taught to expect less, tolerate more, not complain, and not express our discontent? In truth, we have been taught and believe in a world-view that insists we are inherently flawed and need to continually correct those damaged aspects of ourselves, that emotional freedom of expression will hurt or wound those around us. What if living a highly energized, joyous, and satisfying life is possible and we have settled for less?

There are few quotes that better symbolize our challenge of living fully than author Marianne Williamson's challenge to courage.

"Our deepest fear is not that we are inadequate. Our deepest fear is that we are powerful beyond measure. It is our light, not our darkness that most frightens us. We ask ourselves, who am I to be brilliant, gorgeous, talented, fabulous? Actually, who are you not to be? You are a child of God. Your playing small does not serve the world. There is nothing enlightened about shrinking so that other people won't feel insecure around you. We are all meant to shine, as children do. We were born to make manifest the glory of God that is within us. It's not just in some of us; it's in everyone. And as we let our own light shine, we unconsciously give other people permission to do the same. As we are liberated from our own fear, our presence automatically liberates others."

—Marianne Williamson, *A Return to Love: Reflections on the Principles of A Course in Miracles*

So, why are some experiences so energetic while others feel so toxic and depressing? The answer: it is our *response* to those situations that makes them energetic or not; the situation itself only provides the opportunity for us to let go and feel our energetic response to the world. And those other situations and people that trigger feelings of anxiety, depression, or dread are actually the result of our not fully expressing ourselves in the moment, of holding back. Even though we want to give credit to people, circumstances, or environmental factors for producing a positive or negative experience, it is in fact our response to these factors that determines the overall quality and energy of our experience. My conclusions are as follows:

1. Psychological energy is in proportion to self-expression.
2. Self-worth is in proportion to our psychological energy levels.
3. Self-worth is in proportion to self-expression.

You know the formula: if A equals B, and B equals C, then A equals C.

THE FEAR AND THE TWO OBSTACLES

Most people reasonably fear the consequences of open and unrestricted self-expression. The *first* obstacle to embracing genuine, honest and immediate self-expression is overcoming our fear of the *consequences* of being openly expressive. What would actually happen if we went around saying whatever we feel and think and doing whatever we are motivated to do in the moment? Experience tells us that there are certain feelings best left unexpressed, even if they bother us. We rationalize our fear of the punitive consequences of free expression and learn to live a moderately depressed life, safe, but suffering.

The *second* obstacle is more philosophical or theological: Are we inherently moral and good beings, or are we, deep down, self-indulgent animals controlled by a thin layer of social appropriateness? Obviously, if you believe that we are inherently corrupt, the philosophy of self-expression would seem morally inappropriate.

What I have found is that people who are actually destructive or anti-social don't ever hold back, and it is only the compassionate people, concerned with the wellbeing of others, who are self-restricted. It's not that holding back makes us good and uninhibited expression makes us corrupt; it's that good people don't trust their inherent goodness, and by holding back they limit their ability to shape the world for the better. By inhibiting self-expression, our energy and positive influence on the community are compromised. Meanwhile, the truly mean-spirited, self-indulgent anti-socials operate with complete lack of restriction and with complete access to their energetic reserves, to the detriment of society. The challenge of self-expression is really a challenge for the people with true morality and ethics to find their voices and confront and corral the insidious behavior of those who serve the forces of destruction.

So, how do we wake up and claim the deeper energetic reserves of our true Self? There are three essential qualities that we need for personal transformation: *curiosity, courage,* and *commitment*.

Curiosity is needed to discover who we really are and to tap the resources of the unconscious. Without curiosity, we simply lack the motivation to awaken our true nature. The part of our psyche controlled by the ego/personality is in reality a fearful, jealous, resentful, and anxious representation of a truly glorious, creative, spontaneous, and insightful deeper Self. Curiosity is required to proceed on the journey of self-discovery.

Courage is needed to develop the strength and voice that no longer bows to external approval but celebrates the energetic and wise nature of the Self. Without courage, we will shrink from the formidable task of confronting those threats we have suffered throughout our lives. Without courage, we only experience resistance, suffering, and the relentless pressure of the symptoms of our emotional blockages. Courage is the willingness to stand for a deeper moral conviction. Courage is the inner sense of purpose and strength that allows us, in spite of the odds against our voices being heard, to try to represent that growing inner voice authentically. Courage is an aspect of wisdom that helps us differentiate between the pressure of conformity and our duty to the community. Courage is always in service to the greater good.

Commitment is the development of healthy discipline. Without commitment, there is no follow-through, regardless of whether we are prepared or motivated. Commitment is the dedication to the process of awakening. It is the consistent action of expression and experimentation necessary to stabilize emotional chaos, challenge the limits of self-expression, and begin to tackle the formidable task of transforming our world.

The Five Challenges of Waking the Mind

The individual who seriously wants to grow psychologically faces five challenges in order to make progress.

The first challenge of waking the mind is to embrace *hope*: that personal suffering can be resolved and not just accepted. There is a difference between actual *hardship* (the challenges of life, love, and relationship) and the *psychological suffering* that occurs because we:

- agree to a distorted view of the world;
- make repeated errors in judgment;
- encourage predators to feast at our table;
- make excuses for those who persecute and abuse us in the name of love, loyalty, family, and financial security.

These represent the suffering of ego and the false self and the worshiping of the gods of approval.

The second challenge of the waking mind, and certainly the most daunting, is *suffering*: the realization of how much suffering is in the world. Because our fundamental narcissism leads us to take things personally, the awakening sense of suffering in the world is brutal and often temporarily creates a sense of despair. We ask ourselves, "How can I (little me) possibly deal with all this pain?" This despair arises from the limited perception that we are in this life by ourselves. We lack conviction that we are an integral and intimate part of a larger energetic and moral structure and thus still identify with the small ego's perspective of individuality and isolation. This is the view of the child: I have no help; I am tiny and lack power. The truth is that there is an ever-expanding network of people working to transform the world to a higher state of consciousness, and that in spite of the chaos and random violence that certainly exists, there is practical and effective work to be done that will actively move the world community forward. We are not alone. This second challenge is particularly difficult because it raises the issue of interdependence, which leads to the third challenge.

The third challenge of waking mind is *intimacy*: learning that the world acts as a feedback loop that helps guide us in a direction of fulfillment and purpose. Initially, the world appears to be adversarial and threatening; however, as we begin to express ourselves in a more dynamic and direct manner, threatening elements begin to lose their influence over us and we start experiencing a sense of spaciousness and satisfaction in self-determination. Once we begin to recognize that there is a not-so-subtle energetic reward for harmonizing with both our deeper Self and the world, we begin to cooperate with those energetic sources (the rhythms of the world, *feng shui*, *I Ching*) and abandon the small rewards of safety and approval that are mediated through the ego. We develop a deep appreciation and even love for the world; we realize that the world is actually interacting and providing us with the resources to fulfill our path. The energetic attractors of the world seem to be specific to each person's psychological and biological design; thus, the more bravely we attend to the energetic rewards of our personal path, the more the challenges of the path make sense and support our continued pursuit of meaning and purpose in our life. We slowly abandon our attachment to the philosophy of free will and start to actively and aggressively harmonize with those energetic influencing elements in our life. This sense of intimacy immediately leads to a deeper experience of psychological design and purpose.

The fourth challenge of the waking mind is *purpose*: embracing one's psychological design in life. Although almost everyone has the capacity to perform a variety of tasks in this life, embracing and honoring one's design and following the life-path that provides the highest level of energetic satisfaction are among the great challenges of being human. The fourth challenge speaks to a confidence and recognition that each person has purpose and that we are fortunate indeed to discover our deeper design and to fulfill our design destiny. Service to the greater community of life, humanity, and nature is essential to the fulfillment of one's deeper purpose. The Buddhists approach this step as a commitment to compassion and the cessation of the suffering of all sentient beings. But even beyond the moral aspect of this commitment is the more practical and dynamic purpose of accessing the energy of the world community, which leads to the fifth challenge.

The fifth challenge of the waking mind is *energy*: accessing our greater energetic resources and the recognition that service to the world gives consciousness access to a much larger energetic resource. This is a much more subtle challenge in that, without a commitment to an energetic experience, it is difficult to effectively differentiate the energetic potentials of our life choices. If all paths look equal, how can we choose the right path for ourselves? As psychological energy rises, our potentialities begin to differentiate between the higher and lower avenues of self-expression. Part of the challenge of accessing our energetic potential is in recognizing and engaging with larger energetic resources.

In the same way that healthy food, air, water, and environmental safety simply sustain a more energetic body and provide awareness with the energetic potential of one's physical dynamism, the greater energetic resources of the unconscious are directly linked to our relationship with the life force of the human, plant, and animal kingdoms. Without appropriate respect for this essential life force in its myriad forms, our personal energy resources are limited to those social communities with which we identify and from which we actively seek approval. At one fundamental level, it is a question of whom or what we serve. To those who serve the greater good—the healing archetype— the energy we access is in proportion to the service we render.

THE SYMPTOM PROFILE

Throughout this book, I will use the term *symptom profile* as a reference to the set of emotional symptoms that we each manifest as a result of our personality function, which converts emotions into symptoms through three mechanisms: sublimation, repression, and dissociation. For the purposes of this book, I identify eleven major blocked emotional symptoms: *anxiety, tension, stress, guilt, shame, fear, resentment, depression, worry, grief,* and *somatization.* These are symptoms, *not* emotions. Each person has a somewhat unique set of predictable and repeated symptoms that reflect the over-regulation of emotional expression based on the family and social systems by which we were behaviorally shaped in childhood. Most personality-created symptoms are the "acceptable" substitute for emotional honesty, and every family encourages the child to exact this substitution as a convenience to the family pathology. The symptom is not the problem, but it certainly is illustrative of the underlying expressive problem that is contributing to the emotional suffering the client is bringing to therapy. The presence of any of the eleven major psychological symptoms—anxiety, tension, stress, guilt, shame, fear, resentment, depression, worry, grief, and somatization—indicate the presence of an overly restrictive personality structure.

A psychological symptom is the simple substitution for a blocked emotion. The particular symptom profile that we each manifest is predicated on our family and society's support of those symptoms at the expense of the insight and creativity that attend authentic and accurate emotional expression.

Psychological growth requires an important insight into differentiating between feelings, symptoms, and emotions. Although everything we "feel" could be considered an emotion, emotions actually serve very specific functions; they provide information about the world and express our response to that information. In this book's psychodynamic system there are four basic emotions: thought, sadness, anger, and sexuality, and there are five stages of perception through which awareness evolves from unconscious to consciousness: symptom, dream, fantasy, emotion, and insight. (See chapter 2: "Structure of the Psyche," *Reality and The Five Stages of Perception.*)

Personality is different from awareness in that awareness uses personality to engage the world strategically. Personality is how you present yourself in a unique way, whereas awareness is the actual core and truth of who you are and your connection with all that is alive. *You don't have awareness; you are awareness.* However, you have a personality, one that has been shaped by the influences of your family, environment, culture, and gender.

The personality structure is fundamentally an energy, emotion, and information regulating system and has been trained to recognize, interpret, and respond to the phenomena of the world.

Based on the thresholds of perception and expression, personality distinguishes between what is known, what is felt as an emotion, and what is felt as a symptom. When you are hungry, your personality determines whether you feel hunger or whether you feel a pain in your stomach; personality then translates that feeling into knowing what and where you want to eat, or more dramatically, what type of eating disorder you are developing.

Understanding the link between fear, repression, symptomology, energy, and physical health is core to the success of therapy and necessary for any significant psychological growth.

Although the goal of many therapies is to change the symptom profile, no long-term effective personality change occurs without confronting the fears and consequences of emotional expression.

Each emotion has its own particular signature: sadness, anger, pleasure, and thought. However, emotion is but one step in a series that should lead to accuracy of perception (insight) and immediacy of expression (creativity). Psychodynamically, emotion is a transitional stage between experience and knowledge and is, specifically, partially repressed information. Information only registers as feeling when the personality resists the information or is unfamiliar with the experience.

Throughout this book, I will explore the idea that restricted emotional expression is at the core of all psychological suffering. Our personality symptom profile is simply a combination of any of the eleven major symptoms, which are the outward signs of repressed emotions. Too often, these symptoms are treated as emotions and are addressed in therapy as such.

Everyone is brought to a psychological crossroads by the symptoms of suffering that can no longer be ignored. The *Diagnostic and Statistical Manual of Mental Disorders* (DSM-V) is the codebook of the mental health industry and is filled with symptoms and patterns of symptoms, both psychological and biochemical. But remember: symptoms are not emotions and emotions are not symptoms. Unfortunately, many types of psychological treatments are based on symptom relief. This does make sense, but is really a rather shallow and inaccurate way of determining success of treatment. Symptoms are merely the indirect expression of emotions. And the intensity of the symptoms is directly in proportion to the strength of the blocked emotion. In an odd sort of twist, the symptom is actually not the problem. This brings us to a significant psychological rule: The symptom is not the problem; the symptom is the solution to the problem. Why? Because the symptom releases the pent-up pressure of emotional restriction. The unconscious is continually pressuring personality to release both the contents of restricted emotional expression as well as its creative potential. Not expressing one's emotional tension produces symptoms of suffering. The unconscious continually pressures the personality to develop a less restrictive perceptive/expressive structure. All of the emotional responses that personality restricts and relegates to the unconscious remain charged, awaiting opportunity for release, and until that moment, these charged emotions are transformed into symptoms. Ultimately, these symptoms and the repressed feelings that they represent need to be reframed as information about the world and expressed in the fullness of their response. After all, we are just trying to understand the nature of the world and our place in it.

EMOTIONS: A GENERAL OVERVIEW

Much has been written about feelings, emotions, and their qualities, intensities, originations, purpose, and pathology. It is important to make this differentiation: all feelings are not emotions, but all emotions start as feelings. One of the basic capacities of the body is feeling. Fundamentally, feelings are the physical, bio-chemical reactions to external stimuli. Feeling is information about physical function, biological information, external information, and the overall well-being of the body and its relationship to reality. Emotions are a complex and specific subset of feeling. In this book's psychological system theory, emotions are the result of complex neural networks associated with specific areas of the body. Emotion is the specific *set of feelings* associated with each of these specific neural-emotional systems of the body: head, respiratory, digestive, and reproductive.

We all know how emotions feel, but when we begin to examine the mechanism and purpose of emotions, things become a bit more complex. We all know what sadness or anger looks and feels like. And we also recognize that we do not all have identical emotional responses to every situation. What triggers aggression in some triggers fear or laughter or crying in others. What is sexually appealing to some is offensive to others. What is a simple worry to some is an obsession to others. What is sadness to some is depression to others. We certainly experience emotions the same way, but the intensity, meaning, and expression vary significantly from person to person. Culture, gender, family, and social values affect the manner in which we experience and express our emotions. Laughter, crying, and anger all have unique and often humorous expressive variations. Anger can be experienced in intensity varying from mild frustration to homicidal rage. There is clearly a spectrum of intensity in emotional potential. Emotional attraction to others can vary between boredom and a mild interest to strong infatuation, adoration, and even obsession. The mutual attraction between two people seems to be predicated on some specific emotional attractor that is not shared by everyone. This is why we are not equally attracted to the same people.

Emotions that are praised in certain situations are condemned in others. Aggression in sports is generally encouraged up to the point where the rules define controlled behavior. For some athletes, this can present a problem. In 2011, the NFL introduced new limitations on the types of hits that players can deliver to their opponents. The evidence of long-term damage due to concussions led the league to restrict the type and intensity of certain tackles. Some players objected to this limitation, and the league began to fine and suspend offending players.

The consequences eventually began to prove effective in limiting dangerous play.

Families operate in a similar manner. Every family has spoken and unspoken rules about which emotional expressions are permissible and which emotions are not. The rules are enforced with consequences, both verbal and physical. Most families use some variation of physical punishment to limit a child's behavior. The severity, frequency, and style of punishment usually depend on how the parents were raised as well as the cultural and religious beliefs concerning disciplining children.

The issue of how to best discipline children is one the most significant discussions taking place in therapy and research. The evidence of the negative effect that physical discipline has on the child challenges the parental rights to raise a child in this manner. Physical discipline simply has no positive effect on the child, and the use of physical discipline is one of the major factors in turning emotions into symptoms. Instead of the child expressing himself in an emotionally direct manner through verbal communication, opinion, sadness, anger, or sexuality, we now see a variety of symptoms such as anxiety, tension, stress, or guilt.

How we express ourselves emotionally as adults is directly linked to the issue of family discipline. Estimates of the use of physical discipline in American families vary, but figures range as high as 90 percent of American parents who use physical discipline at some point in raising children. At the time of this writing, I am unaware of any research that suggests that physical discipline improves psychological growth in a child. But how harmful could physical discipline be if we have all survived it—and we turned out okay, right? This argument is based on how we like to think of ourselves. Even though we all show signs of developmental trauma, our defensive self-perception is usually, "I am okay, aren't I?" Maybe the next question needs to be: How do I know that I am okay? Then the bigger question becomes: What exactly defines psychological wounding and psychological health? Since we have been taught to tolerate psychological symptoms since our childhood, we all defend our "okay-ness" while simultaneously experiencing obvious psychological and emotional stress. And in some ways we are okay; that is, until our symptoms start to paralyze our lives through sleep interruption, health issues, relationship issues, or simply too much stress. Until we reach a crisis point, as far as we are concerned our symptoms are simply part of our emotional make-up. We don't even realize that the anxiety, tension, and stress we feel are *not* really emotions but are symptoms resulting from blocked emotions, and those blocked emotions are directly related to how we were raised.

Fundamentally, emotion is information, and each emotion represents a different type of information. Pleasure, compassion, thought, and aggression are simply specific types of information about the world. As we are growing up, parents, siblings, and authority figures teach us how to translate emotions into information, which in turn teaches us how to perceive the world and respond to it. Let's say that the body is a receiver, just like a radio. The radio has different channels of information, whereas the body has different emotions of information.

Parents teach the child what each emotion means and how to respond to it. Unfortunately, intermixed with the family wisdom and skillful expression are distortions of reality and obstructions in emotional expression.

THE THRESHOLD OF PERCEPTION

This type of conditioning creates the personality structure, which has two major functions: the threshold of perception and the threshold of expression. The threshold of perception determines the reality that we perceive: what "catches" our attention and sets the level of stimulation required for us to be aware. This means that events in the world will only be perceived when an external person/place/object/event reaches a certain level of intensity, which then catches our attention. Before it reaches this threshold of perception, unique to each of us, it remains a blind spot to awareness; it is simply not noticed. Our inability to read non-verbal communication until it becomes obvious is this type of blind spot. A common example of this blind spot occurs when you are not aware that the person you are speaking with is angry about something until his cues reach a certain intensity. This would be a block in your perception of aggression. Or you might not know that someone likes you until s/he emotionally breeches the perceptual threshold. This might be a block in feeling intimacy. The factors that determine what is obvious are the strength of the external signal and the threshold of perception. Subtle cues, perhaps non-verbal cues, may go unnoticed. You are suddenly surprised by what you now realize, and in looking backward, might even be able to identify the clues that you missed. Another common blind spot occurs in dating. "There's no one to date in this town" (of 70,000 people). This simply means that the individual's psychological filter is set so high that he is unable to perceive potential dating candidates. He is unable to "see" anyone to date.

The question for the therapist is: What purpose does this blindness serve in the person's personality structure? Why would someone be unable to perceive datable people and what protective mechanism is involved? This might be an example of a sexual block, an inability to perceive those individuals who might be sexually available. If it is more important to respect your parents' moral training than to honor your physical desires, then your moral perceptual threshold blocks your erotic perception of available partners. Thus, no one appears on the dating radar. You can see how a therapy designed to help a person learn how to date would be ineffective if the real problem is a moral standard that is too rigid. Working on dating or interpersonal techniques in therapy might improve the client's interpersonal skill set, but ultimately will be rendered useless by the built-in moral authority obstructing the perception and ability to act on those sexual feelings. These types of blind spots are almost always initially associated with anxiety. Perceiving the cues associated with forbidden information produces anxiety, so instead of feeling love, anger, or sexual attraction, the person feels anxiety or another one of the eleven major symptoms associated with blocked emotional expression. These symptoms are a result of the second personality threshold: the threshold of expression.

THE THRESHOLD OF EXPRESSION

The unconscious emotionally responds immediately to all events in our life, and does so initially in proportion to the nature of the situation. In essence, one's unconscious acts like a uniquely personal mirror, reflecting the emotional quality and intensity of the moment. The psychological problem occurs when an individual has been taught to respond to the world in a controlled or restricted manner. Thus, if a fully emotional response to an event represents one hundred percent of a person's emotional potential, but he restricts his emotional response to only fifty percent of his emotional capacity to meet his family standards (don't be angry, sad, sexy, or opinionated), the other 50 percent of the energy is converted into his "symptom profile." This would be his or his family's preferred symptoms: anxiety, tension, stress, guilt, shame, fear, resentment, grief, worry, depression, or somatization.

The threshold of expression is put into place by repeated lessons from the family and culture about what is acceptable behavior and what is not. Unacceptable behavior is met with a threat of consequences, which can be as fundamental as loss of approval from someone important or as dangerous as physical abuse. Usually, the intensity of the symptom is directly in proportion to the external emotional trigger and the threat of consequences. However, even small emotional blocks accumulated over time can become acute or chronic symptoms. The stronger the emotional trigger combined with the family rules and enforcement (the threat), the stronger the symptoms. I call this threat the "Or-Else!" It is the fundamental consequence we all fear, designed by our family or childhood developmental history. This Or-Else is the actual or remembered consequence that triggers the expressive inhibition. The individual's personality, which inhibits perception and expression, is directly shaped by the threats of childhood, which are often accepted and adopted by society. Corporal punishment in school is a perfect example.

The Or-Else is practiced not only in our families but culturally as well and is directed toward the behaviors of certain targeted social groups from country of origin or race to gender and sexual orientation. An example of the cultural Or-Else is how women were threatened prior to the 1960s concerning their expression of the thinking function. "You shouldn't worry your pretty little head about that," was a phrase used both seriously as a cultural prejudice about a woman's ability to think and later in comedic satires illustrating that prejudice. The same prejudice regarding thinking ability was used against black athletes vying for quarterback or coaching positions. This type of repression is often presented as a truth or even as a kindly attempt to protect the person from the emotional distress of overreaching his or her abilities. The underlying message was clear, however: thinking would lead to negative and even violent consequences.

What this type of social bias does on a psychological level is distort a person's ability to trust his own thinking processes or to trigger anxiety when he does activate his thinking. Suddenly, with a single thought, anxiety, guilt, and fear rush to the surface, undermining intellectual confidence and raising the specter of threat. The Or-Else is the consequence of breaking the social rules.

It is no surprise that at the end of the 19th century, psychology as a discipline began to emerge partly in response to the psychological symptoms arising from cultural prejudices against women. And then, in the early 1900s and later in the 1950s, the rising tide of the civil rights movement led to the unthinkable: larger and larger groups of people began to challenge the Or-Else. Instead of cooperating with the social prejudice in order to avoid persecution, women and blacks simply were no longer willing to compromise the quality and integrity of their lives and decided to confront the Or-Else. The response from society was ferocious. The women's right to vote movement in the 1900s resulted in assaults, deaths, and imprisonment; the history of blacks in America is full of the most disgraceful and immoral acts ever perpetrated on a people. The civil rights movement rejected the consequences of suppression and demanded the equality and dignity guaranteed to all through God's moral law. Again, assaults, death, and imprisonment were the social tools used in the unsuccessful attempt to suppress this movement.

One of my psychological truths is that we will not treat anyone else better than we treat ourselves. The deeper truth is that how we treat others is actually how we treat ourselves. The structure of social order reveals the psychopathology of any society. As we look in horror at how we treat people of different genders, races, or religions, it is the children of all these families of the oppressed, oppressors, and witnesses who bear the greatest burden of oppression. We taught these children how to perpetuate injustice, prejudice, and discrimination. Empathy was replaced with hatred or resentment. Love was replaced with prejudice. And fundamentally, truth and accuracy were replaced with distortion and symptomology. To accept and believe in a distortion means that emotional truth is blocked, and that block produces symptoms. These symptoms—anxiety, tension, stress, guilt, shame, fear, resentment, grief, worry, depression, and somatization—are the signs that emotional accuracy and truth have been compromised and that we have a distorted view of the world.

If there were no threats or consequences, most people would simply do and say whatever they felt. But this leads to a massive perceptual challenge. What would the world be like if everyone did and said exactly whatever they wanted? Obviously, the fantasy of this uninhibited reality would vary widely depending on one's religious beliefs, cultural values, family fears, political orientation, and personality structure. Depending on how rigid one's personality is, the vision of that unregulated world would look more and more threatening. Jung suggested that the actual problem with corrupt or dangerous behaviors occurs in those personalities that are the most severely restrictive. Strong inhibition actually produces highly symptomatic, destructive, and self-destructive behavior, and as soon as the individual begins to express himself effectively, his symptomology decreases. The very perfection that the ego seeks by instituting rigid rules of perception and emotional expression is ironically the source of the corruption. It is our perceptual distortion combined with our emotional repression that produce the very behaviors that the "correction" is designed to correct.

> "The unconscious is not a demoniacal monster, but a natural entity which, as far as moral sense, aesthetic taste, and intellectual judgment go, is completely neutral. It only becomes dangerous when our conscious attitude to it is hopelessly wrong. To the degree that we repress it, its danger increases. But the moment the patient begins to assimilate contents that were previously unconscious, its danger diminishes."
>
> —C.G. Jung, *Dreams*

Each person has specific fears associated with his own inhibited behavior based on the consequences he experienced as a child. Although we tend to assume that all of us share the same fears, we do not. Most of our fears are specific to our families. It is true that geographically and culturally defined regions (such as the South) or shared religious values may teach children certain rules of behavior, but the *fear* that each of us experiences when confronted with an emotional dilemma is unique. Even among family members, what we are permitted/taught to perceive or express can vary significantly. This doesn't mean that we limit all of our self-expression, but it often means that we over-control one or two of our fundamental emotions. Those emotions then produce symptoms instead of feelings, and we don't get the energy or the information associated with those emotions. We literally repress the energy and information. We feel a bit more depressed or a lot more depressed depending on how much we are repressing our emotions. At the same time, our perception of the world is more distorted because the information associated with each emotion has been repressed.

In relationships, a partner's irritating behavior that is obvious after months or years of relating to each other was initially completely missed or ignored. The problematic information was simply filtered out for the greater goal of getting a mate. Therapy rooms are filled with clients claiming that they keep dating the same type of man/woman over and over in a seemingly unending cycle. This is because the emotion (information) associated with the blind spot is systematically being inaccurately interpreted by personality. Thus the person is running the same dating experiment over and over. Because the individual is still inhibiting his emotional response to every new situation, it takes what seems like forever to realize that this relationship has the same problem as the last. If you can fully express your emotions, you will be able to access the information missing from the previous experiments. You will still respond to the same attractions, but you will no longer be fooled by them. You will know the specific qualities of the attraction, those aspects unique to your emotional training, and will learn to make a choice based on additional information and not just the attraction.

You stop being the bird repeatedly bashing its head against the window, offended by or attracted to its own reflection.

You begin to shorten the length of time in your dating experiments while simultaneously increasing the information you have about more appropriate mates. Your learning curve is faster and you make better, more expedient decisions concerning your commitment to a relationship.

THE FUNDAMENTAL PROBLEM IN THERAPY

Poor self-image and feelings of guilt and shame are common in human beings. There are hundreds of theories and thousands of books on how to help people overcome their guilt or shame and how to build a positive self-image. Early analysts thought that interruptions in significant developmental stages in childhood led to permanent damage of the personality and that therapy was essentially the method of helping someone identify the damage and learn strategies for compensating for that damage. One hundred years later, we know that personality is much more flexible, and although the nervous system can develop certain stubborn habits reinforcing poor self-expression, the dedicated individual, by adopting a flexible regimen of exercise, diet, spiritual practice, social support, social service, insight, emotional release, and even medication, can effectively and significantly change self-perception and self-expression. Universal to all psychological systems is the need to address perceptual accuracy, emotional self-expression, and emotional regulation (mastery).

I tell my clients there is nothing wrong with them and then they explain in specific detail exactly what is wrong with them. I argue that they are good, fine, healthy, and wonderful, and they express in genuine emotions their anxieties, worries, "bad" habits, sins, dysfunctions, fears, and depressions. I point out what they do well, how they act compassionately, how they care deeply. My clients then argue that they are damaged and self-obsessed; some even argue that they deserved punishment as children. They argue that they are so sensitive that they don't even want to socialize, as the suffering is too much. My clients explain how they set goals to perfect themselves—to change weight, attitude, relationships, finances, diet, education, and employment— which are all ways of perfecting their lives and their self-expression. And yet, each story is marked by a failure to meet expectations. They carefully detail this desire for perfection and the frustrating results of the quest.

With all the literature, workshops, and seminars concerning self-image and self-worth, one would think that the complements of a professional therapist who openly recognizes a person's intelligence, or beauty, or sensitivity, or ability would have a more sustaining impact in the client's view of himself. And yet, in spite of my efforts, my clients cling to a fundamentally distorted self-image. There is no question that people do feel better when their accomplishments and abilities are recognized. The real problem seems to be the inability to sustain those positive, uplifting feelings that emerge with recognition. It's as though there is a gravitational pull toward a feeling of dissatisfaction and discomfort: something inside each of us has been activated briefly and then deactivates on its own.

We live in a culture that loves perfection and the quest for perfection. We are constantly confronted and seduced into accepting social goals that are inconsistent with self-expressive goals. Advertising, in general, is founded on the principle of "There is something wrong with you and this will fix it." We are urged to seek material wealth, physical perfection, emotional balance, prescription medication, improved relationships, and on and on. The underlying message is that there is something fundamentally lacking in our lives. Advertising did not create social self-image, but it certainly takes advantage of and reinforces our flawed self-image. The problem is that we *feel* like there is something wrong with us. And this is our dilemma: What is this feeling that continually creates "dis-ease" in our psyche?

Our willingness to suffer our lower energy-states is a continual challenge when attempting to evolve our consciousness. However, the unconscious is continually attracting us into adventures that will energize us if we are courageous enough to meet the challenge along the way. Our world is filled with one white rabbit after another, leading us down the rabbit hole of psychological adventure.

THE WORLD AS A SYMPHONY OF EMOTION AND INFORMATION

The essence of all phenomena is its particular and specific vibrational characteristics. At the atomic level, all elements on the periodic table have their own vibrational frequencies, their vibrational signature; our bodies are specifically designed to be capable of receiving a significant spectrum of vibrational signals. Every object and event in the material world has a vibrational signature and is known by it. Thus, the world is a symphony of vibrations and our bodies are the receiver for those vibrations. We might then postulate that each neural-emotional complex (except throat/speech) is designed to receive and translate a particular vibration (vibrational information becomes emotion); therefore, the combination of all of the emotions of the four major emotional complexes represents our perception of the world and our response to it: the world symphony as "heard" and translated by our four neural-emotional complexes.

There is a wonderful encounter in the movie about Beethoven, *Immortal Beloved*, in which the composer is explaining the nature of music to his soon-to-be personal secretary. In simple terms, Beethoven says that a composer writes from emotional experiences, and if the musical composition is successful, and the symphony or performer expresses the music effectively, then the audience directly experiences the emotional states of the composer. There is a direct transmission of emotion from composer to audience through the medium of music (vibration). The audience can literally share the emotional experience of the composer. As members of the audience, we are moved, unbeknownst to us, by the emotional quality of the music. Emotion has a vibratory signature, and at some deep level, we recognize/translate those feelings through associations with our own emotional history. We are reminded of and moved by our own memories triggered by the musical vibration. I would further add that the body as a whole has translated the vibratory experience of the music through the four neural-emotional complexes: insight/head, empathy/heart, courage/digestive, pleasure/reproductive. It is obvious that thought, sadness, anger, and pleasure are only the most base aspects of those biological emotional systems and hardly represent the subtlety that our physical systems are capable of perceiving or expressing. Clearly, the matters of the heart—love, devotion, loss, grief, mercy, and more—are more distinct parts of the greater process of the respiratory neural bundle. And each neural bundle has its own perceptual/expressive spectrum. It is the more subtle variations of those neural-emotional capacities that inform music, or art, or philosophy, or theology, and so on. This is the heart and complexity of emotional wisdom.

Each neural-emotional center is designed to translate certain specific types of information and emotions. For example, Wilhelm Reich suggested that sexuality is actually a specific sine wave that occurs throughout the world and that all creatures (including the plant, insect, and animal kingdoms) are attuned to this wave through their particular reproductive organs. It's not that we generate sexual excitement but rather that we tune into and resonate with this sexual sine wave. The more accurately we attune to, or sympathetically resonate with this wave, the more excited we become.

Each waveform is made up of two aspects, emotional wisdom (information) and emotional intensity (quantity of content). The emotional wisdom is the actual feeling represented (anger, sexuality, sadness, thought), and the emotional intensity signals the strength of the emotion. In addition, our attunement to any particular emotional sine wave reveals to us those in our environment similarly attuned to that same sine wave (anger, sadness, sex, thought). We have all had the experience of feeling that someone was generating an emotion and that we were feeling what they were generating, but in this model, we are simply attuned to the same sine wave; we are listening to the same "music." This would suggest that part of empathy or attraction is simply the simultaneous attunement to the same emotional sine wave.

What I find appealing about this idea is that the body may actually comprise a collection of organs whose job is not only to maintain the physical functioning of the body but also to specifically translate what we would call emotional information. This would mean that we don't generate emotions, but rather, we attune to them: that our emotions are the bio-chemical results of the impact of universal sine waves, which essentially produce shared emotional states (dependent on healthy biological functioning and psychological curiosity).

However, when awareness is in conflict with the body, due to family and cultural conditioning, the psychosomatic illnesses that haunt certain organs are specific indeed. Issues of anger have strong representation in the digestive system. Sadness is located within the respiratory system, obsession is associated with the head, and addiction is associated with the reproductive system.

When we begin to examine the nature of the interconnectedness of living creatures, we are biased toward the familiarity of our own species, but we are certainly capable of learning the languages of the plant and animal kingdoms. The sense of intimacy we share with other living beings is actually built into our design; it occurs directly as a result of a common rhythmic language. That language is the emotional wisdom of the vibrations that shape the structure and content of the material world. We are designed to interface intimately with all living creatures through a shared language. Whether we as a species are able to translate the emotional wisdom of that encounter remains to be seen.

CONCLUSION: THE VIEW

Tibetan Buddhists often refer to The View as an aspect of the enlightened state of mind. As personality is brought under the mastery of awareness, there is an openness to our experience of the world, as well as a realization of the interdependent dynamics of the cosmos and consciousness.

The View is the Aha! experience, held in a stable state of effortless concentration.

As we mature, we need to have reality described to us. Cultural myths, faith, and symbols serve as representatives of reality until wisdom replaces superstition and magic. With experience and practice, the world, and our place and purpose in it, begin to make sense and shape The View; symbol and imagination transform into wisdom. Like Helen Keller at the moment she understood that the sign for water and the experience of water referred to each other, Helen realized The View—the expansive, interconnected, and energetic awakening of consciousness.

In psychotherapy, the intimate knowing of how personality works and the simultaneous realization of the complexity and simplicity of the psychological system is part of "The View." We are no longer fooled by symptomology. We are no longer fooled by presentation. We can identify and strategize treatment for the personality structural problems of our clients and not just massage their symptoms. This book is my attempt to describe, through a psychological super-system, how therapy can be an effective tool for evolving consciousness, both in the client and the clinician.

The consumer has the right to expect the therapist to have a more evolved consciousness; after all, that is why the therapist is offering psychological services. To what extent this assumption is accurate will certainly be revealed during the course of therapy. In good psychotherapy, the end result is *truth*. Does the client feel stronger? Does the client have a better skill set for engaging the world? Is there a significant reduction in the client's symptom profile? Is the client healthier? Is the client capable of true intimacy in his personal relationships? Does he see the world accurately? Does he respond emotionally in proportion to the moment? Can you, as a clinician, consistently repeat these therapeutic successes? These are the questions that, when answered affirmatively, provide the greatest truth of all: effectiveness.

CHAPTER TWO

THE STRUCTURE OF THE PSYCHE

PSYCHOLOGICAL SUPER-SYSTEMS

Throughout the short history of psychological science there have been widely varying theories concerning the nature of awareness, personality structure, and the human interface with the physical world. In the same way that physics has had competing theories, there is now a movement within both physics and psychology to find the grand unified theory of our disciplines. As thinking in the psychological discipline evolves, we should be less concerned about whatever current techniques, "evidence-based" or otherwise, are being promoted and more concerned about how these contrasting therapeutic disciplines contribute to our overall knowledge of the infrastructure of the psyche. We have become obsessed with the therapeutic tools instead of the psychological structure of the human being. Imagine surgeons more obsessed with their instruments than with anatomy.

Unfortunately, our excessive dependence on symptom diagnosis and treatment is beginning to retard the progress of psychological thinking, particularly in our training institutions. The influence of the medical model along with the insurance companies' desire to control health care payments has contributed to an ineffective model of psychological symptom treatment. In the medical field, the symptom may well be the problem. But in psychological dynamics, the symptom is often the solution. A volcanic explosion, although it presents a problem, is not really the problem, but rather the expression of the problem, which is the underlying pressure dynamics of the earth. The volcano is simply, literally expressing the underlying problem. In the same way, human beings have similar dynamic pressure systems in the body and psyche. These are the systems that generate the symptoms that punctuate the moods of our lives. The complex emotional interactions between the physical, psychological, and environmental systems are psychodynamics. Just like the physiological system, the psychological system is enormously complex and dynamic. It possesses an intricate network of energetic capacities, perceptual distortions, expressive inhibitions, unfolding potentialities, healing propensities, and health challenges.

There is nothing wrong with teaching dynamically effective techniques as one of the main goals of training; however, this does not replace a sound education in personality structure and energy dynamics.

Since all techniques are not equally effective all the time, knowing when, why, and how to use a technique can improve therapeutic outcome considerably. If you do not have a fundamental training in psychodynamics, then diagnosis and treatment is mostly guesswork.

A psychological super-system is a complete theory of the structure, function, and dynamics of the psyche. Any psychological super-system should contain the following blueprint:

- The structure of the personality and its components
- The developmental stages of personality and emotional functioning
- The psychodynamics of personality and symptomology
- The relationship between psyche and soma (mind and body)
- The dynamic interface between the psyche and the external world
- The nature of psychological perception and expression
- The psychodynamics of psychological energy

- How emotions and thoughts follow predictable patterns
- How personality defense systems are developed, operate, and evolve
- The psychodynamics of resistance
- The psychodynamics of somatic disorders (physical illness)
- How psychological techniques interface with personality dynamics
- The relationship of psychological technique and personality transformation

Without a psychological super-system, the therapist is simply guessing at which strategies and techniques should be used to successfully address the client's underlying problem producing the presenting symptoms. There is no question that with a variety of techniques and sufficient experimentation, a therapist can help provide some psychological relief for his client, if only by trial and error. But how much more satisfying, expedient, and financially respectful would it be for the clinician to be able to identify the correct techniques and timing needed to address the client's specific psychological problem effectively?

THE FIVE COMPONENTS OF IDENTITY

Part of a psychological super-system involves identifying the fundamental building blocks of identity. For therapy to be accurate and successful, the clinician must be able to interact with the whole being, all of the essential components of human identity. Each of these components must be addressed both diagnostically and in treatment strategy.

1. *Awareness:* Who we inherently *are.* The definition and function of awareness continues to be debated in the different psychological schools, varying from the Freudian view that awareness is the byproduct of a complex biological system to the Jungian point of view that awareness is an independent component of the psychological system and has its own structure, energy dynamics, and purpose. Jung further believed that individual awareness is actually an extension of single group/collective awareness. The Buddhists believe that all awareness represents one mind and that the experience of individuality is a by-product of the material world, not of awareness. I would argue that the Jungian and Buddhist perspectives are more accurate and account for more psychological phenomena.
2. *Physical Structure/Body:* The Five Neural-Emotional Centers—the biochemical interface between awareness and external reality. The body carries us through life, transmitting information to awareness

in the form of emotions. The body contains the chemical record of our emotional history, some of which is immediately available to awareness and some of which remains unconscious and difficult to retrieve. In order to simplify this complex interconnection between body and awareness, this book works with five major systems: brain, voice, respiratory system, digestive system, and reproductive system. With the exception of speech, the other four neurological systems are associated with specific emotional function: thinking, sadness, aggression, and pleasure. I consider all emotions as forms of wisdom, and therefore, I treat thinking as the emotion of the brain. These four complexes have two functions, psychologically: to provide perceptual information and to express emotions. Speech illuminates perception by triggering responses in the environment but serves mainly to express emotional responses. Thus, we have four perceptual complexes and five expressive complexes. *These five centers of awareness are the neurological clusters that regulate perception and emotional expression.*

3. *Personality Structure:* The personality structure is the regulating mechanism of the five neural-emotional centers and thus determines how we perceive/interpret the world and the style in which we respond to it. Personality regulates psychological energy, self-expression, self-perception, self worth, insight, intimacy, and creativity. Personality has two major influences: genetic propensities and systematic training received in early childhood developmental stages, reinforced by social standards. The personality structure determines the thresholds of perception and expression. In other words, it governs the threshold at which awareness either perceives external phenomena or suffers from a blind spot, as well as the threshold of expression at which emotions are either expressed or blocked and converted into symptoms.

4. *The Personal and Collective Unconscious:* The personal unconscious contains the content of personal identity that has either not been activated or has been activated and repressed. The contents of the personal unconscious counterbalance and complete the contents of self-expression utilized by the personality structure. There is emotion, information, and energy in the contents of the personal unconscious that put pressure on the personality structure for expression and create symptoms when that expression is blocked. The collective unconscious is the interconnected ocean of awareness that contains the wisdom and energy of all living beings. Its influence can be uplifting and devastating. It is the source of the large shifts of consciousness as evolution waxes and wanes.

5. *Energy Dynamics:* What powers the system. The single most influential dynamic of the psyche is the compensatory nature of

the unconscious; the rebalancing of the psychological structure through a combination of expression of emotion and expression of symptoms. Energy dynamics represents both the physical and psychological energy systems: how we access, distribute, and exhaust energy. This is the key component of psychological growth, creativity, intimacy, and stability. There is no more accurate measure of personal potential, psychological growth, or psychological inhibition than the energy that each of us feels and draws upon on a day-to-day basis.

Awareness: Who We Inherently Are

The soul, awareness, the true self, consciousness, and mind—all of these terms are attempts to define that aspect of identity that "knows." The schools of philosophy, physics, theology, biology, and certainly psychology have each attempted to identify, codify, or simply describe the parameters and abilities of awareness. The perspective of this book is simple: awareness is who we are. That's it. We have a body, but we are awareness. And I fundamentally believe that all awareness is interconnected. Jung's proposition of the collective unconscious is very similar to the Buddhist idea of the "Ocean of Wisdom," and I find both concepts appealing and accurate. There are many aspects of group behavior that simply cannot be sufficiently explained without a theory of interconnectivity. And certainly there are theories of interconnectivity that are supported only by the chemical and hormonal interplay between the individuals in the group. But consciousness seems be at the heart of creation in some dynamic way. As Gary Zukav suggests in his marvelous book *The Dancing Wu Li Masters*, consciousness directly affects the quantum field (the "mother" of reality), and no attempted observation of the quantum field can occur without the intent of the observer affecting the observed phenomena. Atypical but commonly witnessed phenomena such as telepathy, intuitive wisdom, empathy, serendipity, synchronicity, prognostication, coincidence, deja-vu, shared emotional states, group hysteria, and miracles all manifest consistently enough to be a part of human consciousness and history, but inconsistently enough that they are not accepted as predictable phenomena. No effective theory of awareness can be based solely on these outlying states, but the phenomena of such must be included in any thorough theory of awareness.

So, for the sake of simplicity, I bow to Jung and the Buddhists: Awareness is an elemental component of creation that is unique unto itself, interfaces with organic forms, and can be experienced as both singular (the individual)

or as an intimate part of a group (the collective). One might compare this dual
nature of awareness to the dual nature of light: it is both wave and particle.
We are both group and individual.

THE BODY: THE FIVE NEURAL-EMOTIONAL CENTERS
OF AWARENESS

The five neural-emotional centers of awareness are the biochemical
interface between awareness and external reality. The body seems to
be the somewhat reluctant servant of awareness. I appreciate the concept that the physical universe, and the body in particular, are designed
by the rhythmic intent of awareness ceaselessly engaging the material
world, eventually producing the physical forms capable of housing
awareness: the human form being the most recent significant evolutionary product and no less divine due to its late arrival. The human
body has this wonderful ability to decode reality through a broad array
of senses, grouping our experiences into emotional patterns before
revealing the information behind the effect.

One of the core foundations of this book is that there are five major
neural-emotional centers of awareness in the body: the brain, throat,
respiratory, digestive, and reproductive systems. There are four centers
of perception: brain, respiratory, digestive, and reproductive, and there
are five centers of expression when you add speech to the original four
centers of perception. The four perceptual complexes have specific
emotions associated with each physical location whose job is to translate specific types of information to awareness. Each center has three
expressive aspects to its overall function: the biological expression,
the psychological expression, and the pathological expression. The
biological expression is the biological function of that organ. The psychological expression is the specific emotion located at that site. The
pathological expression is the symptom produced at that site when the
emotional expression is repressed by personality or the biological function has been traumatized. The conditioning of these five neural-emotional centers eventually becomes the structure of the personality.

In this model, our emotions are located at specific physical sites, and
psychological dysfunction and physical dysfunction are intimately
related to those sites. Any emotion that awareness is experiencing indicates that a specific physical neurological site is in operation, translating
information into emotion. Although emotion and thinking are often
considered separate functions of the psyche, I regard thought as the
"emotional" expression of the brain, sadness/empathy as the emotional action of the respiratory center, aggression-courage as the emotional action of the digestive center, and pleasure/intimacy as the
emotional action of the reproductive center.

Separating thought from other emotions is a cultural bias. Thought is simply a more subtle emotion. It is functionally no different from the other emotions (as an expression of its host organ), and like the other emotions, performs a specific job in the psychological system.

Thinking, empathy, courage, and pleasure all contribute to the overall landscape of our perception of reality. If any one of these critical psychological functions is limited or missing, massive perceptual blind spots occur in our processing.

Thinking, as an emotion, has its healthy as well as pathological expression. When thinking is healthy, it manifests as insight, clarity of perception, analysis, and strategy. However, when thinking is a symptom of emotional distress, it manifests as obsession, self-criticism, negative self-image, and worry.

Part of the uniqueness of the super-system proposed in this book is that the psychological function of an organ is the emotion of that organ. For example, it is easier to intuitively leap to the observation that sadness resides in the location of the respiratory system; we feel that emotion in the heart area. Does sadness actually reside in the heart? The poets think so! Anyone with a "broken" heart will tell you that the sadness feels like a hole in the chest. But each neural-emotional center has its own specific emotion and its own emotional wisdom. The accuracy of our perception of the world is directly dependent on the effective and efficient function of each of these emotional centers. When the personality restricts the function of any or all of these centers, even a little, it creates a distortion in perception and expression and fuels the symptom profile. Each neural-emotional site has its healthy as well as pathological expression. This will be explored further at the end of this chapter with an examination of my *psychosomatic scale*.

Developmentally, as the baby's body matures, each of the neurological sites activate and awareness begins to translate these chemical cascades of information into symptom, dream, fantasy, emotion, or insight/information. This information can be about external experiences or physical function. Through constant interaction with the world, awareness and the body are simultaneously taught: (1) a description of the world (how to interpret phenomena) and (2) which emotional responses produce pleasure and receive group approval and which responses produce pain and should be repressed or avoided.

The family and society systematically condition our perceptions and expressions. This conditioning is what produces the personality structure, which at its core is an aggregate of patterned neural pathways. These dominant neural pathways, enforced through repetition during childhood, are used by awareness to interpret experience and produce habitual relationship styles.

Essentially, the family teaches us how to feel, what to feel, what emotions are acceptable and what emotions are not, as well as what each emotion means. The family description of reality and expression dictates how accurately we perceive the world, how effectively we interact with the world, and how much overall energy we feel. This is the foundation of our sense of self-worth. This training becomes our family and social mythology or narrative: the stories told to us, and the stories we tell to others, that help us understand and codify the objects in the world, how the world works, and how we should interact with it.

When our family myth (the shared description of reality) is consistent with reality, the family emotional training produces wisdom and ability. When our family myth conflicts with reality, the results are perceptual distortions and emotional instability. Reality is reality regardless of how we've been taught to understand or interpret it. Neurotic anxiety is what occurs when we disagree with reality.

We don't create reality, but we certainly adopt the parameters of reality we perceive and respond to. We may strongly believe and have conviction in what we consider to be reality, as passed down from generation to generation or through religious training, but the presence of any psychological symptomology reveals that there are distortions in our perceptual beliefs. There is a vast gap between conviction and wisdom, and families teach each other, with conviction, how to see and interact with the world. But if that interpretation is in conflict with reality, the individual will fail to achieve his or her potential, intimate relationships will have significant flaws, and suffering will result. Reality always trumps conviction.

The Biological Constraints of Behavior—Neural Plasticity: When we commit ourselves to personal change, there is the unknown factor of how long the commitment needs to be in order to be effective. Current neuroscience as reported by Dr. Ernie Rossi suggests that the nervous system needs four weeks of stimulation in order to activate the neural pathway that will support the "new" behavior/ point of view, but that it will take sixteen weeks of training for the neural pathway to act as a more permanent habit. This is significant information. For example, most diets succeed for a few weeks, and most people can sustain a change in behavior for a few weeks, but to actually accomplish long-term goals, or changes in behavior, or changes in perception, four weeks and sixteen weeks are the absolute minimum amounts of time necessary. Any intervention shorter than these timetables will only be successful in those situations where the external dynamics change and relieve the pressure on the client. We must question the long-range effectiveness of short-term therapy in light of the neurological requirements of change. And these are just the biological requirements for change. The psychological challenge of overcoming our developmental fears is far more significant because we are dealing with the complexities of the nervous system combined with the fear of the negative consequences of our childhood associated with any new behavior.

This time-frame data certainly challenges our current love affair with short-term therapy for permanent personality changes. The prevailing movement in insurance-covered psychological counseling emphasizes brief therapy designed to address specific symptomology or situational crisis rather than the underlying psychological structural problem. Symptom-based therapy is not the same as structural based therapy. Psychological symptoms are produced by an overly rigid personality structure, and there is no question that a symptom can be successfully suppressed, appearing as though it is resolved, without changing any part of the personality structure that is producing the symptom. Since psychological symptoms serve the purpose of discharging blocked emotional energy, reducing a symptom without relieving the emotional block simply requires the personality structure to develop a different symptom in order to discharge the still-blocked emotional energy. The original symptom is gone, but the problem continues.

Treating and shifting psychological symptoms is not successful therapy. It only has the appearance of being successful.

PERSONALITY STRUCTURE: THE THRESHOLDS OF PERCEPTION AND EXPRESSION

Personality is the structure that regulates energy, emotion, and information. It is part of a larger dynamic system in which it interfaces with both the biological drives of the body and the evolving psychological potential of the unconscious. Although the body, the unconscious, and the personality may be viewed as having somewhat competing agendas, when these three systems are operating in concert, awareness is capable of experiencing great insight, intimacy, purpose, and inspired creativity.

The personality structure is carved into the neural pathways from birth. Indeed, the developmental stages of childhood are the training exercises that form neurologically programmed behaviors, which eventually become the personality structure. The qualities of personality that seem to make each of us unique and special are actually the affectations of style based on the self-expressive experiments of infancy. As human beings, the story of our lives, our adventures, our mishaps, and the wisdom we have gained along the path are what make us unique. The dynamic structure of the personality though, is not unique, and shares its functioning with billions of people. The myth of the individual, of free will, and the feeling of separation are the products of ego/personality.

We live in an interdependent reality. Awareness, through its relationship with the body and the unconscious, operates in a collectively shared universe in which the energetic resources, including our actual atomic structure, and wisdoms of the inner and outer realities are exchanged with rhythmic, or cyclical, regularity. There is fluidity to reality when awareness is not a slave to fear or consequences.

In spite of awareness's profound interdependency and interactivity with the external and internal worlds, our limited ability to fully perceive and harmonize with this intimate dynamism has to do with our self-absorption in what I call the pre-Copernican psychological universe: the inaccurate conviction that all external events are directed at, commenting on, and threatening *me*, personally. As a result of the overwhelming level of threat perceived in this state of mind, we systematically block massive amounts of information about the world and our relationship to it. The resulting perceptual blind spots contribute to repeated negative emotional cycles, limit the unfolding of our psychological design, and constitute a major source of suffering and expressive inhibition.

Stylistically, and experientially, we are each somewhat unique, although our preoccupation with fitting into our families, our peer group, our social community, or our corporate systems seems to run counter to actually developing a unique point of view or truly unique self-expression. For all of our desire to be fabulously "individual," particularly in Western culture, almost all of our efforts are directed at being an intimate part of a collective. The curious aspect of the personality structure is that its prime goal is actually to achieve a level of homogenized identity in the hopes of avoiding suffering. In the personality's attempt to achieve this significant level of safety, the energetic potential of the physical body and the wisdom of the unconscious are both severely compromised.

The function of personality is to regulate self-expression in order to avoid punishment and discipline. As the child indiscriminately experiments with all forms of expression, the external world systematically conditions those behaviors that meet, or fail to meet, the expectations, beliefs, and standards of the group. Thus, the nervous system of the child (and adult) is programmed to perceive the world through a cohesive descriptive mythology (what our group believes about the world) and to respond to that description within the boundaries of prescribed emotional expression. Welcome to the personality structure: the guardian at the gates of perception and expression.

If approval is more important than autonomy, personality operates from the goal of gaining approval at the expense of creative self-expression. Ideally, in this circumstance, we are fortunate, indeed, when we receive approval for developing autonomy. We all remember those teachers and authority figures who encouraged us to develop our intelligence, passions, strengths, and insights, who loved us for who we are and encouraged our creativity. And we also remember the legions of authority figures who encouraged only obedience and submission at the expense of critical thinking and passionate participation. They presented a constant threat that hinged on our potential failure to please.

Because it regulates perception and expression, personality operates as an energy regulator. Any perception of threat will constrain emotional expression (energy) to a level that has been pre-determined by family, cultural, and gender roles. Personality's only goal is to establish safety by strategically manipulating the external world, typically through emotional tactics handed down from generation to generation. As far as personality style is concerned, the accomplishments of those who have come before us we receive as gifts of competency, skill, and insight. However, we have also learned shabby family strategies involving perceptual distortions and emotionally chaotic expression. It is this regulating function of personality, in the service of approval and the avoidance of punishment, which causes problematic and predictable symptomatic self-expression.

All of our experiences are regulated through two personality filters: the threshold of perception and the threshold of expression. The threshold of perception determines "appropriateness" of external content, and the threshold of expression shapes an "appropriate" emotional response. As personality inhibits our perception and expression, awareness immediately experiences the restriction as either symptom, dream, fantasy, or emotion, and there is an immediate simultaneous constriction of energy and information. Symptom, dream, fantasy, or emotion are simply the transition states that information goes through before awareness fully engages and perceives these transition states for what they are: information and insight. Each transitional state is directly dependent on the level of restriction imposed by the personality structure. Less restriction produces a more accurate perception of reality and a proportional emotional response. This path leads to the higher energetic states of the psyche.

Personality does not regulate all psychological activity. Even the most restrictive families and cultures approve of specific talents, abilities, and emotional expression, giving complete support to the unregulated expression of those sanctioned expressions of Self.

When the expectations of the group coincide with the abilities of the individual, that person is capable of accessing great wisdom, ability, energy, and emotional capacity. The parts of the psyche that are not regulated by personality are much more in agreement with reality and the dynamic potential of the unconscious. Thus, in those areas of the psyche, the energy is higher, perception is more accurate, and emotions are in proportion to the moment. Less personality, more energy. Less personality, better quality and quantity of information about the world. The individual's overall psychological energy is directly in proportion to the percentage of the psyche that is expressed directly and not regulated by personality.

THE UNCONSCIOUS: PERSONAL AND COLLECTIVE UNKNOWN

Jung's description of the structure, effect, and content of the unconscious is practical and useful. He divides the unconscious into two structures: the personal unconscious, which Jung called "the shadow," and the collective unconscious, both with dynamic contents that pressure the personality structure. The personal unconscious contains the unexpressed emotional responses to trauma that we have endured throughout our lives, the information about the aspects of the world that have traumatized us, and the under-developed expressive abilities of the psyche. The collective unconscious is the interconnected ocean of wisdom/awareness that connects us to all living beings (human, animal, plant), and like the ocean, offers both bounty and chaos. The treasures of the collective unconscious include great wisdom, limitless creative capacity, a sense of intimacy and completion, and a view of the interconnectedness of all "things." The chaos of the collective unconscious is associated with the rolling storms of influence that attempt to balance the universe energetically through combinations of creation, preservation, and destruction. The influence of the collective can move through a community like a virus, infecting those with weaker immune systems (personality structures) and primitive emotional attitudes, or can uplift a community with the power of group empowerment (the home court advantage or the shaping of a community's identity). Religion, religious structures, plague, (perhaps weather patterns?), and war arise from the collective unconscious, as does scientific breakthrough, artistic inspiration, spiritual transformation, and the evolution and de-evolution of culture and consciousness.

Whether engaging the personal or the collective unconscious, we are dealing with material and information that is unknown, either because it is repressed or unfamiliar to us. The contents of the unconscious are like high voltage wires that are sometimes hot and sometimes not but are extremely useful for powering a city. The handling of these contents needs to be approached with respect.

Energy Dynamics: What Powers the System

A theory of energy dynamics is the study of psychological energy in relationship to the design of the human psyche and the personality structure. Because it is energy that activates the necessary resources for creativity, perceptual accuracy, insight, problem solving, and interpersonal intimacy, accessible energy should be the ultimate goal of psychological growth and the major concern of psychotherapy. One of the major theories in this book is that psychological energy is in proportion to self-expression, and the more self-expression is regulated by the personality, the more severely one's energy is compromised. There is a direct relationship between the energy dynamics of the psyche and the role of the personality structure in relationship to awareness's encounters with the internal and external worlds.

One of Jung's key theories of the psychodynamic nature of the psyche is his adoption of Alfred Adler's concept of the *compensatory nature of the unconscious*, a complex idea with a simple function: the unconscious works constantly to maintain an energetic balance between the internal and external worlds. Adler's argument parallels the law of the conservation of energy: *energy can neither be created nor destroyed; therefore, the sum of all energies in a system is constant.* In one form or another, the unconscious obeys this rule thusly: experience in, expression out (in proportion to the experience). However, as far as the psyche is concerned, the energy of any encounter is only available through direct expression of the emotional response. If that emotional response is blunted, energy manifests as symptom and is temporarily unavailable.

The psychological correlate to the law of the conservation of energy states the following: the difference between the amount of energetic stimuli and the amount of energetic response is what produces psychological symptoms. Therefore, that which is not expressed as insight or emotion will be expressed as symptom. Psychological energy will be completely represented by a combination of self-expression and symptomology.

When emotional expression is blunted, the blocked energy is expressed unconsciously as a set of symptoms (usually pre-determined by family rules). If you therapeutically fix one symptom, but do not correct the emotional expressive block, the presenting symptom may recede, perhaps permanently, but the unconscious will have to create another symptom to release the energetic pressure created by the block.

At its most effective energetic potential, the unconscious acts like a mirror, simply reflecting whatever encounter is occurring. Regardless of whether we are expressing our feelings/thoughts in the moment, the unconscious is responding immediately, in proportion to the external event. In this book's psychological theory, the personality regulates energy by directing our emotional expression. Due to personality's regulating role, part of our response to the world will be directly expressed in the form of insight or emotion, and the remainder will be repressed, producing psychological and physical symptoms as *compensation* for the blocked emotional energy.

Personality potentially can be transparent, permitting full expression of our emotional responses to our encounters with the world, or it can be mercilessly repressive, turning emotions into symptoms and health crises.

Most personality structures are a combination of expression and repression. The more broadly the personality represses emotional expression, the more symptomatic and dysfunctional the individual becomes, with corresponding perceptual distortions and a drop in available energy. A personality disorder is nothing more than a personality system that is broadly repressive, compromising many if not most of the emotions of the client. The stronger the repression of emotion, the stronger the symptoms will be in compensation and the weaker the energetic signature.

The overall energetic experience is associated with both physical health and psychological health, requiring both to be operating at the highest efficiency in order to provide maximum energetic resources for the psyche. In the realm of the physical body, energy is translated as health, vitality, and optimal functioning. Although science may want to quantify the bio-chemical process associated with these states of health, most people simply describe health as feeling good, or positive, or "energized." From a clinical psychological perspective, a healthy body contributes to the overall energetic reserves used to create a quality lifestyle. As would be expected, there is an intimate link between physical health and psychological health, each mirroring the other. What is healthy in the body is healthy in the psyche, and vice versa. However, this is not to be misunderstood as poor health always results from poor mental health. Physical health is a complex balance of psychological health, environmental stressors, and genetic priorities. A healthy psyche is simply an important contributor to health and healing.

Anxiety and depression are the two most common psychological symptoms described by people seeking therapy. Each of these symptoms can be viewed as energetic challenges. Depression is associated with too little energy, and anxiety is associated with unstable energy. Except in the case of neurological disorder, both anxiety and depression are symptoms associated with an overly restrictive personality system.

Depression can be physical, psychological, or both. Part of the difficulty of psychological diagnosis is differentiating between the two energy signatures. As far as physical health is concerned I encourage my clients to develop a large support network of health consultants, including a physician, chiropractor, massage therapist, pharmacist, along with an Arsaga's coffee shop (humor) and a Little Bread Company bakery (more humor), and of course to learn how to effectively use the information on the Internet. These services are obviously financially demanding, and yet psychotherapy is often intimately associated with biological challenges, so investing in the wellbeing of the body can be as crucial as investing in the treatment of the psyche.

If you are physically healthy, your psychological energy is directly dependent upon self-expression; the energy that you feel—good, bad, elated, or sad—is a direct result of how you are responding to the world and not caused by the world itself. It may be triggered by the world, but how we respond emotionally determines whether the event is experienced as an energy boost or an energy drain. The natural rhythm of our overall energy is predicated on some predictable and manageable dynamics. Psychological health, like physical health, is a continuum that rises and falls over the course of a day, week, month, year, and lifetime.

ENERGY AND SELF-EXPRESSION

We live in a world that systematically reinforces the belief that external objects and people control our emotions. My wife/husband/boss makes me feel great/terrible/confused. We all experience this phenomena; the world causes my emotion. This is both true and untrue. It is true in that reality impacts us both physically and psychologically, and without a doubt we can feel the world's dynamism. But the energetic effect we feel from those external factors is controlled by our response.

What appears to be the negative effect that someone has on us is actu-ally the result of how we block our emotional answer to that person. Instead of responding spontaneously and honestly, we strategically express ourselves in a manner that is consistent with our family and social "rules." If we repress our aggression, then aggressive situations or people will trigger a draining or anxious feeling in us. If we repress our sexuality, then sexual situations will trigger anxiety or obsession, etc. If we grew up in a family that has anger issues (bullying, cyclical conflict, threats), we might perceive ourselves as morally superior by controlling and limiting our anger. However, the unconscious has no such bias. Anger triggers anger, love triggers love, sexuality triggers sexuality, intellect triggers intellect, but the personality shapes the response based on family and social values, thus retarding the avail-able energy by limiting the intensity and quality of the response. The more a person's personality shapes the emotional response, the more the energetic potential is compromised and the more symptomatic the person becomes.

In simple percentages, let's say that each of the five neural-emo-tional systems contributes twenty percent of a person's energy capac-ity. If all five systems are operating at full capacity, without restriction, then one has access to the maximum psychological energy available. When one's personality restricts spontaneous emotional expression, it has two effects on our energy: we only benefit from part of our ener-getic potential and personality has to use energy to block the part of the emotion that it seeks to regulate. This means that if you block fifty percent of your aggression (ten percent of total energy), you have to use an additional ten percent of your overall energy to block it. This means that you are suddenly deprived of twenty percent (ten percent blocked, ten percent blocking) of your overall energy. Repression is what produces tension, anxiety, or depression. Now imagine that you block all of your anger, or sexuality, or sadness. Those percentages of lost energy become massive. Simply blocking your sexuality (which is unbelievably common) results in a forty percent loss of total energy. (Sexual drive represents twenty percent of total energy, and an addi-tional twenty percent of energy is used to block the sexual response). This is energetically catastrophic and results in chronic psychological depression/symptomology, with the additional possibility of this intra-psychic conflict manifesting as a health issue.

For most people, emotional/energetic response is controlled only part of the time. Family and society provide specific opportunities in which one is given permission to express one's emotions. For example, you can have sex after marriage. You can be angry if someone attacks the character of a family member. The energetic problem occurs because of the inconsistency of the emotional expression. Since the unconscious responds immediately to all of the world's stimulations, all of our emotions are being triggered throughout the day.

Personality is constantly regulating our emotional response based on the rules of engagement learned in our families. As a result, some days are wonderful, and some days are exhausting. We assume this is normal and tolerate these energetic roller coasters. Our energetic variances are the direct consequence of the automatic self-limiting of our personality structure. We are killing our own mood.

Our energy is directly linked to genuine emotional self-expression. I include the word "genuine" because there are many people who express waves of emotion with little benefit. Thought that becomes obsession is energetically exhausting, as is anger that becomes resentment or rage, as is sexuality that becomes addiction, as is compassion that becomes pity. Gestalt therapy, in particular, discovered this during the 70s: unregulated emotion, for some, was very beneficial, and for others, it seemed to reinforce the client's pathology. Specific dynamics that explain this problem will be addressed later in this book.

Since all states of experience are ultimately energy dependent, all joyous and satisfying experiences are determined by awareness accessing the maximum available energy allowed through the personality censor.

If genuine emotional expression is a direct link to our psychological energy potential, then it follows that our highest and most pleasant states-of-mind are regulated by the immediacy, honesty, and accuracy of our emotional expression. Energy follows the expression of emotion. Restricted emotion restricts energetic resources and produces symptoms instead. Although it appears to us that the outside world and external objects or individuals "cause" emotional states, it is our personality, regulating our response to those situations and people, that controls our energetic state and produces emotions or symptoms. It is less what the world is generating and much more how we are responding to the world that determines our energetic or toxic emotions.

THE FIVE STAGES OF PERCEPTION: HOW REALITY BECOMES REALITY

How does the infinite potential of the quantum field appear before us? It seems to be difficult to agree upon what constitutes reality. Philosophers and scientists conflict with each other as to whether we are even capable of perceiving reality in its entirety or whether we can have any confidence in our experience of reality.

As solid as the world seems to be, it is closer to the truth to describe reality as a flexible, rhythmically vibrating, and living arrangement of energetic patterns, co-created and inhabited by a mysterious agent we call awareness.

Quantum physicists might claim that all observed reality is a psychologically patterned interpretation of the dance of atoms, and that our perception of reality represents only a part of the quantum potential, or that our perception of reality actually restricts the quantum potential. Some philosophers have argued that reality doesn't exist outside of our immediate experience. Eyewitness reports assembled by the police during investigations suggest that the accuracy of those reports is vaguely accurate at best and a completely fabricated fantasy at worst, with equal confidence, by each witness, in the accuracy of their description of events.

How is it that this solid and clearly present world that we call reality seems so flexible to interpretation and almost hallucinogenic in its presentation? More like a dream than, well, reality, it morphs in a manner that suggests that reality is completely dependent on the observer and that there is no independent, verifiably present, shared world.

We could conclude that there is no agreed-upon reality and therefore no single, unified reality, or we could conclude that the sum total of all the descriptions are actually the complete representation of reality: one reality as described from multiple points of view.

We certainly do not regard the mythical description of the world as presented by a child as "wrong" reality. We respect how fantasy helps unfold various aspects of the world as well as accommodates the awakening of the child's nervous system. We know that at some point in the child's maturing process they will join the collective agreement about the nature and description of reality. And as a culture, we accommodate widely varying religious interpretations of reality (although we are incredulous at the failure of other religions to perceive the world correctly while having complete confidence in our own myth). And yet, at a very psychological level, every one of these descriptions is true.

Once one considers that reality reveals itself to us through a series of stages, and that our description of the world is more a comment about our stage of development than about competing realities, we begin to develop an appreciation of reality from multiple points of view as well as celebrate the creativity of the human psyche to make sense of a profound and sacred universe. All reality is reality, as mediated by our psychological maturity and physical health.

Human beings are symbol-makers; or rather, the human psyche is a symbol-maker. The human psyche translates the unknown, or the new experience, into a symbolic structure whose nature, meaning, and informational value evolves as we mature, both biologically and psychologically. So, while the psyche uses known descriptive patterns (family or social descriptions of the world), on a deeper level, it employs the mythic patterns embedded in the unconscious (religion, spirituality, magic, superstition, or mysticism) to make sense of the world. When we encounter the unfamiliar, the unconscious immediately organizes this new experience into archetypal patterns of mythic structure. One need spend only a short period of time with someone with a psychosis to recognize that the missing pieces of the personality that normally provide familiar perceptions of the world are supplemented with the mythic structures of the unconscious. Until the neurochemistry is repaired and concentration is restored, there is less of the unique person and more of the deep patterns residing in the unconscious: Bob is now on a mission from God, or Suzy is the Virgin Mary (these are common psychotic identities). Part of personality's job is to narrow the larger "mythic" phenomena into immediately workable patterns that support survival, safety, and reproduction at the most basic level.

Jung suggested that the gods of the past are the unconscious complexes of modern humanity. What were once the deities of mystical and separate realms are now the inner voices of our own psyche. We are now more mystified by our own hopes, dreams, fears, and impulses than we are fearful of the actions of those capricious gods and goddesses of our ancestors. We have become our own mystery.

Our body is a complex bio-computer running multiple programs simultaneously that describe and respond to the world. The body and psyche are capable of perceiving the world accurately, but most of us live in a world that has been endlessly described to us until we perceive that very same description, regardless of its accuracy. The parts of reality that have been described inaccurately, or not described at all, remain a mystery that often results in psychological suffering, superstition, and perceptual blind spots. It may be difficult to accept that we only perceive parts of reality, but in order to attend to survival, massive amounts of reality are simply ignored until we are forced to face them at a later stage of psychological development.

Each of the five neurological complexes discussed earlier in this chapter detects a specific part of the composition of reality. Awareness must develop a relationship with each of these neurological sites and their function through experimentation and practice. Awareness then tries to make sense of reality based on the information from these five complexes.

The specific information at each neurological site is filtered through personality in order to meet the rules of conformity established by family and society, producing an emotionally expressive style and a perspective of reality that is an identifiable, diagnostically specific personality structure.

These neurological complexes are capable of transmitting great energy, information, and emotion. However, for these systems to function at their highest level, awareness must test the perceptual and expressive limits of each of the neurological sites. Without such testing, knowledge of reality is limited, and mastery of self-expression is blunted.

Awareness experiences the phenomena we call "the world" in a series of predictable stages. These stages represent how reality, in multiple disguises, is presented to awareness through the biochemical body and regulated by the personality structure. Any phenomena that we are unfamiliar with, or which has been distorted by personality, is experienced by awareness as symptom (anxiety, stress, etc.) or as some form of magical thinking (dream or fantasy). The phenomena that we are familiar with and that we perceive accurately is experienced as emotion or insight.

These are the stages of perception as reality morphs from symptomatic to symbolic to insight:

- The stage of symptom
- The stage of dream
- The stage of fantasy
- The stage of emotion
- The stage of wisdom and insight

The personality, as a filter, presents neural-site-specific information to awareness as either symptom, dream, fantasy, emotion, or insight. This is a hierarchy of perception with symptom being the initial stage of experience and information/insight being the highest stage of experience. All experiences migrate through every stage, but some experiences perform this migration quickly, and others get stuck and remain fixed at a particular perceptual stage.

Since each person's personality has unique censoring capacities, different people can experience the same reality phenomena in significantly different ways. What is symptom to one person is information to another. What is emotion to one person is fantasy or dream to another. Thus, one person experiences climate change as a scientific phenomena and another person views the same reality as an expression of God's will. A third person may view this reality as God's will acting through science. Each person supports his or her view of reality with conviction, regardless of accuracy. We are all experiencing unique aspects of a shared reality. However, the person with the more accurate view of reality, as it really exists, will have fewer psychological symptoms and more energy.

Distortion of perception produces psychological distress regardless of the confidence in one's point of view. Accuracy of perception and immediacy of expression are the foundation of clarity of consciousness.

This mixture of insight and ignorance exists within each person's psyche, simultaneously. Our intellectual complex may be free of distortion but our aggressive complex may be repressed and biased. Each complex will have its own level of realization. So, at one moment we are completely in tune with the world, and at the next, we are confused and chaotic.

As awareness interacts with the world through these five stages, perceptual accuracy morphs from brilliant clarity into random distortion, and our emotional responsiveness varies from spontaneous and proportional emotional expression into either moody muteness or inappropriate emotional intensity. This shifting can occur quite rapidly, as awareness migrates from neurological site to neurological site, or quite slowly, depending on the perceptual and expressive barriers erected by the personality censor.

The Five Stages of Perception:

Stage One: The symptomatic world is the territory through which we travel when we first wake up: anxiety, tension, stress, etc. (the symptom profile). Any new sensation, unfamiliar circumstances, or newly activated neural pathway is experienced initially as symptom (pressure) and then evolves in proportion to the person's curiosity or the environment's "help" in understanding or controlling that sensation. Children ask so many questions about the world because they are bombarded by massive amounts of stimulation that they do not know how to interpret. They experience reality but lack understanding of the phenomena. These experiences trigger emotions and dreams and fantasies and fears until the phenomena become familiar and the child is capable of rapidly interpreting the information behind the stimulus.

Stage Two and Three: The mythic world—dream and fantasy. As we become familiar with the causes of our experiences, the symptomatic world gives way to the mythic world: the sphere of religion, dream, fantasy, fiction, theater, mysticism, superstition, and fairy tale. In the mythic stage, experiences are organized by archetypes, the deeper organizing patterns of the unconscious. Children make play of their reality; people, relationships, and life struggles are all represented by bringing life to inanimate objects, stuffed animals, dolls, and dynamic play. There is a wonderful book by Dr. Vivian Paley, *The Boy Who Would Be a Helicopter: The Uses of Storytelling in the Classroom,* wherein Dr. Paley describes how children spontaneously symbolize / tell stories of the emotional circumstances of their lives. Through the process of story-telling and play acting, these children naturally heal each other's emotional wounds and find comfort and meaning in the world. What is particularly striking about Paley's book is how children translate emotional experience into the imaginary characters on the stage of the classroom. The children do not differentiate between imagination and reality. However, Dr. Paley noted that adult interference in the spontaneous structuring of the play by the children led to an undermining of the effectiveness of the play in addressing the emotional needs of the children. This flexible interplay between external events and internal emotions illustrates the overlapping of internal and external reality / processes when we were children.

One of the most brilliant features of the human psyche is that when allowed to express itself, the unconscious attempts to harness, master, and heal wounded emotional experiences. The psyche is a self-healing system that, amazingly, we are trained to resist.

Stage Four: The emotional world, which we might also call *the narcissistic universe,* is the realm in which emotion becomes more personal, driving us to satisfy emotional longing, learn to self-soothe, and begin to differentiate between the varying emotions—thought, sadness / compassion, anger / courage, and sexuality / pleasure. Instead of experiencing the undifferentiated wave of physical pressure assaulting the child's psyche, awareness begins to distinguish between the longing for sexual expression and the longing for comfort and love, for example, or between anger and hunger. At this stage, emotion is still magical, and we believe that we are possessed by the emotions of the body. This is the developmental state in which many adults remain; we still believe that others cause us to have emotional experiences.

Instead of the gods of the past who randomly tested and tortured us, we now have our neighbors, family, and workmates. But, as a species, we are less and less bound by magical thinking, and in its place is a more accurate, fact-based experience of reality. However, our feelings tell us that all events point toward us, personally. This was spectacularly illustrated on a collective level when, in 2001, there was an Anthrax attack through the mail on several government agencies in Washington, D.C. As a result, people across the nation became convinced that they were next on the list of victims. Individuals interpreted an incident targeting representatives of institutions thousands of miles away as a potential assault on them, too. They felt the fear. They personalized the fear. And they all avoided their mail.

Stage Five: The insight world. In this stage, reality is experienced as it is, with minimum interpretation, and is responded to immediately and effectively. The experience of living produces little anxiety, except where genuine threat exists or if there is a new and unknown experience occurring. This stage could also be labeled the *mastery stage.* Because reality is perceived accurately, and emotional responsiveness potentially produces the highest possible energetic return, one's will is not in conflict with reality, and one's desires and life's goals can be executed with maximum success and with minimum resistance. One's expectations are in concert with the rhythms and rules of reality.

Self-observation reveals all of these perceptual stages in each of us. Awareness shifts between great clarity and effective function into perceptual blind spots and highly regulated behavior. Each impaired complex contributes to our symptom profile. The parts of our psyche that perceive the world accurately and respond effectively, the components of our psyche that are no longer over-regulated and are free to self-express in response to the world, produce the moments of insight, joy, pleasure, wonder, and creativity. In therapy, the parts of the personality structure that are operating with highest efficiency and emotional responsiveness, thus accessing the highest energetic potential, are, for awareness, the examples of functioning that encourage the evolution of the overly restricted parts of the personality. Awareness needs to comprehend the functional goal of psychotherapy, and identifying and celebrating what works well in the psyche sets the standard of functioning well within the realm of possibility. The experienced therapist will identify these functioning parts of the psyche in order to use them as an illustration of life, energy, and the joy that all experience can bring: that this joy is the normal and sustainable state of mind and not some rare event.

Our psyche requires us to see the world accurately, or at least more accurately, as we mature and to respond to reality in proportion to the moment.

Without this evolving psychological growth, the unknown is eventually experienced as adversarial. If we resist our own evolution, this thrilling universe becomes the stressful and anxious universe. Our only relief from our symptom profile (anxiety, tension, stress, etc.) seems to be to perceive the world accurately and respond appropriately, which means obeying the pressure from the unconscious to evolve.

Personality's Function

Personality is an energy, emotion, and information regulating system. Key to the proposition in this book is the idea that our self worth, self-image, insight, intimacy, and creativity are in direct proportion to our energy level, and that our energy is in direct proportion to our self-expression, which by design, is regulated by the personality structure.

As we discussed earlier, personality has two major functions that regulate information and energy: *the threshold of perception* and *the threshold of expression*. These simple but dynamic "gates" or "censors" rule the function of personality and control how emotional information is experienced and expressed.

The intensity level of these thresholds is determined by three powerful defensive and protective mechanisms: sublimation, repression, and dissociation.

1. *Sublimation* is the redirecting of energy and emotion from one neural-emotional site into and through other emotional sites. Thus, sadness can become anger, or sexuality can become obsession. Essentially, this is an amazingly flexible energy/ emotion re-routing system that keeps the overall energetic signature of the psyche balanced, even though this re-routing is initially less efficient than direct expression and may distort the perceptual information associated with the original site. (See chapter 5, "Psychodynamics," *Sublimation*.)
2. *Repression* operates by restricting perceptual information and emotional expression on a site-to-site basis. Thus, anger may be strongly restricted, but sadness is not restricted at all. Or sexuality is blocked, but thinking is only moderately controlled. Or, even more common, speech is regulated depending on the emotions or thoughts being triggered.
3. *Dissociation* is the most ruthless of all of the defense mechanisms in that it represents awareness completely abandoning a neural-emotional site. The result is a complete conversion of information, emotion, and energy into symptoms. (See chapter 4, "Trauma Dynamics," *Dissociation*.)

48

The threshold of perception determines how intense a stimulus must be before we recognize it. The threshold of expression determines the amount of psychological pressure required before we express how we are feeling. As simple as these two functions sound, they are fundamentally at the source of all suffering and insight. There are five neural-emotional centers of the body (head, throat, respiratory, digestive, reproductive) that serve as the primary centers of awareness, and each has separate thresholds of perception (except for the throat) and expression that govern their operation, both in allowing information into the psyche and allowing an emotional response from the psyche. The throat/speech has no perceptual function, but has a significant expressive function.

The thresholds of perception and expression are arbitrarily set by family, culture, and environmental influence. Through repeated exposure to family values, cultural standards, and artificial gender limits, personality slowly develops a perceptually and expressively restrictive role in the psyche. How much sexuality, aggression, intellect, or sadness are perceived or expressed, and how much of one's voice is expressed, are multiple thresholds of perception and expression that are established by the most dominating or threatening influences in one's environment.

Since each center of awareness is uniquely trained in its function by the family and environment, a complex matrix of perception, expression, and repression result. One neural center might be completely repressed and another might be completely open. For example, one might completely suppress sexual information from reaching awareness, while simultaneously allowing a full accounting of aggression or intellect. In this case, sexual information would be blocked both in perception and expression, while aggression or intellect is both perceived and expressed: complete blindness in one neural center and complete knowledge in another. Typically, most people operate with percentages of their neural centers working effectively. The following numbers represent the percentage of reality that is perceived accurately and expressed effectively. Keep in mind: this is the outline of a psychological personality disorder, in which the "disorder" is the consequence of impaired perception and expressive restriction.

So, we can invent an example that suggests our client has forty percent of his perceptual intellect available but only twenty percent of his expressive intellect, seventy-five percent of his perceptual compassion and sixty percent of his expressive compassion, fifty percent of his perceptual aggression but only ten percent of his expressive aggression, and forty percent of his perceptual sexuality available but only twenty-five percent of his expressive sexuality. Speech is the most complex center to evaluate because it has its own general expressive level—let's say sixty percent—but speech is also linked to each of the other neural centers, and so speech may only have twenty percent function concerning intellect and twenty-five percent function concerning sexuality, etc. The obvious goal is absolute awareness and expression in all five of the significant neural centers, and each of these centers is interconnected to the others; thus, anger can be informed by intellect and/or compassion, or sexuality can be informed by thought or love, etc. In such a state, we would be able to perceive the world accurately and respond effectively and in proportion to the moment.

The thresholds of perception determine the intensity level at which we become aware of external stimuli, and there is a unique perceptual threshold for each of the neural-emotion sites. These thresholds are simply filters that ignore anything below a certain level of excitement/intensity/threat. Thrill junkies need high levels of stimulation to feel alive. A Buddhist master feels the same intensity of "aliveness" with each breath. If you are only seeing the cars that are traveling at one hundred miles per hour, or cost over $100,000, you are missing most of the traffic driving around you.

Considering the massive amounts of environmental stimuli/information that we are exposed to from moment to moment, it is clear that we filter out much of what is not considered (unconsciously) to have immediate value to our physical and psychological goals. And this is, over all, a good thing. Although my dog may be highly aware of a squirrel in the yard, the squirrel's presence is of little consequence to me unless the squirrel is eating my tomatoes, in which case this "squirrel information" is elevated to a level of greater significance in my psychological vetting system. But these types of filtrations of information that the personality performs on a moment-to-moment basis also contain information that may actually be very important to me. What I have been taught to notice is strongly determined by what my family has taught me to perceive and express. Some people are not allowed to perceive/express sexuality, and others are not allowed to perceive/express sadness, or thoughts, or anger. As a result, instead of experiencing sexuality, one simply experiences and expresses anxiety or guilt or shame, etc.

The thresholds of expression determine the levels of pressure we have to feel before we express ourselves, and there is a unique threshold of expression for each neural-emotional site. In some situations we are capable of responding immediately, thus availing ourselves of the information and energy associated with that emotional expression. But, in many situations we hold back, restricting our self-expression until we can't bear it any longer and finally say what we feel. The phrase "the straw that broke the camel's back" refers directly to the threshold at which we give ourselves "permission" to express our emotions. For example, it is a common practice for married couples to restrict self-expression, verbally and otherwise, producing chronic levels of stress, anxiety, and resentment. There often emerges a compensatory fantasy about the freedom that a divorce or affair would produce. The divorce fantasy is always, "Now I am free to do whatever I choose to do and can say whatever I wish to say." But until the individual reaches that threshold of expression, the marriage remains in a static and symptomatically resentful state. When the "dam" inevitably breaks, there is a flood of expression and action, usually with catalytic consequences. With all couples, I immediately recommend a cessation of any and all activities that produce resentment. I require them to commit to a lifestyle that resists compromise without consciousness.

The curious thing about self-expression is that we eventually communicate how we are feeling. It's not a question of "if" but rather "when" and in what manner. We are always expressing ourselves, directly or indirectly, either through communicating emotional information or symptom. The phrase "Something is sure bothering him" clearly illustrates that the mood of the person is surely being expressed, but the content of his distress is still hidden. One of my favorite phrases is "Just because you aren't saying it, doesn't mean I can't feel it."

The amount of pressure / time required to finally "let go and express" depends on the threshold of each emotion. Whereas someone might be able to express opinion and thoughts without much stress, that same individual might require tremendous internal pressure before expressing sadness, or anger, or sexuality. The threshold of expression is very simply set by our level of fear of the consequences.

The effectiveness of self-expression is associated with the quality of the communication. Even at the most pathological levels, expression is occurring, but in a primitive, symptomatic style. The more the emotional content is restricted and retarded, the more obtuse the communication becomes. Narcissistic personalities often believe that those who love them should be able to read their minds and meet their needs without the narcissist having to give voice to any thoughts or feelings. And they will say this directly to their loved ones: "If you loved me, you would know what I need." The narcissistic mother creates a contract with the child that allows the child to be "fabulous" as long as the mother can sustain a role of importance in the child's life. As a consequence, the child needn't ask for what he or she wants, but must remain passive, and mother will determine what will emotionally suffice. Thus, the narcissist, as an adult, is passively waiting for those deeper needs to be met, not communicating the need directly, and in fact, often feeling insulted that they should have to ask for what they want directly.

Overall, one might say that personality is a mechanism that has been taught how to interpret reality or the phenomena of reality. The more accurate that interpretation is, then the more successfully one is capable of pursuing life's goals, because we see the world more clearly. The more distorted the interpretation is, the more difficult to negotiate the challenges of living. If one is not conscious of being attracted to abusive or abandoning personalities, for instance, then one is constantly frustrated with the results of dating and mating. To repeat: "Anxiety is what occurs when you disagree with reality."

At its fundamental, functional level, the personality creates pressure in the psychological system, and although we may try to limit the effect of the pressure through drugs, spiritual practice, and other methods, at best we are only able to redirect the pressure or insulate awareness from the symptomology. Effective long-term symptom relief is only available through replacing the restrictive aspects of personality with expressive aspects. This is the goal of long-term therapy.

THREE-STEP SELF-ANALYSIS

James Masterson once commented in a workshop I attended that if one wants to understand the difference between how we were designed by creation and how we were reshaped by family and society, there is a three-step process we can follow. This is one of the most brilliant observations of psychological process of which I am aware. First: Be your genuine self. Be honest, truthful, direct, spontaneous, and don't hold back. Second: When your anxiety is triggered (being anxious, fearful, stressed, guilty, ashamed, etc.), it means that you are about to do something (express behaviors, thoughts, emotions) that you have been *taught* not to do. Third: Whatever you fear will be the consequences of your actions were the methods used to control you as a child (your fear reveals the type of discipline used on you as a child). For example, if you are afraid that you will have no friends and will be alone if you say what you are feeling, then isolation was the method used to control you as a child.

The fundamental fear is unique for each individual, based on how we were raised. Although there are many shared types of disciplines throughout the families of the world—physical punishment, abandonment, threats of poverty, silence, banishment, or being alone and friendless—*we only fear what we have actually experienced.* Masterson says repeatedly in his books that "self-activation" (genuine self-expression) triggers abandonment depression. I would rephrase that and say that "self-activation" triggers the fear of consequences (threat), in turn setting in motion our personality's repressive editing, resulting in an energetic compromise, and ultimately producing depression (all within minutes or even seconds). This sequence of emotional editing and its energetic consequence is what I have named the Activation-Resistance Cycle. (See chapter 8, "Treatment.)

Our fundamental fear is the memory of how we were punished as a child. We still fear being punished for expressing ourselves. I cannot emphasize enough the importance of this statement: *We still fear being punished for expressing ourselves.* We feel the anxiety attending our childhood training, minus the memory or emotion of those events, so we project the anxiety onto the present moment.

It's not that the world isn't filled with threatening people and dangerous situations; it is. But the psychological fear, trained into our nervous systems, begins in childhood. Of course, there are those fears that are not based in childhood but rather are the products of post-traumatic stress disorder (PTSD), wherein the person has been exposed to ferociously dangerous and threatening situations for extended periods of time, severely stressing the nervous system and producing an unfortunate variety of symptoms of psychological distress. PTSD requires a specific treatment strategy, although many of the techniques are similar to those with which we treat personality problems rooted in childhood.

FEAR AND MEMORY

No one fears something they have not experienced. We understand how pain works and can certainly recognize potential danger without having experienced every danger, but the core fears that undermine our freedom of expression have their roots in family discipline and trauma. When I ask clients what they fear will happen if they simply "let go" and say what they really want to say, I often get the response, "You know." Actually, I don't know. It's as though our personal fear is everyone's fear. But it isn't. We do share certain fears of specific consequences, but each person's fear has been tailored by his or her particular situation as a child, thus resulting in highly personal threats that we take very seriously in spite of the now-missing punishment.

Fears are logical. We don't fear something that is harmless. We fear potentially dangerous situations, people, animals, and environmental threats. The question we must ask is: *Is the emotional fear in proportion to the actual threat of this moment?*

Remember: energy in, energy out. The healthy psyche is capable of bringing no more or no less emotion than is required by the situation. We know when we are over-reacting. We know when our emotional expression is more than the situation requires. We know when someone else is overreacting. We feel it. And we also know that there must be something else bothering that person emotionally that is coming up inappropriately and unfairly in this situation.

The psyche has an uncanny sense of fairness. We can say that "it's the thought that matters," but we know that when we give someone a $100 present and receive a $25 present in return, that something unfair has occurred. It's one thing to give within the limits of our abilities, and it's another to be cheap. The deep psyche knows the difference. That same deep psyche also knows that phobia and anxiety disorders are out of balance. The phobia and anxiety disorders that do not have a biological basis are the result of energy blocked by the repressing of emotions. The intensity of the phobia/anxiety will be in direct proportion to the amount of emotion that has been repressed. Let's imagine that the psyche experiences one hundred watts of energetic stimulation from the environment. If only fifty watts of that energy is reflected back into the world through emotional expression, then the remaining fifty watts of that energy will be expressed through symptoms. All energy is expressed, some directly, some indirectly.

The Psychosomatic Scale

This simple graph contains a wealth of information. Each of the five neural-emotional systems is responsible for two significant functions, biological and psychological. Each of these two functions has a healthy as well as pathological expression. Developmental trauma, abuse trauma, and exposure trauma each compromise both biological and psychological functioning, producing symptomology associated with the functional compromise. I have not included the varieties of biological diseases commonly associated with psychological stress but remind the reader that medical problems play a significant role in identifying the contributing psychological problem. The biological site of disease or dysfunction should alert the clinician to the potential emotional pathology of that site. A symptomatic bio-emotional site is serving either to express the distress of another emotional complex, yet to be diagnosed, or has been psychologically compromised in and of itself. This scale is designed to be a quick reference for the association between biological organ, biological expression, emotional expression, and repression symptomology.

The goal of this graph is to correlate specific psychological functioning with the physical organ that regulates that information. Personality, as we have discussed, determines how awareness will perceive and emotionally respond to this information. There is always some tension in the psychological and physical systems, usually as a result of the personality's resistance to external stimuli (information) or the blunting of emotional response. This tension is site-specific, regulated by the thresholds of perception and expression at that location in the body. Physically, psychological resistance to the expression of anger (situated in the digestive system) will potentially show up as a digestive disorder, ulcer, or other disease of the gut.

Psychosomatic Scale

Physical Organ	Biological Expression	Psychological Expression	Repression Symptom
Head	Thought	Insight	Worry
Throat	Speech	Intent	Silence
Respiratory	Sadness	Empathy	Helplessness Pity
Digestive	Aggression	Courage	Resentment Control
Reproductive	Pleasure Sexuality	Intimacy	Addiction

Repressed emotional expression does not necessarily cause disease, but rather, disease is opportunistic and repression creates stress that gives disease, whether environmentally based or genetically based, an opportunity to compromise organ health.

Psychologically, repressed anger might show up as resentment, being overly controlling, obsessive, or rageful. Diagnostically, the wise practitioner knows that physical symptoms are as valuable to a psychological diagnosis as emotional symptoms. The presence of both the physical and emotional symptomology ensures a more accurate therapeutic strategy upon diagnosis. Resentment combined with a digestive disorder is most assuredly associated with repressed anger.

The psychosomatic scale simply illustrates the healthy expression of a neural-emotional site, as well as some of the emotional and physiological symptoms that can manifest when that site is excessively controlled. Examining the scale, we see the manner in which the body expresses itself at each one of the locations when it is not restricted: insight for the head, intent for the throat, compassion for the respiratory system, courage for the digestive system, and intimacy for the reproductive system. These are the wisdoms of the body, and when they operate in harmony with one another, awareness experiences the perspectives of these emotions as wisdom and clarity of purpose. When each of these neural-emotional systems is operating at full strength, one perceives the world with the highest accuracy possible and responds in proportion to the moment. When the neural-emotional system is repressed, symptomology can include: the head generates worry, the throat generates silence, the heart (respiratory) generates helplessness or pity, the gut (digestive) generates resentment and control, and the reproductive system generates addiction.

Diagnostically, are all addiction problems generated from blocked sexuality? Perhaps not, but it is certainly a good starting point to evaluate sexual functioning when dealing with addiction or pleasure obsessions. Keep in mind that a pornography addiction is rarely about sex as much as it is about the symptomology of fear of intimacy and repressed anger. The Psychosomatic Scale is an attempt to create a quick template for psychological evaluation and therapeutic strategy. Look for a synthesis of physical and psychological symptoms for the most accurate diagnosis and to develop the most effective therapeutic strategy.

CONCLUSION

Attempting to codify personality structure and the relationship between emotion, personality, and one's physical dynamics is a daunting task. The idea that there is an intimate connection between specific emotions and specific neurological sites is not a new concept; I am simply stating this connection directly.

Although many psychological systems attempt to differentiate positive personality versus pathological personality, I believe that it is awareness itself that is non-pathological and that all personality structure is, by design, restrictive and controlling and therefore a pathological obstacle to self-awareness. Fortunately, one's psychological potential is always available by developing a relationship with the unconscious and its contents.

My proposal that awareness perceives reality in five fundamental stages is further explored in my discussion of dream analysis in chapter 11, "Dream-Work." There is a parallel process with how awareness decodes reality and how awareness decodes dreams.

Although reality is experienced through a multitude of perceptions and a multitude of descriptions, what is incredible is our absolute conviction that what we are perceiving is, in fact, reality, and that which we do not know, we supplement with religion, superstition, or magic.

I leave you with these three quotes from Carlos Castaneda.

"The reality of our day-to-day life consists of an endless flow of perceptual interpretations which we . . . have learned to make in common.

What I held in mind as the world at hand was merely a description of the world; a description that had been pounded into me from the moment I was born.

Everyone who comes into contact with a child is a teacher who incessantly describes the world to him (her), until the moment when the child is capable of perceiving the world as it is described. . . . From that moment on . . . the child is a member (of society) . . . capable of making all the proper perceptual interpretations which, *by conforming to that description, validate it.*

—Don Juan to Carlos Castaneda, *Journey to Ixtlan*

PERSONALITY STRUCTURE

In this chapter, we explore James Masterson's proposition that there are four core personality structures out of which all personalities arise: narcissistic, borderline, anti-social, and schizoid. We will closely examine the diagnosis of the borderline personality disorder (BPD) and the theory and application of cognitive behavioral therapy (CBT) as a treatment strategy. We'll explore the limitations of the Diagnostic and Statistical Manual's (DSM) symptom-based diagnostic system and how it undermines the success rate of CBT in treatment of the borderline personality. And finally, we will carefully examine the diagnosis, treatment, and societal challenges of the anti-social personality.

SYMPTOMS VERSUS SOURCE

Much of today's graduate-level psychological clinical training is technique oriented and lacks the psychological superstructure to explain exactly why a technique might or might not work. Without an understanding of personality structure, the application of a technique is simply guessing at a treatment strategy. Symptom treatment continues to be the most common form of therapy practiced in the mental health community, and although the clinician may see a cessation of certain symptoms during treatment, unless the underlying repressed/dissociated emotional material is addressed, the client's psychological problem is far from resolved.

Therapy clients often suffer from a narrow point of view in which perceptual and expressive options are limited or fixed. As cognitive behavioral therapy predicts, opening the client's point of view by asking the client to imagine a variety of possible interpretations of events, as well as possible responses, can be an extremely effective technique. On the surface, it appears that the client is simply using imagination to produce multiple option outcomes. However, in order for the client to accept these new imaginative possibilities and then express an emotional response, the client must overcome some significant psychological obstacles. A simple shift in perspective allows the unconscious to inform awareness with new information, emotion, and energy. This newly acquired relationship with the unconscious, as a result of the CBT technique, is actually the re-engagement of awareness with the dissociated emotional material. When awareness opens itself to a new point of view, it is simply requesting information from the repressed and dissociated neurological complexes. Consequently, awareness begins risking contact with traumatized neural-emotional centers in order to access needed information, emotion, and energy. The client's psychological problem, manifesting as confusion, lack of insight, inhibited emotions, or an array of symptoms, is the result of developmental interruptions, direct and exposed traumas, and biological dynamics.

The theory that wrongheaded thinking or bad thoughts are creating the client's emotional problem is actually a misunderstanding of psychodynamics and a bad diagnostic system. Unless there is a medical problem, mental obsession is not the problem; it is always a symptom of the problem. Correcting the client's thinking will not relieve the pressure of the repressed emotions. Even if you can get the client to parrot a new way of thinking, he will have to develop another symptom to compensate for the still-blocked emotional complex. Emotion will be expressed either directly or indirectly through symptoms.

Years ago, I was referred a client that reported severe obsessive/compulsive neurosis associated with the fear that her pair of prized collies would be stolen and used in dogfights. (There is a history of dognapping and dogfights in my area of the country.) Her property was rather large, more than ten acres, completely fenced but with multiple gates. She could not overcome the fear that her dogs would either escape by digging under the fence and then be stolen or that one of the gates might be accidentally open, leading to the same disastrous loss. As a result, she literally spent her entire day, day after day, walking the fence line and making sure there were no gates left open or holes that would allow her pets to escape. But by the time she was halfway finished with her inspection, she became suspicious that she might have missed something on her first go-round and needed to repeat the inspection again, and again, and again. Her family, friends, and doctor had all attempted to convince her of the unlikelihood of this occurring, but she could not be convinced and remained possessed of the fear. Clearly, simply trying to correct her thinking in this matter produced no results. Medication intervention was equally ineffective. So I received the referral.

In my initial interview, I utilized my standard assessment: (1) environmental pressures, (2) medical history, (3) historical/developmental trauma, and (4) repressed self-expression. My client was remarkably open about her life and we were able to eliminate potential contributing causes fairly quickly. She was happily married, financially stable, and could not identify any significant environmental pressures. Often in extreme obsessive/compulsive disorders, there is an underlying affective or neurological disorder. The client reported good health and no family history of obsessiveness, compulsiveness, excessive worry, depression or mania, or even eccentricities occasionally associated with milder affective disorders. I then considered the possibility that something troubling had happened to her as a child that was emotionally associated to her current situation. She reported no significant trauma, loss, illness, violence, or significant unstable childhood circumstances. All that remained in the evaluation was assessment of the function of the five neural-emotional complexes: thought, speech, sadness, anger, and sexuality. The client was mentally adept with a logical mind and clear thinking and reasoning. Her speech was articulate and lacked inhibition. So I proceeded to the other three emotional expressions: sadness, anger, and sexuality. The client indicated that she and her husband had a healthy sex life and she had no complaints. She reported that she would cry on occasion and did so when appropriate. However, when I asked her about how she expressed anger, she clearly stated, "I never get angry." Surprised by her immediate answer I assumed that I had not been broad enough in my inquiry. So I responded, "No, no,

I mean, like if you are driving and there's someone in front of you frustrating you...how do you express that anger?" She again replied, "I never get angry," in a very matter-of-fact way. "You never get angry?" I asked, somewhat incredulous. "Never," she responded. Still wrapping my head around this perfectly clear answer, I asked again, "Ever?" To which she responded with some detail that she never got angry, ever. Now the little alarms were going off in my head. It's one thing to say that one "doesn't get angry" as a euphemism for attempting to control one's anger, or as a spiritual proposition, but it is completely something else to actually never, ever express anger.

Part of any symptomatic expression is that it often contains within it the solution to the problem. This would mean that my client's fear/ fantasy, might contain the resolution of the obsession. For example, in cases of claustrophobia, there is often a link with repressed anger. If you ask what the client would do if put into a restricted space, such as the back seat of a car, the answer is often that they would simply go berserk. Rarely does the client report a collapse into helplessness. Feeling confined is simply more than the personality can control, and suddenly the aggression that has fueled the symptom of claustrophobia is released in a massive, uncontrolled burst of fury.

Everyone with an expressive inhibition has a threshold that, when crossed, gives permission for the blocked emotion to be released. So, even if you are extremely controlling with your emotions, there is almost always the "straw that broke the camel's back," and the emotion comes roaring out. In psychodynamic theory, it is not "if" the emotion will be expressed, it is "when and how" the emotion will be expressed. With this in mind, I asked my client what her response would be if, God forbid, her precious pets were stolen and put into dogfights. Her response: "I would hunt them (the thieves) down and kill them!" We had found the threshold over which her anger is finally released. If her worst fears were confirmed, she would have permission to act on her anger.

If the obsessive/compulsive behavior is dynamically associated with anger, how does it work? Simple. It is impossible to live in this world and not be confronted regularly with aggressive situations and unreasonable people. By simply living a normal life, one's aggression is being triggered regularly. Most people have psychological strategies for relieving the pressure of their situational anger: exercise, drinking and drugs, angry driving, eating, simply yelling at others, or in some cases, periodic crying or depression. In the case of my client, the fear of the dog thieves was her "tell" or psychological smoke alarm. Every time something happened that made her angry, she experienced it as the fear of the loss of her collies. The situational aggression triggered the only fantasy that could actually permit her to get angry. However, until that horrific moment occurred (the veritable straw), instead of getting angry, she would compulsively check the fence. Something would make her angry and she would immediately become anxious about the dogs.

The therapy did not actually take much time. I explained how the obsession worked, and being bright and desperate, she was willing to practice some simple exercises that would reduce the amount of repressed anger she was carrying around with her. We didn't spend much time on "why" her aggression was so repressed (which is usually required to effect a long-term change), but rather simply applied an emotionally expressive solution to her psychodynamic problem: angry situation triggers anger in client that is repressed, which fuels the symptom (obsessive/compulsive behavior). Solution: express anger more easily and the symptom fueled by the repressed anger is simply no longer triggered. I would say that the simplicity of the solution and its application was as unique as the presenting symptom. In most cases, the simple solution of self-activating and then practicing the expression of the repressed emotion is blocked by the personality (memory of punishment for expressing aggression) and remains symptomatic.

The fear of negative consequences derails simple psychological health. If it were not for the fears associated with childhood, which produced one's personality structure, the psyche would naturally self-express on a moment-to-moment basis; instead, the psyche self-corrects by transferring energy from a blocked emotional expression into and through a symptomatic expression.

Remember, self-activation triggers the symptom profile. Any attempt to express the culprit emotion directly, which of course would be the simplest of psychological solutions, is too anxiety provoking; thus, the symptom remains the lesser of the two "evils." In the above case, the symptomatic obsession proved much more anxiety provoking than learning how to express aggression more effectively, thus, the simpler solution. It is much more common that our symptoms, as awful as they might be, are less problematic than the anxiety we experience when we attempt to break our family and social rules by expressing our emotions directly and honestly.

Identifying the expressive problem rarely takes a great amount of time if you know how to do the differential diagnosis. It is the client's struggle to overcome the fear of the expressive consequences that prolongs therapy.

In this case, the client's moral pride at refusing to express aggression was surely her worst enemy, psychologically.

Narcissism is often marked by an attitude of moral or ethical superiority concerning the importance of repressing an emotion. Not only is the narcissist aware of restricting the emotion, they are proud of it, essentially making the emotional block morally entrenched. This is the curse of perfectionism.

Therapeutic success is directly dependent on the assessment interview and diagnosis. Without addressing the emotional block, therapy could have lasted a very long time, and the likelihood is very high that ongoing medication would have been prescribed. Instead, the therapy lasted about six weeks, and she was satisfied with the results. As powerful as CBT is as a technique, this case precisely illustrates how a CBT approach could have failed. Having the client consider other options and possibilities of how to interpret her fears and thoughts rarely leads to the underlying expressive block. Instead, it reinforces an obsessive defensive mechanism. More thinking, even if it is creative, won't solve this problem.

Personality Structure Introductory Overview

Masterson suggests that there are only four core personality structures that give rise to the complex variations of all personalities: narcissistic, borderline (dependent), anti-social, and schizoid (Asperger's) (parentheses are mine).

Masterson redefines the parameters of the borderline diagnosis, removing the anti-social features so that it has greater consistency with the Dependent Personality. Diagnostically, it appears that schizoid shares so many personality features with Asperger's as to be indistinguishable, and considering that the identification and treatment of children and adults with Asperger's is gaining traction in the psychological community, I prefer the term Asperger's instead of schizoid and will substitute this for Masterson's use of the schizoid diagnosis. Since Masterson derived this system, Asperger's has been identified as a biological presentation of neural diversity rather than an interrupted developmental presentation.

The Narcissists: The Narcissistic personality structure produces three unique presentations: the Grandiose, the Inverted, and the Phallic (the thrill seeker, a variation of the grandiose narcissist, as described by Alexander Lowen).

The Grandiose Narcissist: The narcissist is often bright, accompanied by accomplishment, but has limited interpersonal skills, has an easily wounded self-image, has a secret longing to be loved and accepted, and suffers from a general disappointment at a lack of consistent positive recognition. Alice Miller, in her book, *The Drama of the Gifted Child*, portrays the systematic manner in which the narcissistic needs of the child (the need for positive and confirming mirroring from the environment) have been repeatedly blunted or directed to fill the narcissistic needs of the parents. With little self-confirmation to offer, the parents frustrate large parts of the child's psychological activation, requiring cooperation from the child in order for the child to receive the narcissistic/self-affirming gifts that the parents do have to offer. The classic grandiose narcissist has the favorite child syndrome or at least managed the occasional opportunity to earn the favored child role through specific pleasing.

The Inverted Narcissist: There is always an unconscious compensatory aspect of every conscious attitude, counterbalancing the excesses of ego. Thus, for every grandiose persona (Jung's term for the interactive personality components), there is a hidden wounded aspect of self, The Shadow. This is true of all personality structures: persona and shadow. The inverted narcissist could also be called the wounded narcissist, in that the grandiose self is the part that is hidden in the shadow, where one secretly adopts the attitude that one is special, and that people are idiots, or incompetent. These individuals present much more as lacking self-confidence, with depression or anxiety. Because the inverted narcissist's emotional presentation is so similar to the dependent-borderline, these individuals are often misdiagnosed: treatment is awkward, or ineffective in creating a therapeutic alliance.

The Phallic Narcissist (the thrill seeker): This variant, as described by Alexander Lowen, has a need for high stimulation experiences in order to penetrate the emotional insulation/dissociation by which they feel possessed, the result of a combination of childhood emotional sensitivity and environmental hostility. The result is a hunger for stimulation strong enough to evoke a feeling of "aliveness," mimicking an emotional connection. It is common for this group to have "addictive" behaviors involving sex, drugs, or power (politics, administration, etc.), or behavior as a high-energy exercise fanatic. The addictive habit must involve activities that are sufficiently intense, triggering emotional release. Sexual behavior can briefly provide a sense of relief, connection, and aliveness, but fades all too rapidly, resulting in compulsive sexual/drug/power/exercise reengagement.

The Borderline: Masterson, in my opinion, uses the term "borderline" when he is in fact describing a dependent personality. In order to develop an effective treatment strategy, he has dismissed the anti-social features of the mixed borderline symptom tree. This book presumes a dependent personality whenever discussing the borderline personality, and I will use the term dependent-borderline throughout the text. I

64

give a complete review, in this chapter, of the current borderline diagnosis and how it is contaminated beyond repair.

The Dependent: When we examine the narcissistic personality structure, we are evaluating which components of self-expression are activated and which are repressed. With the dependent personality, the child has been systematically trained to be submissive and dependent by repressing all components of self-expression. Any self-activation has been punished; therefore, the strategy of this personality type is to follow the lead of everyone but oneself. They can be excellent students, performing to the expectations of their teachers, but with little autonomy in expressing their own opinions; thus, a research paper would be all research and no opinion. There is always the possibility that they could come under the influence of someone who takes advantage of their passivity. This could occur in romantic relationships, research fellowships, poorly paying jobs, even criminal activities and abuse: any position where the dependent individual's resources/talents are taken advantage of because of their inability to self-represent.

The general therapeutic goal for both the dependent and narcissistic personalities is for the client to overcome the fear of the consequences of self-activation.

Remember, some parts of a narcissistic personality structure will function reasonably effectively. These parts serve as templates for evolving the more restricted aspects of the personality. Awareness can intentionally return to the functioning of these parts of the personality, getting relief from the symptomology of the restricted parts. This expressive relief is not available to the dependent personality except in pathological submission (which is the relief of safety, not self-expression). There is little refuge for awareness in the dependent personality's structure, because any true self-expression always triggers anxiety. As a result, unconscious passive-aggressive and sabotaging behaviors are common in the dependent personality.

The Anti-Social: This diagnosis has three fundamental forms: the reactionary sociopath, the predatory psychopath, and the neurological psychopath.

The sociopath disguises him/herself typically as narcissistic or DSM-borderline personality disorder. This person presents as having social skills and even a limited moral or ethical code, until backed into a corner, and suddenly, we have a full-blown anti-social personality on our hands. The misdiagnosed sociopath is actually the personality disorder that gives narcissism its bad name and makes the borderline personality so treatment resistant.

The predatory psychopath is simply the aggressive form of the anti-social personality. These people are hunters and users.

The neurological psychopath is the bio-chemical variant of the predator, but in this case, there is a neurological processing problem that presents as a lack of empathy and a willingness to make others miserable simply because they can. Later, this chapter contains a thorough examination of the anti-social personality structure, its prevalence in society, and its inaccurate relegation to the borderline diagnosis.

Asperger's: Asperger's is a neural-diverse learning system that separates itself from "neural-typical" learning styles in that there may be an absence or under-activation of the mirror neuron capacity. In practical terms, this means that people who have a neural-typical, mirror neuron nervous system literally resonate emotionally with their environment, building a psychological inventory of social and emotional behavior. For example, if you have two tuning forks tuned to "G," and you strike one tuning fork, creating an auditory tone, and then slowly bring it towards the other, silent, tuning fork, the silent tuning fork will begin to sympathetically vibrate at the same frequency, sharing the tonal vibration of the first tuning fork. Both tuning forks are now sharing the vibration. Now imagine that this is what a neural-typical, mirror gene nervous system does. The infant is exposed to varieties of emotional vibrations that contain information, specific emotion, and intensity. The child's emotional resonance creates an inventory of information in the unconscious that becomes useful as the child matures, providing an inventory of social behavior that can translate non-verbal and emotional expression in others. In a sense, we are all waiting for our Helen Keller moments.

The person with an Asperger's neural-diverse system learns social and emotional information by studying human behavior and practicing strategies for relating to others. This is a much more labor-intensive style of learning and can become overwhelmed by complex social situations. Although there are certainly pathological extremes within the Asperger's family, I am not convinced that Asperger's, overall, is a disorder as much as it is a parallel operating system that may be significantly more prevalent in the general population than we realize. Some people argue that the number of people with Asperger's is increasing. I would argue that there is probably a cycle of increase and decrease between the neural-typical and neural-diverse operating systems in the past five thousand years, with each cyclically dominating local cultural values with their rising tide. These two neural systems may be subtly reflected in the difference between *moral order* (Asperger's) and *moral responsibility* (mirror). In the past one hundred years, there does seem to be a strong increase in the number of people with the neural-typical design, leaving those with an Asperger's learning system feeling like everyone else is speaking a language they don't understand, or in some extreme cases, don't respect (a general disregard for the suffering of others).

It is premature to say that empathy is a byproduct of certain neural processing, including the presence or absence of neural mirroring, but there may be a link. This raises a sticky issue concerning some similarities between Asperger's and psychopathology as defined by Dr. Robert Hare (*Without Conscience*). Limited emotional resonance does not imply inability to love, but it certainly affects the presentation of that love. It is possible that the large non-criminal spectrum of Hare's psychopathic research is actually extreme Asperger's. Since personality function is predominantly strategic for the person with Asperger's, the type of personalities that these children are exposed to will have a strong impact on the style of self-expression adopted as an adolescent and adult. Thus, there really is a developmental aspect to the personality style that someone with Asperger's presents, but the psychological method used to come by any particular personality style is significantly different from the neural-typical empathetic resonance.

I suspect that there will come a time when medical science can track and identify the genetic underpinnings for the evolution of the neural-typical and neural-diverse structures, much like we are recently capable of doing with Neanderthal genetic signatures in modern people. This will not, however, change the developmental challenges faced by those with an Asperger's perceptual and expressive design. They still have to figure out how to socialize and express their psychological gifts.

THE DEVELOPMENTAL FORMATION
OF PERSONALITY

The theory of *developmental activation or interruption* describes the series of stages through which the infant's nervous system unfolds, activating certain perceptual and expressive potentialities. This theory predominantly applies to neural-typical process. Neurodiversity, such as Asperger's, proceeds along a unique parallel path (learning style), and thus, needs to be evaluated by different expressive markers.

Since Asperger's is a genetic, neural-diverse learning variant, we are left with three neural-typical *developmental* structures as the foundation of all personalities. We need to abandon the sloppy and inaccurate method of symptom-based diagnosis and replace it with an analysis of the personality components that are revealed in a person's relationship style. The relationship tools that each person uses to interact with others reflects the components of his or her personality that have been activated or repressed. These relationship styles are what identify the personality structure, as well as which parts of the personality structure are expressed and which parts are producing the symptoms of suffering.

Diagnostically, the three neural-typical personality structures are: narcissistic (partial activation of psyche), dependent-borderline (activation is limited to submission), and finally anti-social (adversarial activation of psyche).

Assuming a healthy biological system, the child travels through a series of stages of neural activation in which they learn perceptual interpretation and practice self-expression.

If one considers the possibility that the Self contains all the potentialities of the individual, then the role of the environment, and in particular, the family, is to activate, cultivate, and encourage the child in adopting a perceptual schema and an expressive style.

However, no family, well intentioned or abusive, operates without imposing self-concerned needs on its children. When the family or social system finds fault with a child's interpretation of reality, the child learns to suppress his or her experience and adopt a shared point of view. When the family or social system finds fault with specific forms of self-expression, the child learns to regulate the expression of these emotional aspects of Self. The personality structure is specifically designed to control perception and self-expression in order to meet the approval of the family and social systems. This approval becomes a self-expressive contract in which the child views the world and/or expresses herself in a manner that provides protection from punishment or attack and simultaneously receives tacit approval for the expressed behavior. Essentially, the child perceives and acts in a manner to please the environment and reduce the risk of trauma.

Thus, personality structure is nothing more than a series of perceptual and behavioral contracts with the world. It is the learned expectations of this personality structure that we project onto the world, anticipating the same results from the world as those we experienced in our family, both fearful and hopeful.

The curious thing about our childhood psychological training is that we have full confidence in our perceptual accuracy and emotional expression, in spite of the amount of suffering that we experience due to our psychological obstructions.

If we are fortunate enough to have been given permission to perceive parts of reality accurately, and express parts of our psychological potential, we will utilize those functions at every possible opportunity, taking full advantage of those perceptions and specific skills. Meanwhile, our perceptual blind spots continue to undermine our life experiments (why do I repeatedly date the same type of person?) and the unexpressed emotions relegated to the unconscious continue to create symptoms.

Awareness does not ultimately require personality except as a means to avoid threat and prevent punishment, and there seems to be an inverse correlation between self-realization (insight, emotional fluidity, and psychological energy) and the interference of this protective personality structure. Personality is functionally pathological: designed to inhibit perception and expression in order to promote self-protection. This means that for awareness to achieve its highest potential, personality must have its influence significantly reduced.

Masterson proposed an object relations approach to diagnosis that simplifies identifying personality disorders and improves outcome (if you know what you're fixing, there is a much better chance of succeeding with the repair). He argued that the client's transference, or style of relationship, is a much more accurate diagnosis of personality structure than the symptom profile. The implication is that the style of relating to others is uniquely shaped by the personality structure, whereas symptoms are almost universally shared by everyone. Thus, how a narcissist relates to others, or how a dependent personality relates to others, or how an anti-social personality relates to others, or even how an Asperger's personality relates to others, is unique to the personality structure behind the relationship.

Since each of these four personality types share the complete symptom profile: anxiety, guilt, shame, resentment, etc., a symptom-based diagnosis can easily confuse and intermix these personality structures.

Psychological symptoms are universal and can be shared by any rigid personality structure. However, the transference style (submissive, charming, helpful, resentful, studied, strategic, adversarial, or passive), or the specific transference itself (merging, mirroring, idealizing, erotic, strategic, or adversarial), is, in fact, the unique signifier of the personality structure of the client. (See chapter 8, "Treatment," *Transference*.)

In the initial therapeutic assessment and the ongoing treatment, the therapeutic alliance and transference are more important than the content of the complaints. This is because the complaints are part of the symptom profile.

In many, if not most clinical cases of psychological impairment, it's not that the client lacks ability or information to handle his problems; it's that the client resists self-activation and doesn't trust his perception, judgment, or his emotional response.

SELF-ACTIVATION AND PERSONALITY STRUCTURE

With the dependent-borderline personality, self-expression is completely repressed. Self-activation (opinions, creative initiatives, pursuit of self-interests, etc.) have all been threatened and punished, and thus the dependent personality waits for instructions from the world, and patiently, if not fearfully, cooperates with the demands of everyone in the environment. In the case of the narcissist, parts of his psyche have been activated, and the narcissist attempts to meet all emotional and energetic needs through the overuse of those few active parts of the Self. Narcissists can self-activate, but only within the parameters of the family-approved forms of self-expression, which are often performance based. Unfortunately, when those approved personality traits (charming, smart, disciplined, intimidating, etc.) fail to gain the anticipated response from environment, the narcissist is left with the same symptoms of the repressed self as the dependent-borderline, the wounded child. The major difference between the narcissist and the dependent is that the narcissist has been given permission to express a greater quantity of features of the Self, but only within the context of seeking approval and praise from others. Without this approval, the narcissist is just as frustrated and blocked as the dependent-borderline.

For example, if a person is born with ten major personality traits, the dependent-borderline is permitted to express only one of these traits: submission. The narcissist may be permitted to express three or four of these traits (charm, intelligence, ability, seduction, etc.).

The challenge for both the narcissist and the dependent is to overcome their fear of social disapproval and then to access and develop the unexpressed contents of the unconscious. The narcissist may present as successful, educated, well married, or professional, and this is due to the successful use of the activated parts of the Self. What brings the narcissist and the dependent-borderline to therapy are the constant nagging feelings of loneliness, isolation, persecution, emotional insulation, depression, or anxiety associated with the languishing parts of the Self, still confined to the unconscious.

The anti-social personality is relationally adversarial, even when acting charming or seductive. In the anti-social family system, the child's need for love, affection, and confirmation, is responded to with neglect, cruelty, and abuse. The child begins to develop a hostile response to any form of potential affection or compassion. Regardless of how much of the Self has been activated or repressed, self-expression is always predicated on survival and avoidance of punishment. The underlying relationship dynamic is inevitably adversarial, with a utilitarian approach to relationship, economic opportunity, and group membership.

The Asperger's personality style is predominantly strategic, studying behavior and developing tactics and strategies for social interaction. Thus, they can present as any of the other three core personalities, which is probably an indicator of the type of family in which they were raised. They can adopt narcissistic, dependent, or anti-social features that often interfere with the accurate diagnosis of Asperger's. Social awkwardness in this population is predominantly due to a limited set of social strategies and leads to a much more significantly introverted life-style.

A variety of presenting symptoms—frustration, depression, anxiety, alienation, lack of fulfillment, etc.—are potentially present in all of the personality structures. However, each of these personality structures will respond to a relationship with the therapist (therapeutic alliance) in a unique manner: the dependent-borderline will be submissive, the narcissist will perform (tragedy is a performance as well), the anti-social will eventually be adversarial, and the Asperger's will be cautious and strategic.

The presumed expectations of relationship are unique to one's personality structure, and therefore, diagnostic: no activation (dependent-borderline), partial activation (narcissist), punitive activation (anti-social), or strategic and distancing (Asperger's).

THE NARCISSISTIC PERSONALITIES

The narcissistic personality is common, with three predominant variations: grandiose (performer), inverted (wounded), and phallic (thrill seeker).

The *grandiose narcissist* presents as one who is relatively high functioning, both emotionally insensitive and emotionally needy, rarely feels deeply connected to others, personalizes comments, opinions, and emotions different from his own, and is constantly frustrated by his lack of recognition by significant others. He displays his "shiny" side (the parts his mother approved of) to the world in an attempt to win approval while hiding his wounded side, except in those situations of significant disappointment. The *inverted narcissist* presents as the opposite of the grandiose type. He is typically misdiagnosed as a dependent or borderline personality, presenting depression, anxiety, emotional volatility, and hyper-sensitivity to rejection or criticism, and often accompanied by severe passive-aggressive traits. As a result, unlike the actual dependent-borderline personality, he responds *adversarially to confrontation*. The *phallic narcissist* is the thrill seeker in this group, having discovered that sex, drugs, or power can temporarily relieve him of his crushing depression, feelings of isolation, and anxiety. This is the personality structure behind many of the high functioning addicts (sex, drugs, gambling) and thrill seekers. Rule out bi-polar in the phallic narcissist diagnosis.

The narcissistic personality varies widely in rigidity, suffering, and symptom. The percentage of the psyche compromised by the inhibiting effects of the personality structure (20 percent functionality versus 90 percent functionality) determines the severity of the symptoms.

The narcissist specifically suffers from partial activation of his or her psychological potential. Any perception or expression that is not approved is sublimated, repressed, or dissociated. The rejected parts fuel the symptom profile.

The approved and activated components are linked to an expectation that the world will love and approve of him in a manner mirroring the mother's response. When the world (marital partner, child, boss, employee, teacher) fails to meet the responsive expectations, the narcissist is thrown into an agitated state, leading to emotional acting out, depression, anxiety, combative or threatening behavior, passive aggressive sulking, drinking, drugs, affairs, compulsive buying, etc.

The acting out is usually done in a style shared in the family or at least in a style permitted by the family. Even though the narcissist may perform in certain areas of his life at quite a competent level, he constantly feels wounded by the stress of his blocked self-expression and the lack of environmental positive mirroring he once experienced with his mother.

The difference between healthy mother approval and pathological mother approval is that in the pathological approval, the mother is supporting her own narcissistic emotional needs through the specific performance of her child. The child adopts his/her self-expression as a way of achieving love, approval, and safety. It is a contract for love. The mother makes the performance request and the child attempts to fulfill that request; the mother then reinforces or punishes the child's performance. The acts of affection and approval are performance based *versus* autonomous self-expression arising from curiosity, creativity, and courage. The child, now an adult, although having received permission to express certain parts of his psyche, is bound to the expectation parameters (performance style and expected approval or punishment) of the mother, transferring these expectations to the world in general:

work, romance, self-activation. However, no amount of performance approval by the environment will compensate for the chronic, and often acute, symptomology arising from the blocked psychological components. As a result of their unconscious search for, and need to find, that external approval (established by mother), they unconsciously allow themselves to be taken advantage of. These individuals become prime targets for psychological predators who are able to morph into a variety of emotional reflections capable of providing strategic support (grooming) as part of a seduction to access resources (home, money, travel, social position, etc.). These predators are capable of sustaining the desired emotional mirroring for as long as it takes to "seal the deal," (marriage, baby, money, social status), and then, look out!

Although narcissism can present as symptomatically complex, the formation and structure of the narcissistic personality is easily identi-fiable and treated. What Masterson's diagnostic system does is discard the complexity of the symptom diagnosis and ask a simple question: "What did the parents love and support in this child?" (obedience, per-formance, dependence, brilliance, creativity, helplessness, submission, aggression, cleverness, rescuing behavior, whining, etc.). There is a significant correlation between mother's approval, even if the approval is narrowly selective in its emotional support, and the formation of the narcissistic personality structure. The mother simply supports the activation of parts of the child's psyche that make her feel "proud" and systematically suppresses the parts of the child's psyche she finds unac-ceptable. In the narcissistic system, self-expression is a performance contract that never consistently or completely fulfills the expressive or acceptance needs of the person. No amount of approval compensates for the inevitable perceptual blind-spots, emotional volatility, and ener-getic depletion.

The Grandiose Narcissist: The initial presentation for the *grandiose narcissist*, although depressed and anxious, is typically pleasing, cooper-ative, or even charming, depending on the client's narcissistic "rules of relationship." They are testing the therapist for the hoped-for mirror-ing of love and approval. The narcissist's wounded side is identical to the dependent personality; there are potentially large amounts of the client's self-expression that have been strictly denied expression by the parents and family system. The narcissist will reveal these depressive/avoidant features later in therapy, but, typically, not in the beginning presentation. Expressing these repressed complexes will be part of the long-term therapeutic goal. What is unconscious must become conscious.

The Inverted (disguised) Narcissist: Masterson also proposes a variant of the narcissist that he has labeled the "inverted narcissist," in which the client presents his wounded and depressed side to the therapist rather than the cooperative, charming, and grandiose side. In these cases, the inverted client may appear to be more in the dependent-borderline diagnostic category. Masterson suggests a simple differential diagnostic technique: a mild confrontational question. Narcissists take offense at confrontation, whereas the dependent personality will simply consider the question. The offensive response to a mild confrontation is the marker of the narcissistic personality structure. It's that simple.

The dependent-borderline can only express submission and dependency by crushing self-activation and self-expression. The narcissist differs in that a variety of psychological gifts can be activated and expressed, but only within the parameters of mother's approval. The narcissist and the dependent personalities are perennially seeking the mother's approval through any and all authority and intimate figures in their lives, to their continued disappointment and anxiety. The only difference between these two personality types is the behavior they expect to be approved: dependency versus performance.

The Phallic Narcissist (the thrill seeker): Alexander Lowen MD, in his wonderful book, *Narcissism*, describes a sub-type of narcissism that he calls the "phallic narcissist." This person is identified by a need for high levels of stimulation. Lowen felt that this variant of the narcissistic personality, through a combination of developmental wounds and a particular psychological sensitivity, is wrapped in a cocoon of emotional insulation that protects him or her from emotional insult. The problem is that the thicker the insulation, the greater the need for high levels of stimulation to penetrate the emotional barrier so that the narcissist can feel alive. It is safe to say that the "cocoon" Lowen is describing is more accurately identified as dissociation, in which awareness simply retreats from the area(s) of the body being traumatized. Severe developmental insults (isolation, control, discipline) radically increase the dissociative effect and produce the insulation that shields awareness from emotional wounding. But it also shields the narcissist from feeling loved, connected, and alive by constricting perception and expression.

The pulse of life is only experienced through the fullness of the function of the body. The rhythmic reality that sings around us is silent for those who have abandoned their emotions or are possessed by resentment and rigid emotional control.

These individuals, insulated from their own feelings, sometimes become thrill seekers as a way of reawakening their connection with their bodies. However, the thrill is only temporary as the awareness immediately retreats from any emotion that might make us vulnerable to being hurt. There are three types of stimulation that the phallic narcissist is particularly attracted to: sex, drugs, and power. Each of these methods can be increased in intensity to the point where the individual begins to literally feel alive again, and these methods provide a brief respite from the narcissist's emotionally isolated cell. Due to the temporary nature of the thrill, the narcissist develops a compulsive need to repeat the experience in order to feel connected to life. Without working through the emotional trauma that keeps the narcissist isolated and blunts all emotional experiences, the narcissist repeatedly seeks succor in those behaviors that often undermine their families, careers, and financial security. In this sense, however, the behavior of the phallic narcissist points to the solution: a need to feel emotions. This type of acting-out is simply the method that has worked, regardless of how poorly, to keep the individual connected to the life force and provide some meager sense of feeling.

A diagnostic challenge that might arise with these individuals is differentiating between the phallic narcissist, a bi-polar spectrum disorder (or both), or a sociopath.

The phallic narcissist has developed a strategy for feeling alive that is compulsive only in that, through repetition, the effect of the emotional insulation can be breached, providing relief from the chronic emotional isolation.

The anxiety or depression that occurs between the ritual events (sex, drugs, power) is the direct result of awareness losing emotional vitality when avoiding emotional pain by dissociating. The bi-polar spectrum behavior, in contrast to the phallic narcissist, is driven by an unstable biochemical disease manifesting as impulsivity, risk taking, lack of concentration, and a high sex drive. The phallic narcissist will at least gain some sense of connectedness and satisfaction from his or her "addictive" behaviors, whereas for the bi-polar spectrum individual, there is only temporary stress relief, requiring repetition without any sustainable satisfaction.

Therapy with Narcissists: Narcissists are extraordinarily tuned to the emotional states of others. The problem is that this information is usually taken personally, thus rendering this emotional sensitivity useless and painful. With the narcissistic personality, confrontation at the beginning of therapy is usually, if not always, experienced by the client as insensitive and wounding. Narcissists take everything so personally that even mild confrontation, or humor, is viewed as an emotional insult. The best starting tactic with narcissists is empathy. Quickly try to identify the genuine abilities of the narcissistic client: intelligence, emotional sensitivity, and specific skill sets. Narcissists are notorious for being emotionally insensitive to others while being hypersensitive to how they are being treated. This is because they personalize the emotional behaviors of others, as though the emotional expressions of

75

other people are somehow specifically directed at them. The narcissist is certainly tuning into the emotional states of other people, which can actually be a real advantage when this emotional information is de-personalized, but initially it is experienced as painful personal commentary. The narcissist needs the world to constantly affirm him, and when this doesn't happen, and some less comforting emotion is being expressed by others, the narcissist immediately reacts defensively. Anything less than positive emotion is experienced as a personal wound.

Much of the narcissist's personalizing of the emotions of others arises from insufficient positive mirroring of the child by the parent, during childhood.

All children personalize the emotions in their environment. This is a predictable developmental stage. We all start with the developmental perception that the world is "all about me." However, delayed or absent gratification, constant emotional frustration, inconsistent or missing positive regard, and limited or absent praise leaves the child stuck in this self-absorbed stage for life.

Insufficient and inconsistent positive regard, combined with a parent who overlooks, rationalizes, or simply disregards the needs of the child, or who may just need to feel needed, thus demanding some helplessness or incompetence from the child, leaves the child narcissistically wounded.

Even though narcissists personalize others' emotions, actual sensitivity to the emotional state of other people is ultimately very useful for reading the moods of those around them. Ironically, though narcissists are notorious for being completely insensitive to the feelings of others, they respond this way precisely because they are hypersensitive to the feelings of others.

One of the therapeutic challenges is to teach the narcissist how to accurately read the emotions of others without being trapped in the perceptual and interpretive distortions that make those emotions feel personal.

Narcissists are often quite intelligent, professionally skilled, or gifted in some area (although this is certainly not a requirement). Once the therapist has identified the client's actual gifts, the next goal is to create an alliance by acknowledging these features and how they are often underappreciated, overlooked, and a cause of distress due to emotional sensitivity. On the face of it, it sounds like this technique reinforces the often obvious grandiosity and whininess of the client. In fact, in order to create a therapeutic alliance, the therapist is mirroring that narcissistic nurture with the intent of eventually exploring the narcissistic wound (inhibited self-expression).

Because narcissists personalize other people's emotional expression, these clients are often emotionally isolated and lonely. They can't bear the constant failure of the environment to mirror a consistently positive regard. Narcissists have the same self-expressive wounding that the dependent personality has: the components of their psyche that would give them an internal self-soothing system are too highly restricted, held prisoner by anticipated punishment or rejection. The results of emotional repression or dissociation are the same for everyone: symptomology, reduced energy, distorted perception, and wounded self-image.

The therapist needs to do some positive shared-functioning with the narcissist to create a therapeutic alliance. Ultimately, the therapist knows that the deeper problem is compromised self-expression associated with one or more emotions. The client may actually deny childhood difficulties, but it is not a complicated task to identify which emotions are not being expressed and eventually track the client's symptom profile to those repressed emotions.

A Short Diagnostic Review: Theoretically, each neural-emotional site (thought, speech, sadness, aggression, sexuality) contributes twenty percent of the overall information, emotion, and energy of the psyche, thus one hundred percent functioning of each neural-emotional center would represent the full perceptual and expressive capacity. However, most people have varying percentages of functionality at each site. One's normal energetic capacity represents the total combined functioning of all of the neural-emotional centers. Each center has its own regulatory rules affecting perceptual accuracy, emotional expression, and energy level. As the child is experimenting with the perceptual and expressive abilities of each neural emotional site, the significant members of the child's environment encourage or discourage the function of that site, affecting perception, emotion, and energy. We are being systematically conditioned by our world as to how to perceive and express, or repress, each of our major neural-emotional complexes: thinking, speaking, sadness, aggression, and sexuality. One or more of these complexes might be operating quite well, while several others might be rigidly controlled and symptomatic. We need a thorough analysis of each complex to develop a therapeutic treatment strategy. Here are seven basic evaluation goals:

1. The overall function of each neural-emotional site. Simply ask the person how well he thinks he functions in thinking, speaking, sadness, aggression, and sexuality.
2. Accuracy of perception at each site: Can he read specific information about the world through the five complexes? Is the

person aware of intellectual, empathic, competitive, or seductive cues from the environment?

3. Effective emotional expression at each site
4. Style of expression at each site
5. Overall symptom profile (anxiety, tension, stress, guilt, shame, fear, resentment, worry, depression, compulsion, somatization).
6. Identification of which symptom attends which emotional restriction. What specific emotions are fueling the client's symptoms? (e.g. crying when angry, anxiety instead of sexuality, etc.)
7. Specific fear of consequences at each site (the Or-Else). (The formula for horror movies is often: if you have sex, you will be killed fairly quickly in the film.) What is the underlying fear of the consequences of expressing one's thoughts, sexuality, sadness, or anger? Whatever you fear will be the consequences was the method used to control you as a child (Masterson).

The therapist needs to create a therapeutic alliance that will eventually reveal the developmental compromises and the lonely childhood that resulted. Keep in mind, the family has only activated specific parts of the client's personality, and the client has attempted to accomplish all of life's complex challenges with these few activated components (exactly in the same manner in which the dependent personality tries to negotiate all of life's complexities through a submissive attitude).

In those positive relationships, where the expectations of the parents actually align with the abilities of the child, the child experiences a free flow of self-expression and little immediate psychological suffering. However, when the child's experimental behavior does not meet the parent's emotional mirroring needs (what will the neighbors think about me because of my child's behavior?), the parent systematically requires the child to repress any behaviors that seem contrary to the parent's self-image.

These are the parts of the psyche that will be necessary for healthy human interaction but are unavailable due to fear of expressive consequences. The suffering occurs when the world requires broader emotional expression and the needed psychological components are repressed. The narcissist remains frustrated, emotionally blocked, and unable to live up to his own expectations of excellence due to blocked self-expression. So, narcissists often use drugs, cars, sex, thrills, gambling, and other potent symptomatic distracters to occupy the psychological energy that is imprisoned. These efforts provide temporary relief from the rigidity of the personality structure but fail to address the deep anguish associated with their childhoods and the resulting emotional inhibition, the release of which would liberate their emotional expression and allow for creativity and authentic joy.

The real problem for narcissists is that they are attempting to accomplish all of their psychological tasks through a very narrowly expressive personality. If the problem cannot be resolved by being charming, or hyper-functional, or wounded, or domineering, or "brilliant," they have no complementary psychological abilities and their emotional defenses kick in and ruin the moment. Rage, defensiveness, depression, moodiness, drug abuse, and isolation overtake the potential for authentic engagement with people and events. The psychological components that would be helpful and appropriate have been repressed and offer only symptoms.

THE ASPERGER'S PERSONALITY

Diagnostic differentiation: If your client is presenting as narcissistic but can't read the emotions of others, consider high functioning Asperger's instead. Asperger's clients can very successfully mimic a narcissistic personality, especially if one of their parents is narcissistic. The "wounding" of the Asperger's client is not from personalizing the emotions of others, but rather from the anxiety of not being able to read the emotional language of those around them or being irritated by the failure of the world to act as expected.

If emerging research findings are accurate, the high functioning Asperger's diagnosis will turn out to be much more prevalent than currently reported. The inclusion of Asperger's as part of the autism spectrum and the continued use of schizoid as a separate category in the DSM-V is questionable at best. The original Asperger's diagnosis was finally achieving some social traction and we are making headway in the identification and treatment of adult Asperger's. Unfortunately, this unique genetic operating system will have to persevere independently from the blessing of the DSM-V committee, and unfortunately, many clinicians will have to adjust their diagnosis in order to provide treatment. A colleague of mine bumped into Dr. Temple Grandin, the world-renowned autism activist and animal ethicist, in a Florida airport and asked how Dr. Grandin felt about the anticipated placement of Asperger's into an autism spectrum disorder in the upcoming DSM-V. Dr. Grandin was reportedly disappointed.

There are many Asperger's individuals who present superb mental ability, charm, highly functional professional abilities, and only a little quirkiness, until someone starts looking at the behavior closely. Asperger's behaviors are tactical and strategic, designed to effectively operate in social situations. It is often much easier to identify the Asperger's personality in children with complex social difficulties and then work back to the parents to identify the source of the Asperger's. I've been surprised more than once about my assumptions of the presence of a narcissistic or anti-social personality in a new client, when in fact, Asperger's with narcissistic or anti-social traits/presentation is a much more accurate diagnosis.

The Asperger's client is often brought to therapy for marriage counseling or by a family member hoping to improve the client's awkward and often "insulting or cold" behavior. The highly intelligent person with Asperger's will often have developed very sophisticated social strategies and appear to have few obvious social problems. These individuals tend to dedicate themselves to hard, even obsessive work regimens to limit social anxiety (you can't socialize if you are constantly working). They can be superb in their professional field, marry, raise families, and for all purposes, look typical. These are the narcissistic Asperger's and can be extremely high functioning. This population may be much larger than we have previously estimated. Remember: If a family has a child with Asperger's, there is a good chance at least one parent is in the Asperger's spectrum.

When analyzing the challenging Asperger's personality traits, it is difficult to ascertain whether the oft-present aggression, stubbornness, resentment, and combative nature of the Asperger's adult are due to genetics, social conditioning, or both. The characteristic emotional blind spot in regard to the emotions of others, combined with an almost utilitarian approach to the function of others in their lives, can present itself as an emotional disconnect and portray the individual as insensitive and self-absorbed. There seems to be an underlying aggression toward those who do not meet the utilitarian roles to which they have been assigned, resulting in combativeness that seems particularly linked to the Asperger's genetic pattern. Thus, I have come to call the Asperger's "operating system" (genetic design), the "law and order gene."

Asperger's clients frequently demonstrate great difficulty with social interaction and are often moody, petulant, withdrawn, and stubborn. Due to the fundamental inability of the Asperger's client to read non-verbal communication, social blunders abound. The simple give and take of a conversation becomes excruciating. Often, self-imposed avoidance and isolation is the practical solution for the Asperger's client to reduce his or her anxiety and stress. This means that in the case of married Asperger's individuals, the emotional work of the family is being done by the other partner, or in the case of the child with Asperger's syndrome, the work is handled by the siblings and parents. Child Asperger's are much more likely to receive and accept treatment than the adults, who are more set in their ways, and in some sense, have become stubborn due to the lifetime of misunderstandings at the hands of their community. One of the more effective therapeutic strategies is for the therapist to provide information, tactics, strategies, books, and resources for the supporting family members so that they can understand the nature of the loved one's operational system. Knowledge can relieve the stress of the unknown. Often it is more practical to offer therapy to the family members in order to give them the skills necessary to understand and deal with their challenging loved one.

Recently, from 2012-2014, several brutal gun violence mass murders have been linked to a killer with, allegedly, an Asperger's diagnosis. There is no evidence that someone with Asperger's is any more prone to extreme violence than someone with a typical neural-typical operating system. There are psychopathic outliers in those who are neural-typical, as well as those with an Asperger's (neural-diverse) genetic variant. However, I am convinced that a person's style of aggression, whether they have Asperger's or not, is learned at the hands of someone treating the child with violence and aggression. People with Asperger's mimic behaviors that they have been exposed to, and although everyone has a built-in capacity for aggression, we are all capable of being taught how to be aggressive in the extreme. Someone with Asperger's who is raised in a physically abusive family, and whose family members support violence, combined with a genetic predisposition to aggression, and lacking empathetic emotions with people, would be a formidable foe and a cold and dangerous enemy.

THE ANTI-SOCIAL PERSONALITY

Sociopaths and psychopaths trust no one. Typically, these clients have been severely abused or neglected by the very people who should have cared for and protected them. These children are "groomed" for use and abuse by their families. As a result, empathy, compassion, and kindness are interpreted as a prelude to abuse. It's not that the developmental anti-social personality (versus biochemically impaired psychopath) can't feel empathy or compassion. They do. It's just that they interpret these feelings as warning signs of imminent danger. And because they experience intimacy as threat, any attempt by the therapist to create an empathetic alliance will simply trigger acting out by the client. As a result, confrontation is the only effective treatment modality.

It is sometimes difficult to differentiate between the charming nature of the narcissist and the seductive nature of the anti-social. However, you can quickly determine the difference when you confront the client. The narcissist will be highly offended, while the anti-social will accept the confrontation as long as it is not experienced as disrespect.

Non-criminal anti-social personalities generally present a cautious alliance initially but are in therapy because they are being required to go to therapy (divorce, separation, legal system, out-patient). Because the sociopath ultimately responds adversely to the empathetic bond offered by the therapist, confrontation becomes the only method of therapeutic work. It is important to note that confrontation in this context is not the same as the form practiced in cognitive behavioral therapy. Confrontation of the anti-social personality about his or her self-destructive risk-taking is the type of confrontation that a gang member might provide when one of the members is putting the gang at risk. It is what is known as pro-social confrontation: fit in, don't draw attention to yourself, don't take risks with negative social consequences, control destructive impulses, don't be an idiot, avoid confrontations with the police and justice system, avoid activities that will put you in prison or cost you heaps of money. The sociopath will provide a therapeutic alliance as he tries to seduce you onto his side. It is not uncommon for the therapist to be temporarily seduced by an anti-social, and it is not until the client feels threatened or simply impulsively acts out that the true diagnosis is revealed. The therapist needs to take very seriously the client's volatile relationship history, criminal or intimidating behavior, or verbal indulgences (rationalization of outrageous behavior, grandiose and unlikely or inaccurate stories, inappropriate personal comments). These are the cues, usually expressed early in the treatment, that reveal the anti-social personality. Any attempt by the therapist to rationalize the youth, impulsivity, or poor judgment by the client will lead to suffering for everyone. The anti-social personality will be further explored in the borderline diagnostic section.

The Dependent Personality

The inability of a client to self-activate and direct therapy is often the initial presentation of the dependent personality. The client's childhood training to be cooperative and submissive will be the dominant feature in the early stages of therapy. The passivity and willingness, if not passive-aggressive demand, that the therapist initiate and drive the therapy agenda is a significant diagnostic tell. The immediate problem that presents in therapy occurs when the therapist requires the client to be proactive in his or her own therapy. The client's anxiety will immediately spike due to the unconsciously remembered and feared consequences of self-activation.

Submission and passive cooperation are the only self-expressive features allowed in the dependent personality structure: developmentally, all autono-

82

mous expression has been met with punishment and threat by the mother and the family, who continue to reinforce this inhibited interactive style at every family encounter.

Accurate diagnosis is critical in that the therapeutic strategy is specifically designed for the diagnosis. Because the predominant transference type that the dependent personality uses is merging, the therapist has to limit all helpfulness that would increase the client's desire to use shared functioning, encourage dependency, and trigger a regression. The dependent client has been repeatedly taught to use the parents' higher functioning at the expense of his or her own autonomous, self-activating potential. Self-activation has been punished while dependency has been rewarded, and the client will systematically attempt to get the therapist to agree to this expressive family contract. The more "helpful" the therapist is, the more passive and dependent the client will become, eventually regressing into some significantly disturbing behaviors.

Cognitive behavioral therapy (CBT) is an effective strategy with the dependent personality. It requires the client to self-activate, repeatedly returning to his or her own internal processing rather than deferring to the therapist's problem solving ability. Using CBT will eventually prepare the dependent client for the working-through phase of the therapy (discussed near the end of this chapter).

There is possible counter-transference during treatment of the dependent personality. The narcissistically "helpful" aspect of most therapists, counselors, and social workers is simply the role arising from their own family dynamics. They are rescuers, fixers, and helpers. It is easy to see how a person with this personality feature would be drawn to the "helping" professions: teaching, counseling, social work, medicine, etc. And to be honest, would I prefer one hundred "helpful" narcissists to one hundred self-centered anti-social personalities? Of course. But the helpful feature doesn't make the helping activity any less unconscious. The problem is not that the individual is being helpful, but rather that the individual is being compulsively driven to be helpful by his or her personality dynamics. The dependent personality wants the therapist to be helpful, to problem solve, to give the answers to life's challenges. Unfortunately, this can create abundant counter-transference. The more helpful the therapist is, the more the client becomes functionally disabled. The dependent personality strategically positions him or herself to be needy in order to fulfill his or her dependent contract, allowing significant others dominance. Dependent personalities will feign helplessness and inadequate problem solving skills in order to elicit the helpful behavior of the therapist. Cognitive behavioral therapy is particularly helpful with this population. The dependent personality will be further explored in the borderline diagnostic section.

THE BORDERLINE DIAGNOSIS: DEPENDENT vs. ANTI-SOCIAL (ASP) SUB-TYPES

Each of Masterson's four major personality structures can be identified by its unique relationship expectations, with the exception of the borderline personality (as defined by the DSM). The borderline personality is that chameleon of personalities that one moment looks dependent and fearful of abandonment and the next is assaulting the object of affection, or harassing a partner, or is involved in some self-destructive or self-mutilating behavior that simply freaks the heck out of everyone. This combination of behaviors simply does not make clinical sense. For too long, the therapeutic community has tolerated the DSM diagnosis of borderline personality in spite of its treatment-resistant legend.

The inconsistency of the behaviors demonstrated by the borderline personality disorder actually reveals not a difficult patient, but a flawed diagnostic system.

Several years ago, I attended a lecture by then senior trainer for the Beck Institute, Dr. Leslie Sokol, on the psychotherapy of the borderline personality disorder (BPD) using cognitive behavioral therapy. Dr. Sokol began her presentation with a colleague's research on BPD subgroups and identified three subtypes (paraphrased): dependent, mixed, and anti-social (ASP). In the past ten years, it has become obvious to both clinicians and researchers that the DSM-defined borderline diagnosis is seriously flawed. The borderline personality is almost legendary in its resistance to therapy, unpredictability, and chaotic nature. BPD, as a diagnostic criterion, illustrates the limits of a symptom-based diagnostic system.

Symptoms are too widely shared among the major personality disorders, and a symptom-based diagnostic system is fraught with inaccuracy. And, if the diagnosis is flawed, the treatment will be flawed. As a result of the treatment challenges of the borderline personality, research is beginning to examine the subgroups within the BPD diagnostic criteria. We are finding that the BPD diagnosis is contaminated with several personality disorders that are grouped together symptomatically as one disorder. It would not be unreasonable, then, to predict treatment success/failure rates consistent with a flawed diagnostic category.

84

Dr. Sokol presented research (the evidence in "evidence-based therapy") indicating that CBT had achieved a long-term symptom-free treatment result in fifty percent of those clients meeting the DSM criteria for BPD. I found myself somewhat startled by this statistic. A fifty percent failure rate is arguably spectacular. However, a fifty percent success rate is also significant. Evidently, CBT is very, very effective with one BPD sub-group and completely ineffective with a different BPD subgroup. If we could quickly differentiate the subgroup that responds to CBT, then we could theoretically achieve a one hundred percent success rate utilizing CBT in the treatment of borderline personality disorder. This research dilemma illustrates the limitations of the current professional drive to utilize "evidence-based" theories. The evidence in this case suggests that CBT fails as often as it succeeds with the borderline personality diagnosis.

Herein lies the problem with the DSM diagnostic criteria. If we diagnose a borderline personality according to the standards of the DSM, and then apply a CBT strategy, we will be successful, statistically, fifty percent of the time. However, if we can separate the wolves from the sheep, diagnostically, we won't get bitten as much (therapeutic failure) and we can improve our therapeutic success rate. So who are the wolves parading as sheep in this diagnostic mess?

THE DIFFERENTIAL DIAGNOSIS

When deconstructing the DSM borderline diagnosis, consider the social contracts of the dependent personality vs. the anti-social personality. The dependent personality has been trained to submit to authority, and in most cases, to relinquish most decision making to others. Dependent personalities rarely, if ever, self-activate, and if they do, the self-actualization produces such anxiety as to discourage any consistent autonomous self-expression.

All personality structures are based on threat-assessment and operate in a manner to reduce the possibility of emotional or physical assault.

The dependent personality is simply the natural result of an upbringing by a parent who requires complete submission to the parents' authority. Any autonomous self-activation by the child receives immediate negative reinforcement by the parent; thus, submission, deferment to others, lack of opinion, and inability to self-activate are the common markers of the dependent personality.

The anti-social personality (ASP) produces a completely opposite transference and relationship style: the adversarial transference. There are three subsets within the ASP spectrum: developmental sociopath, developmental psychopath, and biological psychopath. In this diagnostic system, the sociopath is a reactionary anti-social, whereas the psychopath is the predatory anti-social. These are developmentally produced personality systems. There is also a biological variant of the psychopath, as outlined in Dr. Robert Hare's brilliant book, *Without Conscience*. Dr. Hare describes a complex set of biological "processing" impairments that produce an individual who does not share an empathetic bond with other living creatures. Without the emotional mirroring that occurs through empathy (and the neurochemical pathways that support the empathetic experience), the psychopath lacks the shared interaction that produces concern for others' wellbeing. For those with a neural-typical nervous system, what happens to you also happens to me. We share the experience through a sympathetic resonance at the neurological level. We mirror each other's emotional experience. Without this, the neurological psychopath remains isolated in emotion and experience, and through a standard anti-social family environment, becomes the predator who cares for no one. This leaves the psychopath with a broad capacity to take advantage of anyone. Without the capacity to empathize with other living creatures, there is an absence of an awareness of the needs and rights of others. For psychopaths, the world is simply their hunting ground. Their personality operates without any internal moral or ethical conflict. This group is often offended by any attempt to limit their abuse of others, simply confounded by any rules of social behavior. Hare estimates that the biological psychopath is one percent of the general population, and, interestingly, four percent of the corporate hierarchy.

The anti-social personality variant simply avoids intimacy and perceives any act of compassion as threatening and, therefore, lacks sympathetic resonance with the rights, needs, and autonomy of others. Since sociopaths perceive threat everywhere, they view the world as theirs for the taking. Inappropriate behavior is always justified by blaming the others involved: "She was asking for it," "He started it, I just finished it," "The cop was just looking to pull someone over," "He was mouthing off," "What I did was legal," etc. Sociopaths are simply attempting to get those around them to submit to their will.

The psychopath variant of the anti-social personality spectrum is simply the shark in the fish tank. These are the predators of the human species, contending that rules are for suckers and trust is for the weak. Whereas the sociopath's deepest pathology is not apparent until they are threatened (this is why they are often diagnosed initially as narcissistic or borderline), the psychopath is a hunter. Rules that bind humans to a greater social good are simply the fences that contain the prey and make it easier for the psychopath to pick off the weak ones.

The anti-social personality's style of relationship is markedly self-activating and operates as though the world is filled with resources to be used as desired. There is little emotional bonding, and although a "romantic couple" with an ASP member can present as "emotionally close," these relationships are predicated on mutual need and shared functioning, rather than intimacy and love.

The parent that produces the developmental anti-social personality used consistent cruelty as a response to the child's attempt at emotional bonding. Thus, as the child grows up, any emotional exchange with others is viewed as a prelude to abuse, neglect, or even assault. The biological psychopath can be born to almost any family and any style of parenting, although I would argue that there is family pathology that increases the more cruel aspect of this anti-social variant.

The sociopath/psychopath anticipates cruelty to follow emotional intimacy, and thus acts out through violence, threats, abuse to self or others, drugs, cutting, or abandonment, in response to compassion or empathy.

As a result, the anti-social group is considered treatment resistant and often described as unable to feel empathy, love, or compassion. Contrary to how ASPs are portrayed in the media, the developmental ASP feels the full range of feelings everyone feels, but it is how they interpret the feelings that makes treatment, and relationships in general, so difficult. Love is viewed as a prelude to abuse. Kindness leads to abuse. Compassion brings about abuse. Consequently, when developmental sociopaths feel that someone is offering emotional availability, they become suspicious and begin to act out destructively to protect themselves from what they fear is coming. As a child, the ASP was treated in such a consistently cruel manner that emotional interplay came to be perceived as threatening and potentially violent.

Continuing with our deconstruction of the borderline diagnosis: On the other hand, the *dependent personality* has been specifically trained to repress self-activation and autonomous action. Any self-activation required by the environment (school, romance, social activity, employment) immediately triggers anxiety and panic. The dependent personality fears and avoids self-expression. The primary caretaker, usually the mother, has made it clear that she is dependent on the needs of the child to give her purpose and identity, and therefore requires the child to remain completely dependent on her for most psychological functions. Any action by the child that threatens the mother's sense of purpose will not be tolerated. Obedience and submission are the only pleasing behaviors the parent accepts.

Thus the hallmark of the dependent personality is of submissive cooperation to the point of simply following the expectations of everyone else in the room. In a clinical setting, this client will not know how to start therapy or have an opinion about almost anything. Instead, he waits for the therapist to direct the therapy session and provide the therapy content. In contrast, the hallmark of the anti-social is to control the session and limit true intimacy from occurring. Thus, the sociopath will distract by simply directing the therapy based on what will control the therapist's interests.

Since true dependent/borderlines are unable to self-initiate, any behaviors that show capacity to initiate action or self-activate should encourage the clinician to consider an alternative diagnosis.

Good therapists, being fundamentally narcissistic by nature ("I'm going to heal the world"), often view "therapy failures" as their fault. In fact, this is not a bad starting place in order to improve one's skills as a therapist, but in those cases where the therapy is struggling, increased effort on the part of the therapist, without a more accurate diagnosis, often produces more of the same. The anti-social borderline will begin therapy like everyone else. The lack of true intimacy and trust suits this type of client just fine. They can be charming, depressed, anxious, drug-dependent, frustrated at lack of social or economic success, paralyzed by performance anxiety, or afflicted with any number of commonly shared frustrations. There are no immediate pathological "tells" until misrepresentations, fabrications, and grandiose stories begin to occur. Anti-social personalities, and certainly psychopathic personalities, are often skilled at reading what the therapist expects to hear during therapy. "Disclosures" by the ASP client are often tailored to fit therapeutic expectations. The client is "reading" the therapist and providing content consistent with perceived therapeutic expectations. As the therapy proceeds and the therapist attempts to secure a therapeutic alliance, the client will begin to act out. The therapy that was proceeding smoothly now starts to derail. Missed appointments, unpaid bills, self-destructive acting out, increased drug usage, cutting, and general regressive behaviors are common in this anti-social group (classic borderline behavior). The therapist, assuming that he is failing his client based on the growing difficulties and the client's seemingly regressive behaviors, redoubles efforts at connecting with the client, infusing sessions with more compassion, more empathy, and more emotional resonance. This simply increases the already unbearable anxiety of the ASP client, and the acting out gets worse. The anti-social, when feeling threatened, acts in a manner to discourage intimacy and closeness. S/

he wants distance and acts in a way that is consistent with producing emotional distance from his target.

As a therapist, if you honestly find yourself wanting to escape your client, it is time to review the diagnosis.

CUTTING BEHAVIOR

One of the classic features of a borderline diagnosis is cutting: self-abusive scarring. It is not uncommon for clients to display certain physically self-assaultive behaviors when in distress, and the act of cutting or mutilating one's skin is well known in therapeutic circles. As odd as this may seem to people outside the medical and mental health fields, cutting and self-mutilation has attended human beings throughout history and seems to be cross-cultural. Pathologically and diagnostically, cutting can be divided into two different categories: hidden/shameful cutting and exhibitionist cutting. These two categories also correspond with the two major subsets of borderline personality disorder: dependent and anti-social. The dependent personalities are the hidden/shameful cutters, whereas the anti-socials are the exhibitionistic cutters.

The hidden/shameful cutters operate from a more compulsive motivation, unable and in many cases unwilling to control the behavior, and yet feeling terribly shameful about the action, hiding the cuts and mutilations from public view. These cutters are reluctant to reveal this behavior; it is simply too shameful. It is always a positive therapeutic sign when this behavior is brought to therapy. The therapist needs to use a combination of reframing, deguilting, grief work, emotional expression, body work (yoga, T'ai chi), or possibly medication, to reintegrate awareness into the dissociated physical sites and release the emotional chaos the client is feeling and expressing through cutting. The purpose of this shameful type of cutting is to counteract the dissociation caused by trauma, and reawaken the body. (See chapter 4, "Trauma Dynamics," *Dissociation*.) These types of cutters only cut until they feel and then stop. When the dissociative numbness becomes too intense, the cutting reoccurs. There is nothing exhibitionistic about this behavior. It feels shameful and compulsive.

The second category of cutter, the exhibitionist, is more closely aligned with the anti-social subset of the borderline diagnosis. Cutting, in this personality group, is designed to alarm the observer. The cutting is often on public display and even proudly declared: "Look what I did this weekend!" Remember, part of the agenda of the ASP is to limit intimacy and emotional closeness. Because sociopaths fear that intimacy will lead to abuse, many of their psychological defenses are specifically adopted to create emotional distance. If the target of this distancing ignores these signals to withdraw, the acting out will escalate, becoming more severely self-destructive, threatening, chaotic, or even violent. This behavior is designed to create anxiety or fear in the target (in this case, the therapist). When clients display behavior that significantly raises the anxiety of the therapists, it is crucial that therapists trust their instincts. Predatory clients project very clear emotional signals that many professionals simply ignore in an attempt to provide some "ideal" emotional availability, in spite of what the therapists' emotions are telling them about the client. Do not avoid or suppress your survival instinct. You will pay for it later if you do. Do not be ashamed to admit that you don't like a client. Do not do ongoing therapy with a client you do not like, and certainly not with one by whom you feel threatened or do not trust. It will undermine the effectiveness of the therapy, not to mention put you in real danger.

The fundamental goal of the dependent personality is to align with the will of the "significant other" by repressing self-expression, thereby avoiding the anticipated punishment associated with autonomous self-activation. The anti-social personality limits the possibility of emotional intimacy to avoid the anticipated cruelty associated with emotional closeness.

Anti-Social Personality Traits

The following is a list of ASP traits. If any of these features are prevalent in a client, and certainly if several of these features are prevalent, a diagnosis of anti-social should be seriously considered.

- Instability and volatility in relationships
- Obvious and exhibitionistic cutting behavior
- Severely physically abusive family history
- Family history that includes long-term, repeated sexual abuse
- History of dangerous drug abuse
- History of marital/family physical violence
- Criminal history
- Chronic lying, fibbing, and rationalizing bad behavior
- Volatile emotional history, particularly aggression
- Predatory sexual behavior
- Unstable employment history
- Client "freaks-out" the therapist

The single biggest challenge in treating the ASP is in creating a therapeutic alliance. Compassion and empathy are viewed by the client as a prelude to abusive behavior. If the clinician uses empathy with the sociopath, it will trigger acting out: self-destructive behaviors, missed appointments, outrageous stories, and failure to pay the bill. All of these acting out behaviors are designed to disturb the therapist and create emotional distance. This is why clinicians need to trust their reactions to their clients.

The Adversarial Transference

In general, adversarial transference typically occurs in therapy for one of three reasons:

1. The therapist has made a timing or judgment error, jeopardizing the therapeutic alliance, offending the client.
2. The client is moving into a more autonomous phase and is testing his or her ability to express an opinion or begin to break free of the transference dependence with the therapist.
3. The client has an anti-social personality structure.

Most therapists, again being narcissistic, treat the presence of the adversarial transference as a product of the first reason: their own failure as a therapist. The adversarial transference is interpreted as needing correction, which typically means realigning with the client through an empathetic resonance with the client's emotional needs. If the adversarial transference is occurring because of therapeutic error, this strategy is usually successful and therapy continues. If the adversarial transference is the result of client progress, any attempt to realign the transference "back" to a "positive" interaction (mirroring, idealizing, merging, which are all dependent transferences) will promote a regression in the client and undermine progress and therapeutic effectiveness. This is the same error that parents make to keep their children dependent. Conflict with others is normal as we gain strength of identity and begin to express ourselves directly. Therapists and parents who resist this phase of the relationship create a greater challenge for the child/ client who is attempting to expand his or her autonomy by testing his or her growing independence and relationship boundaries. However, if the client is anti-social and the therapist attempts an empathetic realignment, the client will escalate the acting out, which triggers empathetic realignment from the therapist, which, of course, triggers more acting out. It is not until the therapist revisits the diagnosis and interprets the personality structure as anti-social that the acting out can be brought under control with an appropriate therapeutic alliance through *confrontation.*

When we begin to examine the dependent-borderline versus the anti-social borderline personality subgroups, it becomes immediately obvious how the two groups are significantly different in developmental history, emotional expectation, and social contract. The contamination of the borderline diagnosis by an unusually high number of anti-social personality disorders, misdiagnosed as borderline by the current DSM criteria, is illustrative of one significant problem in the mental health community and society in general. There is a fundamental denial of the prevalence of the ASP in our culture and treatment facilities. If our relationship with other living creatures and our social contract as human beings to be responsible for each other is the best method of evaluating personality structure, then I estimate as high as ten to fifteen percent of the general population is within the anti-social spectrum, with five to ten percent in the psychopathic predatory or biological spectrum and ten to fifteen percent in the reactionary sociopathic spectrum. These estimates are usually met with disbelief, and with the extreme symptomatic criteria of the DSM required for an ASP diagnosis, it is no wonder that the spectrum anti-socials are being buried in the borderline diagnosis. However, shifting from a symptom-based diagnosis to a transference-relationship-based diagnosis reveals the prevalence of the anti-social personality disorder.

The Anti-Social Personality in Society

The college campus is the perfect setting to examine ASP behavior. Spend any time on the Internet researching predatory sexual behavior on college campuses and you'll find the results startling. Estimates of between six to fifteen percent of college students openly admit to predatory sexual behavior. These self-reports include a willingness to take advantage of anyone who is drug impaired, psychologically weak or passive, physically weak and incapable of self-protection, or isolated from a support group. Researchers express amazement at their subjects' brazen acknowledgment of their readiness to use others for their own purposes. Anticipating deception and lying to be factors in the accuracy of their estimates of predatory behavior, the data revealed a complete willingness among the subjects to unabashedly admit to these ASP behaviors. This is actually consistent with the ASPs threat assessment orientation. If the researcher does not display an obvious threat, why would the interviewee resist admitting to taking advantage of others? Without guilt or shame, there is no emotional resonance to inhibit blunt self-expression. Jon Ronson, in his entertaining, informative, and shocking book, *The Psychopath Test*, describes an encounter with an ex-corporate CEO in which Ronson reads to him from the list of Hare's Psychopath Test. Each attribute of this test reveals an aspect of psychopathology. The CEO takes each question and reframes it as a quality of strong leadership or good business practices. Not only does the CEO not refute these qualities, he promotes these qualities as desirable leadership or business principles.

If we take the mid-range of estimates of campus predatory behavior and say that eight percent of any college campus population is sexually predatory (both men and women), on a campus of 20,000 (the size of many typical state colleges), there would be an astounding 1,600 sexual predators enrolled. If we consider this ratio on a nationwide level, we would first have to account for those less than ten years old as not yet pathologically fixed and subtract them from the population total. With 308 million Americans in the 2010 census, and approximately 45 million children under the age of ten, we would have a measurable population of 263 million adults. If the ASP spectrum is near eight percent, approximately 21 million anti-social people live in America. Of these 21 million anti-social personalities, perhaps as many as three to seven million people fit the criteria of psychopath, either developmental or bio-chemical in origin. In my opinion, this partially explains why society struggles to deal directly with issues of human suffering versus economic opportunity. The belief that large parts of the population can be used for economic gain, with no responsibility for their health care or education, is more than a little anti-social. It is psychopathically opportunistic.

Society's Submissive Response

For decades, the borderline personality disorder diagnosis has been the dumping ground for the spectrum anti-social personality masquerading as a mixed personality disorder. Our denial of the statistical prevalence of sociopaths and psychopaths is partially rooted in our acceptance of this behavior in business, politics, and religion. ASPs want power and influence over others and often seek positions of influence in society. The empathetically empty rhetoric of the predator can be found at every level of society and public influence. The ASP can be identified by callous disregard for human suffering and by fear mongering.

Exposure to this ASP type of aggression often produces a submissive response from those confronted by it. We marvel at how someone is able to take advantage of another person, but con artists, seducers, abusers, and manipulators generate an emotionally threatening signal. This signal seems to provoke a submissive response from the general population. We find ourselves considering and accepting ideas that, when carefully considered, make little sense, or worse, are transparently mean-spirited. Jung observed and commented extensively on the Nazi movement in Germany and the public's willingness to go along with fundamentally anti-human policies. The underlying threat to those who objected or resisted was immediately demonstrated, thereby encouraging all others to cooperate passively, at the very least, in crimes against humanity.

The submissive response in human beings is at least a partial result of learning to submit to parental authority and discipline. Whether or not there is well-meaning intent behind our parents' actions, we are taught how to submit to implied (or remembered) threat or consequences and to suppress questioning authority. Our willingness to deny our own abuse and to submit to the manipulations of those who take advantage of our childhood training is partially responsible for the mental health community's inability to perceive and diagnose anti-social personality disorders.

It is ridiculous to have a diagnostic criteria (borderline personality disorder) in which sub-groups of the disorder are so treatment-resistant that we pity the clinician who ends up treating this population. Our passivity can only be a part of the overall social problem of accepting these individuals as "difficult" rather than threatening and dangerous. Our hope that "deep down, everyone is good" is completely inconsistent with reality. We may all start with basic goodness as a potential, but developmental training creates the saints and the monsters, and no amount of hopefulness will turn a monster into a saint. These predators will never be good citizens, but they may be taught to be cooperative citizens. The majority of ASP people are not criminals: they are our neighbors, political and religious leaders, teachers, school administrators, businessmen, and Boy Scout leaders. Anywhere influence over others exists, the ASP will be present. Thus, when a clinician receives a referral of a local business executive, religious leader, or medical professional, he cannot assume that because the client has social success that they are also psychologically healthy. Our bias is to assume that ASPs are deadbeats, economic failures, overtly violent or threatening, or drug addicts. Certainly, sociopaths and psychopaths are represented in these marginal social roles, but do not be fooled. The great majority of ASPs are successful, with families and social positions. ASPs do have a capacity for interpersonal connection as seen in gangs, closed family systems, and cults, and anti-social personalities can show great loyalty to their "clan," but they lack actual intimacy and emotional resonance. These groups are bonded together as much by who is not a part of the group as by who is. Groups founded on racism, religious and political extremism, or vigilantism are excellent examples of this type of bonding. Because so many sociopaths have social status, it is more socially or politically convenient for clinical professionals to diagnose these individuals with borderline personality than as what they really are: anti-social personality. This leads to a statistical upswing in the borderline diagnosis, which is viewed socially as a difficult personality type, rather than the accurate diagnosis of anti-social, which is of course viewed by society as, well, anti-social.

Clinicians tend to use the borderline diagnosis when they are clinging to some false hope that anti-social behavior is a result of impulsive action or poor judgment or youth. These excuses for anti-social behavior are what perpetuate therapeutic failures and tacitly allow sociopaths and psychopaths to wreak havoc on society.

CONCLUSION

The borderline diagnosis may be too contaminated at this point to be a useful diagnostic category. It is clear that the borderline spectrum contains two significantly different personality structures that emerge from different developmental disruptions: the dependent personality and the anti-social personality. Confrontation, as a therapeutic strategy, can be effective with both of these disorders, but the similarity ends there. When one of my supervisees seeks guidance concerning a difficult "borderline" client, I require the clinician to identify which end of the spectrum is involved: submissive / passive (dependent) versus resistant / adversarial (anti-social). The use of dependent and anti-social diagnostic categories is simply a more accurate diagnosis. Distinguishing between the two leads to a more effective treatment strategy and predictable, if not outright positive, outcome. With this separation in the borderline spectrum, cognitive behavioral therapy could theoretically be one hundred percent effective with the dependent personality, and only marginally effective, if at all, with the anti-social personality.

Ultimately, we must face the truth. While the actual prevalence of anti-social personalities is disturbing, we must consider the ethics of masking them in a false diagnosis, and through our submission, permit them to operate unchecked in our communities and in society as a whole.

CHAPTER FOUR

TRAUMA DYNAMICS

TWO TYPES OF TRAUMA

Trauma dynamics is the study of the interaction between awareness, the body, and the environment and how these experiences shape perception and emotional expression. Trauma might be described as any overwhelming experience in which the personality structure restricts perception and expression as a method of reducing threat but unfortunately increases internal suffering and symptomology at the same time. As clinicians, one of our concerns is the identification of current or historical trauma and its perceptual and expressive consequences in order to form a diagnosis and treatment strategy. To do this effectively, we need to understand how trauma works and the psychological protective mechanisms that arise in response to trauma.

There are two basic types of trauma. *Direct trauma* is the actual physical insult in many forms, including physical and/or emotional abuse, medical emergencies, childhood surgeries, childhood illnesses, direct threats, intimidation, sexual assault, or any predatory or hostile activity directed specifically at the person. *Exposure trauma* is the result of dysfunctional, volatile, or threatening environmental situations, such as family alcoholism, family violence, extreme poverty, neglect, grief, illness, family upheaval, environmental disaster, neighborhood violence, systematic family transition (moving frequently), and any unstable home dynamic. These are extreme forms of both types of traumas, and there are certainly variations that impact our developmental experience in a less obvious manner.

The family does not have to be grossly dysfunctional for a child to suffer some form of developmental or expressive interruption.

Most families are really trying to do their best. Protective and loving parents, reasonable financial security, minimum alcohol or drug problems, normal competitive sibling relationships, extended family relations, childhood friendships, loving pets in the family, and positive school experiences are all part of many families. And yet, developmental trauma occurs even in these optimal situations. Serious illness, adoption (loss of the birth mother), separation from mother for more than a few days at particularly important developmental phases, nutrition challenges, chronic health problems, and many other normal and common childhood experiences are all significant factors that impact personality development in young children (those under 24 months). Bad dreams, difficult separations from the family, and a variety of common family challenges that affect the child's sense of security are examples of lesser, and yet significant, childhood traumas. These types of experiences also compromise the nervous system and train us to be hyper vigilant for threats from our environment, often undermining the development of higher psychological function while producing a personality structure that is more rigidly concerned with feeling safe than self-expression. In these cases, the unconscious remains the repository for those aspects of the self that have yet to be activated or were activated and repressed.

When the survival strategy of pleasing others becomes a higher priority in psychological development than the activation and mastery of one's psychological potential, the undeveloped components of the unconscious continue to press on the personality structure for expression. Thus, the unmet needs of the child often become the priority goal of the adult and can lead to repeated relationship dramas or life challenges.

How can we recognize the severity of the trauma that we have endured? Simple.

The frequency and intensity of one's non-medical symptom profile (anxiety, tension, stress, guilt, shame, fear, resentment, worry, grief, depression, and somatization) reveals the difficulty of one's childhood and the presence of an expressive disorder. Psychological symptoms are in direct proportion to one's trauma.

Non-medical, psychological symptoms are always in proportion to trauma (whether that trauma was intended or not). A commonly asked question is: How can children in the same family be exposed to the same family dynamics and emerge with completely different worldviews and self-expression strategies? The uniqueness of each child, and thus the child's sensitivity to trauma, is due to a number of factors: the child's genetic code (neurodiversity spectrum), parental expectations and discipline, sibling order, childhood traumas, environmental factors unique to each child, and perhaps even, as Jung would propose, the personality temperament of the child (the natural tendency of a child to be extroverted or introverted, etc.). These factors, combined with the client's symptom profile and relationship expectations, become the foundation of therapeutic diagnosis and treatment.

Absent a medical disorder, the most significant therapeutic problem resulting from trauma is the continued suffocation of emotional self-expression.

Because we associate loss and pain with specific emotions, we restrict the expression of those emotions as a way of trying to ward off potential threat. Curiously, although the trauma is the *cause* of the psychological problem, it is the resulting inhibition of emotion, as a result of the trauma, that forms the expressive problem. This is why two people can be exposed to the same traumatic experience, and one is traumatized, and one is not. The energy behind the blocked emotion produces symptoms in the place of emotions. The intensity of those symptoms is in proportion to the type and intensity of the traumas we have suffered.

Although these traumas form the narrative of the therapy, it is the expressive blocks of the personality structure that are the source of the symptoms and the targets of the therapeutic intervention.

Think of psychological trauma as a virus that infects personality by redirecting emotional energies from creativity and intimacy into priority protective systems that constantly survey the world for threats and dangers and produce symptoms instead of genuine emotions.

THE FOUR TRAUMA FACTORS

We are attempting to measure several issues in our clinical evaluation and diagnosis, or even in our self-evaluation. Which neural-emotional sites have been traumatized and thus are being perceptually and expressively compromised? How seriously restricted are these sites? Finally, we have to get a sense of the history of the trauma at these sites. Complete repression of any neural-emotional site is less common, but most people have multiple sites that are at least partially restricted and severely limit expression of at least one or more sites.

There are four basic trauma factors that contribute to personality rigidity. These determinants help to predict the severity of perceptual and expressive restriction and to identify which neural-emotional sites were likely compromised.

1. *Developmental Stage*: At what developmental stages was the child traumatized? Inventory all medical history, with particular emphasis on the first seven years (neural-emotional development); the approximate ages when significant family developmental events occurred; any and all separation events, with emphasis on the first three years of life (object relations); and any additional events, siblings, and major changes in the child's environment that would have raised the anxiety and tension level of the family.

2. *Intensity*: How intense was the trauma? The more severe the symptom profile, the more severe the trauma. Family stories and family interviews are surprisingly helpful. Sometimes there are stories that are told about us in the family of which we are surprisingly unaware. Clients often rationalize their own trauma as normal or attempt to protect their parental introject by criticizing their own childhood behavior. As a result, trauma intensity can be a difficult factor to establish. Be aware that any attempt to get the client to prematurely criticize his or her parents may trigger an adversarial transference. The examination of parent-child relationships is not a question of blame; it is an assessment of the accuracy of perception of the client's childhood experiences.

3. *Intent*: What was the aim of traumatic situation? Was it *predatory* (deliberate and dangerous) or *situational* (swept up in family or health dilemmas)? The intent behind the trauma has real significance. The cruelty of the predator produces a very different emotional block than the accidental or unfortunate trauma of circumstances or the impact of careless or indulgent parenting. Since childhood discipline is usually a repeated attempt to control

the child's behavior, the style, intensity, and frequency of discipline is extremely important.

I am unaware of any families that never used physical discipline. I have listened to protestations that the physical discipline was inconsequential or extremely rare. However, simply because a clever child was capable of avoiding repeated physical discipline does not mean that the child did not compromise his or her self-expression in order to avoid punishment.

Regardless of the most common forms of discipline used in the family—such as silence, disappointment, time-out, guilt, grounding, neglect, or other types of emotional manipulation—most clients have at least one memory of spanking or physical discipline which made it clear that failure to obey parental demands had physical consequences. These corporal acts are the foundation of emotional inhibition.

4. *Repetition:* Single episode traumas, unless life threatening, usually do not severely affect personality structures. However, repeat patterns of abuse, neglect, abandonment, family chaos, health problems, and physical discipline all contribute to a personality structure pattern that prioritizes safety over self-expression, producing symptoms instead of emotional self-expression.

As a result of developmental trauma, the energy dedicated to self-expression gets diverted to more obsessive pursuits of safety, security, and avoidance. Activation of traumatized emotions trigger memory, which triggers anxiety and resistance. (This is the Activation-Resistance Cycle (ARC), which will be fully explored in chapter 8.) For example, if we have blocked aggression due to family discipline, when we attempt to use our aggression under natural and reasonable circumstances, the activation of that emotion triggers the fear or anxiety associated with the anticipated (and remembered) punishment of childhood.

The activation of a repressed emotion triggers symptoms instead of emotion.

Personality converts emotion into symptom rather than risk the feared negative outcome of expressing the emotion. Specifically, the expression of forbidden emotion triggers the fear of danger. We literally associate emotional activation with threat. As adults, this personality-protective mechanism is triggered on a regular, if not daily, basis. To be a normal human being is to experience thought, speech, compassion, aggression, or sexuality constantly, simply by conducting one's life in an active and highly stimulating society. The emotional stimuli that surround us are not all significantly strong enough to trigger the anxiety of a repressed emotion, but through repeated stimulation (several frustrating events, for example), the threshold of perception is crossed, the emotional response is triggered, and the blocked emotion is transformed into a set of symptoms (the symptom profile).

Every time one experiences any of the eleven common symptoms—anxiety, tension, stress, guilt, shame, fear, resentment, worry, grief, depression, and somatization—the personality is blocking self-expression due to an unconsciously remembered threat associated with specific emotions.

Herein lies one of the most difficult aspects of self-expression and trauma. Psychological injury is organ-specific. Our psychological wounds are experienced as threats against specific emotions and the physical sites associated with those emotions: this is neurological site-specific trauma (and the associated emotion). This site-specific trauma is true, except in the case of post-traumatic stress disorder (PTSD), a condition that involves massive (rather than localized) neurological trauma. When severe trauma leads to PTSD, specific factors result in more universal damage to the nervous system. Brutal aggression, life-threats, near-death experiences, war, imprisonment, and adoption are all of such an intense nature that they have a vast negative effect on the whole body and psyche.

One might describe PTSD as the result of a multi-organ assault.

The percentage of the body affected by the trauma determines the PTSD's pervasiveness, intensity, and treatment requirements. PTSD is almost always a combination of medical, situational, and psychological trauma. A medical disorder like anxiety or depression, for instance, combined with an ongoing threatening situation such as financial disaster, war, famine, disease, familial assault or threat, combined with a rigid personality system due to childhood developmental challenges, is a high-risk combination that may result in PTSD.

In non-catastrophic circumstances, childhood developmental interruption is associated with very specific emotions and the physical organs associated with those emotions. The trauma remains mostly localized, physically. Thus, for example, the threshold of sexual perception and/or the threshold of sexual expression might be blocked or highly regulated by the personality structure. If our families taught us not to notice or express sexual activity, our personality has a sexual block; this produces a perceptual distortion and expressive inhibition. This same personality mechanism operates with all of the five centers of awareness: thought, speech, sadness, aggression, and sexuality.

Our physical organs have three psychological functions aside from their physical functions: to provide specific information about the world, to generate specific emotional responses, and to provide specific quantities of energy. This means that the five major organ systems of the body (brain, throat, respiratory, digestive, reproductive) likewise serve as delivery systems for information, emotion, and energy. Each organ/emotion provides part of the overall perception and response to the world. (Speech obviously lacks a perceptual function.)

Information is organ specific. Emotion is organ specific. Trauma is organ specific. Energy is organ specific. Dissociation is organ specific (the issue of dissociation will be explored in greater depth later in this chapter). The quality and energy of our lives is severely compromised if even one emotion/organ is blocked. For example, the reproductive system is also the psyche's compass for pleasure. Without a healthy pleasure system, the world becomes bland and without preference. One job is as good as another. One career is as good as another. One partner is as good as another. One car, one house, one life, is as good as another. Without pleasure one wanders the world with little preference or purpose. One might say that the reproductive system is not just related to sex; rather, it is the meaningful compass for one's life path. It is the pleasure system that declares which activities, people, environments, thoughts, and feelings are attractive and feel energetic. And, to be sure, pleasure has meaning. Without pleasure, life is a big "so what!" I've often thought that Existentialism is the philosophy of men lacking a fulfilling sex life. If you have a fun sex life, you know the meaning of life. It's not a big mystery.

The significance of developmental trauma versus adult PTSD is that the personality structure is created from the childhood developmental experiences.

Developmental trauma determines the architectural plans of the house of the personality, whereas PTSD is usually associated with the areas of the house that have been damaged after completion.

The fundamental rule is that developmental trauma produces the personality structure; the more significant the trauma, the more rigid the personality. Thus, all people have some form of personality "disorder" because a percentage of everyone's perceptual and expressive systems have been compromised and restricted. The question is: How much of a person's awareness is now regulated and controlled by the trauma-spawned personality structure?

The psyche, by design, responds immediately to every situation, moment to moment, by mirroring the emotion of the situation. So, anger in, anger out; sex in, sex out; love in, love out: a simple mirroring mechanism. What trauma and training do, however, is redirect this mirroring response through the personality so that it will be expressed in a way that will reduce or neutralize perceived, remembered, or actual threat from the environment. Unfortunately, personality is not very flexible and has a tendency to use the same defensive strategies repeatedly, regardless of the outcome. We use personality tactics we learned from our mothers with our friends, and where those techniques may have been moderately successful with Mom, they really fall short with our intimates. This is because our intimates have different goals and emotional requirements, and though we sense the pressure to please them, our capacity to succeed in this goal is limited by our inflexible emotional expression system. Our personality systematically eliminates too many emotional strategies. It's as though we are performing in a play, reading the lines we have been taught, and realize that our loved ones are performing in a completely different play. Most marriage and intimate couple conflict is about whose "play" is going to be performed in this relationship.

The Three Consequences of Blocked Emotions

When cosmologists originally theorized the existence of black holes in space, they realized that the challenge of locating such an object would be extremely difficult. Black holes have such strong gravitational fields that they emit nearly no signal of their presence. We now know that these all but invisible black holes exist by the effect they have on their environment. The presence of the black hole distorts the surrounding celestial phenomena. We don't see the black hole, but we can see the distortion it creates. The same is true of the influence of repressed emotions: they affect what we perceive and how we respond to reality. We identify these emotional "black holes" by the effect they have on our lives.

There are three primary indicators of blocked emotions:

1. Symptom dynamics
2. Perceptual blind spots
3. Self-destructive behavior

1. *Symptom Dynamics*: Symptoms are not the problem; they are the solution to the problem. The energy of any emotion that has been repressed or dissociated will continue to exert pressure on the psyche in the form of symptoms: anxiety, tension, stress, guilt, shame, fear, resentment, worry, grief, depression, or somatization. The psyche is in a constant battle between attempting to wake up and live responsively

in the moment and going back to sleep and trying to repress any and all symptomology of psychological distress.

The fundamental rule of symptom dynamics is what is not experienced as insight or expressed as emotion will be expressed as symptom.

2. *Perceptual Blind Spots*: Emotions have two features: energy and information. When personality becomes too restrictive, it redacts critical information about our world and our options in the world. We don't realize that we are seeing only part of reality. We are certainly experiencing all of reality, but we are only acting on a portion of it, the portion we have been trained to see and to which we have been taught to respond.

This information about reality is not missing: it is stored in the body, and personality restricts awareness from easily accessing that information. One might say that wing of the library is closed, and the librarian enforces that restriction.

Perceptual blind spots are directly in proportion to emotional over-regulation.

It is as though part of the data stream of reality has been redacted, and awareness is trying to conduct life based on only a portion of the information needed to see the world accurately and respond creatively. Thus, parts of our lives have insufficient information and insufficient expression to be successful and effective.

Our failed experiments in living are the result of obscured information combined with inhibited response, creating emotional blind spots.

Because it does not have the means to connect with vital information, due to repression or dissociation, awareness perpetuates cycles of unsatisfactory relationships, relationship roles, employment dynamics, and educational challenges, with limited success. These patterns repeat themselves until we access or retrieve the knowledge that will resolve the challenge. Once awareness begins re-engaging with the dissociated neural-emotional complexes holding the "hidden" information, we become aware of how we can resolve the cycle. The information, although always available, is now accessible, and new options and choices become obvious.

Analytic psychology encourages the clinical therapist to resist offering the "missing" information to the client as a quick fix for the perceptual blind spot. Although the client may feel that the absent information is the problem, the deeper problem is the client's personality structure that created the informational blind spot.

It is a simple task for the clinician to offer informational solutions (problem solving therapy) or to even have the client offer his or her own varied solutions (cognitive behavioral therapy). The real challenge in therapy is for the client to overcome the fear of the consequences of self-activation and genuine self-expression and thus recover or simply perceive the missing information directly. S/he still has to develop the curiosity and courage to express those forbidden thoughts and feelings openly. Half the battle is locating (in the fog of dissociation) the missing information/emotions, and the other half is the expression of said feelings and opinions. Even if we know something, it is the ability to express our true thoughts and emotions that creates change in our world, our energy, and our self-image.

Even with subtle perceptual and expressive blind spots, awareness knows that it is missing critical pieces of information.

Awareness expects the world to make sense. Even if we don't like reality, human beings are much more capable of negotiating life's challenges if we know that our perception of the world is accurate.

The devastating effect of lying, misleading, and manipulating other people's perception of the world is that the distortion creates tremendous amounts of anxiety in the recipient. Our confidence level in our perception of the universe is directly linked to self-image, self-worth, and self-expression. The more distorted our perception, the more we doubt ourselves, criticize our judgment, and express ourselves symptomatically.

The entire philosophy of the "randomness" of life is founded on perceptual blind spots. Reality is reality, and simply because we suffer from the apparent randomness of reality due to our blind spots, we can be assured that there is one unified reality that integrates all the descriptions of reality. This does not mean that we all agree to what that reality is. Most people can describe and experience only parts of reality. It's as though each person in the world has a part of the greater jigsaw puzzle of reality, and until we each contribute our piece of the puzzle and appreciate everyone else's contribution to the puzzle, our worldview will be incomplete.

A myth, far from being fictitious, is a narrative describing the universe and our place in it. Myth is the universal story of humanity. However, part of the challenge of myth is that it is attempting to describe a greater truth that is only partially understood. In this case, myth is an interpretation of fact, with some of the pieces missing. Most of our sense of reality is filled in with perceptual and expressive myths taught to us by our families, culture, and religious institutions. Unfortunately, the pieces of truth that are missing from our family's myth of reality produce suffering cycles, self-destructive behavior, superstitious notions, and magical religious thinking. We are literally attempting to describe, in symbolic terms, aspects of reality just beyond our understanding. Instead of accurate information, we have beliefs about the unknown.

The presence of any of the major symptoms is the signal that we are operating with limited information and trapped in a perceptual blind spot. Although we can speak of these symptoms as problems in and of themselves, each is predicated on an underlying fear of the consequences of self-expression and self-activation. Fear is the most common symptom of a perceptual blind spot.

We have been trained through family discipline and consequences to fear the response of the world if we express ourselves in a forbidden way. Part of the blind spot is not even being able to remember accurately how we have been taught this fear. We are unable to track our fear of self-expression back to the lessons learned at the hands of the authority figures in our lives. Yet, our skewed perception that our parental experience was without fault is betrayed by the symptom array that punishes us on a day-to-day basis. As adults, our psyches simply believe that the world will reject certain forms of self-expression and self-activation, including anger, sexuality, sadness, personal opinion, creativity, playful behavior, self-centered behavior, or emotional expression. We have universalized the specific lessons of our family, especially the punitive lessons. Fear is the greatest constrictor of self-expression. You will know you've broken your family's rules of self-expression when your anxiety spikes. Every time we break our family rules and express ourselves in a direct and honest manner, our anxiety goes up and we immediately begin to scan the environment for the imminent punishment.

Anxiety alerts us to scan for danger. Our problem is that we are not sure what we are scanning for! Because we have a perceptual blind spot, we are unable to identify, specifically, what is causing our reaction. We can only feel the effects of the blind spot. Most of the time, the anxiety is due to self-activation rather than an actual outside threat. To quote the first cartoon Zen master, Pogo, "We have met the enemy and he is us!"

3. *Self-destructive behavior:* There are four predominant styles of self-destructive behavior:

1. Acting out
2. Putting ourselves to sleep
3. Distraction
4. Thrill seeking

1. Acting Out: Acting out, in general, is simply a category of behavior that symptomatically and temporarily discharges psychological stress. This behavior is often emotionally chaotic, self-destructive, indulgent, habitual, insensitive, abusive to ourselves and others, or distracting: impulsive drugs, sex, or tantrums are common. Acting out is stress-induced behavior that temporarily relieves the anxiety that one feels without fundamentally changing the situation or improving self-expression. This behavior can be identified in both individuals and groups. Family systems often share the responsibilities of acting out the family stress. The identified patient in family therapy, often a child, is usually acting out (risky behavior) in response to a dysfunctional marriage or a transition phase failure (the family's inability to adjust to a difficult challenge: birth, death, illness, graduation, divorce, marriage, separation, relocation, etc.). The patient is simply the canary in the coalmine, the first to show signs of a toxic environment.

Acting out behaviors are usually associated with self-destructive actions and thus are problematic. Sexual and financial problems, drug use, academic failures, combative conduct, and all types of passive aggressive, obsessive, compulsive, or impulsive behaviors are common forms of acting out. For example, an affair is a common type of acting out. The affair provides temporary stress relief to the participant, thus permitting the person to tolerate living in a dysfunctional marriage or relationship for a longer period of time. Essentially, it is stress management without a change in the situation. This means the individual will continually be living in a dysfunctional family system, continually be in a stressful relationship, continually be unhappy with existing circumstances, tolerating pain and suffering, but experiencing some temporary relief on the side. Although relationship affairs, sexual and otherwise, are often manifestations of acting out, this does not mean that all affairs are ultimately bad. They are not. In some cases, an affair blows up a stuck relationship so that the couple is forced to work on their communication, problem solving, sexual life, financial crisis, or face whether they actually want to be together. Or, an affair provides comfort in a situation where keeping the family together is the priority, but the emotional connection is severely damaged. An affair also reminds the person who has lived in desperate emotional depression how strongly and passionately he or she is still capable of feeling. Affairs at least involve relating to people. However, as far as stress dynamics are concerned, acting out is simply the stress relief mechanism that sustains a dysfunctional psychological/social structure without effectively changing it. Often it is the acting out that triggers the crisis that leads to change.

2. *Putting Ourselves to Sleep:* It's not a question of *if* we will wake up; it's a question of *when* we will wake up. Unfortunately, the more toxic our body becomes with blocked emotions, bad eating habits, no exercise, too many drugs, and physical injuries, the more difficult and painful it becomes to wake up. Drug abuse can function as a form of acting out, but it is at the top of the list of methods of staying asleep. With drugs, one simply does not feel, and therefore the symptoms of psychological distress can be further ignored until they reach the threshold that cannot be further suppressed. The sooner a person commits to cleaning up his or her act, the easier it will be for awareness to access the emotions and information contained in those neglected parts of the body. I mean, really, who wants to live in a toxic waste dump?

When I begin therapy with any client, I request that they keep a dream journal and begin exercising. It's a combination of detoxing both the emotions and the body simultaneously. We often fight the rhythms of the body in the same way we fight the rhythms of emotional self-expression. Aligning with the rhythms and cycles of the body (sleep cycles, digestion and elimination cycles, and respiratory cycles) can reduce physical tension significantly and increase overall energy levels. Since one of the fundamental goals of therapy is to transform symptoms back into energy, information, and emotion, respecting the rhythms of the body is a rapid method of healing years of bad habits and self-abuse.

3. *Distraction: Behavior,* in general, can be divided into several broad categories: creativity, stress management, intimacy, and productivity. Humans thrive with patterned behavior. Repetition can be reassuring up to the point of boredom. Once one has mastered a task, however, the security of repetition lacks sufficient energy to positively reinforce the repetition. Essentially, we repeat an activity until it is boring, and then we either intensify the activity or migrate to a new endeavor. Thus, there is a tension between the safety of repetition and the need for an energetic challenge. Distraction behaviors such as unnecessary shopping, overeating, worry, absorption in television watching or computer activities, and so on, can be obsessive or compulsive behaviors that direct our attention away from our psychological suffering.

Even though we seek to soothe ourselves with the distraction, it is only a temporary comfort and we find ourselves immediately returning to the anxiety as soon as the activity has finished. The diversion loses its effectiveness. On a positive note, distraction behavior is a form of concentration wherein we block out our psychological symptoms by concentrating on the activity. The Internet and electronic games are widely used to ease stress through concentration. The fact that we are able to find any comfort in distraction indicates the potential to develop consistent relief. The next step is actually addressing the emotions triggering our anxiety so that we can find a more permanent relief in self-expression. Addressing the underlying causes leads to liberation from suffering. By actually attending to the emotions, or biochemistry, that are triggering our anxiety, we can find relief in self-expression. It's no longer a question of whether or not we will feel anxious in our lives, but rather, how long we will feel anxious.

4. *Thrill Seeking:* Thrill seeking is common to the human species. In our desire to feel alive and connected to the life force, we expose ourselves to experiences that break our emotional insulation threshold and produce strong emotional responses. As a result of the emotional dissociation learned in childhood, adults require higher levels of stimulation to trigger an emotional response to produce a feeling of being alive. In any situation, there is a correlation between the intensity required to feel awake and vital and the depressing trauma of our childhood. But there is a somewhat tragic cycle involved in thrill seeking. Any surge of energy or emotion eventually triggers the painful emotional memories stored in the body. What was dormant is now awake. Energy activates memory. Now the dilemma is how to re-repress those unresolved emotions: this cycle of boredom/depression, thrill seeking, emotional activation, anxiety, repression, and boredom/depression is one example of the Activation-Resistance Cycle. (See chapter 8, "Treatment.")

In Alexander Lowen's book, *Narcissism*, he suggests that the painful experiences of childhood create an emotional insulation, and the narcissist must place him/herself in thrilling situations in order to feel emotionally reconnected to the world and others. He describes this type of person as the "phallic narcissist" because of the sexual compulsivity that often attends these emotionally insulated individuals. Lowen suggested that there are three methods commonly used by the phallic narcissist to penetrate the emotional insulation: sex, drugs, and power. Each of these methods has the capacity to be escalated to the point where the activity will penetrate even the most cocooned individual. The problem is that the feeling of "emotional aliveness" produced by the activity is fleeting and must be compulsively repeated in order to

sustain the emotional experience. The person is attempting to wake
up, while his or her personality structure is simultaneously doing its job
by attempting to keep the emotional anxiety asleep. This, again, is the
Activation-Resistance Cycle.

The Three Control Tactics

When people get into emotional conflict, there are three primary tactics used to control the situation: *attack*, *abandon*, and *act helpless* (fight,
flight, freeze). Although much has been written about human emotional defensive styles, they are all complex forms of these three basic
strategies.

The first one, *attack* (fight), is simply a straightforward aggressive,
threatening, and in some cases, dangerous style of dominating others.
It is a direct attempt to get others to submit to our will. This strategy's primary goal is to control people's behaviors and to threaten, with
major consequences, if the subjects do not cooperate. Physical violence, grabbing, pushing, intimidation, throwing objects, emotionally
intense yelling, threatening, tantrums, and aggressive physical gestures
are all part of the inventory of the attack intimidation style. These
actions produce immediate fear, anxiety, intimidation, and severe emotional inhibition in the victims.

The second strategy, *abandon* (flight), is simply the act of leaving
the area of the conflict. Storming out, slamming doors, deserting the
children, walking away, ignoring, withdrawing, or hanging up the
phone are all part of the abandon strategic style. Its purpose is straightforward: to punish others and control the situation by abandoning.
Abandonment can produce high levels of anxiety and, naturally, fears
of abandonment in their targets.

The third style is equally as aggressive as the first two, but appears
to be the complete opposite: *act helpless*. This is where the person
plays the victim. Crying, complaining, acting pitiful, feeling miserable,
never expressing happiness or allowing things to get better, whining,
or playing stupid are all examples of this insidious form of aggression;
the passive aggressive defense. These people drive everyone crazy
while playing the victim, and their actions are designed to produce
guilt, shame, and pity in their targets. Fritz Perls (founder of Gestalt
therapy) often warned of the power of the "victim."

In order to tolerate any of these three forms of intimidation, we
suppress our natural response to choke the life out of them. Overall,
take any obnoxious, offensive, pushy, insulting, demanding, punitive,
helpless, and controlling behavior and it will fit into one of these three
categories. Even adults experience these tactics (from others) as highly

stressful, but imagine how a small child would react. It would be terrifying.

Our personality is designed, from birth, to strategically control the environment in order to reduce exposure to these three threats. When any of these threats is present, we have a prescribed set of responses, advocated by our family system, with which we automatically respond, regardless of effectiveness.

Each of these threatening behaviors attempts to accomplish the same goal: to silence and manipulate the target into cooperating with the expectations of the other. Every family has an unspoken contract concerning how to respond to these three threats: "We would prefer that you were fat rather than angry," for instance, or "Depression is preferable to anxiety," or "Illness is okay, sadness isn't."

Once you begin to inventory your own symptom profile, and then honestly evaluate what emotions you express well and what emotions you don't express well, you'll find exactly what you've repressed to meet your family expectations. As we discussed in chapter 2, in order to evaluate how you have been compromised by these three major defensive tactics, simply execute Masterson's three-step analysis:

1. Be yourself, be genuine, don't hold back. Speak honestly, speak truth, and be authentic.
2. When your anxiety begins to increase, it means you are about to do or say something (express an emotion or opinion) that you've been taught *not* to express. Your anxiety does not mean that you are about to do something immoral or unethical, but rather that it has to do with being afraid. You've been taught to avoid certain self-expressions in order to avoid punishment.
3. Whatever you fear will be the consequences of your actions (friendless, no job/money, all alone) was the method used to control you as a child. Simple, but brilliant! What we fear is what we have experienced personally during our childhood. We simply do not fear consequences we have not experienced.

There are a number of common fears that we experience in the process of becoming fully expressive of our emotions and opinions. Loss of income, fired from jobs, abandoned, alone, broke, attacked, and humiliated are only some of the more common fears shared in my office. However, our fears are unique to our personal history and though many people in fact share these fears, it is our particular emotional history and its consequences that are awakened when we try to express ourselves more fully. These fears and inhibitions are the direct result of our parents', families', and social pressures' use of these three aggressive tactics: attack, abandon, and act helpless.

TIME DELAY AND TRAUMA

There is immediacy to health: the rapid, flexible, and appropriate response to our experience of reality. Trauma introduces a time delay into the equation of our personality. The psychological and physical response to trauma produces dissociation, which delays our perception and expression. When we are psychologically impaired, it simply takes longer to perceive the world accurately and to respond appropriately. What is potentially immediate perceptual accuracy (or as Malcolm Gladwell would label the "blink" moment) might actually take minutes, hours, days, weeks, months or even years to accurately remember, understand, and integrate. The same is true of emotional expression; our design is to respond immediately and in proportion to the moment. Unfortunately, our personality structure, in an attempt to protect us from harm, retards or simply blocks our emotional expression. The greater the trauma, the greater the time-delay between experience and insight, or experience and response. This issue of time and trauma plays a significant role in diagnosis and treatment of personality expressive disorders.

The parts of the personality that are easily expressed versus those parts that are inhibited or retarded determine diagnosis and treatment. For example, it might take a woman six months to break up with a boyfriend that she knew within six weeks was a bad fit. This is an obvious example of the time delay between experience, knowledge, and action. From a Gestalt point of view, the diagnostic question is whether it took six months for perceptual information to reach awareness, and thus for her to see the hopelessness of this match, or whether it took six months to act on the information that she was aware of six months earlier, or some variation of the two. ("I knew it was a bad relationship within a month, but it took five months to act on that information.") Time is the marker of a restrictive personality (blocked perception and/or expression) in any of these variations.

It is possible, therefore, to measure a certain amount of therapeutic success through the deregulation of self-expression. Reducing the time between stimulus and response provides access to additional information and increased energy (in spite of our fear).

However, in verbal self-expression there is a much subtler interplay of time. Thought blockage, emotional censoring, verbal censoring, scanning for threat, and general approval-seeking behaviors can manifest as verbal inhibitors that cause verbal hesitation or verbal interruption. The verbal pause or interruption of a thought is the personality censoring process in action. Every experienced therapist pays close attention to communication blocks and expressive interruptions in order to identify a processing problem.

THE FOUNDATION OF FEAR

We don't invent fears, we relive them.

This cannot be overstated: We are only afraid of what we have experienced. As the fundamental purpose of personality is threat assessment, personality is designed to monitor and regulate emotional experience. But since the unconscious responds immediately and in proportion to every situation, the best personality can do is to convert the perception or response into symptoms as quickly as possible to avoid possible negative consequences. Thus, anxiety or fear replaces emotion and information. If expressing a sexual feeling got us in trouble as children, then any feeling of sexual attraction might immediately be crushed by personality and replaced with the same amount of energy in the form of one of the eleven symptoms: anxiety or headaches, for example.

External conditions and internal responses can both trigger the personality censor. A simple solution to reducing the triggering of this censor might be to avoid *all* potentially emotionally triggering situations. However, this strategy leads to a painfully isolated life, and ultimately avoidance will produce its own psychological symptoms arising out of our failure to follow and master our own psychological design. Remember, the unconscious is not passive and puts pressure on awareness to evolve and fulfill our abilities and gifts.

It is better to master one's fear rather than to be confined by it.

Personality is triggered by emotional responses linked to memory and not necessarily by a real and present threat. The censor tends to restrict emotional expression even when there is no improvement to one's actual safety. We carry the fear of the negative consequences within our emotional memory and apply those fears to the current circumstances. For example, if, as a child, expressing an opinion was viewed by your parents as "talking back," and as a result you were punished for what was seen as disputing your parents, eventually the simple act of forming an opinion—much less the voicing of that opinion—could trigger the fear of negative consequences. This is a conditioned reflex, made famous in Ivan Pavlov's experiments with his dog. In Pavlov's experiment, Pavlov trained his dog to drool when presented with a bowl of food, and then Pavlov would ring a bell as the dog was responding to the food. Eventually, all Pavlov had to do was ring the bell and the dog would drool, even when the food was not present. The dog's neural memory trained him to drool when the bell rang, food or not. And although it may seem insulting to suggest that human beings are as equally easy to train, the fact is that the human nervous system is designed to be trained in just such a manner. We are conditioned to respond in a way that is helpful to our survival. If we are hit for talking back, personality eventually restricts our talking back...to anyone. And, often, simply considering "speaking up" triggers great anxiety.

It is the activation of the emotional function, not the person, place, or situation, that triggers the anxiety (unless, of course, you are being directly threatened).

For those people who have difficulty expressing an opinion—or starting a conversation or holding a position in a discussion—they can be assured that they have been trained to repress this normal and natural function and the energy behind the opinion has been diverted into some form of symptom. Social situations can become highly stressful due to the broad activation of a variety of emotions and thoughts that should remain repressed. As a result, social avoidance becomes the simpler, if not more lonely, solution. (The clinician needs to differentiate between a social expressive disorder and Asperger's, which is known for social anxiety.)

Consider this: Whenever we attempt to self-activate a part of our psyche that has been punished, the effort triggers a symptomatic response, and awareness then begins to scan the environment for potential threats. Awareness narrows the world into those variables that confirm our sense of danger or risk. Thus, what starts as an amazingly open and complex reality is reduced to only the factors that confirm our fears. However, even though we certainly can find potential threats in our environment at almost any time, these threats certainly do not represent the whole of everything occurring at this moment. It is the personality that collapses the magnificence of the world into a narrow set of factors that personality has been taught to perceptually prioritize. When Buddhist philosophy suggests that we each create our world, it is probably more accurate to say that we each perceptually narrow reality to see the world we've been taught to see.

Our personality is the filter that creates, out of the larger more magnificent universe in which we live, the small world that we experience. Personality sees the world it expects (and has been taught) to see, and although this world is real, it is only part of the world.

THE DOUBLE BIND AND THE STOCKHOLM SYNDROME

I am inhibited because I am afraid: perceptual accuracy and honest emotional expression versus threat assessment and the sacrifice of personal truth in the quest for safety or approval.

The double bind is a spectacularly insightful theory developed by the brilliant team of multi-disciplined theoreticians: Gregory Bateson, Jay Haley, Don Jackson, and John Weakland. An aspect of this theory can be applied to how people, and children in particular, are constantly placed into situations where they have to choose between their emotional experience of the world and the world as it is being described and imposed on them by others.

A fundamental tenet of this book's super system is that there is in fact one reality, but many descriptions of that reality, and that our energetic reservoirs are directly determined by our perceptual accuracy and emotional immediacy.

As human beings, we are constantly describing the world to each other based on the interpretations taught to us by our family and culture. Sometimes these descriptions are completely accurate, but often these descriptions are partial or incomplete distortions of what is actually happening in reality. In essence, we are receiving mixed signals. When a parent says, right before disciplining a child, "I don't know why you make me do this," or "This is going to hurt me more than it hurts you," every child knows that this is total baloney. We know who is in charge and who is getting hurt in this situation. But we are being challenged, and even threatened to abandon our point of view, which is based on the emotional and even factual truth of the moment, and instead adopt the parent's point of view. Due to the unfairness of the power differential, the child replaces an honest angry response with guilt, shame, and fear in order to perceive this moment from the parent's distorted description of reality. Until the child is capable of surviving life on his own, the child will consistently choose to perceive the world through the adult's distorted reality in order to secure his safety. This is the submission response to external threat: a key element in the Stockholm syndrome.

When external and internal information are in conflict, the child's worldview and self-image are challenged, and often undermined, which produces anxiety in the child. When children are confronted with an angry parent who says she loves the child, the child gets a mixed message, a "double bind" message. The child hears, on the external/ language level, that the parent loves him; however, on the internal/

emotional level the child senses tension, threat, anger, and rejection. The child now must choose between the parental point of view and the child's own emotional experience, which represents internal truth. Due to dependency or fear, the child will usually disregard his emotional internal truth (which is accurate) and accept the conflicting parental message as reality. Depending on how often these double-bind messages take place, the child's once accurate view of the world is slowly replaced by the parental point of view (description of the world).

The more emotionally unstable the parent is, the less accurately the child is able to interpret the world later in life, for s/he is continually attempting to understand and interact with the world through the parent's interpretation of reality while resisting his/her built-in emotional clarity. Essentially, the child is ignoring his/her truth and attempting to live in Alice's Wonderland, where very little makes sense.

This is why parental abuse and neglect create such blinding gaps in an individual's ability to accurately understand the world. Much, if not most, of an individual's point of view is an interpretation of the world and only partially correct. Religion, cultural values, family identity, and regional or gender biases all contribute to a view of the world that is distorted to some degree, leaving the individual with a history of missed messages and confusing results. All therapy starts with a listing of these confusing experiences: "How could I have missed that?" or "Why did it take me so long to realize what was going on?"

There are two questions I ask clients repeatedly as therapy progresses. The first question: "At what point did you first become aware of what you now know for sure?" This question is designed to establish that the client's emotional radar was, in fact, working correctly, but was being ignored (for a variety of reasons). This question is particularly useful in identifying the source of poorly functioning relationships. The second question: "How long did it take for you to act on this information?" This question has to do with the client's psychological learning curve. Healthy lifestyles are associated with a quick learning curve, the ability to identify those non-working aspects of our life, to assess the problem and make corrections. The therapy concern is how much time passes between realization and action: the time delay. In each therapeutic relationship, I am attempting to establish that the client has always possessed the information he or she needed to live life effectively and happily, but that the client was taught to ignore specific types of information (based on imposed emotional blind spots), or that the client was taught to tolerate, and therefore not act upon, dissatisfactory circumstances and relationships (submission).

Everyone wants to avoid negative relationships, sometimes abandoning any form of intimacy whatsoever. The truth is that it is very difficult to predict relationship compatibility without actually engaging in a relationship. I do recommend a technique called "The Interview," in which we simply seek pertinent personal information right from the start on the first date. This is lesser version of a standard therapeutic assessment. Your date's childhood, previous relationships, relationship with parents, sexual history, style of emotional fighting, and ability to negotiate or apologize. A favorite movie or book can speak volumes about how your date views the world and what motivates him or her. As one of my colleagues "famously" says, "When someone tells you who they are, believe them." To this, I add the famous adage, "The devil can't cross the threshold of your home unless you invite him in."

A favorite movie, book, or fairy tale can represent the myth that the person lives by, or at the very least, metaphorically describes the world in which he or she lives. I usually ask for the top two or three movies to get a broader view of his or her unconscious.

The only successful way to take emotional risks is to improve one's ability to recognize when the relationship is not working and to take action to transform or dissolve the relationship. We will always be attracted to whom we are attracted, but we can improve our chances of success by abbreviating our love learning curve. (See chapter 15, "Love's Shadow.") The only way to do this is to learn to listen to our emotions carefully and trust them.

The amount of time that passes between perception and insight is the learning curve of the threshold of perception. The amount of time that passes between emotional reaction and emotional action is the learning curve of the threshold of expression.

We almost always know the truth (of who we are with) very early into the relationship, but resist acting on that knowledge until it is unbearable (the threshold of expression). So you can imagine how helpful it would be to lower the thresholds of perception and expression. We would see the world more accurately, more immediately, and we would be capable of responding more rapidly, thus improving the quality of our life.

Our emotions are our information network; thus, our selective acceptance of our emotions leaves us with blind spots that keep us locked in neurotic relationships and neurotic self-expression. We either have been taught to "not see" the alternatives or we are afraid to challenge the limitations of our current situation out of fear of remembered retribution (physical/emotional discipline). We are unable to perceive, either in ourselves or in our environment, what we are doing incorrectly.

The famous Stockholm syndrome, although typically associated with life-threatening circumstances, is a variant of the double bind. This is a very famous case in which bank robbers take a group of bank employees hostage while negotiating their surrender. During the five days of captivity, the robbers repeatedly threatened the lives of their captives as part of the negotiation. The standoff ends without tragedy, but in the ensuing trial, the defense for the robbers called a few of the captives as witnesses *for* the kidnappers. *The victims defended the captors.* This is called "aligning with the aggressor" in psychological terms. The victim essentially agrees to the point of view of the perpetrator in order to reduce the danger. In many cases of kidnapping combined with long-term captivity and abuse, the victim adopts an internal protective mechanism that begins to "agree" with the perspective of the person doing the endangering. We will even defend those that have proved to be most cruel to us. If this type of threat can fundamentally, if only temporarily, change an adult's perspective, then we begin to understand how profound the effect that a parent has on a child's point of view of the world. Children often abandon or distrust big parts of their experience in order to adopt a parent's point of view. The more controlling the parent, the higher percentage of the child's personality reflects the parental priorities and perspectives. Usually, these perspectives are only partially accurate or true, and as a result, the unconscious is continually attempting to correct this inaccuracy by pressuring the personality to see the world in a more complete description.

As we mature, despite the suffering arising from this tension between unconscious and the personality, our fear of the consequences of breaking the parental rules of perception and expression keep us locked in neurotic emotional cycles and failed repeated experiments. The individual simply clings to the inaccurate point of view out of fear. This is the result of the parental, religious, or cultural threat. The pressure of the unconscious is experienced as symptoms (anxiety, tension, stress, etc.) instead of information. When these symptoms are present, it indicates that we are *perceiving the world incorrectly* and certainly *not expressing ourselves fully.*

DISSOCIATION

Dissociation is one of the major elements of the psychological periodic table. It represents awareness' ability to avoid direct suffering by simply abandoning parts of the body that have been traumatized. This loss of feeling, however, is not without consequence. After all, feeling is information and energy, and the compromise of these two significant dynamics will negatively impact our quality of life. We must also be aware that dissociation is a spectrum disorder, from the smallest loss of consciousness due to boredom to those stunning psychosomatic conversion and somatoform disorders: physical numbness, body dysmorphia, eating disorders, sexual dysfunction, or psychosomatic disorders.

Ever find yourself driving and realize that you haven't been aware, at all, of driving the car the last five miles, and yet here you are, safe and still on the road? This is a relatively harmless form of dissociation in the sense that it is dissociation associated with boredom or distraction. We might say, "My mind was somewhere else (and don't ask where…I don't know)." There is also a form of dissociation that occurs during trauma. When the body suffers significant shock and suffering, it shuts down the ability of awareness to experience the physical record of the moment directly. People frequently describe the experience of an automobile accident as suddenly going into "slow motion." Or, a person who has endured a traumatic event only has a few memories from before or after, but remembers nothing of the episode itself. Sexual assault is often reported with these types of disconnected memories, feelings, and disembodied experiences.

Although awareness seems to inhabit the entire body, it is probably more accurate to say that awareness can be located anywhere in the body, but not necessarily everywhere at the same time. If you direct your attention to the various parts of your body, you will probably be able to "feel" what that part of your body is experiencing. However, to make a point, put your fingertips together lightly as though you are praying. Now, feel the pulse of your blood at your fingertips. This should be a fairly simple experience to accomplish. Now, put your awareness in your toes and try to feel the pulse of your blood pumping in your toes. Not such an easy task, but with practice one can tune into this basic function with ease. Breathing is another exercise: Sit still and breathe deeply for a few breaths, and then allow your breathing to return to its natural rhythm. Awareness can control, for a brief amount of time, one's breathing, but it is much simpler for awareness to lightly participate in how the body wants to breathe on its own. Awareness simply rides the inhalation/exhalation wave. Awareness can learn to experience natural everyday biological functions; however, it does best when it doesn't interfere with natural function but rather cooperates with the rhythmic function of the body.

Since it is clear that awareness can move from place to place in the body, gathering information (in the form of feelings), the next challenge is to try to expand our awareness throughout the entire body, reaching to the furthest outline of the physical form. Even when we try to be everywhere in our body at the same time, we're still checking in from place to place in the body, taking inventory of the activity at each location. To experience the entire body all at once is quite difficult and can be sensorially overwhelming. Awareness is location-oriented, and a rapid shifting of awareness's location might feel like a simultaneous experiencing of multiple locations, but actually, one is just rapidly shifting the location of experience. This is normal. The real challenge is being able to attend consciously to every location in the body: first to each organ separately and then to all of the organs simultaneously.

Remember, memory is organ-specific, emotion is organ-specific, energy is organ-specific, and information is organ-specific. Most people simply avoid the feelings at certain locations in the body. As a result, awareness is present in the organs and with the emotions that function well and aid our psychological evolution, and awareness avoids the sites of suffering. Old physical injuries, emotional upset, and developmental trauma are all organ-specific. Thus, those areas that contain the painful memories are often avoided by awareness to prevent from feeling or remembering those ordeals. This is dissociation.

Our experiential history lurks within our bodies, and awareness unconsciously knows the locations of those memories. Awareness seeks pleasure and avoids pain, and when the body starts to become filled with more pain than pleasure, awareness retreats further and further away from the organs that are traumatized. Awareness simply withdraws or abandons any of the organs of the body that remember and feel too much suffering. This is trauma-based dissociation. *This is the dissociation of the personality structure built from our history of physical suffering.*

Years ago, after a particularly difficult knee surgery, I was asked by my doctor to raise my leg into the air to reduce the possibility of blood clot. As much as I tried, my leg simply was not going to perform the task. The problem was that I did not have conscious control of my leg. Why? Well, every time I would place my awareness into my leg, I became acutely aware of the pain and damage that had been done in the knee area, and I didn't like how it felt and simply fled the area. The doctor said he couldn't leave until I performed this feat and eventually I sorted it out by tensing my entire body and rolling to the opposite side, thereby lifting the wounded leg into the air. Clearly, my awareness had a "mind of its own" and had no interest in experiencing the pain in my leg. On a fundamental level, since this was my first knee surgery (of five), I had no way of putting into context what was happening in my healing process. I could not translate the pain into knowledge and thus relied on dissociation to keep from feeling damaged. Rehabilitation is essentially coaxing awareness to re-inhabit the area of the body that has been traumatized and then retraining the neural pathways.

The difficulty of any rehabilitation, whether it is physical or psychological, is the ability to tolerate the pain while reanimating the damaged area. The advantage in psychological rehabilitation (therapy) is that when the body is working appropriately, we are simply resisting the emotional memory stored at the traumatized site. Awareness needs to reclaim the traumatized area, whereupon regular exercise of the emotional and physical functions promotes healthy reintegration. I say this with one caution: Emotional expression alone produces limited results. Emotion requires memory to heal.

Emotion and memory are both required to reduce the trauma impact and prevent future activation of dissociation.

Dissociation is simply when awareness avoids or abandons any physical organ that is storing offensive memories and emotions. Thus, children that are repeatedly hit about the head often resist activating the functions associated with thinking and opinion. Awareness doesn't want to attend to the site of the assault and thus avoids consciously entering into the head. You know the people with "dead eyes"? Awareness is simply avoiding activating the non-verbal communication of the eyes, due to the parents' warning: "Don't give me that look!" With sufficient ongoing threat, the parent simply demands that the child deactivate the non-verbal communication at that particular site. The same can be said about tremendous sadness and dissociation from the respiratory system or dissociating from the digestive system in the case of repressed anger.

Repeated abuse and life threatening experiences trigger such emotional disruption and physical pain that awareness abandons the site in order to "tolerate" the offending feelings and memories. Although awareness is not directly feeling what has happened to that part of the body, the automatic and unconscious emotional reaction to the trauma continues to physically express in the form of symptoms. Instead of actively remembering the emotional information or the physical assault, we are now aware of a variety of symptoms that are expressing the distress of those experiences.

Our personal experience of the world is comprised of two processes: memory and emotion. Dr. James Masterson has suggested that when trauma occurs, there is a split between memory and emotion, and to diffuse the full brunt of a painful experience, awareness bonds to one and abandons the other. This means that one might have full memory of his/her traumas but not feel anything about those events. Or, one might have a variety of strong emotions that are usually out of proportion to the moment but have no recollection of the events that put those feelings into play. It's either *I remember but don't feel* or *I feel but don't remember*. Awareness has dissociated from the organs that integrate memory and emotion. In trauma, these two functions are split, with one aspect remaining in consciousness and the other relegated to the unconscious. Therapeutically, some people need to access dissociated feelings, and others need to access dissociated memories. This is *not* like "recovered memory syndrome," which has proven to be contaminated with the therapist's agenda (iatrogenic) and which I find to be a superstitious and inaccurate psychological theory. It is the rare client, indeed, that suddenly remembers an event, or events, that were completely blocked from memory. Almost every person can provide an emotional or symptomatic "trail" that indicates a history of trauma or abuse, and although we often attempt to ignore these psychological wounds, we are certainly aware of their cycling presence. I look for confirmation of psychological wounding by the presence of three signs of trauma: physical dissociation, traumatic dreams, and an obvious symptom profile.

Wilhelm Reich proposed that emotional trauma created what he called *body armor*, the tensing of muscles and joints. He further argued that this body armor stored the emotional information connected to the offending event(s). He proposed that body work (massage, etc.) would release the emotional information stored at the site, thus restoring the body to its original health. This essentially became the first mind/body integration attempt in psychoanalysis, and the theory's impact on popular consciousness has been profound. There isn't a massage therapist in the world that doesn't know that working on a person's body releases a variety of intense emotions as the musculature releases tension.

The mind knows, but the body also knows.

Childhood developmental stages are important for many reasons, and for our work as psychotherapists, it is these critical early childhood stages that establish body wisdom or body ignorance. When the nervous system is first activated in sequential stages throughout the body, each newly aware organ serves as an information and data collector.

As children, we learn and are taught how to translate the information processed by each organ as it "comes on line" (myelination). We learn how to interpret the feelings and emotions that the body produces. For example, at approximately three to four years old, the genital region of the body "wakes up" and the child begins to sense aspects of the sexual universe that previously were ignored. Until the genital region is activated, the child has a "sexual blind spot" and simply does not process sexual information. Prior to awakening, the child may witness sexual behavior but interprets it from a non-sexual point of view. It is often reported that very young children who witness people engaged in sex describe the activity as fighting. The lack of sexual information, or even the lack of sexual "translators," simply means the activity has to be understood through the limited knowledge and experience that the child has. As the child matures and all the physical circuits are activated, and the child is taught how to interpret and understand these feelings, then the child is at least in physical possession of sufficient data necessary to understand the world more accurately.

But consider this: As each organ becomes fully activated, it is particularly sensitive to stimulus, and all environmental experience is experienced strongly through the newly acquired neural pathways. During the unfolding of the oral stage, or the anal stage, or the genital stage, life's experiences are associated and stored at the location of the awakening body. Memories of joy or suffering are associated with the stimulation of that area of the body. So, in families where there is significant suffering or chaos, the child is constantly being exposed to painful experiences, and the newly awakened neural pathways, in particular, are being bombarded with these powerful feelings. A history/memory of this time period is stored in the area of the body that has newly awakened. For example, during the anal stage (the activation of the musculature around the anus that allows for successful toilet training), the joy or pain occurring in the child's life is associated with digestion and elimination. Any trauma occurring at this time period (approximately fifteen to thirty-six months) can lead to adult symptomatic behavior around eating and elimination. Or during the genital phase of neural myelination, between the ages of three to six years old, the genital region of the body becomes activated and the child becomes aware of newly acquired sexual feelings/knowledge/desire. The newly activated physical organs are simply "recording" the emotional events occurring in the child's world. Joy and pain are being stored particularly strongly in this newly activated site. Ongoing anxiety about safety or threat is stored in any of these organs during the activation stage, creating exposure trauma. These memories and feelings are activated when these physical sites are stimulated. (For sexual dynamics, see chapter 15, "Love's Shadow.")

In direct trauma, abuse results from actual physical contact. This is the standard perception of sexual abuse. However, in exposure trauma, it is the child's repeated exposure to an unstable and threatening environment that creates the memories and feelings stored throughout the body. These types of exposure traumas are common and lead to sexual inhibition later in life, even though the client reports no inappropriate sexual contact as a child. The "sexual" site has been traumatized by exposure to a hostile environment during a key developmental stage. The events that occur as our nervous system is first awakening become significant memories in the body. Instead of first love, it is first fright.

Most children are not sexually active (besides playing with themselves) between the ages of six and twelve years old. As a result, the genital region of the body remains fairly dormant, and the disruptive emotional memories of environmental/family craziness might be expressed only as social anxiety, introversion, passivity, isolation, and other low to moderate symptoms of trauma. There is little evidence to predict a future sexual inhibition. But upon the advent of sexual exploration as a young adult, the sexual site reawakens, and the memories and emotions of earlier environmental experiences manifest as part of the symptom profile: anxiety, tension, stress, etc. "Slasher" type movies are notorious for combining teenage sex with serial killers, further suggesting that the awakening of sexuality also awakens the memory of frightening experiences.

There are obvious cases where direct-contact sexual trauma immediately triggers acting out and the child begins involving other children in "sex play," imitating the acts of the abuser in an attempt to learn to regulate the overwhelming feelings associated with the abuse. In the same way that physical punishment teaches the child to act out physically, sexual abuse triggers either acting out sexually or dissociating sexually, producing regressive developmental behaviors, and in particular, regressive eating and elimination behaviors. The acting out behavior is simply the child's attempt to master brutally powerful feelings that are beyond the child's ability to stabilize. This acting out is the psyche's way of attempting to discharge the highly anxious response the child is having to the traumatic experiences. Remember: energy in, energy out, either as emotion or symptom. There is always a spectrum of how trauma affects us, ranging from mild depression, anxiety, or worry to the extremely destructive acts of sexual predation, fire setting, cutting, assault, theft, drug dependency, and other behaviors dangerous to self and others. Unless there are biochemical factors contributing to symptomology, the symptom profile will always be in proportion to the developmental suffering.

Emotional trauma produces symptoms until the trauma is remembered, emotionally experienced, and expressed. Clinical diagnosis and treatment usually starts with the symptom profile and works backwards to those fundamental historical emotional events that have shaped personality. In most cases, it is not an issue of *if* symptoms of emotional and physical abuse will come to the surface, but rather *when* and *how* this material will be reactivated. For emotional trauma stored at the genital site, this re-activation often begins at puberty. When teenagers begin sexual exploration, along with the pleasure associated with that physical site, all of the emotional memories of that site are activated as well. Suddenly the individual finds him or herself in a very real, and sometimes highly anxious, wave of conflicting feelings. Pleasure and anxiety arise together. This exact scenario takes place with the development of ones' confidence in aggression, thinking, speaking, and trusting others. Each of these significant informational and emotional sites has a combination of psychological perceptual and expressive potential, combined with a history of frustration, anxiety, and fear.

The quest for pleasure and emotional immediacy conflicts with the avoidance of anxiety and emotional memory. This tension becomes a lifelong conflict until the emotional memories stored at the traumatized site are realized and expressed, freeing the body for pleasure without triggering conflict or anxiety.

A word about medication dissociation: Pain medication and anti-anxiety medication are forms of chemical dissociation. These meds insulate awareness from offensive feelings/symptoms, providing temporary relief from the symptomatic pressures of anxiety, tension, stress, etc. However, long-term treatment with dissociative medications encourages drug dependence as a way of controlling emotional suffering, which can become a problem unto itself. There is nothing wrong with temporary medication intervention using dissociative meds (benzodiazepines) or social inebriants such as alcohol and marijuana, but this is not a successful long-term treatment strategy. The more the body is impaired, the more our perceptual and expressive abilities are limited. We may not be feeling the discomfort of the symptomology, but we are nonetheless suffering the consequences of these physical blind spots. The treatment of chronic pain often requires the long-term use of pain medication, which can interfere in effective psychological treatment at the deeper levels of integrating the components of the unconscious. Awareness needs access to the memories and emotions stored in the physical body, and the use of medication to blunt the painful effect of those physical sites can potentially impair deeper analytical processes.

Further, therapeutic effectiveness is limited for any drug-dependent client. Active alcoholics will impede therapeutic progress every time they drink. In-depth psychotherapy requires rehabilitating neural pathways to sustain new perceptual and expressive abilities, a process which is neutralized by the effect of the drug habit. It's as though every session is the first session. The client may be fully active and committed to therapy and work hard during the session, but the overall benefit of the work is undermined by the effect of the drug on the nervous system. Each session is drawn on an Etch-a-Sketch. Every drink simply erases the work done in the previous session. There is no long-term gain. If my clients are taking anti-anxiety medication under their doctor's orders, I request that they not take their meds immediately prior to the session. I want to be able to evaluate their anxiety levels in response to the emotional work during the session to determine how much of their anxiety is situational, historical, or medical. Rehabilitation therapy for clients with severe affective disorders (bi-polar or depressive disorders with psychosis) usually combines psychotherapy with medication. In these cases, in-depth analysis is suspended until the nervous system is stable and the medication regimen is optimal.

Emotional Toxicity

We are all familiar with toxic emotions: those emotional experiences we have with people that make us feel exhausted, depleted, tired, and even "poisoned." This is emotional toxicity. How many of us have spent time with people who manage to crush the life out of us and leave us feeling depleted and depressed? Everyone knows this experience. And yet we seem to be helpless to correct the problem other than avoiding those people. However, not everyone affects each of us equally. What exhausts one person doesn't bother someone else. Massive energetic deflation in one person doesn't even register on someone else. How is this possible?

The curious thing about real poison is that it affects everyone more or less the same way. A bee sting for one person is essentially a bee sting for everyone. So, how is it that we are not equally affected by "toxic" people the same way? We can certainly find agreement among people of similar points of view on a shared "toxic experience" by certain members of our community, but it would be nearly impossible to find universal agreement on the emotional effect of one person on everyone. This suggests that *how we respond* to someone is a significant factor in the effect that person has on us.

Family members are almost universally recognized as having skills at poisoning us emotionally, at least some of the time. A popular therapy joke suggests that one visit home for the holidays can ruin six months of good therapy. We find ourselves feeling exhausted, depressed, or frustrated after a significant holiday visit with our kin. Again, what is causing this energy drain? How is it possible that our families can penetrate even the best training or therapy and leave us exhausted and frustrated? The center of our energetic experience seems to be how we respond to these people and situations.

When we examine those experiences that have particularly high levels of energy, like falling in love, one of the commonly reported experiences is the absolute freedom of self-expression in that magic moment. How many newly met lovers have claimed early on that they "talked for hours and hours without stopping" or marveled, "I can really be myself"? Let's face it: If you are carrying on a conversation for hours without any loss of energy, you're basically saying anything that comes into your head or heart. You're "going for it," so to speak. This highly responsive interaction seems to be directly associated with higher energy states, whereas muted, withdrawing, and resentful behavior is associated with energy depletion.

We almost always give credit for any type of energetic experience to an external source for "producing" this effect in us. Whether it is positive and exciting energy or negative and depressing energy, we believe that the external person or situation is creating this feeling. In love, we start by believing that the subject of our affection is creating a wonderful feeling, only to blame them for the toxic feelings we experience later. Infatuation becomes resentment.

In toxic marriages, the fantasy of divorce almost always contains the fulfillment of self-activation, of finally "being free to be myself again." No holding back. No compromising behavior for anyone. Toxic marriages are founded on partners filled with resentment based on feeling that they cannot do what they want, or say what they want, or for that matter, be who they truly are. One has to make resentful compromises that slowly strangle the life out of the marriage.

When newly graduated counselors and social workers are beginning to do clinical counseling, there are many types of clients that are capable of triggering anxiety in the therapist. Emotionally chaotic or explosive clients with high levels of self-destructive behavior can be emotionally and energetically taxing to those professionals new to this work. However, seasoned professionals simply do not have the same level of anxiety or depression at the end of the day, working with exactly the same types of clients.

Through experience and emotional self-knowledge, the more experienced therapist has learned how to interact with "toxic" clients without becoming emotionally poisoned by them.

The difficulty of being a psychotherapist is that we do not have the luxury of avoiding emotions that don't fit our personality rules. Each client brings a new expressive challenge into our office, triggering both conscious and unconscious emotional responses from our own psyche. This is, of course, also true for everyone, but the therapist intentionally exposes him/herself to a much broader spectrum of emotions, with little opportunity to avoid uncomfortable or unconscious emotions.

Everyone experiences any activation of their repressed emotions as a hostile threat, and the repression of our response produces the toxic effect. When we block our emotional response to uncomfortable client emotions, we create a proportional depression in our psyche: burn-out. One solution to the toxic effect of emotional conflict is the Buddhist practice of compassion, which is intended to be an antidote to the painful/toxic effect of emotional interaction. Compassion is a spiritual reframe that eventually permits one to interact with the emotions of others without the negative effect. Although compassion provides relief by training awareness to abandon specific ego patterned responses, the practice of compassion does not transform the structure of the personality; it simply bypasses it and gives the practitioner a "taste" of resistance-free perception. But in psychotherapy, we are not simply looking for a reframe that can be applied to emotional situations. Instead, therapy is looking for an expressive correction that eliminates the repressive pattern producing the toxic effect.

If unrestricted emotional flow is the answer, you might logically ask, "Then why does someone who is uninhibited with anger or sexuality or sadness seem so unbalanced and unhappy, since that person should have so much energy?" The answer is in how the psyche operates as a whole. Each emotion contributes only a part of our energetic whole. Aggression, sexuality, or compassion only contribute a part of the total energetic experience. Someone who has been given permission to be angry, but not to cry, is missing a large part of his or her energetic potential. All of our emotions are required to see the world accurately and to access the full potential of our psychological energy. It is impossible to live a successfully dynamic and creative life on only a portion of our emotional energetic capacity. You can't "anger" yourself into health, "sexualize" yourself into health, "cry" yourself into health, or "think" yourself into health unless those are the neural-emotional centers that are obstructed, in which case the expression and mastery of those emotions will have a significantly positive effect on your psychological health. We habitually overuse the emotional centers that are working (the emotions we feel comfortable with) in an attempt to sustain our energy, eventually exhausting their energetic capacity, leaving us feeling drained. The unexpressed emotional centers remain bound by our developmental fears, producing symptoms instead of emotion, information, and energy.

Psychological energy is dependent on self-expression, not on the external situation or people. The universal constant in psychological energy depletion is repressed self-expression. Since our personality is what determines what is expressed and the style of that expression, our personality is responsible for the energy depletion. Open expression: more energy. Restricted or guarded expression: muted energy.

The World as Enemy or Ally

Eric Erikson, in his brilliant outline of psychosocial developmental stages, describes the foundation of trusting or mistrusting the world as occurring in the first year of life. Repeated disappointment and frustration during these first twelve months of life inevitably leads to a fundamental distrust about the world. The world is not our ally. This basic view of the world has stunning consequences later in life as we develop a belief system that reinforces our expectations.

We scan the environment for confirmation of our point of view and simply edit out any information that does not confirm our expectations. Fear creates massive perceptual blind spots. Fear edits mercy and hope.

But what if the world is actually an ally instead of a random, and often ruthless, enemy? There is certainly a case to be made that the world can be a significantly dangerous place. But these fearful dynamics hardly represent the full spectrum and beauty that reality offers just as readily. Our personality, and its orientation to threat, simply redacts the environmental stimuli to that which reinforces our expectations. However, each of us has a history in which love, mercy, kindness, and joy have impacted us and challenged our fearful narrative. Perhaps it is the inconsistency, or the cyclical nature of these nurturing experiences, that prevents them from redefining our fearful expectations and cautious approach to living. And yet, these brilliant moments of feeling connected and having purpose leave their impact on our psyche and call to us to seek more meaningful moments in life. So, in spite of our fearful beginnings and our anxious anticipation of a heroic disaster, we cautiously, or even courageously, continue to seek connection and meaning in our lives.

One of the principle markers of personal/spiritual growth is when we shift from the point of view that the world is a chaotic and random environment to the point of view that there is a universal feedback loop in which the world actually reinforces healthy, creative, and positive decisions. As human beings, we are so invested in rationalizing and tolerating our stress that we miss the subtlety of the positive feedback loop between the environment and ourselves.

The threshold of perception, for most of us, is so restrictive that we simply do not see the helpful information that sits just below the threshold of awareness. The information is there, but we simply can't register it. The positive, energetic signal is present, but our tension level is so high that we don't experience it.

The curious aspect of operating as though the world is an ally is the possibility that the world has "intent," that there is a direction for consciousness, indeed that evolution is not accidental, but intentional. Maslow's *hierarchy of needs* theory suggests that consciousness is moving toward an expressive goal, yet to be fully revealed. Over the past ten thousand years, the advancement of civilization is obvious. Each cultural accomplishment evokes the next cultural accomplishment. Social stability provides the opportunity for the body and the psyche to transform (the advancement of physics, nutrition, medicine, etc.). If we accept Maslow's theory of the hierarchy of needs, then each level of social stability means that the energy of our collective and individual psyches will migrate, naturally, to the next expressive goal. Each evolutionary thrust leads to the next psychological challenge. The possibility that the individual and the collective consciousness are actively evolving the world in which we live is quite intriguing.

From this vantage point, the world is no longer viewed as an ongoing personal threat. Instead, the world is an arena in which humankind is invited to develop and express deeper and often unveiled aspects of the Self.

The world literally seeks to wake us up. This evolutionary exchange can be rude, but it is quite effective once one realizes that the world has more of an interest in our service potential than soothing our fears.

In fact, the aspects of the world that seem threatening are often the components of the Self that have been denied expression. Every emotional blind spot is experienced or perceived as inappropriate or corrupt. It is our prejudice toward any particular emotion that filters out the positive aspect of the emotion and reinforces, through selective scanning of the environment, the negative side of the blocked emotion. And it is true that every emotion has its corrupt aspect. But every emotion has its wisdom aspect as well. (See chapter 2, "Structure of the Unconscious," *Psychosomatic Scale*.) For every abusive husband, there is a brave first responder using the same emotional energy, each represented and expressed with significantly different results. The emotion is not good or bad. It is the intent that corrupts or elevates.

The corrupt aspect of any form of emotional self-expression—worry, silence, pity, aggression, or addiction—is the direct result of repression to the point of distortion. One cannot hold hostage the natural form of emotional expression without the consequence of its emerging in a warped form, upon initial release. Emotions that have been repressed for years produce significant pressure and instability. The concern that "letting go" might have some worrisome consequences is most likely correct. But without the release of these emotional contents, and their eventual mastery, the danger further increases. Isolating oneself from the world is certainly one method of regulating emotional reaction. Simply remove oneself from a conflictual or seductive environment and the internal emotional conflict will reduce significantly. If nothing is triggering your anger, your problem with expressing anger will be greatly reduced. But this is hardly a realistic way of living except when dealing with psychosis, severe PTSD, or in those rare monastic traditions that attempt to control the influencing environment to aid the practitioners' struggle to live emotionally regulated lives. For most of us, taking time off from interacting with the world provides a brief relief from emotional tension. A much more realistic solution is to discover how to come to terms with how we have been emotionally designed and quit trying to improve (restrict) upon a system that is actually quite amazing.

CONCLUSION

Trauma occurs when the nervous system is either overwhelmed by external stimuli or simply systematically trained to inhibit self-expression under threat or seduction (pleasing authority). Extreme stimuli (neglect, violence, sex, threats, malnutrition, war, abandonment, and environmental extremes) flood the psychic system with pain, and awareness retreats from the sites of the insult (dissociation). Systematic trauma is simply the imposition of social or family system designed expressive styles that inhibit, interfere, or replace a more direct healthy style of self-expression.

The emotional results of *single episode trauma* (any life threatening experience) can be as mild as anxiety or as ferocious as post-traumatic stress disorder, depending on the intensity of the offending event. *Systematically repeated trauma,* prior to ten years old, actually shapes the personality structure, affecting emotional expression and perceptual accuracy. The distinction between these two types of trauma is significant. Systematically repeated trauma, such as domestic violence, will actually shape the personality directly, whereas single episode trauma will shape personality choices but not the personality system.

As members of the animal kingdom, human beings respond to painful experiences initially by fight (attack, defeat, dominate, or destroy the negative stimulus), flight (abandon, retreat to a safe location), or freeze (attempt to be invisible or act helpless). When we are children, due to our profound dependency on our families, we learn to harness these three basic protective responses in order to secure our long-term safety. We are too small to defeat the source of pain, and we are too dependent to strike out on our own. We are left with "freeze" which is simply the "wait it out, hopefully" strategy for dealing with unfortunate circumstances. As a result, we endure repeated exposure to offensive stimuli from parents, siblings, neighbors, classmates, and circumstances, and our emotional responses to these physical and psychological insults are eventually shaped into a pattern of expression that releases this emotional tension through symptomatic behavior. We convert these emotional and physical insults into our symptom profile: anxiety, tension, stress, guilt, shame, fear, resentment, worry, depression, grief, and somatization.

When trauma is systematically repeated, awareness begins to develop a pattern of somatic avoidance; awareness withdraws from the physical site of the pain. This produces two major effects: Awareness dissociates from the neural-emotional site of the trauma (psychological "numbing"), reducing the information available from that site and creating a perceptual/informational blind spot and progressively restrictive emotional response that converts/transfers emotions into symptoms. This is the foundation of the personality structure: perceptual redaction and emotional restriction.

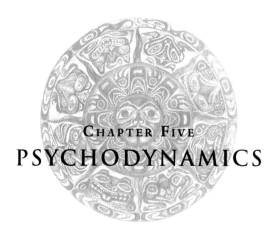

CHAPTER FIVE
PSYCHODYNAMICS

INTRODUCTION

Whereas the *psyche* represents the totality of the components of personal identity—awareness, personality structure, the body, and the unconscious, *psychodynamics* is the study of the structural dynamics of the psyche—the energetic interaction between the components of the psyche and the internal and external worlds.

Personality, by design, has multiple components that create its ultimate structure, some working together with other parts for the greater good of psyche and soma, and other parts clearly in conflict with each other, creating psychological distress. In general psychological theory, personality structure can be healthy or pathological. A healthy personality has accuracy of perception and is emotionally expressive in proportion to the moment. The pathological personality has too many developmentally (or biologically) introduced distorted perceptions and/or restricted emotional responses creating symptomology and provoking/driving destructive behavior toward self and others.

This book takes the attitude that any and all personality is pathological, redundant, and inefficient. Although the psychological habits that one develops as a child to aid in survival or avoiding danger can certainly be viewed as helpful to the overall goal of staying alive, the patterns of perception and self-expression that are created by these highly stressful circumstances ultimately inhibit psychological health, replacing autonomy and growth with approval seeking and compliance. And although this certainly helps one survive childhood, the limiting factors of the personality structure interfere with the psychological potential of the adult.

Since awareness does not seem to require personality to operate successfully in this world, (and I would argue that those moments in life that are filled with joy and creativity, or even spiritual breakthroughs are personality free), then perhaps we need to view the personality structure as a redundant, less efficient system of perception and self-expression, formed exclusively out of the trauma dynamics of our childhood environment. Thus, as adults, our expectations of how the world works, both accurately and distortedly, as well as our styles of response to those expectations, illustrate the fundamental personality structure that our awareness is using to negotiate life. Where there is accuracy of perception and proportional emotional response, there is little personality interference, and our lives typically demonstrate creativity and balance. Where our personality distorts perception and restricts self-expression, our lives seem to produce cyclical chaos, suffering, and symptoms.

The challenge of psychodynamic psychotherapy is in (1) identifying the personality structures that constrict perception and self-expression, (2) discovering the history of emotional training and modeling that produced that specific personality structure, (3) binding accurate memory to accurate emotional history in order to reduce emotional contamination in the present, and (4) expanding the boundaries of self-expression and perceptual accuracy in order to more effectively interact with the world.

THE FIRST TEN YEARS

Childhood is a continual experiment in perception and self-expression. The childhood behavior that meets with *approval* becomes a repeating pattern of perceptual interpretation and self-expression and shapes our expectations of how others should relate to us: our relationship patterns. The self-expression that meets with disapproval and punishment is eventually systematically repressed. The aspects of perception that are denied or challenged begin to create blind spots where information about reality is dissociated.

Personality becomes the predictable pattern of expression and repression. The repressed aspects of the Self, along with the unfolding/untapped aspects of the Self, are still active in the unconscious, producing the energetic pressure that fuels the personality symptom profile. The greater the quantity of material that is repressed in the unconscious, the stronger the personality symptoms. Where symptoms are present, traumatic history is present.

Typically, the first ten years of our lives are lived practicing and perfecting the style of relationship (personality structure) that we have learned from the principle people in our lives: parents, siblings, and social partnerships. The most significant contributor to our style of relating is our primary caretaker (usually the mother). She has the dominant role in limiting or supporting self-expression for the child's first four years of life. This does not mean that the father or siblings don't contribute to the particulars of how we relate to the world, but the mother's bond is significant and pleasing her is the highest priority in a child's early life.

By the time the child is ten, the nervous system has been considerably "programmed" by the environment, and the personality structure is solidified. The experience of adolescence is more concerned with experience and confidence and does not significantly alter personality structure. The potentialities of personality are established and the environment begins to press the adolescent into more adult relationships. Certainly, the adolescent can be encouraged to pursue a variety of life possibilities, and without a doubt, guidance, mentoring, and support are necessary at this crucial stage of development, but the personality structure is already in place. The concept that personality is fixed by ten years old may be concerning to some readers, but I will share this experience with you: I once had the opportunity to ask James Masterson and Otto Kernberg (arguably two of the most influential clinicians and theorists in object relations theory), in an open-question panel discussion at the Evolution of Psychotherapy conference, how they felt about the idea that a person can't have a personality disorder before the age of eighteen (the limit of the DSM). They both started laughing at the same time.

The DSM suggests that for a diagnosis of anti-social personality at eighteen years old, a diagnosis of conduct disorder needs to have been established by fifteen years old. Robert Hare's work on the biological psychopath shows that psychopathic behavior is demonstrated as early as five years old.

Since the 1950s, we have clung to an idea that adolescence is a time of developing personality, when in fact it is a time of gathering experience and information that contributes to our expressive skills but does little to rework the fundamental structure of personality. If you have a murderer or violent assailant at thirteen years old, he is, psychologically, a killer. This does not mean that he can't learn more appropriate social skills and stay out of prison, or not kill or assault anybody else, but do not be fooled that the fundamental personality will be changed in any way. It will not. Behavioral change, or the avoidance of punishment is not the same as personality structural evolution.

True psychological change occurs in the context of interpersonal, empathetic relationships, in which we increase our ability to share emotional experiences with others. Anti-social personalities view intimacy as a threat to their safety. Without the ability to form an empathetic bond there is little psychological growth, only skill-set development, and these are two fundamentally different capacities. As a result, adolescence is a time of skill-set development, not evolution of the personality structure; personality disorders can certainly be in place throughout childhood.

Although we certainly learn new relationship skills after ten years old, a significant portion of personality is no longer flexible. These "fixed" aspects of personality are perceptions and expressions associated with the family relationship contract. This "contract" represents the perceptual and expressive rules of the personality. It defines how we interpret the world and how we respond to that perspective. We will repeat this approved family behavior with every relationship and act as if everyone knows and abides by the relationship contract set by our family. We will use this style of relating in most situations in our life with moderate success.

However, we are at a loss when our "approved" behavior (whether charming, strategic, submissive, or adversarial) is not socially effective. We have no psychological back-up plan, no back-up styles of problem solving, no back-up emotional expression, and no back-up relationship skills. The unconscious tries to provide access to a more appropriate form of expression (self-activation), but we are already under "contract" (personality structure) to repress these components. The tension between the unconscious and the personality struc-

ture is what triggers our symptom profile. This failure to safely negotiate social pressures activates anxiety along with our particular variety of symptoms.

When the environment places us in situations where the family style of relationship is inadequate, the unconscious immediately offers access to the underdeveloped components of the psyche that might more effectively deal with our social dilemma. These components were initially experimented with in childhood, but were met with discouragement or discipline and were subsequently repressed out of fear of consequences. These components are necessary to negotiate the complex situations of adulthood but are nonetheless repressed in childhood, and remain so. As adults, when that component in the unconscious is triggered by external events, the tension between expression and repression triggers our particular symptom profile: anxiety, tension, stress, guilt, shame, fear, worry, etc. out of fear of remembered punishment for expressing that forbidden emotion.

Obviously, it would be to the best interest of the individual to have complete access to all of the skills, abilities, and wisdoms repressed in the unconscious, but instead, until specific effort is made to overcome our psychological fears and express those sublimated, repressed, and dissociated components, what we have is only partial activation of our psychic potential and a complimentary set of symptoms.

APPROVAL AND SELF-EXPRESSION: THE FOUNDATION OF PERSONALITY

Under most circumstances, children are born with access to a complete set of perceptual/expressive potentialities (the Self) that respond to activation, expression, and regulation. The environment not only triggers these potentials, but behaviorally determines which will be developed and which will be repressed and replaced with symptoms (and usually with specific symptoms).

Fortunately, there are many situations and relationships in which there is a match between the expectations of the parents and the abilities of the child. In these cases, the child simply excels and the parents are delighted. Parental approval is the natural result. Thus, parental approval can be supportive and encouraging without being pathological (in the service of the parents' neediness). A parent can be genuinely curious about the child's growing self-expression without personalizing that growth as a sign of the parent's self-worth. However, even in ideal cases, the child leaves home with the anticipation that everyone will be delighted at his or her "good" behavior. When this positive mirroring does not occur, there will be an immediate increase in anxiety. The individual inherently has the capacity to meet a variety of social and interpersonal emotional requirements, but often the family has limited access to some of these emotions, and the unconscious produces anxiety instead. So when the standard operating behavior fails to meet the social challenge, the activation of an unused part of the psyche produces anxiety, at least initially.

The pathological aspect of approval occurs when the parent requires certain behaviors from the child in order for the parent to feel valued or respected. In many cases, the child's responses provide the parents with a sense of meaning with regard to their values, parenting goals, and even self-worth. When the child's behavior is no longer an aspect of self-expression, but rather becomes the way in which the child can curry favor with the parent or other authority figures or a way to avoid a punitive response, the child's personality becomes oriented to strategically manipulating the world to produce praise and avoid punishment. Approval becomes the goal rather than creative self-expression. Security trumps creativity, and until the child feels safe, approval-seeking behavior will rule.

One of the key aspects of psychotherapy is the development of one's confident self-expression. This open, or less regulated form of communication is *self-activation*. Self-activation is the art of engagement, creative response, independent intellectual functioning, and adherence to a set of internal values separate from the need for approval to avoid punishment. Self-activation also involves a spontaneity of living that is capable of interpersonal intimacy, interdependency, and autonomy, without compromising personal perspective and emotional honesty.

Ultimately, self-activation is the unimpeded flow of information and expression between the unconscious and consciousness in spontaneous response to our encounter with the world and the evolutionary cycles of our unconscious (psychological potential).

This ability to self-activate is one of the key measurements of a healthy adult psyche. Every person's personality has its own rules of self-expression and self-activation but is constrained by the fear of the consequences of activating a part of the psyche that has been restricted by the family and social system.

Almost all fear of consequences is founded in actual experiences of our childhood, whether we remember them or not. The body remembers and alerts the personality to the dangers of certain self-expressions. It is these defining fears that create the personality structure that emerges in all relationships. When a restricted part of the psyche is triggered, either through social pressure or self-activation, the emotional energy of the response is blocked and turned immediately into symptoms.

THE FIVE CENTERS OF AWARENESS

As discussed in chapter 2, there are five neural-emotional complexes that rule personality. Each complex is organ specific, information specific, emotion specific, and trauma specific. To review, personality is predominantly defined by the thresholds of perception and expression of each of these five major neural-emotional complexes: thought/insight, sadness/empathy, anger/courage, and sexuality/pleasure, with the addition of speech as a purely expressive function of the psyche. Each neural-emotional center (minus speech) has a psychological function that perceives information, holds memory, and expresses emotion. Each of these complexes is associated with a specific location in the body and performs two tasks: regulation of perception and regulation of expression.

1. A Perceptual Threshold:
   A. How intense an experience has to be before we recognize it
   B. What experiential information is recognized, defining the parameters of reality
   C. What information is blocked, creating blind-spots

2. An Expressive Threshold:
   A. How intense an emotion has to be before we express it
   B. The amount of time that passes between recognition and response
   C. The intensity and style of the emotion when it is expressed

These psychological thresholds simply retard information or expression until the pressure to respond becomes sufficiently strong and the resistance is overwhelmed temporarily, producing a rush of attitude, opinion, emotional intensity, and impulsive behavior. The individual is suddenly aware and expressing all of the repressed content in an unstable and intense rush. There is little difference between an anxiety attack and falling in love, except for how the individual is interpreting his or her feelings. It's never "if" you are going to express yourself or see the world accurately, it is only a question of "when" this will happen and how long will this be sustained. Once the emotional pressure exceeds the threshold of inhibition, resistance gives way to expression, often out of proportion to the moment.

Emotional expression is usually based on social, gender, and predominantly, family styles. We were taught to express anger, sadness, sexuality, thought, and speech by the examples around us, and the constant reinforcement of perceptual and expressive distortions that have been handed down for many generations. And to be fair, all the good, insightful, and wise expressions of the family are passed down as well, although often not equally among the children. Families often bias their perception of a child's abilities and encourage certain features in one child while discouraging those expressions in others.

Sibling order and gender contribute greatly to the projective content of each parent's expectations of the child. Thus, the child is carefully crafted to express him or herself in a style that is reinforced by the family. Through reinforcement, both positive and negative, the fundamental structure of perception and expression forms the personality and becomes the operating script in all relationships. This style of perception and expression is simply the result of neural training. We are taught to see the world through a specific bias, and certainly to express ourselves with a specific bias. Even though we have available to us a nearly infinitely evolving set of information and an equal number of expressive options, personality is, by design, a strongly restricted set of controls that interferes with our perceiving the world fully and accurately and severely limits the amount of energy available to us through self-expression. We experience the denied informational and expressive potentialities as pressure and symptom.

Our families then teach us which symptoms to use when repressing our emotions. This is why guilt is so strongly used in some families, whereas others use anxiety, shame, or worry. These combinations of symptomatic expression are founded in solid family tradition. So when we watch some child throwing a deafening tantrum in the local department store, and we wonder why that parent doesn't teach her better behavior, the answer is that the parent has taught the girl *that* behavior: that girl's behavior is the direct result of systematic training. The girl's conduct is the result of psychological stressors and internal emotional pressure and reflects the expressive design of her forming personality. By the time she is ten years old, this expressive system will be, for the most part, fixed.

Further, each of this girl's neural-emotional complexes has been compromised in some manner. Disruptive and emotionally chaotic behaviors are the signatures of psychological pressure from one or more of those emotions. Remember, emotion is organ specific, information is organ specific, trauma is organ specific, dissociation is organ specific, energy is organ specific, repression is organ specific, and symptom is organ specific. Each neural-emotional center is uniquely trained in its function of perception and expression.

With four perceptual complexes and five expressive complexes, all children are constantly and continuously experimenting with how they see the world and how they respond to it.

We, as family members and cultural representatives, *shape* what gives each child pleasure and what creates fear and anxiety. How children initially come to view the world, what will be significant and what will be ignored, and how they will respond to those experiences, are all founded in the quality of the relationships we offer that child. Thus, perceptual blind spots and expressive disorders result directly from social conditioning.

Each neural-emotional center has a varying dynamic potential (energy and information) based on one's genetics, activated and developed potential, and environmental support; energetic "wattage" varies depending on each neural-emotional site as regulated by one's personality structure and developmental history. These high-energy neural-sites might be viewed as natural gifts: intelligence, sexual desirability, a competitive spirit, or the gift of "gab." When these energy-emotion-information complexes are compromised, limited, or repressed, they can produce significant symptomology. For example, the energy of one's dissociated sex drive can produce significant symptomology, such as worry, anxiety, bothersome headaches, skin rashes, digestive disorders, or any of the common symptoms associated with repression and dissociation.

In psychodynamic therapy, the therapist needs to resist the distraction of the symptoms, and focus on the diagnosis and treatment of the expressive dissociation. With the greatest respect and skillful means, the therapist needs to continuously redirect the therapy back to the blocked emotional expression and the memories associated with the original psychological insults.

Awareness continuously seeks reasons for all feelings registered in the body. If the current situation is triggering some historically repressed emotions, awareness still treats those emotions as though they are being created in this moment, which is only partially true. Because we experience all emotions in this very moment, we assume that all emotional content has been created in this moment.

Awareness has two ongoing specific goals: accuracy of perception and immediate proportional emotional expression.

Both of these goals are compromised by repressed emotions that have been activated by, and then contaminate, this current moment. One of the major goals of therapy is to link those historical emotions with their experiential history so that awareness perceives our developmental history accurately and responds appropriately emotionally to current events and past events.

Emotions are blocked for a reason: usually a history of direct or exposure trauma. And there is high anxiety associated with the therapeutic examination of that trauma. After all, who wants to feel and think about all those unfortunate experiences of our childhood? Thus, it is not unusual for the client to avoid the memories and feelings connected to his or her childhood history. But the therapist, having diagnosed an emotional expressive block, must help keep the client wrestling with those repressed emotions and memories. Otherwise, the treatment will never successfully resolve the limited self-expression. The client's symptoms may be the obsessive concern of the client, but have little to do with the actual problem: blocked self-expression.

Most psychopathology involves inhibition of speech in association with blocked emotional function. We are simply not allowed to speak of our underlying emotional problems. Thus, activation and expression of the voice plays a significant role in therapy. The initial therapeutic alliance always involves the client's commitment to simply describe, talk about, and discuss a variety of thoughts, feelings, and emotions. Verbal communication becomes one of the cornerstones of psychological healing.

PERSONALITY'S EXPRESSIVE SCALE

If emotion expression can be quantified on a 1-10 scale, with 1 being the lowest level of emotional intensity (calm, clear, socially comfortable), and 10 being a massive emotional intensity (assertive self-defense, in love, accountability), most people's personality structure allows them to operate emotionally within the 1-3 range (covering most social situations) and then again at the 8-10 range (complete expression with little or no inhibition). So, in the 1-3 range, emotions are available and communicable. In the 8-10 range, the emotional pressure has become so significant that we finally "say what we've been wanting to say all along." The 8-10 range is the result of "the straw that broke the camel's back." However, in the 4-7 range, (the therapeutic target range) we are mute, frustrated, anxious, and generally symptomatic, without direct expressive release. Until our emotional pressure reaches level 8, we are stuck with our symptoms. If we were more flexibly expressive in the 4-7 range, we would only reach the 8-10 level in very rare moments (unless, of course, you play competitive sports).

These three levels also apply to perceptual data: the reality we experience is directly related to the intensity and subject matter that our personality structure unconsciously permits. On a perceptual level, personality permits us to detect all phenomena in the lower (1-3) and higher ranges (8-10), but we are "blind" to the qualities of the world in the 4-7 range. There are aspects of the world that are perceptually redacted. We may fully admire a great athlete, ignoring his brutality on the field until he murders someone in his private life, and suddenly, we see the whole picture. That athlete has been illustrating his anti-social behavior at every emotional level, but we missed the more brutal acts until a truly immoral act has taken place. Our perceptual blind-spots occur most frequently in our personal relationships wherein we "miss" some very obvious cues as to the qualities of some of our "friends," colleagues, and business associates, until they abuse us in a very obvious or repeated manner.

These blind spots and responsive obstructions have serious energetic consequences. The amount of effort that is required to continually filter reality into a prescribed and approved script is an energetic drain. We all eventually become exhausted with the symptomization of our emotions, and at the tipping point, a sudden stream of memory and emotion replaces our symptomatic "silence." By the time our emotions reach their breaking point (threshold of expression), we are also aware that the intensity of emotion pouring out of us is probably more than the situation requires, but there's no stopping us now. The explosion of emotion possesses awareness and will continue until the emotional charge is released: this could be minutes, hours, days, or even weeks, depending on the amount of repressed content. Awareness will be "possessed" by this attitude, until magically, we return to our previous selves. Our personality has been hijacked by the very emotional material that personality has been restricting for years. Essentially, the prisoners have taken over the prison; sometimes it's a fight-fest, and sometimes it's a love-fest. Falling in love is also the result of crossing the expressive threshold. (See chapter 15, "Love's Shadow.")

By working on our memories and the emotions associated with them, particularly in relationship to our family of origin or unresolved trauma, we begin to reduce the emotional content and pressure in the unconscious, which then allows our normal emotional responses to be in proportion to the moment.

When there is a minimum level of repressed emotional content residing in the personal unconscious, our perception and emotional response to the moment are accurate and balanced. There are no big fluctuations in mood, attitude, energy, or insight, because there is only the expressive and perceptual content of the moment.

How Much Personality Disorder is Really a Personality Disorder?

A personality disorder is the result of a rigid perceptual and expressive system: distorted in perception and out of proportion in emotional expression (too much or too little affect). Considering that personality has five major neural-emotional components that each contribute to the overall quality of functioning of the individual, the severity of the personality problem would be in proportion to the number of the personality components that have been compromised (sublimation, repression, dissociation), and the severity and type of the restriction.

The DSM diagnostic manual typically requires extreme symptomatic behavior in order to be classified as a personality disorder. For behavior to exhibit consistent or rapidly cycling symptomology, a large percentage of the personality structure needs to be rigidly fixed in perception and expression in order to qualify. The problem with this diagnostic method is that, in reality, the behavior of mildly, moderately, or severely symptomatic individuals is essentially the same with the exception of the amount of time the individual stays in a pathological state. This means that the person with an eighty-five percent expressive block is potentially symptomatic eighty-five percent of the time. And the person with a twenty percent blockage is potentially symptomatic twenty percent of the time. For the person with the eight-five percent block, it is nearly impossible to live a consistently happy and energetic life with access to only fifteen percent of one's psychological potential. Symptoms replace self-expression and the world is reduced to a cruel environment. In those moderate cases, when our pathology compromises only twenty percent of our psyche, awareness is still being one hundred percent regulated, but only twenty percent of the time. The fact that eighty percent of the personality works quite well makes little difference when you are under the control of the impaired twenty percent. The influence of that twenty percent psychological obstruction may not last for several weeks or even months, as is the case in severe personality disorders, but during the hours and days that the wounded complex is in control, we are completely compromised. For the DSM to suggest that one is required to have months of continuous suffering to qualify for a personality disorder is ridiculous. It's like suggesting that someone who is drunk only twenty-five percent of the time does not have a drinking problem. Certainly someone who is drunk ninety percent of the time has a more disruptive problem, but the dynamics of the disorder are the same. If you repress your sexuality only twenty-five percent of the time, it essentially means that you are one hundred percent repressed twenty-five percent of the time. You might enjoy your life more than someone who represses his or her sexuality seventy-five percent of the time, and certainly your symptoms will be less than those experienced by the person with the seventy-five percent restriction, but you are still completely restricted twenty-five percent of the time, and you will produce similar psychological symptomology while under the influence of that obstruction. Personality disorders certainly have varying intensities of constriction and acting out, but the diagnosis and treatment of those wounded personality components is the same. The therapy potentially takes longer for those with the higher percentages of compromise.

Awareness may have complete access to several neural-emotional sites while suffering from complete dissociation from several other sites. There are multiples of combinations of integration, sublimation, repression, and dissociation possible in human personality structures. For example, speech is a critical and complex expressive component of the psyche. One might be able to integrate speech and thought, but not speech and sexuality, or sadness. Our capacity to verbally express ourselves may vary considerably depending on the neural-emotional complex involved. Ultimately, the healthy psyche has interconnectivity between all of the neural-emotional complexes, so that each complex informs and energizes every other complex. Pleasure informs thought, courage, speech, and compassion. Compassion informs aggression, speech, thought, and sexuality. Thought informs speech, sadness, anger, and sexuality. Courage informs thought, speech, sadness, and sexuality.

The personality, like any great stage play, has a variety of characters (emotional complexes) coming to the forefront, or receding into the background, who are influencing the direction and mood of the play. Awareness, like the audience of such a play, is most affected by the presentation of the actors with the dominant roles. Those with the loudest voices, and a majority of the dialogue, have the greatest influence on the audience's perspective and response to the action. But unlike a well-performed play, in the personality structure, the parts of the psyche that are relegated to smaller parts or whose influence is muted by a biased and controlling director (personality), those "actors," when off stage (repressed or dissociated), are often tearing down the sets, getting into fights with the other actors, or periodically harassing members of the audience.

If the personality were truly a stage play, it would shift between Shakespeare and Mel Brooks, unless of course this personality had no sense of humor (severe narcissism), and in that case, it would generally rotate between each of Shakespeare's tragedies. Imagine living in the world of Othello, Hamlet, King Lear, or Romeo and Juliet. The question we should ask of ourselves and our client is, "What theatrical play are we participating in?" For a wonderful answer to this question, I refer the reader to Kurt Vonnegut Jr.'s marvelous short story, "Who Am I This Time?" found in his short story collection, Welcome to the Monkey House, perhaps my favorite book of fiction.

In the Beginning: The Infant's Point of View

The child's point of view is formulated from the activation of the neural-emotional sites, unfolding in sequence, with each site contributing specific information about the world and producing an emotional response to that information. The child is initially incapable of interpreting or regulating the waves of sensory information cascading through his or her body. Awareness, unable to recognize or decode the information, feels only pressure or tension, producing dreams, fantasies, and anxious symptoms. At this stage, the baby borrows much of the mother's emotional stability for emotional comfort; however, until there is object constancy (around twenty to thirty months) the child's sense of safety or comfort is fleeting and dependent on the availability of the mother. If the mother is unavailable, or inconsistent, the baby responds to the world with anxiety and fear.

The baby's initial personality traits are really the result of a subtle (and sometimes not so subtle) interplay between the external world, the mother (principle caretaker), and the child's awakening nervous system. The mother recognizes and responds to certain traits in the child and encourages or discourages these expressive traits. A mother's fears shape the child's personality as much as do a mother's hopes.

The mother's emotional stability, recognition, and response to the child's needs and expressions significantly form the expressive style of the child's personality, as well as the child's relationship expectations of the world. These expectations are the fundamental contract (relationship pattern) that every child/adult brings to all of his or her relationships. It is this relationship pattern that is diagnosed and treated in therapy.

This is the beginning of the neural feedback loop, which gives perceptual information to awareness and expresses our emotional responses. This loop has the capacity to be nearly instantaneous, but as we have discussed throughout this book, perception and expression become retarded by the regulation of the personality structure emerging from family and cultural training. During this early development, the child is taught how to interpret and perceive reality and how to express emotions "appropriately." In ideal circumstances, we are taught to perceive the world accurately and respond effectively. However, under most circumstances, we receive a combination of truth, superstition, and social ritual, rendering reality and our interaction with it somewhat confusing and anxiety provoking.

The child must learn to fit into the family and culture and adopt approved social and gender roles. This inevitably clashes with the need of awareness to perceive the world accurately and emotionally respond fully to experiences. Personality is created from the compromise: biased perceptual interpretation and restricted emotional response. Personality is truly the guardian of perception and expression.

The child's world is a world of symbol and imagination. From the infant's point of view, the body's developing neural-emotional complexes each contribute mysterious input from an unknown and undecipherable world that seems to self-organize in mythic patterns. Imagination precedes knowledge and provides a flexible working structure of reality. The family and culture eventually teach each child how to interpret and respond to reality through shared language and behaviors. Every culture relegates portions of reality to a mythic structure of religious beliefs that are eventually challenged by experience, insight, or a new developmental stage.

Awareness has to the learn the language and meaning of each of the five neural-emotional centers, beginning with hunger, pleasure, pain, frustration, anxiety, loss, comfort, thought, and even desire, which later develops into the adult experiences of analysis, sexuality, friendship, loyalty, grief, courage, patience, and intimate relationship.

As awareness wrestles with the massive amount of information flooding the child's newly activated neural circuits, anything familiar is experienced as emotion or insight, and everything new and unfamiliar is experienced as mythic (symbol-fantasy-dream-imagination) or symptom.

With each developmental stage of the child's maturing body, newly activated neural pathways provide shocking and energetic experiences. Awareness is taken on a journey of biological unfolding, information without interpretation. When the child tries experiments that are considered inappropriate, morally questionable, or situationally inconvenient (opinions, sexuality, comfort), the family and society are quick to instruct the child to ignore or repress those feelings, thoughts, and actions and to adopt behaviors that are socially acceptable based on gender, economics, race, religion, and other current social standards. This behavioral training is the foundation of personality, expressing those behaviors that receive praise, and repressing perceptions and self-expressions that elicit punishment, rejection, and disapproval.

For human awareness to function in the world, reality must be repeatedly described and behavior repeatedly modeled and reinforced. Instead of, as with most animals, having a genetically built-in recognition and behavior inventory that is activated by experience, humans mirror behaviors or adopt expressive strategies that are designed to prioritize survival and group approval.

TRUTH VERSUS THE MYTH OF REALITY

Everybody who participates in a child's life describes the world, emotional responses, relationships, and physical functioning. As a result, we are vulnerable to all types of creative distortions of perception and expression. However, people are born with one significant gift—the ability to recognize truth—and *truth* has energy. Of course we can get children (and adults) to believe all sorts of fantasies and distortions, but adopting a point of view that conflicts with reality triggers anxiety. Distorted perception or inhibited self-expression compresses our energetic response and redirects our emotions into symptoms. As a result, when we experience the truth, there is a psychological energetic surge that accompanies it, even if the truth is painful.

We inherently know what is truthful and can differentiate truth from "presentation" or distortion. We may be forced as children to accept and adopt distortions about the world and to suppress and repress healthy emotional responses to dysfunctional family systems, but at our core, we know what is a lie. However, when our built-in lie detector is repeatedly challenged, threatened, and intimidated, we often substitute symptoms and perceptual distortions for truth. Awareness is caught between self-protection and self-expression.

We unconsciously repress curiosity, emotional expression, and effective self-defense in order to embrace the lesser gods of approval, submission, and safety. We begin life open to (if not overwhelmed by) the amazing possibilities of the world, but as our curiosity and courage lead us into a variety of experiments, testing the limits of our experience of reality, we begin to develop the ability to differentiate truth (reality) from description, or even deception. When someone offers us a distorted description of the world, we know it when it happens. We know it's false because it evokes anxiety in us. Deception is always reinforced with an implied threat, which triggers fear. In a sense, reality is reality, and we know the difference between reality and someone's hallucination, no matter how many people agree to believe the hallucination. However, most family and social systems require submission to the agreed-upon "myth of reality," with severe consequences for those who resist acculturation (the Or-Else). (See Chapter 1, "The View," *The Threshold of Expression*.) Significant aspects of the known universe are ignored, denied, reframed, or simply attacked, all at the expense of the child's later quality of life. And it's not that the descriptive distortion is a fabrication of a universe that doesn't exist; rather, it is often the condensing of reality into an extremely narrow set of variables and values. Each generation literally sees only the narrow bandwidth of reality they've been taught to see by their community and then avoids those broader "facts" of reality that result in punishment. Rules concerning danger, sexuality, social behavior, self-expression, eating habits, food bias, and religion have been carefully passed down from generation to generation, with typically only a few upgrades to higher perceptive and expressive accuracy.

PARTIAL DISSOCIATION: THE LOSS OF THE MIND-BODY CONNECTION

As discussed in Chapter Four: "Trauma Dynamics," *Dissociation*, dissociation represents the most common, automatic, and unconscious psychological defense; awareness simply abandons parts of the body that are wounded, contain trauma memories, or are providing information that makes the person feel uncomfortable. Dreams are filled with the images of emotions, associated with specific complexes that have been ignored, or completely rejected. Dissociation, by design, increases the amount of time that neural information requires to reach awareness and provide a response. As one would expect, there is a direct correlation between time delay and symptom intensity. From seconds to minutes, hours to days, and weeks to months or even years, the severity of the trauma causes increasingly larger time gaps in perception and response. The interactive time required by each neural-emotional site varies based on the severity of the dissociation. One can be mildly, moderately, or severely dissociated from the biological and/or psychological function of each organ.

When the nervous system is newly activated during the early developmental phases, the effect of the environment can be profound and long lasting. If the child experiences repeated trauma and suffering, the pattern of response eventually becomes a fixed personality pattern. There is a significant difference between single-episode trauma (emergency room visit) and repeated episode trauma (abuse by an older sibling). The personality structure is formed by the repeated episode trauma. However, PTSD caused by a single episode extreme trauma (threats to life), can significantly affect the overall functioning of the personality structure, much like a virus invading the body.

The effect of any dissociation is measured by four factors:

1. The time involved in awareness accessing the site-specific information (dissociation)
2. The percent of that information that is distorted or missing (repression)
3. The time required producing a response (emotional processing)
4. The intensity of the symptoms associated with the blocked/ inhibited emotional response

The nervous system has the capacity to rapidly form repeating patterns of recognition and expression, as well as "hold" a traumatic emotional charge. It is this painful emotional "charge" that awareness seeks to avoid through dissociation. So, awareness retreats from the site of the trauma, and the emotional information at that site is temporarily lost, while the energy of the charge is converted into symptoms, signifying traumatic history and an emotional/perceptual block. What's curious about this rather straightforward trauma-dissociation-avoidance-symptom cycle (See chapter 8, "Treatment": *The A.R.C.*), is that there are a series of protective mechanisms surrounding the trauma site. In the same way that the heroes and heroines of ancient Greece fought their way through a series of challenges/tests in order to retrieve the "treasure," we, the seekers of psychological treasure, will encounter anger, helplessness, exhaustion, anxiety, forgetfulness, and many other "guardians at the gate of wisdom." Only through curiosity, courage, and commitment will we be able to defeat the psychological challenges and acquire this deep wisdom.

Dissociation is automatic, immediate, and usually ongoing, producing perceptual blind spots, emotional inhibition, and energetic depletion. Dissociation is the personality protecting awareness from negative circumstances and consequences.

INTEGRATION OF SPEECH

The lack of full integration of speech presents a problem in the expression of any and all emotion. Verbal communication produces a significant energetic release and shapes our impact on the environment. Although non-verbal communication is a significant part of human expression, verbal communication can be used not only for stress release, but also as an expression of will and intent. As Don Miguel

Ruiz states in his masterful book, *The Four Agreements*, "Be impeccable with your word, speak with integrity." He implies throughout his book that one's voice and intent literally shape the quality of one's world.

We might have full and accurate perception at any neural-emotional site and be aware of our emotional response without being able to verbally communicate our emotions or intent. Speech plays a singularly important aspect in all emotional expression. Any block or delay associated with the voice will retard emotional expression and create increased symptomology. In many of these illustrations, because speech is at least partially repressed, the full expression of any emotion will encounter some verbal resistance and create some symptomology instead of direct communication.

For each of us, the capacity to include speech in the communication of our emotions varies depending on the emotion. One might be able to verbally express thoughts or anger, but not sadness or sexuality. Verbal dissociation is emotion specific.

There are certainly personality structures where speaking is disconnected from all psychological functions—*"children should be seen and not heard"*—and the person is essentially silent most of the time. This is a very common symptom in the dependent personality, and thus, what should be the simple process of directing one's own therapy by verbal interaction instead produces excruciating amounts of anxiety. Finding one's voice is a critical aspect of psychotherapy (the talking cure). The simplest method of evaluating the severity of a verbal block is to identify the symptoms that appear when called upon to speak up and give a verbal response to the world. Word blockage, thought blockage, loss of focus, avoidance, agitation, shame, guilt, memory loss, immediate anxiety, and sweaty palms, etc., are all immediate symptomatic responses to a verbal inhibition.

Because one's verbal response to the world, especially in childhood, can trigger immediate retaliation, verbal communication is often one of the very first victims of childhood discipline and dissociation, which is ironic, considering how excited most parents are when their children begin to speak.

Structural Sublimation

Sublimation is the psychodynamic task of transforming one emotion into a different emotion. Personality performs the task of "appropriate" emotional expression; thus gender rules and social rules, but mostly family rules, dictate the intensity level of most emotional expression, so that when the threshold of expression is exceeded, personality converts the "inappropriate" emotion into a more "acceptable" emotion.

Sublimation occurs when our emotional response—for example, anger—exceeds the threshold of "approved appropriate behavior," and the personality structure redirects the "excessive" aggression through sadness, and the person begins to cry, even though he is furious. Up until the aggression is sublimated, the person may have complete access to, and expression of, his or her anger. Emotional expression only becomes a problem when the aggression exceeds the threshold of expression designed into the personality structure by social standards.

All personality structures start with awareness having perceptual and expressive access to all of the neural-emotional centers, but as the emotional pressure exceeds the perceptual and expressive thresholds, the structure shifts into a protective mode that converts emotional expression into symptomatic expression, protecting the person from anticipated threat.

Sublimation, repression, and dissociation become the mechanisms that handle the energetic tensions associated with threat assessment, restricted expression, and production of symptoms. Sublimation is simply the less offensive (energetically) restrictive mechanism.

Sublimation is one of the wonderful features of the human psyche, essentially re-routing emotional energy through emotional or physical expressions other than the original neural-emotional complex. Thus, for example, sexuality is re-routed through anger, sadness, worry, athletic competition, or the job at hand. Sublimation is a marvelously flexible and therapeutically challenging psychodynamic (energy/emotion/information) program. It is not as brutal as repression or dissociation, because in sublimation, the energy behind the original emotional response is still available for productive psychological use and has not become purely symptomatic.

Sublimation is one of the most interesting and practical aspects of personality dynamics. We are raised in family systems that prefer certain forms of expression, and most people have been encouraged to develop specific emotionally expressive abilities. In plain terms, we're either good at crying or anger, but rarely both. The permitted emotional expression (thought, speech, sadness, anger, sexuality) often serves a dual role: to express the genuine emotion and to express the other repressed emotions. For instance, repressed and sublimated anger could be expressed as sadness, or repressed sexuality could be expressed as mental obsession. Some people express their anxiety by becoming very talkative, while others become withdrawn and mute.

Gender roles in American culture teach women to cry when they are angry and men to be angry when they are sad. Thus for many women, anger is sublimated through the "empathic/sad" neural pathways. Instead of blocking the anger completely and creating more somatic symptoms (headaches, rash, depression, "the vapors"), the anger is redirected through sadness. The sublimation only occurs when the anger exceeds a specific intensity level and then suddenly, anger becomes tears, or if repressed or dissociated, a symptom or a somatic complaint (headache, stomachache, rash, anxiety attack).

The problem with redirection/sublimation of any emotion through another emotional expression is that the transfer is inefficient, so part of the energy and information is lost, leaving part of the emotional charge in the unconscious, producing some symptomology. In general, restricted emotions build up pressure in the unconscious, contaminating the emotions that are being expressed, creating unhealthy and disproportional emotional responses in our present situation. Learning to express all of our emotions is a good start to mental health; however, since any emotion can be a symptom for another emotion, it takes real courage and mastery to allow our natural emotional response to re-emerge in place of the learned expressions and symptoms of our childhood.

Let me say this again: *sublimation makes it possible for any emotion to be a symptom for another emotion.* You may be expressing the heck out of anger but never feel better or resolve your emotional tension. This means that you are blocking a different emotion, and it is the other emotion that is creating the dis-ease in your psyche. A major rule of psychotherapy is that when a person finally expresses the emotions that are repressed, s/he will feel better. If significant emotion is being expressed and there is no improvement in the overall mood and energy in the client, either the wrong emotion is being released or there is a biological problem. Sadness will never be resolved if it is only being expressed as anger. You can rage all you want, but the problem still remains that your sadness is blocked and you need to learn how to cry and grieve in order to relieve your symptoms. And, of course, no amount of emotional expression will cure biological depression, mania, anxiety, or other neurological disease, in the same way that no amount of medication will fix an emotional problem.

There are many circumstances in which sublimation can be very helpful. If one member of a couple has a high sex drive and the other has a moderate sex drive, in order to maintain peace in the home there are negotiations that will need to take place to resolve how the couple will deal with the sexual tension. Eventually, the individual with the higher sex drive will need to sublimate some of that energy into other activities so that it doesn't continue to create frustration and conflict, and the person with a lower libido will need to increase his or her sexual flexibility. The energy behind the sex drive can effectively be used for many purposes, just like all emotional energy: creativity, developing new skills, education, sports, etc.

THE STRUCTURE OF PSYCHOLOGICAL OBSESSION

Most psychological obsessions and compulsions are the result of the overdeveloping of at least one neural-emotional center at the expense of the other three (thought, sadness, aggression, or sexuality). The obsessive personality structure processes all feelings through the head (thought). This is very common among "thinking" types of people.

When angry, they worry. When sad, they worry. If sexually approached, they worry. Awareness resides almost exclusively in the head with brief forays into other parts of the body when highly stimulated or when anxiety is reduced through medication, drugs, alcohol, or courage. Almost all feeling is redirected to the thought process, with predictable results: heightened, ongoing anxiety and worry that rarely releases its grip. Until the "thinking" type is willing to get angry or sad, or feel sexy, their obsessions will possess their attention. They have sublimated all feeling into predominantly obsessive expression. See Chapter Three: "Personality Structure," *Symptoms versus Source,* for a good example of a non-medical obsessive-compulsive disorder.

If you are a worrier by nature (something learned and supported by your family) and you do not suffer from a biochemical disorder (depression, mania, obsessive/compulsive disorder, anxiety), you probably do not express your feelings very well. The pressure created by blocked emotional expression drives the obsessive worrying. You will never find permanent relief by trying to resolve all the challenges that worry you. Instead, supplemental emotional expression is required.

When awareness is dissociated from the speech center, an obsessive person could be relatively mute. If your family discouraged verbal communication, you could very easily be a quiet worrier. A lack of verbal communication seems to be a critical feature in many psychological blocks. Remember, as an energy distribution system, personality prioritizes what type of information is consciously recognized, which emotions are expressed, and how long it takes for each of these functions to take place. The more repressed or dissociated an emotional complex is, the longer it takes for the information gathered by that complex to reach awareness, and the longer it takes for the emotional reaction to be expressed. Instead, the complex that is permitted expression does the heavy lifting for the psyche, processing a majority of the psychological energy and symptomizing the rest.

Chronic worriers are often good students, very disciplined, capable of great responsibility, careful and methodical, and normally unlikely to be impulsive. In spite of potentially great accomplishments, chronic worriers suffer from poor self-image and poor self-worth. Remember: self-image is in proportion to self-expression, and in this case, the only emotion working is thinking: the other eighty percent of the psyche is compromised, negatively affecting self-image.

The shadow side of the personality is indulgent and obsessive about food, alcohol, and drugs—and when the chronic worrier does cutloose, look out! He is capable and willing to indulge all of his feelings when drunk or high, and drinking often becomes an antidote to such an obsessive and rigid lifestyle. The obsessive thinker is in search of passion and purpose.

THE STRUCTURE OF INTEGRATION

Integration is the presence of awareness at all of the major neural-emotional sites, simultaneously, with accuracy of perception and immediacy of emotion in proportion to the moment. There are no lingering historical emotional contaminants in the psyche to obscure and color our experience of reality.

This illustration represents awareness having simultaneous access to all of the body's processing and emotional expression centers. Perception and expression are immediate. Information is unrestricted, and emotional response is spontaneous and proportional. The goal of the integrated personality is to produce accurate assessments of the world, to express oneself emotionally in proportion to the moment, and to provide awareness with full and immediate access to all the processing power of the physical body.

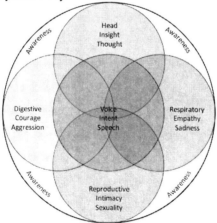

Complete integration, accuracy of perception, and immediacy of response. Each of the neural-emotional centers has complete access to the resources of every other center. Thus, the specific information available to any of the emotional sites is available to all of the other emotional sites; sexuality is informed by compassion, compassion is informed by courage, thought is informed by passion, and dozens of other combinations. And, they all have a voice!

Dissociation, as we have discussed, is awareness avoiding traumatized parts of the body, thus losing access to some or all of the information and feelings associated with those physical sites. One of therapy's main goals is to talk the client "back into his or her body," where memory, feeling, information, and energy can be accessed. When historical emotions are reconnected with their historical memory, the body regains much of its original flexible functioning. No longer are current situations triggering old emotions and recollections stored in unintegrated sites. The body is essentially clear of past emotional debris. The client is free to fully experience the moment and respond to it spontaneously, liberated from all of the symptoms associated with self-activation. Since there is no fear of the consequences of actions based on past threats, the individual is free to fully self-activate and self-express. As a result, we are no longer tolerating the tensions and repressed emotions of our past relationships, and our toleration for current inappropriate people and meaningless activities is significantly reduced, as well.

Most people check in with the various parts of their body, bouncing from emotional site to emotional site, depending on the intensity of the external trigger or emotional response. When true integration takes place, awareness fully inhabits the body and has immediate and simultaneous access to all the neural-emotional sites and can differentiate between them. All emotions work for the overall evolution of the psyche.

Every neural-emotional complex needs an interactive relationship with each of the other four complexes in order to offer the most effective, balanced, and complete counsel for the psyche.

Thought without speech isolates. Thought without empathy lacks compassion. Thought without aggression lacks courage. Thought without pleasure is sterile. Empathy without thought is short sighted. Empathy without speech is mute. Empathy without aggression can be manipulated. Empathy without pleasure lacks joy. Aggression without thought lacks strategy. Aggression without speech is unable to negotiate. Aggression without empathy is brutal. Aggression without pleasure lacks direction. Pleasure without thought lacks creativity. Pleasure without speech is lonely. Pleasure without empathy lacks love. Pleasure without aggression lacks intensity.

The specific relationship of each complex to each of the other complexes represents the exchange of emotion, energy, and information. As each complex contributes its emotional and energetic potential, the intensity of the experience increases. Thus, the most intense sexual experience is associated with the participation of all of the components of the psyche. For example, if each complex contributes twenty percent of the psychological energy, information, and emotion of every experience, then all five complexes would need to be engaged in order to have the highest energetic, most informative, and emotionally satisfying experience possible. If a sexual encounter is being conducted only with sexual energy, although it may be satisfying, it only represents twenty percent of the experience possible. If you care about the person you are with, you are adding the additional twenty percent of the empathic neural-emotional center, further energizing the experience. It is not difficult to see how the contributions of thought (sexual creativity), assertiveness (sexual boldness), and speech (direct verbal communication) could add a significant amount of energy to the experience.

If you own a computer, you know how nice it is when the various applications and programs communicate and interface with each other seamlessly, as well as the frustration that occurs when the applications function in an isolated or erratic manner. The human psyche interacts with itself very similarly. Each complex serves a specific function and contributes specific energy, emotion, and information to every encounter with reality. The better the access to all of the complexes, the more accurately we perceive reality and the more appropriately we emotionally respond to reality.

CONCLUSION

There is an old T'ai Chi description of mastery that says: "You do the form, and you do the form, and you do the form, and then one day, the form does you." When the protective and predictive functions of the personality structure are resolved, we begin to trust and serve our deeper internal wisdom, which has always been available, but highly restricted. We permit this greater wisdom free access to communicate itself without strategy. Ego ceases to protect its "wounded" self by manipulating the environment through strategic and unconscious emotional tactics, and instead, inner wisdom gains traction and voice, allowing awareness to develop an appreciation for the world as it is and confidence in the spontaneous and creative appropriateness of our response. There is a growing curiosity about one's own process: a sense of being present and stable even in unpredictable circumstances, and yet, ready and capable of being spontaneous in the moment. There is an accuracy of perception and an immediacy of emotional response. Our creative potential is available at each encounter, and there is a transparent quality to reality that reveals the environment without comment or corruption, engages the interactive strategies of others, and engages the world with an emotional depth that is appropriate and in proportion to the moment.

To be psychologically healthy, emotional energy must be more equally inclusive of all of the neural-emotional centers—a balance of perceptual and expressive capacity immediately available to the individual in proportion to the moment.

The information contained at each of the neural-emotional sites is critical to healthy accurate functioning in the world: each organ is a part of our world "radar" and describes specific aspects of our experiences in nature. Without that information, we have perceptual blind spots. We go through life running the same experiments over and over with the same results, but because we are not permitted to be aware of the needed information, it is simply ignored once again. It's not that we don't have the information. We do. We're simply not allowed to access that information without triggering predictable and cyclical symptoms: anxiety, tension, stress, guilt, shame, and other forms of suffering.

As the nervous system, and in particular, the neural-emotional complexes, attune to reality through their specific perceptual and expressive capacities, awareness will spend a lifetime learning to master the interface with all the complex organs of the body and how to translate the very specific information associated with those organs.

Maybe the most important feature of a healthy mind is the development of a flexible sense of humor. The highest level of humor is the ability to laugh at oneself, and to do this, one has to abandon the point of view that one is the center of the universe. At a conference in 1991, I heard Dr. Masterson say, (and I paraphrase), that when he treats dependent-borderline personalities, he mostly tells jokes, because their lives are so unhappy, but you can't do that with narcissists because they take it personally and think you are laughing at them. Now I know that Dr. Masterson was pushing our rigid perception of the borderline personality with his comment, and of course, his therapy is much more sophisticated than just "telling jokes." But even the comment requires a sense of humor. Narcissists do take almost everything personally. And for the narcissist, developing a sense of humor in which he can laugh at his own predicament is a huge leap forward in therapy. I'm not saying that the world is not worthy of serious respect, but certainly without humor the world can feel significantly oppressive.

Ultimately, the integrated mind has the capacity to see how our lives have purpose, direction, a built-in moral and ethical compass, and personal authority rooted in our service to the evolution of humanity.

THE ARCHITECTURE OF ATTITUDE

INTRODUCTION

This chapter will outline and describe the building blocks and expressive functions of the personality structure. We will examine the universal sub-structure of the personality, identified as the four functions. We will also explore the unique content/presentation of personality, comprised of a group of introjects associated with developmental environmental influence.

The second half of this chapter covers diagnostic identification, core issues, expressive fears/blocks, social contracts, and treatment styles of the four major personality structures (dependent-borderline, anti-social, narcissistic, and Asperger's) as they would present in therapy.

A Brief Structural Review: A *neural-emotional complex* is one of the five major neurological clusters of the body (head, throat, respiratory, digestive, reproductive). Each complex serves a specific perceptual and expressive function for the personality structure and contributes to our overall interaction with the world. The *four functions*, the subject of this chapter, are the sub-structures of each neural-emotional complex and represent the attitude presented by the personality. An *introject* represents the relationship style utilized by the four functions; essentially the content of personality. An introject presents itself as a sub-personality. For personality, the neural-emotional centers are the structure, the four functions are the attitude/presentation, and the introjects are the contents of each function.

The Sub-Structure: The Four Functions

When examining the architecture of the personality, we begin with the five neural-emotional centers (See Chapter 2, "Structure of the Psyche," *The Five Components of Identity*,) and then sub-divide each neural-emotional center into a quaternity of *relationship interactive functions*: the architecture of attitude.

- The Rewarding Function (RF)
- The Punishing Function (PF)
- The Seducing/Pleasing Function (SF)
- The Wounded Function (WF)

This quaternity is associated with James Masterson's object relations theory. Masterson uses a gender-neutral terminology to describe each of the four functions. He refers to the rewarding object relations unit to describe the split of the rewarding function and the seducing/pleasing function (parent's rewarding introject and child's pleasing/seduction response) or the withdrawing object relations unit to describe the split in the punishing function and the wounded function (parent's punishing introject and the child's hurt response). Masterson is extremely careful to be technically neutral due to the possibility that people other than mother are capable of playing the role of the most significant object relations unit (influencing person) in the child's early development. I find Masterson's terminology, although technically correct, to be a bit sterile; therefore, I am using a more descriptive terminology for the four functions in this object relations theory.

It's helpful to consider these four functions as relationship strategies, shaped in childhood and unconsciously applied throughout life. Personality is fundamentally an unconsciously applied tactical mechanism designed to automatically influence the outcome of every relationship encounter. Each of these functions can perform as a healthy expression of self or as a pathological and unconscious defensive mechanism. Initially, these are simply the styles of self-expression learned from one's family and culture, and with diligence, one can transform the limiting strategies of these neurologically embedded operating systems.

These personality functions are neurological patterns of behavior, instilled in the child through repeated contact with positive and punishing reinforcement. The particular *style* of each of these four functions is based on those most intimate of relationships (introjects) in early childhood and reveal how we have been permitted to, or even required to, perceive and emotionally respond to the world. These relationship patterns become our personality structure, our method of relating to others and our self. (See Chapter 1, "The View," *What If.*)

The evolving nervous system learns to quickly replicate our recognition and response to any repeating situations; thus, those first significant relationships establish the initial relationship patterns coded into our neural pathways. As a result, our emotional associations with our historical relationships contribute to our expectations of the current, and every future, relationship.

Not only do we perceive and respond to the world through these early relationship patterns, these perceptual and expressive tools are also how we self-evaluate. Thus, our internal critical voice is often an amalgam of those critical voices we heard in childhood. That noisy, punitive, and harassing voice in our heads is the *learned* critical style of those we were subject to in childhood.

The primary caretaker (initially the mother) contributes the greatest influence to the content and style of the four functions and, thus, is the dominating relationship pattern that will be utilized with greater frequency throughout life. Other significant people in the child's life who have the powers of praise and punishment additionally contribute to the overall confidence and style of the child's personality and psychological operating system.

The strength and longevity of the child's extended relationships (father, siblings, relatives, teachers, etc.) help create the sub-personality introjects that rule self-confidence, self-worth, perception, and expression, and eventually become the complex features of the personality. This means that in addition to the mother introject (primary caretaker), any significant, long-term relationship, when experienced during our early developmental stages (up to seven years old), contributes to the child's operating system and expression style.

Each of the five major neural-emotional complexes (See chapter 2, "The Structure of the Psyche," *Physical Structure*,) has this underlying quaternity structure (rewarding, punishing, pleasing, wounded), but the specific content of each complex will vary depending on how the child was treated and the experiences s/he accumulated during the developmental stages associated with each function. For example, how each significant person interacts with the child's aggressiveness will often be uniquely different from how each person interacts with the child's thinking process, sexual expression, or loving expression. Thus, the fundamental *organizing structure* (four functions and neural-emotional complexes) is shared by everyone, but the content (introjects) is unique to the individual and based on the dominant relationships of childhood.

What each child unconsciously constructs are a set of perceptual and expressive patterns (introjects/sub-personalities), displaying unique levels of confidence or reluctance, symptomology, perceptual accuracy or distortion, and expressive freedom or inhibition, each with varying capacity to be expressed through speech. Thus, how the personality perceives and responds to sexual issues may differ significantly from how the personality perceives and expresses thoughts, sadness, or aggression. The four functions simply provide the outer presentation of these emotional states, depending on the unconscious strategy the child is using to secure approval or safety from the world. Each of the four functions is simply a negotiation tool in social interaction.

Because personality structure is based on multiple neurological sites, and then is sub-divided again into four additional functions at each site, it produces the effect of multiple personalities. This assemblage of emotional introjects presents in a variety of states of integration or dissociation: one moment flexible and dynamic, the next, rigid and moody. All personality structure has multiple personalities, and they are rarely all working together. At best, they are fluid in their influence on perception, rising and falling in their informational, emotional, and energetic impact, and flexibly expressive in their response to environmental stimuli. At worst, perception is fractured and distorted, superstition replaces wisdom, symptom replaces emotion, and the world appears to be a chaotic mess.

Gestalt therapy addresses the personality's varied composition in a particularly instructive way. One of the standard beliefs of Gestalt therapy is that personality is actually an assemblage of sub-personalities (introjects) interacting (internally and externally) in a variety of states of conflict and cooperation. The Gestalt therapeutic goal is for awareness to "own" all of its sub-components, assembling a flexible, efficient, and cooperative structure: a seamless availability of information, emotion, expression, and energy.

PERSONALITY CONTENT: THE PARENTAL INTROJECTS

Every personality structure (narcissistic, dependent-borderline, anti-social, Asperger's) is comprised of a collection of psychological introjects that serve as the expressive patterns of personality (sub-personalities). Based in object relations theory, these neurologically trained patterns seem to be the underlying mechanisms behind relationship presentation (how we relate to others), and thus, personality structure. An introject is a personality cluster of perceptions, behaviors, and styles of relating associated with significant authority figures (parents, siblings, or caretakers) that the child has incorporated into his/her psychological structure. Since each parent, or significant authority, "imposes" their specific style of function and relationship expectation on the newly forming nervous system of the child, the child usually adopts several unique introjects, starting with the mother introject and the father introject. One parental introject might have a dependent style, and another might be anti-social, alcoholic, narcissistic, or Asperger's, thus producing the appearance of a borderline type personality structure in the child, in which awareness rotates between these significantly different expressive styles: one moment, dependent and needy, and the next (take your pick), anti-social and threatening, narcissistic and insulted, or Asperger's and aggressive. In the same way that an adult child of an alcoholic might present an "alcoholic style" of emotional expression (even if s/he does not drink), the child will mirror or mimic those emotional styles that are repeatedly imposed upon the child. These introjected styles of relating are different from the actual personality structure and should be viewed as sub-personalities. However, each introject has an entrenched quality and will strongly represent the individual's point of view and emotional style when it is activated.

In truth, these significantly different introjects (sub-personalities) are fighting for domination of the person's operating system. These styles of expression are distortions (some slight and some gross) of natural emotional expression and must be evolved if the individual is to align with his/her natural design and creative potential. If the dependent traits are not subdued, the individual will compulsively submit to the will of others, becoming highly anxious when required to self-activate. If the anti-social traits are not subdued, these individuals will become unreliable in their relationships, constantly testing the people in their lives, suspecting betrayal, manipulation, abandonment, or callous disregard. If the narcissistic traits aren't subdued, the individual will constantly seek to seduce the attention and praise of others, all the while feeling lonely and underappreciated. If the Asperger's personality style is not evolved, the individual will be socially avoidant, isolated, inappropriately aggressive with others, and will misread non-verbal cues. With the Asperger's personality, evolution occurs by dedicated and disciplined learning of social cues, emotional regulation, and practiced interactive strategies.

THE PATHOLOGY OF THE FOUR FUNCTIONS

The four functions have both healthy and pathological features. At their core, the four functions are psychological strategies that we inherited from significant authority figures and are our main techniques for interacting with the world. They are utilized to promote and reinforce specific behaviors, externally and internally. Initially, we are caught in the judging, punishing, pleasing, and helplessness associated with our childhood. Although these unconscious and automatic strategies can be useful in specific circumstances, they lack the creative flexibility, or intent, to be utilized as effectively as needed in the complexities of our lives. These behaviors are not necessarily destructive or even inappropriate, but they are triggered automatically and are limited in scope, effectiveness, and flexibility. When these behaviors are ineffective at controlling the environment (or even our own behavior), there is an automatic cycling between the four functions and/or a burst of symptomology. In the next two sections, we will examine the limitations of the unconscious use of these functions, and then we will explore the healthy evolution of these psychological features.

THE REWARDING FUNCTION: THE PERFECTIONIST

The pathological aspect of the rewarding function is the conformist, the perfectionist. The rewarding function sets the standards for acceptable behavior, and the punishing function expresses the emotional backlash for failure to please. The parental rewarding and punishing functions work together to form the foundation of self-expression that every child then uses throughout life. In psychoanalytic terms, the rewarding and punishing functions are the ego ideal and the super-ego: internal confidence versus internal criticism. Keep in mind that the rewarding function often unconsciously rewards inappropriate, dependent, and emotionally chaotic behavior. I watched a mother and son interaction at a local mega-store in which the child, around five years old, standing next to a "wall" of candy as they were in line to check out, asks his mother, in a very straightforward and non-whiny voice, for a candy bar. The mother says, "No." The child then, in a whiny voice, says, "I want a candy bar." Still, "No." The child escalates emotionally and vocally, "I want a candy bar." Again, "No." And then, in a near shrill cry, whine, complaint, yells, "I want a candy bar!" The mother then gives in and gives him a candy bar. Obviously, this is positive reinforcement of a negative behavior, and completely unconscious; the mother simply wants some peace of mind. However, a few more engagements like this between mother and child, and the child will skip all those earlier more appropriate requests for candy and go straight to the "outrage" stage of communication, fully expecting to get his way. Everyone witnessing this interaction is probably wondering what is wrong with that child! Nothing, really. Yet.

The rewarding function is simply the part of everyone's personality that rewards the behavior in others who please us. It maintains a standard of behavior that is completely self-serving, without being aware of its selfish intent. This is the part of the personality that encourages specific behaviors, whether or not those behaviors are healthy or pathological. It's how we encourage others to meet our psychological goals. Since parental/authority approval is so powerful, the child (and later the adult) seeks to elicit a continuous stream of positive reinforcement, and will avoid, inhibit, abandon, or conceal those qualities of self that conflict with the approval goals. This is normal; we seek approval and avoid punishment. This really only becomes an issue when the rules of approval are so narrow and constrained that a significant proportion of the child's psyche, creativity, and self-expression become blunted. In this type of relationship, the child's inner critic (mother's punishing introject) ruthlessly suppresses any behavior that does not meet the standard of perfection. One might say that the child's rewarding function and punishing function will be in inverse proportion to each other.

The mother's rewarding function encourages specific psychological expression in her child. The child attempts to conform to the rewarding function in the mother by developing his or her own seducing/pleasing function, designed to meet mother's approval, thus creating a safe outcome in the relationship. Through positive reinforcement, the child develops an expressive style that will become the foundation of all future relationships.

Whether the mother knows it or not, she is subtly, and sometimes not so subtly, training her child to please her and conform to her performance and expression goals. This, obviously, can be positive or pathological, depending on the psychological needs of the mother. If the mother is curious and supportive, the child has the opportunity to develop his or her curiosity, intelligence, and emotional confidence. When the mother is fearful and trains the child to only act, think, and perform in a manner that is designed to reinforce her need to feel valued, wanted, and important, then this creates a personality structure in the child that performs in order to avoid disappointment or punishment from the mother. One child's behavior emerges from joy and curiosity; the other emerges as a strategy to avoid disappointment or punishment. The behavior of the child produced by each of these styles of mothering may look similar, but the internal motivation of the child is significantly different.

If the mother lacks self-confidence or suffers from some self-expressive problems, the child will often become an integral part of the mother's internal drama. The child will be encouraged to express those emotions, affectations, attitudes, prejudices, skills, and talents that make the mother feel "worthy" and will be discouraged from expressing those traits and emotions that upset the mother. Thus, the identity of the child becomes directly associated, and potentially fused, with the expressive or controlling parts of the mother's psychological structure. The rewarding and punishing aspects of the mother binds the child to her will as a part of her self-expression, and can vary in intensity depending on how "needful" mother is. The mother is simply seeking emotional relief through her child's emotional expression. This relationship eventually becomes the mother introject and will continue to operate within the child's personality with the same effect and perceptual bias.

This type of psychological interdependency is called *shared functioning,* wherein several people perform the functions of a single psyche, with none of the participants capable of operating fully emotionally independently. Most family systems operate from this model. The relationship between mother and infant always begins with shared functioning but hopefully leads to the child eventually demonstrating a growing capacity for autonomy and self-motivation. In most cases, the child's personality structure eventually has some autonomous features combined with shared functioning features (introject).

The Seducing/Pleasing Function: The Performer

This is the part of our psyche that tries to seduce the world into approv-ing our behavior. The child simply wants the mother's approval and protection and so will adopt what-ever style of self-expression that will produce the approval. I call this agreement a performance contract, which defines a major part of our interactive personality structure. However, this pleasing behavior is not just a response to the rewarding and punishing functions of the mother's personality but is also uti-lized by the child to attempt to trigger the rewarding function when the mother is depressed, ill, or otherwise emotionally or physically impaired. As children, we are attempting to heal our parents' wounds so that they might love us. Until the child is seven or eight years old, the child personalizes the mood of the parent. The child literally uncon-sciously takes credit for the emotional state of the object of his affec-tion. If mother is depressed, the child blames himself and will attempt to transform mother's emotional state. If the child is unsuccessful, and the mother, due to her psychological or physical condition, remains in a depressed or agitated state, the child will begin developing an inade-quate self-image: the child imagines that, somehow, he or she lacks the power or importance to heal the wounded mother. This can lead to a life-long quest to heal those wounded individuals (similar to that aspect in our mother) that we invite, attract, and allow into our lives.

This seducing/pleasing behavioral/personality style is used every-where with everyone. To paraphrase Jung, this is the part of the per-sonality (the persona) that greases the wheels of social interaction. Whatever worked with mother becomes the dominant relationship strategy with the world: the performance contract. Due to the moth-er's rules of behavior, there is limited flexibility in the child's personal-ity structure concerning self-expression. When this seducing/pleasing strategy does not work, we typically have limited expressive options: instead of emotional expression, we begin expressing symptoms (anx-iety, tension, stress, guilt, shame, etc.). The psychological components that would be situationally helpful are restricted from perception and expression, and the child becomes symptomatic as a result. This is particularly obvious in social situations in those individuals with an Asperger's operating system. Symptoms are triggered when the approval seeking behavior/strategy fails to work.

Failure of the seducing/pleasing function to control the environment triggers the punishing function or the wounded function. These are secondary tactics to secure safety or control the environmental dynamics.

THE PUNISHING FUNCTION: THE ENFORCER

The punishing function is part of the personality that holds other people accountable for behavior we don't like. Its most common styles are attack, abandon, or act helpless, learned in childhood and taught by those with power over us. It is both our internal and external critic and bully. It is how we criticize ourselves and others. It is shaped predominantly by the parents and older siblings. The punishing function is the Or-Else. (See Chapter 1, "The View," *The Threshold of Expression.*)

The more the mother fears the child's autonomy (who am I without my child to define me?), the broader the effect of the mother's punishing function and the greater the percentage of the child's psyche that is sublimated, repressed, or dissociated. In the dependent-borderline structure, all autonomous activity by the child is abandoned in favor of submission and dependency. However, in the narcissistic structure, there are widely varying percentages of activation and repression of psychological potentials, depending on the specific behaviors of the child that the mother actively controls. So, although the overall structure of the personality may be narcissistic (partially activated but not overly submissive), the amount of repressed psychological content will vary in each child, even in the same family system.

If there are other significant authority figures in the child's life (father, siblings, grandparents, caretakers), and the relationships take place early in life, these relationships will also produce introjects that will offer additional expressive options, thus giving the child a variety of rewarding, seducing/pleasing, punishing, and wounded tactics. When the mother distances from the child, or is impaired and unable or unwilling to sustain the original bond, the child will automatically seek intimate interaction from a secondary source. Even if successful, the original separation leaves a traumatic impact on the child's psyche due to the premature loss of the first bond.

It is the mother's punishing function that produces the repressed components in the child's personality structure. Although interdependency is normal and healthy in the mother-child relationship, it is the mother's ongoing reinforcement of the child's neediness, dependency, and symptomatic expression that makes this interdependency pathological. Whether the mother realizes it or not, she is responding in a punitive manner to a predictable set of her child's self-expression, undermining the child's normal rising autonomous capacities. This creates, in the child, a rigid self-regulation, repression, or even dissociation, based on the fear of the consequences (mother's punitive response). The punishing function is the part of our psyche that reprimands behavior that doesn't meet our expectations (mother's expectations). The punishing function utilizes three methods of aggressive manipulation: attack, abandon, and act helpless. (See chapter 4, "Trauma Dynamics," *The Three Control Tactics*.)

This external relationship drama not only serves to activate or suppress self-expression in the child. As the relationship is internalized, the punishing mother introject becomes the critical inner voice that the child hears throughout life.

Our perfectionistic tendencies, failures to meet our own standards, and unreasonable accomplishment goals all refer to the standards learned as a child at the feet of authority and our fear of the consequences.

THE WOUNDED FUNCTION: THE VICTIM

The wounded function: helpless, furious, grief stricken, self-destructive, symptomatic. This is the part of our psyche that expresses our hopelessness, anxiety, helplessness, loneliness, sadness, alienation, etc., when we feel rejected. Each person has his own personal variation of his wounded self, his sense of being a victim.

The particular style of expressing our "woundedness" is always tolerated by the family system, so that even our way of being depressed, sad, frustrated, or anguished requires approval of the family system and the rewarding function of the mother. Her willingness to tolerate certain behaviors affirms the style of "brokenness" the child is allowed to express.

The wounded function symptomatically expresses the diverted energy of those aspects of self that conflict with the pleasing/punishing mother.

EVOLVING THE ROLES AND GOALS OF THE FOUR FUNCTIONS

The initial presentation of our four functions is typically unconscious and is triggered automatically. These are behaviors and attitudes that seem to be our "normal" way of experiencing the world and responding to it. But in truth, these are family and cultural habits, conditioning, designed to fit into the expectations of our gender, race, religion, and country. This means that we are instinctually engaging in one of the four functions depending on our behavioral training and our unconscious assessment of the social environment.

When we become conscious of our interactive behavior, we may utilize many of these originally unconscious behaviors, but in a more consciously strategic and effective manner. For each human being to achieve his or her design potential, these four functions must evolve to a more efficient and effective interactive strategy that sustains our energy and successfully promotes our will in the environment. With work, these four functions can help us develop insight, intention, and emotional balance, producing an evolved method of self-expression, challenging the unconscious behavior of our intimates, and mentoring those underdeveloped expressive qualities in others. We begin to authentically explore our world and our psychological and physical potentials. We eventually develop a moral and ethical standard that considers the well-being of all living beings. And finally, we learn to negotiate as a part of our effective navigation through life.

Here are the four functions and their evolutionary goals:

- From rewarding to mentor
- From seducing/pleasing to explorer
- From punishing to guardian
- From wounded to negotiator

Mentor, explorer, guardian, and negotiator: these are the evolved aspects of the four functions and represent the expressive goals we need to seek in order to fulfill our psychological design. These are qualities of the personality that will naturally arise out of the evolution of the pathological quaternity.

THE REWARDING FUNCTION: THE MENTOR

The rewarding function needs to evolve from "demanding" conformity or perfection into the mentor: one who appreciates creativity, cleverness, intelligence, ingenuity, affection, loyalty, and all healthy traits of self-expression. This is a broadening of the narrow rewarding function. To transform from the conformist/perfectionist to the mentor requires curiosity and compassion. The challenge for the rewarding function is: how much of other people's psyches do we find interesting? This requires genuine curiosity and compassion about the stunning diversity of human expression. Without curiosity, we are driven by conformity. Without compassion, we lack mercy.

The mentor role is continuously attempting to support and encourage direct, honest communication. Thus, when the child asks directly for something, he has earned an honest and direct response. The mentor will encourage the negotiation function in the child instead of the victim function, even in those situations when the child will not get what he wants. Most behaviors are the result of unconscious parental support for the behavior, healthy or helpless. The mentor supports negotiation, intelligent reasoning, patience, compassion, assertive interaction, respect for the rights of others, courtesy, politeness, and self-soothing.

THE SEDUCING/PLEASING FUNCTION: THE EXPLORER

The seducer is a manipulator, even though s/he may be quite brilliant, pleasant, cute or clever while doing it. It is designed to win people over and reduce environmental threat. It is a strategy for getting along. The seduction/pleasing function represents the child's style of emotional expression that pleased the mother and kept the child both safe and feeling loved. It is a straightforward contract with the mother to get approval. This aspect of personality is the part that contains the skill sets that will later lead to educational success/failure, career tracts, and relationship acquisition. These start as automatic behaviors, designed to win the support of others; when they prove to be inadequate in seducing social approval, they trigger the wounded or punishing parts of the psyche. The seduction/pleasing aspect of personality can vary significantly, even within the same family structure: one child becomes a doctor, another becomes a drug addict. The child's behavior that supplies the mother with a sense of satisfaction is reinforced to a degree that the child will unconsciously use these behaviors for all socially complex situations, producing varying results. The child learns to perform in a specific manner in order to elicit praise or secure safety. The underlying psychological problem is that any aspect of the psyche that has not received "support" from the child's significant authority figures remains inactive, or repressed and symptomatic, limiting the child's, and eventually, the adult's psychological expressive options.

When the approved-of aspects of self-expression are too narrow, the child consistently feels inadequate or imperfect, in spite of every effort to perform well. The parts of the personality that have not been given approval to be expressed lay languishing in the unconscious, pressing on consciousness for recognition and expression. These are the components that produce the psychological symptoms.

It is the pleasing function that isolates behaviors that fail to meet the approval of the parents. This means that the pleasing function could theoretically be as broad as eighty percent of the psyche, or as little as twenty percent (these are randomly chosen numbers; it could be as much as ninety-nine percent or as little as one percent). This is why narcissism is a spectrum "disorder," wherein significantly different amounts of the psyche are compromised but still operate with the structure of the narcissistic relationship contract. It is only later in the therapy that we are capable of assessing exactly how much of the psyche has been compromised (although the extent and intensity of the symptomology does point to the size of the psychological wound needing to be addressed).

The seduction function needs to evolve from the automatic pleasing behavior (afraid of seeing the world as it is and unconsciously trying to manipulate the environment into a recognizable response) into the conscious, curious explorer: always seeking new information, new self-expression, new talents, new abilities, new gifts, new insights, and new relationships. The explorer provides the curiosity needed to motivate psychological growth.

The Punishing Function: The Guardian

The punishing function needs to evolve from the punitive enforcer/perfectionist into the guardian, wherein the child sustains an inner sense of being protected rather than punished. The guardian still expresses aggression, but it is in service of the growth and safety of the child, and not directed at the child unless protecting a higher standard: the rights of others, personal safety, respect for life, self-defense, etc. It is the indulgent and unconscious use of punishment that produces a child who becomes anxious and fearful, does not develop a sense of boundaries, or becomes pathologically self-indulgent (a quality often culturally associated with a lack of discipline, when in fact it is the very discipline that produces this quality). The Asperger's child does display anxiety out of proportion to the moment, and this is usually when his or her natural pattern or desire to isolate is derailed by social requirements.

The pathology of the punishing function is illustrated as the judge, jailer, and executioner: the function that attacks the child's emotional expression that fails to meet the mother's criteria for cooperation. Inappropriate discipline and bullying almost always result in a systematic repressing of parts of a child's self-expression and can create the rigid aspects of personality, and thus, personality symptoms: anxiety, tension, stress, guilt, shame, fear, resentment, obsession, and depression (depending on which symptoms are acceptable in the family system).

The guardian displays dignity, discipline, self-defense, and the defense of those who are vulnerable. The guardian serves human ideals: social justice, equality, fairness, and courage. The guardian also identifies corrupt behavior and inappropriate actions in self and others. It is convenient to use super-hero/heroine illustrations for this function: the guardian of good. However, the guardian must always be on alert to shield against rigidity and conformity. The greater good is an excellent starting point, as long as evolution of thinking and expression is permitted. Rarely are culturally transformative ideas welcomed with open attitudes, and yet, the guardian must embrace curiosity to remain open to the unfolding of human potential.

THE WOUNDED FUNCTION: THE NEGOTIATOR

At a fundamental level, the wounded function is simply the sum-total of the symptomatic expressions of frustration, loneliness, passivity, abandonment, fear, neglect, and abuse. The style of this wounded expression is whatever the family permitted; even our style of suffering is regulated. Hard to believe, but even the most obnoxious or dangerous behaviors may be given tacit approval by parents and siblings. Remember, personality is selective expression, and somebody, somewhere, reinforced the use of helplessness, whininess, incompetence, inadequacy, stubbornness, inhibition, and all the other spectacularly irritating personality styles.

The wounded function needs to evolve from the complainer into the negotiator: the capacity to negotiate being treated fairly in personal relationships, work, education, and social dynamics. The wounded function needs to develop a voice with which to negotiate. The negotiator is the active part of the personality that evolves interactions towards a more fair interchange rather than complaining about the unfairness of it all. The pathological aspect of the wounded function is the passive acceptance of inhibition and suffering. The negotiator needs to be proactive in resolving suffering circumstances. The skills of the negotiator require logic, verbal expression, a sense of fairness, courage, and a willingness to see the world as it is, danger and all.

NEURAL-EMOTIONAL STRUCTURAL REVIEW

The four functions, discussed above, are the sub-structure of each of the five neural-emotional complexes, which are, in turn, the sub-structure of the overall personality architecture. This multi-location structure, associated with specific organ function as well as perceptual and expressive functions, is our source of emotional wisdom: the site-specific intelligence of the body.

The structural function of each neural-emotional complex:

1. Site-specific biological function
2. Perceptual perspective (the threshold of perception)
3. Memories
4. Emotional expression (the threshold of expression)
5. Relationship style (the four functions in congress with multiple introjects)

    i.   *Site Specific Biological Function:* The five neural-emotional centers: thinking, speaking, respiration, digestion, and reproduction.

    ii.   *Perceptual Perspective:* Our view of the world. As each neurological site is developing, the child is experimenting with translating experience into recognizable patterns (knowledge) and exploring and expressing the feelings and curiosities of each site (emotional response). The manner in which the world is explained to us as we attempt to understand new experiences contributes to our overall accuracy of perception of the world. It is not uncommon that superstition, psychological symptom   Ds, and magical beliefs are substituted for an accurate perception of the world. The predictable result is limited success in negotiating life's challenges (employment, education, relationships).

        Each site contains the memory of what experiments worked, how the world responded to that self-expression (encouraged or punished), and the level of confidence in one's perception of the world through that neurologically specific perspective: sexual perspective, compassionate perspective, courageous perspective, analytic perspective, and dynamism of speech. Each physical site performs its function, regardless of whether awareness is embracing or dissociating. It is each site's energetic information, when blocked, that simultaneously creates perceptual blind spots and expressive symptoms. A simple example: someone who has been raised in a sexually conservative home may be unable to perceive the presence of sexual attraction towards him/her (perceptual blind spot) and remain sexually frustrated (emotionally symptomatic) due to an energetically charged, but repressed, sexual neural site. The same case could be made for repressed aggression, compassion, and thought.

iii. *Memories:* Our life memories are emotionally charged and are predominantly stored at the sites that served as that specific emotional interface. Sexual memory is stored at the genital region. Aggressive memories are stored in the digestive system. Sad memories are stored in the respiratory system. Thinking memories are stored in the head.

All experience is essentially information, grouped by emotional content and neural-chemically coded and decoded by the appropriate neural-emotional sites. This means that trauma and joy are associated with the same location.

Awareness chooses one of two solutions for negotiating the energetic charge associated with site-specific trauma. The first symptomatic solution is hyper-activation and possession: a significantly strong activation of a neural-emotional site (sexuality, aggression, obsession, helplessness). The energy of the traumatic experience (energy and information) produces a gravitational seizure of awareness by the site, producing obsessive fantasies, and behavioral acting out in an attempt to discharge and/or master the energetic charge located at the site. The second symptomatic solution is dissociation from those hyperactive neural-emotional sites, which produces significant symptomology instead of information and emotion. For example, repeated assaults to the child's head (slapping, punching, hitting, pulling hair) either triggers aggressive fantasies and acting out that mimics the abuse or dissociates awareness from the head, producing a significant reduction or delay in the development and mastery of thought, logic, opinion, etc. Awareness often simply avoids inhabiting, or visiting, the sites where insult or trauma has repeatedly occurred.

Until awareness systematically re-inhabits those dissociated organs, the individual will suffer from perceptual blind spots, emotional possession/inhibition, and energetic compromise.

iv. *Emotional Expression:* Each site has its specific emotional expression: brain/opinion, speech/intent, respiratory/sadness, digestive/aggression, reproductive/pleasure. When a person's emotional expression is compromised or his or her perception of the world is inaccurate, awareness has dissociated from the specific neurological site that is in charge of processing that information and emotion.

Our experiences either rise to the level of insight or regress to the level of symptom, depending on awareness's relationship with the neural-emotional site doing the translation.

The emotion of a particular site is simply the transitional expression of information as awareness negotiates its familiarity with that information. Remember, all stimuli is experienced as either insight, emotion, fantasy, dream, or symptom.

As awareness abandons the physical sites that have been traumatized, site-specific neurological information is reduced to symptom.

v. Relationship Expectation: The history of how our mother and significant others related to us during each childhood developmental stage establishes how the child expects others to relate to him/her throughout life. The developmental relationship with family members is the dominant source of relationship style and expressive confidence or impairment that will be carried into adulthood. Support, or even a neutral response from the world, gives the child confidence in the function, perception, and expression of that neurological site. Punishment triggers dissociation/possession at that neurological site and begins to create an inventory of symptoms in the place of self-expression.

The four functions (rewarding, punishing, pleasing, wounded) rule the relationship style of each neural-emotional site, specifically. This means that emotional perception and expression, as well as our interactive confidence with reality, varies from site to site.

Awareness rotates between the five neural-emotional complexes, gathering information and emotionally responding to a variety of environmental stimuli. The effective function of each site determines the accuracy of the perceptual information as well as the emotional, self-expressive confidence at that site. The more a neural-emotional site is ruled by an unreasonable introject that sublimates, represses, or dissociates the information and emotion of that site, the stronger its symptomatic expression becomes, until those symptoms hijack our mood, attitude, and expectations. The emotional charge that builds up at the dissociated site creates a type of gravitational field that eventually pulls awareness into its influence, holding it in that prejudicial perspective and attitude until the emotions are discharged, releasing awareness to the next strongest emotional gravitational field. Through a history of repression and symptomatizing, the repressed neurological sites begin to dominate our quality of life and skew perceptual accuracy and emotional balance. In spite of how complicated this process sounds, we experience this gravitational dynamic as emotional attitudes that we can't "shake off." The phrases "waking up on the wrong side of the bed" or "being in a cranky mood" are cultural expressions of being possessed by a repressed attitude. Severe diets can trigger brief reactive food "addictions." Rigid sexual upbringing can trigger self-destructive risk taking when under the influence of drugs. Teenage sex abstinence programs have led to higher teen pregnancy in that group. Repression creates an energetic charge at a particular site that eventually seizes control of our behavior, if only temporarily.

This cyclical pattern of capture and release can be resolved by reducing the intensity of the dissociation, which co-creates the energetic charge in combination with environmental stimulation. This means that awareness needs to regularly and intentionally "check-in" with the body's feeling network. Meditation, yoga, exercise, diet, sex, verbal communication, intellectual stimulation, participatory sports, acts of compassion, massage, Reiki, simple body awareness, and a variety of other kinesthetic approaches provide the opportunity for awareness to connect and re-connect to its body. By intentionally attending to the expressive requirements of the entire body—but in particular, the neural-emotional sites—the energy, emotion, and information of those sites are available without delay or without creating energetic tension that would capture awareness. This means that by systematically extending awareness throughout the body, neural-site by neural-site, we reduce the tension at each site and make ourselves available to the specific informational-emotional-energetic dynamics of the body's sub-systems.

Whereas trauma is imposed on the body's organic systems, healing is a natural outcome of cooperating with the rhythmic designs of these five central organs. Consciousness can participate in the tension and release at each site by respecting and participating in each of these dynamic rhythms with a minimum of resistance and withholding. Thought arises and releases. Speech arises and releases. Breath arises and releases. Hunger arises and releases. Desire arises and releases. The greatest healing benefit is in aligning consciousness with the natural rhythms of the body. Any resistance to these cycles will produce tension, anxiety, symptom, and attitude.

Specific Personality Pathology Dynamics

The following is a checklist of dynamics associated with the dependent-borderline, narcissist, anti-social, and Asperger's personality structures. The first three pathologies (dependent, narcissistic, and anti-social) are all developmental psychological expressive disorders that emerge from a neural-typical operating system. The neural-diverse Asperger's personality structure develops styles of behavior by studying and imitating the personalities in the family system, combined with a fairly rigid set of biologically driven priorities, perceptions, and responses.

Each of the following four personality types will outline specific functioning and emotional dynamics based on the following list:

- *Presentation*: a general approach to the world. The style and tactics of each unique personality system and how they create relationship alliances.
- *Differential Diagnosis*: separating similarly presenting personality structures
- *Self*: the individual's relationship with his or her deeper Self (the repository of our psychological and physical potential)
- *Contract*: the style of relationship learned from the mother
- *Expressive Block*: those aspects of the psyche that are highly regulated
- *Fear*: specific anxiety triggers
- *The Four Functions*: (rewarding, punishing, seducing/pleasing, and wounded) how each of the four functions is designed to express itself
- *Curse*: blind spots, inhibitions, and limitations associated with this personality type
- *Transference*: the relationship style, usually associated with therapy that denotes the diagnosis
- *Therapeutic Goal*: perceptual and expressive goals
- *Treatment*: the strategies and techniques most effective in treatment
- *Challenge*: common obstacles that arise during treatment

These personality structures and treatment strategies are fully explored in Chapter Three: "Personality Structure," Chapter Eight: "Treatment," Chapter Nine: "Therapeutic Strategy and Technique," and Chapter Ten: "Therapeutic Stages and Goals." What follows are simply shortcuts to understanding the underlying dynamics of the four personality structures (dependent-borderline, narcissistic, anti-social, and Asperger's).

THE DEPENDENT-BORDERLINE PERSONALITY

Presentation: Dependency and submission. Passive, often helpful, open to guidance, doesn't trust one's own thoughts or insights, delays or resists taking the initiative to action, will follow orders, potentially a hard worker with minimum initiative or creative thinking available, any self-activation triggers symptom profile.

Differential Diagnosis: The borderline diagnosis is contaminated with both dependent and anti-social personality pathology. Both respond to confrontation, therapeutically, but the dependent personality is unlikely to initiate any activity that would undermine relationship stability. Dependent personalities rarely seek their own psychological needs other than to maintain a submissive attitude to the alpha personality in their world. Revisit the diagnosis if the individual is creating too much chaos in his or her life.

Self: Completely restricted but available: self-activation is developmentally severely restricted by the environment; thus, a broad range of psychological abilities are trapped in the unconscious, producing a variety of symptoms.

Contract: Stays dependent to avoid threat. The mother supports dependency and submission and punishes autonomy and self-activation.

Expressive Block: Any autonomous action or self-activation evokes anxiety and the psychological symptom profile.

Fear: Fear of self-activation.

Fear: Hyper vigilant for environmental threats. Constant environmental scanning for potential threats. Always waiting for the "other shoe to drop!"

Fear: The unconscious is systematically responding to the environmental dynamics; thus, the individual is in a constant state of unease and anxiety resulting from repression of the reflective emotional response being triggered by the environment.

Fear: Anticipates being punished for any behavior other than submission.

Rewarding Function: Unconsciously rewards those who are controlling.

Punishing Function: Self-activation produces anxiety. Highly self-critical. Constant internal attack about being selfish or self-centered.

Seducing/Pleasing Function: Passive. Feels safe only in dependent mode. Will become highly anxious if not supported in relationship dependency.

Wounded Function: Terrifying fear of any autonomous action/ thought. History of being punished for autonomy. Required to *need* another. Anxiety is triggered when autonomy is expressed. Any form of self-activation by the dependent-borderline triggers fear of abandonment (or other punishment). Dissociation is common. Passive-aggressive symptomology is always present.

Curse: Avoids self-expression. This person presents as passive and cooperative while secretly undermining psychological growth.

Curse: Anticipates punishment if not allowed or encouraged to be dependent.

Curse: What pleases mother (any authority figure) kills autonomy.

Transference: Merging, shared functioning, adversarial. Client uses therapist or significant other as the decision-making ego component of his or her psyche to avoid being attacked for self-activation. Client seeks to incorporate the therapist as an active, regulating part of the client's personality, simultaneously degrading the client's ability to operate autonomously. Intimacy offers fantasy of safety at the cost of functioning as an adult.

Therapeutic Goal: Courage and curiosity. Overcome fear of consequences. Punishing function needs to evolve into the protective function, producing an ability to be directly confrontive and assertive. Aggression needs to be utilized to set limits with others and not for brutal self-criticism. Wounded function needs to learn to negotiate for what the client needs, instead of passively cooperating with everyone else, regardless of self-benefit. The pleasing function needs to develop skills in the interest of self-expression, not to avoid conflict. Needs to develop curiosity and courage in order to tolerate anxiety triggered with self-activation. Needs to be capable of acting on autonomous desires and needs. May need to fire therapist at some point if the adversarial transference is too stubborn. Any act of autonomy or self-activation is progress.

Treatment: Confrontation. When therapist does not reinforce client's dependency, the client will become depressed and potentially self-destructive/impulsive. Adjusting to the depression. Grieving the personal history. Confront client's ability to run his or her own life.

Treatment: Mild confrontation to self-activate. Cognitive behavioral therapy is very effective with this group. The mild confrontive style of CBT allows expansion of the perceptual and expressive potential. This will trigger a symptomatic response even in a "safe" therapeutic environment. However, the therapist needs to continually remind the client that the source of his or her anxiety is the activation of self-expression combined with memory of the consequences of childhood. Gradually, anxiety transforms into low-grade excitement by the risk taking of self-expression.

Challenge: Therapist must differentiate between client's self-destructive, dissociative behavior (dependent) and behavior designed to manipulate and control (sociopath).

Challenge: When there is also an affective disorder (depression or mania), cutting and other forms of physical pain stimulation are often used to re-activate dissociated neural pathways. Cutting behavior will be shameful (dependent personality) or arrogant-exhibitionistic (anti-social personality). It is important to differentiate between these two significantly different uses of cutting behavior.

Challenge: Therapy degrades into problem solving, which confirms the client's fear that he or she is not capable of running his or her own life, producing a regression to lower developmental state.

Challenge: Therapist may inadvertently encourage dependency by continuing contact when client distances. Rising adversarial transference may trigger termination of therapy. This may be sufficient therapeutic success.

THE ANTI-SOCIAL PERSONALITY: SOCIOPATH (REACTIVE) AND PSYCHOPATH (PREDATOR)

Presentation: Charming, even friendly up to a point, suspicious, manipulative, passive, passive-aggressive, seductive, avoidant, threatening even when acting helpless or emotionally wounded, shares inaccurate information, even compulsive fibbing (although this is much more prevalent in adult children of alcoholics). Trust is for suckers! (These are the individuals who give back-handed compliments—they draw you in, just to wound you. Malicious gossipers: will pretend to let you into their inner circle while throwing someone else under the bus.)

Differential Diagnosis: Anti-social spectrum—psychopath versus sociopath.

> PSYCHOPATH: Predator. Proactively abuses others.
> SOCIOPATH: User. Emotional distance, reactively abuses others when triggered.

The Developmental Anti-Social Personality: The developmental variation of the anti-social personality emerges as a result of parental abuse: using the child's natural bonding empathy to severely abuse the child. Thus, the child associates the empathetic/compassionate bond with abuse. Contrary to the biological psychopath, the developmental anti-social feels empathy or compassion, but they interpret that feeling as threat! This is the developmental aspect of the anti-social personality.

The Biological Psychopath: There is evidence that critical brain functions associated with emotional identification with other beings, as well as social behavioral agreements that lead to moral/ethical functioning, are impaired in biochemical psychopaths, thus promoting an emotionally isolated and opportunistic personality associated with the anti-social personality. This is the biological aspect of psychopathology. The biological psychopath may represent the criminal element of the neural-diverse operating system.

Self: Isolated, the collective is perceived as threat. People are useful, that's all.

Contract: Avoid punishment, use or be used.

Expressive Block: Can't deeply trust anyone.

Fear: Intimacy, empathy, and compassion from others are misperceived as imminent threats.

Fear: Intimacy has always resulted in severe wounding. Reactively uses others for one's own need.

Rewarding Function: Relationships have limited intimacy based on "useful" object-relations. Life is dangerous but useful.

Punishing Function: When pushed into a "corner" emotionally, financially, employment, education, etc., they reveal their true ruthless nature, displaying a broad distrust of everyone and a willingness for revenge, punishment, or crime.

Seducing/Pleasing Function: Bonds with those who are useful. Gang dynamics are common. The anti-social personality bonds with others by forming relationships in response to a mutual enemy or shared anti-social goals. Prefers inconsistent intimacy.

Wounded Function: Authority, structure, confinement, or intimacy trigger acting out, which will escalate until the perceived threat is relieved or removed.

Curse: Compassion or empathy from others is experienced as threatening and dangerous.

Transference: Adversarial (manipulative/avoidant/seductive/threatening). If a therapeutic alliance is created, it is because the therapist (spouse, friend) is perceived as having joined the client's gang, not because they have joined your gang.

Therapeutic Goal: Help them become socially appropriate (how to avoid going to jail, not get caught in bad drug deals, abuse family members, or choose friends who will harm them). Identify behaviors that lead to social punishment. Respectfully confront self-destructive behaviors. Must pay bill on time; no appointment reschedule; no fee agreements; no drugs or drinking. Limit setting provides the anti-social client an exit from therapy when the "intimacy" triggers fear. They are likely to miss appointments, owe money, or push the boundaries in other ways as a way of creating distance, thereby reducing threat of intimacy and emotional vulnerability.

Treatment: Confrontation is the only method that reduces the client's threat threshold. Pro-social treatment goal: the client needs to learn to strategically fit into appropriate social behavior to more effectively avoid punishment. Reduce self-destructive behavior that often invites the intervention of social services and law enforcement.

Treatment: Confrontation and strategic problem solving in association with reducing social threat.

Challenge: Intimacy triggers acting out. Strategic, respectful confrontive therapy is recommended.

Challenge: Rarely comes to therapy willingly.

Challenge: Do not confuse client cooperation with intimacy.

Challenge: Psychopath is often mistakenly misdiagnosed as narcissist.

Challenge: Sociopath is often mistakenly misdiagnosed as borderline (DSM).

THE NARCISSISTIC PERSONALITY: GRANDIOSE AND INVERTED

Presentation—Grandiose: Clever, smart, charming, industrious, athletic, competitive, but above all, sacrificing autonomy for praise. Classic narcissistic selfishness appears self-centered or self-obsessed. Unfortunately, this type of selfishness is imbedded in self-denial and broad emotional repression, producing depression, anxiety, poor self-image (in spite of the grandiosity) and inappropriate drug and sexual behavior. Grandiose narcissism could be summed up as talent and intelligence in chaos.

Presentation—Inverted: Depressed, anxious, resentful, stubborn, and passive-aggressive. When narcissists present the "wounded" function rather than the "seducing/pleasing" function, they mimic the dependent-borderline profile and are usually misdiagnosed as borderline due to their capacity to self-activate and the boiling resentment/disappointment.

Differential Diagnosis—Dependent-Borderline versus Inverted Narcissist: Avoid treatment failure (the recommended confrontive technique used with dependent personality will fail with the narcissist, and the reflective supportive technique recommended for the narcissist will fail with the dependent personality). Masterson recommends a form of mild confrontation that will evoke insult from a narcissistic disorder and self-examination from the dependent-borderline.

The narcissist requires a supportive and empathetic strategy for therapy, and the dependent-borderline requires confrontation for successful therapy. For the narcissist, any interaction that does not provide (narcissistic supply (empathy)) is experienced as wounding criticism. For the dependent-borderline, treatment that is supportive rather than confrontive tends to encourage regression in the client. However, the inverted narcissist presents very similarly to the dependent-borderline. A simple confrontation during treatment will reveal the core structure of your client. The narcissist will be offended and the dependent-borderline will examine the confrontation. A quick and neat differentiation.

Self: Partially activated psychological potential, thus narcissism is a spectrum disorder with severe, moderate, and mild pathology: pathology and symptomology are in proportion to obstructed self-expression. The percentage of the Self that is repressed varies.

Contract: Perform for praise.

Expressive Block: Self-worth is dependent on external praise; most expressive behavior is a form of seducing praise from the environment.

Fear: I will fail to please and not be lovable.

Fear: No one will truly know and love me (because narcissists do not truly love and respect themselves—hidden shame).

Fear: Perpetual loneliness and never consistently feeling truly loved or appreciated.

Rewarding Function: Mother values herself through the performance of her child; thus, the narcissist requires that the environment meet specific performance goals to receive praise.

Punishing Function: Enforces the contract through attack, abandon, or act helpless.

Seducing/Pleasing Function: Can perform at very high levels; however, self-worth requires constant praise.

Wounded Function: Depression, anxiety, loneliness, sexual interference, restricted libidinal expression, passive-aggressive behavior, drugs, sex, power, and control dynamics.

Curse: Expects the world to value him or her in the same manner as the mother.

Curse: Displays sexual intimacy or loyalty issues due to mother's rules of conduct.

Curse: World is divided into allies and enemies.

Curse: Emotional insulation: Alexander Lowen, in his book, *Narcissism*, proposed that the emotional insults of childhood lead to a layer of "insulation" (dissociation) that protects one's emotions against painful experiences, and thus the individual requires heightened levels of stimulation to breach the insulation. Lowen found that a common solution to emotional insulation is the use of sex, drugs, or power to provide sufficient stimulation to make the narcissist feel "alive." He labeled individuals with this presentation as "Phallic Narcissists" due to the common use of sex as a method of overcoming the dissociation. These methods (sex, drugs, and power), due to their temporary relief and habitual repetition, present as addictive behaviors. It is important to clinically differentiate physically addictive behaviors and the phallic narcissistic "solution" to dissociation. This "narcissistic insulation" is probably more accurately described as the severity of dissociation associated with the narcissistic personality, which requires a heightened level of stimulation in order for awareness to re-awaken the traumatized areas of the body (five neural-emotional centers).

Curse: Energy activates memory. Environmental stimulation, and intimacy in particular, energizes the body, activating the trauma memory at specific neural-emotional sites, triggering dissociation and other psychological symptomology, as well as the cyclical search to re-activate the body through some form of intense stimulation.

Transference: Mirroring/idealizing/adversarial. The therapist is either perceptive, sensitive, or stupid.

Therapeutic Goals: To overcome the fear of the loss of approval. To shift the relationship goal from seeking approval to be genuinely curious about others, and not personalizing external emotional interactions. To activate and develop the parts of the psyche that have been sublimated, repressed, or dissociated. One therapeutic goal is for the client to develop real selfishness instead of the compromised self-centeredness.

Treatment: Alignment: Therapist uses empathy, praise, support, and identification of client's skills and abilities. This will eventually evoke the underlying self-attack/shadow that is often directed at others. Grief is frequently the hidden feeling. Anger is usually misplaced or inappropriate. Identifying the developmental threats used to control the child's behavior is critical. It is crucial to pinpoint the feared consequence(s) for autonomous behavior (memory). The narcissist needs to practice truly selfish behavior as opposed to the indulgent selfish behavior he or she presents. The development of the neutral observer is critical for successful therapy. The narcissist will need to develop some self-nurturing skills to cope with the depression associated with the great grief of childhood.

Challenge: The perfect childhood. Sometimes the relationship with parents is so enmeshed that the client is unable to initially understand the relationship between his or her current relationship and performance crisis and how he or she was raised.

Challenge: Client is highly defensive of parents, particularly mother. Client suffers a general inability to critically evaluate childhood parenting and to differentiate between those family learned healthy expressive qualities and the subtle methods (and sometimes not so subtle) that were used to undermine self-expression.

Challenge: Adversarial transference. When the therapist "breaks the desired narcissistic mirror" through loss of idealized reflection, due to the evolution of client's autonomy, or when empathy and practicality therapeutically compete, the client will become adversarial. This is inevitable. If the therapist has erred, apologies are in order first to repair the damage from the insensitivity, but secondly, to model apologetic behavior in order to demonstrate sensitivity to the emotional needs of others. If the client is adversarial as a result of developmental growth, the therapist needs to follow the rules of appropriate conflict resolution, including crediting the client for his or her risk-taking.

NEURODIVERSITY: THINKING OUTSIDE THE BOX

The manner in which the majority of human beings biologically function (which may actually be a smaller majority than we think) is often referred to as neurotypical, suggesting that the current, and widespread, mirror gene operating system is the dominant and most common human neurological system at this juncture in history. This assumption may not be accurate, however.

The term neurotypical suggests that there is one correct neural-psychological operating system for human beings and that currently the mirror neuron system is the correct one. This is a bias partially based on an insufficient assessment of the distribution of neurodiversity, and Asperger's in particular, in the general population. It is probable that there is a large population with Asperger's who function well within social norms and are misdiagnosed when they come to therapy. Only the most severe examples of Asperger's are identified in childhood. By adulthood, high functioning Asperger's have the typical appearance of either a narcissist with anger issues and/or poor people skills or an introvert with social anxiety.

There has been, for several decades, an attempt among the mental health treatment community and the families of the neurological "outliers" to re-label these individuals as "neural-diverse." Neurodiversity suggests that there may be multiple neurological operating systems within the human community, each with functioning advantages and disadvantages. The Asperger's operating system may be the largest of these neural-diverse systems. Due to poor diagnosis and highly symptomatic requirements (DSM-V) for diagnosis, estimates of the distribution of Asperger's in the general population differ significantly. Current thinking places the occurrence of diagnosable Asperger's syndrome in children at around two percent of the population. Robert Hare, in his book, *Without Conscience*, estimates neurologically impaired psychopaths at one percent or more of the population, and this is certainly the extreme wing of neurodiversity. Dr. Hare does not label these neurologically impaired criminals as having Asperger's, but the parallels are significant. These two groups truly are the "outliers" and represent extreme versions of Asperger's. With nearly four percent in the extreme category, it would not be outrageous to consider the general population to have a fifteen to twenty-five percent distribution in the Asperger's spectrum, perhaps even higher. Twenty-five percent of the current population of the United States would translate to 75 million people with some variant of Asperger's. Even at ten percent, we're speaking of 30 million people. I am not claiming that these numbers exist, only that our diagnostic criteria is so ineffective that we have yet to assess how broad neurodiversity is.

Unfortunately, the Asperger's outliers are often how the mental health professionals view the entire Asperger's spectrum, as if Asperger's is *only* pathology. If we describe the neural-typical operating system only through the lens of developmental sociopaths and extreme narcissistic and dependent personality structures, we would only have a grossly dysfunctional perspective of the neurotypical system. When we broaden the parameters of Asperger's to include common Asperger's traits, it becomes evident that this is a very common, and widely distributed, genetic system.

Imagine that the operating traits of your personality arose from the careful and diligent study of the human beings in your environment. In particular, the most significant or dominating personalities in your family were the personality styles that you mimicked (mother, father, older siblings, grand-parents). But also consider that you had a few specific neurodiverse (Asperger's) traits associated with your personality presentation: introversion; cautious eye contact; hyper aggression (often referred to as narcissistic rage); stubbornness; social anxiety; an obsessive-compulsive learning mechanism; specific time schedule; rigid rules concerning the conduct and function of others (law and order); and a hyper-sensitivity to a variety of sensory information (this varies by person), including sound sensitivity, taste sensitivity, skin-touch sensitivity (fabrics, physical contact), pattern attraction (varying from how food is arranged on a plate to animal behavior and environmental patterns). This is the high functioning Asperger's operating system and it produces researchers, doctors, administrators, librarians, engineers, architects, lawyers, law-enforcement specialists, farmers, naturalists, and computer programmers, to name a few.

Regardless, the Asperger's neural-diverse system certainly has greater representation in the general community than the pathological percentages would lead us to believe. When we split off the seriously impaired people of the Asperger's system or the mirror system, we are left with a great majority that have moderate impairments in their psychological functioning, and these middle-of-the-road individuals are the population who can make great progress in psychotherapy.

THE ASPERGER'S PERSONALITY: NEURAL DIVERSITY IN ACTION

Presentation: (These traits vary depending on the person.) Introversion. Meyer's Briggs Type: INTJ. Social anxiety when interacting with people who are unfamiliar. Awkward conversation skills. Awkward phone skills. There is often avoidance of extended eye contact. Some physical awkwardness including hand and arm gestures when talking. An initial difficulty with creating a therapeutic alliance, combined with anxiety, social difficulty, awkward eye contact, nervousness, haughtiness, inappropriate aggression, and an underlying adversarial/fearful transference should lead the clinician to consider an Asperger's diagnosis.

Differential Diagnosis: High functioning Asperger's can present as narcissistic, anti-social, or dependent-borderline. The Asperger's expression hyper-aggression is often misdiagnosed as narcissistic rage or borderline instability. A lack of interest in the opinions or the life stories of others or the inability to carry on a "give and take" conversation is often viewed as narcissistic self-absorption. The Asperger's propensity for emotional disconnectedness can be viewed as anti-social or social anxiety disorder. Most Asperger's present with social anxiety, even though they may have adopted extroverted personality techniques. Self-medication (alcohol, pain medications, marijuana) is often present as a way of controlling anxiety. Curiously, marijuana may not be a bad choice for this group.

Self: The self is the great, undiscovered interpersonal world, which represents a great ocean of confusing information. Due to a lack of training in human social behavior, too much emotional information is missed and anxiety replaces insight. If we were to use Sherlock Holmes as a practical example of someone with Asperger's, it is his fascination with deciphering the subtle information about his world that leads to his interaction with others. Social cues and non-verbal communication need to be studied as a science.

Contract: Everyone, and everything, has a job to do. In the Asperger's universe, it is your function that determines your value or attraction. Everyone needs to perform according to Asperger's expectations or suffer the aggressive consequences.

Confucius, and the "natural laws" of "correct" or ethical relationship, (a balance of power, position, duty, and responsibility) perhaps represents some of the highest Asperger's values. I have come to view Asperger's as the "law and order" genetic system.

Expressive Block: Social anxiety leads to interpersonal avoidance. Needs to develop strong curiosity about human non-verbal communication in order to overcome the inhibition that leads to relationship avoidance.

Fear: Strong history of being ostracized in family and school. Social awkwardness triggers predatory treatment by bullies and authoritarians.

Fear: Obsessive fascination in narrow subject matters is not shared by others, and often disrespected and interrupted.

Fear: There is no one else like me.

Fear: No one shares my interests.

Rewarding Function: Do your job (meet my expectations) and we'll be ok.

Punishing Function: Perfectionist. Aggression out of proportion to the moment. Emotional intensity is often viewed as escalating and adversarial.

Seducing/Pleasing Function: This is the most underdeveloped function. Very awkward at positive reinforcement. This function is a good therapeutic goal—the client's family members will thank you.

Wounded Function: Highly anxious, isolated, obsessive.

Curse: Lack of patience in relationships.

Curse: Holds grudges.

Curse: Difficulty learning anything that is not particularly fascinating.

Curse: Isolates, thus limiting learning social skills.

Transference: Initially anxious. Will often dominate the conversation without providing opportunity for feedback from therapist. Will literally talk the entire hour with no opportunity for dialogue. Discussion is awkward. Stable eye contact is anxiety provoking and usually avoided.

Therapeutic Goals: Creating an alliance is a great step forward. Expand interactive skill set. Client needs to develop curiosity and patience in dealing with his or her human community. The therapist needs to take time to assess exactly what the interactive deficits are.

Treatment: Effective communication. Shared appreciation for the opportunity to interact. Work on interactive skills. Practice give and take. The interactive process is therapeutic in and of itself. Obsessive skills can be applied to strategies of relating.

Challenge: Difficult diagnosis, particularly high functioning Asperger's.

Challenge: Finding the comfort zone in the therapy interaction.

Challenge: Client becomes easily bored or distracted.

Challenge: Therapy could become boring for the therapist.

Neurodiversity and the Rise of the Mirror Gene

When we examine how the Asperger's (neural-diverse) and mirror gene (neural-typical) operating systems present themselves in the social history, and not just as individual dynamics, we might be able to identify the cultural contributions, as well as a general time-table of the influence of each operating system on world culture.

I suspect that the Asperger's genetic structure was one of the dominant human operating systems until the last two thousand years of human evolution, where we see several tipping points that gave the mirror gene a reproductive foothold.

With the rise of agriculture ten thousand years ago, which led to small settlements, then larger cities, and then city-states, the great accomplishment of the Asperger's genetics may have been the establishment of law and order at a large group level. The institutionalization and administration of social roles (the variety of cast systems) could represent the genetic strength of the Asperger's type. However, with the rise of large city-states in the past 2,500 years, these world societies may have permitted those with a mirror gene operating system the opportunity to begin establishing, philosophically and religiously, cultures based on the importance of human relationships and spiritual interconnectivity versus social duty and cast function. Buddhism, and its underlying philosophy of interconnectedness (mirror operating system), versus Confucius, and his philosophy of duty and social stratification (Asperger's operating system), may be a good representation of the philosophies arising out of these competing genetic systems. Jesus's teachings about our moral responsibility towards one another and his conflict with the social representatives of his time who held the law above all may also illustrate a major tipping point in the influence of mirror genetics versus Asperger's genetics.

In Maslow's hierarchy, the mirror gene operating system may have only gained traction due to the fulfillment of the evolutionary role of the Asperger's system. The Asperger's traits of aggression, hyper-focus obsession, duty, social position, law and order, and limited emotional attachment could have been highly advantageous in those early human cultures where group survival required highly focused hunting and fighting skills, leadership was stratified, and death and emotional loss were commonplace. The attributes common to Asperger's may well represent the foundation layer of Maslow's hierarchy, at least at the group level, creating structured civilizations around the world.

At what point can we identify the influence of the mirror gene perspective? It is possible to view the teachings of the Buddha and Jesus as the first major codification of the mirror gene experience. The foundations of psychological interconnectedness, equality of all peoples, compassion towards others (versus fairness, a strong Asperger's trait), and perhaps even non-violence certainly represent the values of a mirror genetic system that sympathetically resonates with the emotional life-force of those living around them, including nature.

Recently, the massive world wars of the past 250 years may have played a large part in providing the mirror gene system its biggest opportunity to gain broader representation in the general population. With the Asperger's propensity for aggression and duty, they are the likely candidates to serve in the military and be resistant to post traumatic stress disorder (the limited ability to register the emotional distress of your enemy would be highly desirable in war). With the mass war deaths of those young men of prime reproductive age (seventeen to thirty years old), the Asperger's genetic code may have suffered an evolutionary tipping point. The call to duty and conflict, hallmarks of the Asperger's system, may have resulted in a much higher proportion of Asperger's deaths, giving the mirror gene reproductive traction. We might consider the possibility that these wars shifted the world psychological balance from the Asperger's genetic system to the mirror genetic system, which would, in turn, give strength to the philosophies of interconnectedness, non-violence, social responsibility, and collective well-being versus law, order, and social stratification.

The social revolution in Western culture between 1900 and 1980 (the suffrage movement up until President Ronald Reagan) may actually be the trumpeting of mirror gene morality in its rising demand for social equality, social justice, non-violence, ecological responsibility, and the war on poverty.

Regardless of etiology, the mirror gene operating system is in the ascension across the world. It would be fascinating to be able to identify the trends in our evolutionary history of the cyclical dance of dominance between the Asperger's operating system (law and order) and the mirror gene operating system (shared emotional intelligence) in the unfolding of civilization.

CONCLUSION

Although psychotherapy in action seems to have a seamless and even conversational appearance when observed, we can only hope that the therapist is paying attention to the variety of personality strategies that are being employed by the client. Approaching personality as having multiple functioning components that regulate perception and expression and can be triggered by specific environmental stimuli is critical in creating a therapeutic alliance and the effective transformation of a rigid personality structure. Of course, there are many psychotherapeutic techniques that are effective when applied, even if the therapist is unaware of the underlying components shaping the experience. But for maximum results (the client's mastery of his or her perceptual and expressive abilities), it is better for the therapist to possess a complete knowledge of the client's psychological operating system.

A successful therapeutic experience hinges on several key factors: (1) the honesty, curiosity, and courage of the client; (2) the creation of a therapeutic alliance; (3) the accuracy of the diagnosis; (4) the application of effective therapeutic techniques; and (5) the resolution of the client's therapeutic dependency.

CHAPTER SEVEN

THE RULES: THE PERIODIC
TABLE OF THE PSYCHE

D URING THE FORTY YEARS of my clinical training and practice, I've assembled a set of clinical psychological truths I call "The Rules." These principles outline fundamental psychological dynamics that will aid the clinician, or anyone with a general curiosity about psychological growth, in understanding the entire personality process, providing accurate diagnosis and successful therapeutic outcome. This is an integrative super-system borrowing from self psychology, Jungian analytic psychology, Gestalt integrative therapy, Masterson object relations and diagnostic theories, psychodynamics, Erickson Strategic Therapy, and Buddhist mindfulness. I would call it a positive system in that it views psychological suffering as a product of repression and that the inherent potential of the individual, in terms of wisdom, self knowledge, interpersonal intimacy, creative ability, and an energetic life, is completely intact and pressing awareness for expression. There is nothing inherently missing or corrupt about human nature. But there are certainly corrupt forms of self-expression, distorted views of reality, and poisonous emotional relationships, all arising out of a too-restrictive personality structure. This is the psychopathology that is systematically taught to every child and reinforced by conditional approval, discipline, or threat of discipline.

In spite of this type of inhibitory neural training, there is within each of us our original healthy design and energetic potential. The job of the therapist is to help the client overcome his or her fear of the consequences of self-expression and to continue with the evolution of the Self that began at birth but was interrupted in childhood. Each of the following psychological rules is fully explored elsewhere in the book. It is my hope that the fundamental truths I use as a foundation for my work will serve as a useful reference for readers as they establish their own approach to psychological growth and/or clinical practice. Note: "The Rules" assume that the therapist has identified and recommended treatment for any biological disorders, freeing the client to work on his or her personality structure and psychological expressive system.

1. **THE PSYCHE IS COMPRISED OF FIVE MAJOR COMPONENTS**: (See chapter 2, "Structure of the Psyche.") (1) awareness, (2) personality structure, (3) the physical body, (4) the unconscious, and (5) energy dynamics. I reject the proposition of many in the medical community that awareness is a byproduct of a complex bio-chemical organism. I believe that Carl Jung and the Buddhists correctly identified awareness, as part of the great ocean of awareness, independent but interdependent with the biological mechanism, as the actual source of identity, but regulated by the personality structure.

2. **ENERGY IS THE PRIME DIRECTIVE**: (See chapter 2, "Structure of the Psyche," *Energy Dynamics*.) The client's energetic state, not symptomology (anxiety, tension, stress, etc.), is the most accurate measure of psychological health and progress. Instead of viewing the highly energetic state as a peak experience, we need to view energy as a result and representation of the expressive capacity of awareness, liberated from the restriction of the personality structure. Energy is brilliance, unedited. Although energy may be a term that is missing from psychological literature as a measurable dynamic, it is a neutral way of describing the arc of our emotional experience. From depressed to thrilled, awareness experiences points along the arc as states of energy. My clients have found the term to be a practical tool in describing their overall mood, concentration, and attitude toward life in the moment. The quality of our energetic experience is the result of the tension between expression and repression. It is our personality structure that defines the quality of our experience.

3. **YOUR MOST JOYFUL MOMENT IS YOUR NORMAL STATE OF MIND**. (See chapter 1, "The View," *Our Natural Ally*.) When personality's repressive/protective role is temporarily suspended, joy, creativity, intimacy, love, and insight immediately arise, replacing caution, fear, and inhibition. These breakthrough moments of connectedness and joy are our normal state of mind, available on a moment-to-moment basis. The personality structure, having been formed out of the fear and suffering of childhood, inhibits awareness' access to these higher energetic states. When we begin

to expect joy and connectedness, these opportunities reveal themselves in the environment, having been hidden in perceptual blind spots.

4. **IF AN EXPERIENCE FEELS ENERGETIC, IT IS ENERGETIC**: (See chapter 2, "Structure of the Psyche," *Energy and Expression*.) Energy is simply a measure of health and happiness and is a part of the everyday language many of us use to describe our state of being. Learning to differentiate between energetic and non-energetic experiences allows us to identify those people, places, and experiences that have personal psychological significance. Likewise, our capacity to perceive and respond to the energetic attractors in our world is a significant measure of psychological and spiritual growth. Although many energetic attractors, such as beauty, intelligence, and athleticism, are universally recognized, most of the energetic attractors in our lives are the contents of our own unconscious reflected on the mirror of reality. The energy associated with the relationships that hold a charge for us becomes the foundation for insight and creativity, perceptual accuracy, expressive immediacy, and general psychological growth.

5. **THE PSYCHOLOGICAL LAW OF THE CONSERVATION OF ENERGY**: (See chapter 2, "Structure of the Psyche," *Energy Dynamics*.) The psychological correlate to Newton's Law of the Conservation of Energy states: the difference between the amount of energetic stimuli and the amount of energetic response is what produces psychological symptoms (the result of personality censoring). (See chapter 1, "The View," *Symptom Profile*). Total psychological energy is represented in a combination of self-expression and symptomology. The most highly efficient psychological translation of experience is insight. The least efficient psychological translation of experience is symptomology, with dream, fantasy, and emotion representing transitional states between symptom and insight. This law is at the core of psychodynamics.

6. **THE NATURE OF THE UNCONSCIOUS IS COMPENSATORY AND SELF-HEALING**: (See chapter 2, "Structure of the Psyche," *Energy Dynamics*.) This is perhaps Alfred Adler's single greatest insight, which was then adopted by Carl Jung as the fundamental psychodynamic of his psychological energy theory, discussed in Jung's *On the Nature of the Psyche*. Jung and Adler proposed that the unconscious is always attempting to bring balance to the psyche by compensating for the restrictions of the personality by producing a complementary attitude in the unconscious. Jung specifically identified this pairing as the persona (personality) and the shadow (personal unconscious). This is the actual dynamic that produces

the psychological law of the conservation of energy (Rule Five). Awareness is caught between these two polarities, attempting to access the energy and information of both.

7. **THE FIVE STAGES OF PERCEPTION**: (See chapter 2, "Structure of the Psyche," *Reality and The Five Stages of Perception*.) There are five stages through which perception travels, moving from external stimulus to "internal" knowledge: (1) symptom, (2) dream, (3) fantasy, (4) emotion, and (5) insight. Awareness experiences the bio-chemical cascade/translation representing the stimuli of reality as symptoms with which to start, then as the dreaming/fantasy stages, then as emotion, and finally as insight-wisdom-knowledge. The symptom stage is represented by our symptom profile (anxiety, tension, stress, etc.). Dreaming and fantasy are associated with the mythic stage because information is shaped by the archetypal structures of the unconscious. Emotion is also a transitional stage in which information reveals a particular neurological character (thought, sadness, aggression, sexuality). The final stage, insight, is simply the accurate knowing of any phenomena. This final stage is also part of the uninhibited psychological loop that then expresses a response with energy equal to the stimuli. Perceptual accuracy is combined with responsive immediacy.

8. **THE ROLE OF THERAPY IS TO BRING ABOUT PERCEPTUAL ACCURACY AND RESPONSIVE IMMEDIACY**: (See chapter 4, "Trauma Dynamics," *The Three Consequences*.) From birth, we are taught how to view the world and how to respond to it. However, we are trained to see and respond to only a small percentage of reality, an indoctrination that leaves us with massive blind spots and an unstable energy supply (fluctuating self-expression). One of the clearest descriptions of this dilemma is Gregory Bateson's description of the double bind. In the double bind, a child is repeatedly put in relationship situations where the child is required, partially out of need for survival, to choose between his or her experience of reality (the truth) and someone else's conflicting description of reality. When circumstances repeatedly force the child to reject his or her experience (and the associated physical senses) in favor of the described distortion, it becomes more and more difficult for the child to successfully negotiate the experiences of life. Perception of reality is distorted, which simultaneously produces a symptomatic response from the psyche. ". . . What I held in mind as the world at hand was merely a description of the world; a description that been pounded into me from the moment I was born." (Carlos Castaneda, *Journey to Ixtlan*)

9. **TRUTH HAS ENERGY:** (See chapter 8, "Treatment," *Progress.*) Truth has energy; a simple rule that has magnificent implications. It is a great breakthrough in personal psychological evolution to realize that all experiences are not equally energetic for us, and we are selectively attracted to those encounters with people and places and even objects that are uniquely energetically charged by our unconscious. There is one reality, one truth, that we all share, though we are only able to know it in a partial way due to psychological filtering. As we accept the truth, as we accept reality, we receive an energetic reward: the *Aha!* experience. *It is what it is.* The reasoning behind Rule Eight is that accurate perception is energetic and distorted perception is symptomatic, and therefore, energetically compromised. As we perceive reality more accurately and respond to that experience emotionally uninhibited, we approach our energetic potential. The truth that speaks to each person will be specific to that person's psychological developmental design in the moment. Emerging from individual truth, our unique psychological design ultimately evolves into perceiving the world *as it is.* We move toward a singular truth, one we share with all humanity, and the result is a shared sanity.

10. **PERSONALITY STRUCTURE IS CREATED OUT OF CHILDHOOD DISCIPLINE, FEARS AND TRAUMA:** (See chapter 3, "Personality Structure") Personality structure arises from the need to restrict self-expression due to the repeated threat of negative physical and emotional consequences.

11. **PERSONALITY IS AN ENERGY, EMOTION, AND INFORMATION REGULATION SYSTEM:** (See chapter 2, "Structure of the Psyche," *Personality's Function.*) Personality has two dominant functions, regulating perception and regulating expression. Personality determines how intense environmental stimulation needs to be in order to be perceived and how much internal pressure has to occur before we express what we feel. These two thresholds hold the key for understanding psychological blind spots, repetitive behavior, explosive emotions, inconsistent emotional behavior, and unstable psychological energy.

12. **ALL PERSONALITY IS MULTIPLE PERSONALITY:** (Chapter 5, "Psychodynamics," *The Five Centers of Awareness*). A fundamental tenet of Gestalt and Jungian theory is that personality is actually an assemblage of many sub-personalities or complexes that contribute to thought, mood, emotion, energetic capacity, and particular style of expression (parental/sibling/authority introject). This book proposes that these sub-personalities correspond to five fundamental neural-emotional systems: brain, throat, respiratory,

digestive, and reproductive. Each complex has its own unique combination of biological and psychological functioning, with healthy and pathological manifestations. These five complexes form the dominant structure of the personality, and each has the potential to operate as a sub-personality system, complete with its own perspective of the world, expressive capacity, and style of expression.

There is an expressive and perceptual overlay at each site that is associated with the dominant parental and sibling influences. We will utilize the style of expression of those with whom we had the most significant relationships. The five neural-emotional components are the substructure and content of personality, but the parental/sibling introjects will supply the style of expression.

Ideally, the five components would contribute equally and unrestrictedly to perception and expression, providing a complete and accurate view of the world, an immediate and appropriate response to the world, and a consistent supply of energy. However, when any of these neural-emotional systems are repressed, the energy of the restricted complex builds until awareness is seized by its influence, producing rigid perceptions and chaotic emotional expression, until that point when the emotion is sufficiently discharged and awareness is released to be influenced by the next highly charged complex. As each of these complexes is allowed free-flowing expression, without significant regulation, awareness gains access to all of the energetic and informational potential of the psyche.

13. **SELF-IMAGE AND SELF-WORTH ARE IN PROPORTION TO SELF-EXPRESSION**: (See chapter 8, "Treatment," *Introduction*). A positive childhood permits the child to be self-expressive, which in turn produces the experience of self-confidence and self-worth. A restrictive, punitive childhood produces restricted self-expression, resulting in poor self-image and poor self-worth. Since all childhood has its challenges, most adults suffer self-worth and self-image issues. A self-image is not something you get because someone likes you: it is the result of expressing oneself directly and without inhibition. Consistent positive self-image is predicated on full expression of all of the neural-emotional complexes, not just a few. Each complex produces a portion of the emotional and energetic response that contributes to overall positive self-image. As awareness utilizes the five emotional complexes for processing and expressing, the complexes that are less restricted produce a confident feeling, and the systems that are more restricted produce less

self-confidence. Thus, self-worth is dependent on the accumulated function of the five emotional systems and varies accordingly.

14. **ENERGY IS IN PROPORTION TO SELF-EXPRESSION:** (Chapter 2, "Structure of the Psyche," *Energy Dynamics*). Although most people believe that external circumstances produce energetic or toxic experiences, it is in fact our response, and only our response, to those events that determines their energetic and emotional quantity and quality.

15. **IT IS THE PERSONALITY, NOT THE SITUATION THAT PRODUCES SYMPTOMS**: (See chapter 1, "The View," *Our Natural Ally*, and *Symptom Profile*). The personality restricts emotional response in specific situations based primarily on childhood training, which produces symptoms as a by-product of repression. The situation is not "toxic" or "bad," or even "good," for that matter. The situation is simply a trigger for an emotional response that the personality either permits or represses. It is the act of repression that produces the toxic feeling, not the person or situation being encountered.

16. **SUBLIMATION, REPRESSION, AND DISSOCIATION ARE THE DOMINANT PSYCHOLOGICAL DEFENSES:** (See chapter 2, "Structure of the Psyche," *Personality Function.*) *Sublimation* is the redirection of emotional energy through a different neural-emotional complex than originally was triggered: anger is expressed as sadness. Repression is the conscious or unconscious subduing of an emotional response, converting the emotion into a variety of prescribed symptoms (anxiety, tension, stress, etc.). Dissociation is when awareness abandons the physical sites that have been traumatized. Since emotion is organ specific, and information is organ specific, and trauma is organ specific, the strength of the dissociation (organ abandonment) determines perception, expression, and symptom production.

17. **WE DO NOT INVENT FEARS: WE RELIVE THEM**: (See chapter 4, "Trauma Dynamics," *The Foundation of Fear.*) Except in circumstances of overwhelming stimuli, our fears are based on past experiences. We are only afraid of what we have already experienced.

18. **SELF-ACTIVATION TRIGGERS EMOTIONAL MEMORY: THE ACTIVATION-RESISTANCE CYCLE (ARC):** (See chapter 8, "Treatment," *The ARC.*) The ARC (Activation-Resistance Cycle) is the five-step process through which the personality structure, which regulates perception and expression, copes with the energetic surge that attends self-activation. As circumstance requires us to self-activate (express ourselves, initiate action or opinion)

and expand our expressive boundaries in order to handle life's challenges, the neural-emotional complexes are pushed past their expressive thresholds, triggering anxiety associated with punishment or past trauma. Personality then rigidly regulates our response to reduce anticipated environmental retaliation. The sublimated, repressed, or dissociated response immediately produces symptoms, and the energy associated with the emotional surge is immediately compromised. This is the Activation-Resistance Cycle: transition or intimacy activates the body, which activates memory or emotion, which triggers resistance, which activates symptoms, which reduces energy.

19. **BLOCKED EMOTIONS FUEL SYMPTOMS AND SELF-DESTRUCTIVE BEHAVIOR**: (See chapter 4, "Trauma Dynamics," *The 3 Consequences*.) Assuming biological/neurological health, the energy that drives symptoms and acting-out is derived from sublimated, repressed, or dissociated emotional responses.

20. **SYMPTOMS ARE NOT EMOTIONS**: (See chapter 4, "Trauma Dynamics," *The 3 Consequences*.) Anxiety, tension, stress, guilt, shame, fear, resentment, grief, worry, depression, and somatization are the dominant psychological symptoms of repressed emotions and perceptual distortions and should not be considered emotions. They are the symptoms of repressed emotions.

21. **THE SYMPTOM IS NOT THE PROBLEM; IT IS THE SOLUTION TO THE PROBLEM**: (See chapter 1, "The View," *Symptom Profile*.) A symptom is the indirect expression of the energy of a blocked emotional response. The symptom is not the problem; it is the expressive solution, although it is certainly experienced as problematic. Symptoms are points of entry to the underlying mechanisms that inhibit expression and distort perception. Without the presentation of symptomology, dissociated memories remain undetectable and thus untreatable.

22. **PSYCHOLOGICAL SYMPTOMS ARE IN PROPORTION TO REPRESSED OR DISSOCIATED EMOTIONS**: (See chapter 1, "The View," *Symptom Profile*.) When there are no biological complications, the quantity, frequency, and intensity of psychological symptoms are directly in proportion to the energy of the repressed emotions. Symptom magnitude can be used as a gauge for identifying the level of trauma hidden in the unconscious and its accompanying potential as an energetic resource upon release.

23. **REPRESSED OR DISSOCIATED EMOTIONS ARE IN PROPORTION TO DEVELOPMENTAL TRAUMA**: (See chapter 3: "Personality Structure"). The clinician should expect to uncover childhood or adult trauma in proportion to client's emotional diffi-

culty. Assuming biology is healthy, developmental or adult trauma produces dissociated neural-complexes and repressed emotions.

24. **THERE ARE THREE REQUIREMENTS FOR PSYCHOLOG-ICAL GROWTH:** (See chapter 1, "The View," *The Fear.*) The "Three Cs," curiosity, courage, and commitment, are vital to the challenging work of freeing energy by addressing personality blocks. Initially, the client seeking psychotherapy is driven by the desire to stop suffering. The simple act of being true to oneself and trusting one's emotions can bring about significant changes and improve living conditions. However, addressing the deeper personality structure that has led to the compromises now creating much of life's difficulties requires a stronger commitment than the passive desire for emotional relief. The three C's (curiosity, courage, and commitment) are the qualities of self that catalyze that deeper personal transformation.

25. **IDENTIFYING AND NEUTRALIZING THE CORE DEVEL-OPMENTAL FEARS ARE CRITICAL FOR SUSTAINABLE PSYCHOLOGICAL PROGRESS:** (See chapter 1, "The View," *The Fear.*) It is nearly impossible to grow psychologically without a commitment to overcoming some of the basic childhood fears of retaliation, punishment, poverty, control, abandonment, or even assault. These fears are associated with specific emotions and are triggered by day-to-day emotional requirements. Curiosity helps us identify the expressive block, and even the history behind the expressive block, but it is courage that helps us move from repression to expression. Neutralizing the core fear formed in childhood may require effectively arming oneself in adulthood, emotionally and/or physically. Psychological growth and the ability to defend oneself are directly related.

26. **THE MISSING EMOTION IS THE THERAPEUTIC TARGET:** (See chapter 5, "Psychodynamics," *Sublimation.*) If a client is capable of expressing anger, sadness, thought, sexuality, or speech in response and proportion to the stimuli that trigger those emotions, then there is little therapeutic usefulness in the repeated expression of these emotions in therapy. The clinician should instead be searching for the emotions that are not well developed and are overly regulated by personality. For example, if a client can express sadness (sexuality, anger, thought) easily, then spending a great deal of therapeutic time supporting the client crying (discussing sex life, anger, thoughts) will produce minimum therapeutic change. Instead, identify and exercise the emotional complexes that are underdeveloped.

27. **ANY EMOTION CAN BE A SYMPTOM FOR ANOTHER EMOTION**: (See chapter 5, "Psychodynamics," *Sublimation*.) We express the emotions that have been encouraged by our family. The less comfortable emotions, those controlled or repressed, are often sublimated and expressed through feelings that we do express. Anger might be expressed as sadness, sadness might be expressed as worry, or anxiety as sexuality. The emotion that we feel comfortable with will do the "heavy lifting" for the overall emotional regulation. In order to access our maximum energy and to perceive the world with the greatest accuracy, all of our emotions must be expressed authentically, not redirected into seemingly safer outlets. We will always express the convenient emotion first. The repressed emotions will be available only in circumstances where the trigger is overwhelming and overrides the repressive circuitry, or we intentionally give ourselves permission to express ourselves more fully.

28. **ACCURATE EMOTIONAL EXPRESSION WILL REDUCE SYMPTOMS**: (See chapter 5, "Psychodynamics," *Sublimation*.) If expressing an emotion does not reduce symptomology and raise energy, it is not the problematic emotion (or there is a medical condition). Find the repressed or sublimated emotion, bring it to the surface, and begin working on expressing it in proportion to the moment.

29. **EMOTIONAL REGULATION IS AS IMPORTANT AS EMOTIONAL EXPRESSION**: (See chapter 9, "Therapeutic Strategy and Technique," *Emotional Regulation*.) Although repression is usually described as negative, the principle of regulating self-expression is important. Repression should be intentionally applied to hostile internal dynamics: negative self-talk, habitual self-criticism, anticipating negative outcome. If we can repress the good stuff, why not learn to repress the bad stuff instead and free the mind of that chronic negative mental chatter.

30. **YOU GET THE RELATIONSHIPS YOU ALLOW**: (See chapter 9, "Therapeutic Strategy and Technique," *Repression*.) Our energetic attraction to the people in our environment is associated with the charged contents of our own unconscious. The unconscious, in its attempt to bring balance to the psyche, seeks to release repressed emotions or creative potentials. We are thus selectively attracted to those individuals and situations more likely to act as emotional triggers. The relationships we develop serve to awaken these unconscious components within us. Attraction and rejection are specifically charged emotions or psychological potentialities in our unconscious associated with environmental "triggers." The external attractor is merely the mirror reflecting the unconscious

contents of our own psyche. Thus, the relationships we develop in association to these attractors serve to awaken unconscious components within us. As we use difficult current relationships to identify and release historical pain, we become able to elevate the richness and beauty (and ferocity) of our connections with others.

31. **FREE WILL DOES NOT EXIST**: (See chapter 5, "Psychodynamics," *Integration*.) This rule causes more conflict when I lecture than does any other idea that I propose. Both psyche (awareness) and soma (body) obey the structural and expressive rules of their design. Physiology seeks biological satisfaction, moving from one area of tension to the next in order to satisfy the cycling needs of the body. It is extraordinarily difficult to "demand" that the body perform a behavior that is inconsistent with its biological tensions. It can be done, but mostly this type of "free will" is using our will against the natural course of self-expression the body seeks, and ultimately will have limited success if it does not fail outright. In these cases, free will is nothing more than resistance to the flow of our biological "river," which is inevitably a temporary condition due to the stress it produces.

The psyche (awareness) also has an unfolding developmental agenda as well. The psyche is not a passive by-product of complex biology, but rather is a dynamic ocean of expressive intent. The drive of evolution is intimately associated with the unfolding intent of the psyche to shape the environment and provide expressive opportunities for the life force.

In the same way that an acorn is designed to express its potential, both structurally (shape) and dynamically (function), the human psyche has an expressive designation. When the design of a person's psychological journey is served well, energy and purpose emerge. When the design is resisted, there is suffering. There is no greater sense of energetic satisfaction than to abandon what we imagine to be free will in order to fully serve one's purpose and then to experience that purpose as a life's work.

The energetic reward of cooperating with our biological and psychological designs suggests that free will is nothing more than the resistance to this unfolding energetic matrix. Unless free will can be described solely as resistance to evolutionary intent, or as a set of choices with a very limited field of options, then free will, as we theologically, philosophically, and psychologically define it, does not exist.

Section Two:

TREATMENT AND TRANSFORMATION

Treatment

Therapeutic Technique and Strategy

Therapeutic Stages and Goals

TREATMENT

INTRODUCTION

Milton Erickson is reported to have said that the goal of therapy is "not to make the client feel better, but to make the client feel stronger." When you examine Dr. Erickson's life and his struggles with polio, one can understand the confessional aspect of this goal. However, Dr. Erickson was a master in dealing with resistance in therapy. It was his strategy to neutralize therapeutic resistance before it manifested in the work. Dr. Erickson knew at a very fundamental level that clients were not acting in their own, long-term best interest when they resisted the influences of the unconscious mind.

On a daily basis, we are all confronted with a choice between spontaneous, genuine, self-expression *or* a strategic repression of our emotions. We almost always choose the latter, which leads to living with a variety of symptoms that drive us crazy. What can possibly be so threatening that we would choose systematic suffering over self-expression? The simple answer: fear of the consequences. Fear of what happened to us as children and adolescents, as we experimented with self-expression while growing up at home and in school. We fear the punishment, being ignored, the intimidation, the physical domination, the retribution, the revenge, the Or-Else.

Personality is the servant of fear. Personality simply operates to protect awareness from the hostile experiences of childhood.

It takes curiosity, courage, and commitment, in equal amounts, to overcome those limiting life lessons of childhood. The shift from suffering to curiosity marks a significant evolution in one's psyche and produces the greatest results in psychological growth. Courage is the component that enables us to overcome our fears of the consequences of expressing forbidden emotions and behaviors. Without courage, we remain servants of social approval and will never effectively challenge the perceived/remembered threat of the consequences of self-expression. One simply remains locked in a psychological structure that distorts reality, compromises creativity, and undermines intimate relationships. That constricting structure is your personality.

Personality is the regulating system whose primary function is assessing threat and protecting awareness and the body from punishment by redacting perception and inhibiting emotional expression.

Personality styles, whether charming or destructive, disciplined or indulgent, humorous or humorless, are the direct results of positive and negative reinforcement at the hands of those with power in our lives. Even the more socially appealing personality styles: charm, humor, wit, competition, or even beauty turn out to be social strategies for accomplishing a variety of conscious and unconscious psychological goals: love, reproduction, sex, financial security, education, etc. And strategy, whether pleasing or not, takes psychological energy to execute.

Personality determines whether our social strategy is energy efficient or energy draining. When personality becomes too rigid, it grossly inhibits self-expression, which in turn creates moderate to severe energy depletion.

In an ironic twist, we view distorted emotional behaviors resulting from punitive family dynamics as examples of why we should control our emotions. In an attempt to monitor our own moral behavior or self-expression, we often view the worst social examples of emotional expression as illustrations of the negative potentialities of the unconscious, when in fact these distorted, self-serving, and even cruel behaviors are actually the result of

1. psychological repression due to developmental neglect or abuse;
2. bio-chemical impairment arising from neural or brain dysfunction; or
3. post-traumatic stress disorder, also associated with neurological trauma.

Unfortunately, the quest for moral perfection distorts our perspective of natural expression. Our attempt to achieve higher levels of moral and ethical behavior often lead to an imposition of restrictive expressive goals. This is our quest for perfection. It is this restriction that actually creates the internal conflict and the predictable unstable emotional relationships with others that we are attempting to correct through these moral/ethical exercises. It is the imposition of self-restriction that fuels the psychological distress. It is our adversarial attitude toward our own natural self and self-expression that causes our psychological suffering.

The intent to live as a moral and ethical person is to be admired. The problem occurs when our self-analysis is flawed. I do not teach my clients to abandon self-criticism, which is necessary to evaluate the effectiveness of one's talents and self-expression, but I do encourage them to listen to that "still and quiet" voice of the unconscious that honestly and compassionately answers their questions of self-worth, self-image, and lovability.

Perfection is a state of mind, not a state of performance. Our inability to see the inherent perfection in our design is what causes the psychic conflict.

Eric Neumann, in his book, *Depth Psychology and a New Ethic*, suggests that the quest for perfection is flawed in both intent and execution. By rejecting parts of one's self as "flawed" or "base," one fractures the self into conflicting and competing components. Personality then attempts to correct the perceived imperfection by regulation (sublimation, repression, and dissociation) which, of course, fuels the psychological symptoms.

Every emotional complex has its own specifically distorted and symptomatic expression. Most spiritual/religious/ethical/moral disciplines target one or more of these emotions as the source of spiritual conflict. Compassion, sexuality, aggression, speech, and thought are regularly targeted for improvement or perfection. What begins as learned inhibition for the convenience of the family is eventually adopted by religious institutions and social structures as appropriate and desired moral behavior. Most behavior is taught for the good of the group, not the good of the individual. Thus, personality worships at the altar of group approval.

What we need to keep in mind is that the unconscious is always attempting to counterbalance the repressive effects of personality. What is denied expression consciously by personality is expressed indirectly by the unconscious in the form of symptoms, dreams, fantasies, self-indulgence, and risky behaviors.

The psychodynamics of the unconscious apply not only to the individual but also to humanity as a whole. The genius of Jung is that he understood that these same personality dynamics apply to social/group dynamics. When people support values and behaviors that are out of balance to the whole of human potential, the repressed/dissociated components emerge in social conflict. These social corrections counterbalance distorted social values. When homosexuality was demonized during the 2004 presidential election of the United States, there was an almost immediate counterbalance response from the media to portray homosexuals as our neighbors and family members (sometimes eccentric and often comedic, but nonetheless beloved). The whole of awareness is attempting to continually heal the artificial psychological distortions of personality and society.

To this end, we witness the recent arrival of psychological treatment, which is the evolution of the role of the shaman in community. The role of the shaman is to asses how the individual or community has fallen out of balance with the cycles and powers of nature and then to orchestrate rituals and practices that are designed to re-establish the natural balance, bringing about the needed correction. Psychology has specifically identified those diseased structures of culture and personality and specified techniques and rituals to correct the "dis-ease."

So, what are the goals of psychological treatment? First, *to perceive the world free of perceptual distortions, and* second, *to express oneself without restriction and in proportion to the moment, freeing self-expression from the tyranny of personality.*

This concept of spontaneous and unrestricted self-expression is often met with horror at the perceived consequences of a society filled with unregulated people. Religion often preaches that the base character of humanity is corrupt and, if left unregulated, will throw society into a primitive frenzy with the immoral feeding on the weak. Ironically, those with anti-social tendencies are already operating freely in this mode. These psychopaths, anti-social personalities, criminals, and extreme narcissists are already completely unbound by ethical and moral principles. They do what they wish, to whom they wish, without limit. While many of those who populate prisons are relatively easy to spot as dangerous, those who populate boardrooms and political arenas tend to present as charismatic, dynamic, effective, charming, and even threatening. Their presentation as "normal human beings" is simply the seduction by the predator seeking gratification at the expense of any and all who cross their paths. It is not the lack of moral discipline that produces these anti-social parasites. It takes a biological processing problem, like psychopathic neurodiversity, or a ferocious level of physical punishment, abandonment, rejection, and emotional disregard to produce a person capable of rejecting the higher interconnection between all living creatures. It is not the unregulated base human emotion that undermines ethical and moral behavior. Rather, it is the abuse at the hands of others that produces the eventual disregard for the value of others. In most cases, we have created the predators ourselves.

Some psychological monsters are, in fact, born monsters, but for the most part, we create our own social monsters during the child's early developmental stages and then pretend that it is the nature of humanity that is corrupt. We teach our children and family members exactly how to act and behave. We see the lack of moral or ethical behavior in others and suggest that a lack of religious or family discipline is at the heart of the problem, when in fact it is this discipline, or the indulgence of the parents and family, that produces the problem.

Those of us with a concern for unregulated self-expression are precisely the ones who need to deregulate: to open to the spontaneous response in the immediate moment. Those with a moral rationalization to restrict self-expression need to find the courage to be who they were ultimately designed to be, without repression. Just like any prisoner who is suddenly set free, any emotion that has been buried for years will need some time to achieve equilibrium. But with practice and patience and courage, all emotions find a balance of expression in proportion to the moment.

Ironically, it is the actual normal person, seeking to be a good person, who overly restricts self-expression and produces the suffering that leads to therapy. Suspicious of their own psychological intentions, these symptom-prone clients seek a new way of seeing themselves and their life goals. They view the events of their lives as random and chaotic, repeat emotional frustrations, and suspect a more satisfying life is available, but find themselves unable to achieve or sustain that life. In these cases, the primary goal of psychotherapy is to raise the client's energy level. Although this can be accomplished through a variety of strategies and techniques, as noted in Chapter 1, there are several specific parameters that guide therapeutic intervention.

These are three of the more important elements of the psychological periodic table:

1. Self-worth is in proportion to one's overall energy;
2. Energy is in proportion to self-expression;
3. Self-worth is in proportion to self-expression.

THE ENERGETIC ATTRACTOR

Psychotherapy has long been associated with disorders of the psyche that result in destructive behaviors, chaotic moods, and emotional volatility. The goals of therapy have often been defined as the absence of symptoms rather than the presence of insight and creativity. But what if all of our descriptions of symptomology or creativity are actually attempts to describe our energetic state, and our mood is reflective of that energetic state? Essentially, we are our own "battery tester." We are capable of assessing our energetic level by mood, creativity, symptomology, insight, emotional availability, and stability of mind. The truth is, *if it feels energetic, it is energetic.* Although emotional and mental states are ultimately subjective measures of health, human beings describe them as energetic experiences. "I feel depressed." "I feel really pumped-up today." "I have really low energy today." Energy is simply a measure of health and happiness and is a part of everyday language describing our state of being. Learning to differentiate between energetic and non-energetic experiences is simply a matter of identifying those people, places, and experiences that have personal psychological meaning.

The term *energy* is the only consistent, reliable descriptor of a healthy, stable, creative personality, and ultimately all therapeutic strategies and techniques have the common goal to raise the energy level of the client. The personality structure, the main object of diagnosis and treatment in psychotherapy, is essentially an energy regulation system that is designed to limit self-expression and thus compromise our energetic experience. I would also add this caveat: energy must have stability to be effective and productive. The difference between joy and terror is stability and balance. We are all familiar with the bi-polar/ manic depressive who has massive amounts of energy, but little stability or balance. But the martial arts master, the yogi, the great athlete, the guru, and the experienced psychotherapist all demonstrate balance and stability in the face of chaos: they reside in the eye of the human emotional "hurricane."

Ultimately, all psychological experience can be described as providing access to a quantity of energy. Falling in love is a quantity of energy. A spiritual experience is a quantity of energy. Depression is a quantity of energy. Insight is a quantity of energy. Anxiety is a quantity of energy. Each of these states of mind represents a different quantity of energy; the low energy states are associated with suffering, and the high-energy states are associated with joy.

It is a significant measure of psychological and spiritual growth when we begin to perceive, and respond to, the energetic attractors in our world: those people, places, and circumstances that seem to generate a desirable energetic experience. Although many energetic attractors are universally recognized, such as beauty, intelligence, and athleticism, most of the energetic attractors in our lives are personal: those people, places, and events that we associate with personal significance. They are reflections of the contents of our own unconscious in the mirror of the world. As we pursue and engage with these attractors, the energy associated with these relationships is released from the unconscious and becomes the foundation for evolving insight and creativity, perceptual accuracy, and expressive immediacy. Although we often give credit to the energetic object, it is actually our willingness to self-express freely that produces the actual burst of energy.

In the Beginning

Therapy always begins with the client's story: depression, anxiety, worry, life crisis, personal loss, life transition, or some equally important motivating experience. Although often filled with loss, pain, grief and, too frequently, horror, these human experiences are the foundation from which personality arises and transforms. Over the course of therapy, the client will need to build a fundamental trust in his or her perceptual abilities: the courage to express thoughts and emotions and negotiate love, loss, employment, education, transformation, and even develop spiritual wisdom. If therapy is successful, there will be, within the client, a growing confidence that the world has structure and purpose and is not just a random set of events.

TYPES OF THERAPY

For the therapist, it is imperative that s/he be able to diagnose the presenting problem and the underlying causes that bring a client to therapy. The nervous system has the unique ability to mimic symptoms that could be biological and/or psychological. Depression, for example, may be the result of a rigid personality structure that represses emotions to the point of distress, producing a psychological depression: dysthymia. But depression can also be the result of an underlying medical/biological problem, indicating a health problem that is potentially very serious: an affective disorder such as major depression or manic-depression, or a disease process. And to further complicate the diagnosis process, depression could be a result of both psychological and medical problems. It is not unusual for an individual growing up in a family with medical depression to inherit the medical problem, as well as an emotionally repressive personality. In this case, the diagnosis and treatment is initially complicated. Since the psychological aspect of depression usually takes longer to resolve, the clinician needs to be sure that the client isn't suffering needlessly from a medical condition that a physician, nutritionist, chiropractor, or exercise program could treat fairly quickly. The medical professional faces the same diagnostic challenge. It has been the habit of physicians to treat all symptoms as part of a biological process and to treat those symptoms with medication. Since psychological depression presents similarly to biological depression, too often patients are misdiagnosed and given a variety of medications in the attempt to treat a stubborn problem, when in fact the patient suffers from a psychological condition and requires psychotherapy, not medication. If the client does not have a biological depression, then anti-depressants are at best harmless, and at worst, expensive and cause a variety of side effects. But when a client has an affective disorder (biological depression, etc.), months of psychotherapy will not address the biochemical problem, and the longer the client waits for effective diagnosis and intervention, the longer the client and his or her loved ones suffer.

This is where a holistic and inclusive attitude helps achieve one's health goals. With most people having access to the Internet, many resources have become available for staying healthy and reducing stress. At minimum, the Internet information can point you in the direction of health professionals and health resources in your area. I always laugh when a client asks me if I believe in alternative or holistic health treatment. I tell them that I believe that talking can reduce suffering and increase health and energy, and that's about as alternative as one can get: the "talking cure," as psychotherapy is often referred.

THE FOUR TYPES OF THERAPY

Medical, rehabilitation, short-term, and long-term therapies are designed to diagnose and treat unique and specific types of psychological problems. Medical therapy addresses biological challenges. Rehabilitation therapy is designed to precede actual psychotherapy, providing a fundamental groundwork for healing neurological complications. Short-term therapy is an abbreviated and strategically oriented variation of long-term therapy, which addresses expressive disorders, perceptual blind spots, rigid personality structures, and dysfunctional family systems.

MEDICAL THERAPY

Medical crises are due to physical disorders that have emotional features, such as affective disorders (bi-polar or depression), anxiety, immune disorders, attention deficit and concentration problems, hyperactivity, hormonal disorders, obsessive/compulsive disorders, post-traumatic stress, and many more. Once the client has been diagnosed with a medical disorder, appropriate treatment through medication, nutrition, or physical therapy usually brings relief to much of the symptomology. Psychological intervention may be necessary if the condition has been active for a long time. It is often difficult to differentiate between the psychological and physiological aspects of a psychological disorder. Medical doctors misdiagnose psychological symptoms and mental health specialists misdiagnose physical symptoms. The best service we can offer to our clients is to provide an accurate diagnosis, effective treatment strategies, and a solid and effective referral network with other professionals in the community.

Rehabilitation Therapy

This small section on rehabilitation therapy is presented simply to illustrate some of the more significant factors in symptom treatment and therapeutic outcomes. Rehabilitation therapy is primarily associated with circumstances of medical crises such as psychosis, addiction, eating disorders, or catastrophic trauma, usually associated with the diagnosis of post-traumatic stress disorder (PTSD), which is a combination of psychological overload and neurological damage.

In the case of PTSD, rehabilitation therapy, both psychological and medical, is usually required as the nervous system is slow to heal after a severe shock, abuse, or psychosis. PTSD can occur after assault, violence, home invasion, kidnapping, war, robbery, auto accident, near death experiences, life-threatening illness, and financial disaster, to name a few. Treatment progress is typically measured in terms of six-month increments, often with several years of treatment to return to "normal" functioning. With insurance limits, mental health gate-keepers pressing for cessation of therapy, and even families wishing for the patient to appear "normal" by a quick return to work and social activities, these vulnerable PTSD clients often suffer catastrophic results when social re-integration occurs too quickly. Healing has its own timetable and is to be respected.

In the case of manic-depressive individuals who have suffered a psychotic break, effective treatment can give them ninety-five percent or more of their lives back, with minimum psychological symptomology. However, if the therapy places them back into overwhelming situations in which the nervous system is re-traumatized, the resulting additional psychosis can be devastating. After the second or third psychotic break, the client often "integrates" fixed delusional material as part of the psychological functioning, looking more schizophrenic than bi-polar. Many patients who end up with a schizophrenic diagnosis are the product of multiple manic psychoses. Ideally, to complete a more effective rehabilitation, a short-term disability ruling that would allow slow recovery over at least six to nine months would be ideal. This cost would be minimum compared to a lifetime of disability after multiple psychotic episodes.

Manic-depressive psychosis, schizophrenia, schizoaffective disorder, or long-term major depressive disorders are several examples of diagnoses requiring rehabilitation psychotherapy. Rehabilitation psychotherapy is significantly different from all other forms of therapy in terms of how it views symptomology, stability, the client's ability to handle stressful stimuli/situations, and the step-by-step reclamation of the client's major neural-emotional centers. A damaged nervous system is very, very slow to heal. A psychotic break can do serious emotional damage. Part of the problem is that unlike a broken arm, which you put in a cast and stop using for several months to allow it to heal, you can't stop using your nervous system for several months.

The closest that we can come to a "neurological cast" is medication that insulates the nervous system from overwhelming stimuli, paired with restricted social interaction in order to reduce exposure to intense stimuli.

Once the nervous system has been isolated from over-stimulation, rehabilitation begins by therapeutic monitoring of mood, emotional expression, physical symptoms, anxiety level, sleep patterns, perceptual accuracy, and concentration capacity. Sleep may be the most important factor in healing the nervous system, particularly when mania is a factor in the treatment. Psychological rehabilitation therapy is the road to health through boredom. The therapist must *discourage* emotional exploration, dream work, relationship confrontations, or any other emotionally stimulating activity.

Working on concentration and emotional regulation becomes paramount in the early stages of rehabilitation therapy. Depth therapy can resume when the medication regimen is significantly reduced and the client has demonstrated the ability to tolerate emotional stimulation without regressive symptomology, sleep interruption, break-though primary process, excessive anxiety, or concentration difficulties.

SHORT-TERM THERAPY

Short-term therapy is usually "solution-focused," and the dominant goal is problem solving. As noted elsewhere in this book, short-term therapy is being used more and more often to offset the expenses of long-term therapy and insurance limitations, as well as to address certain types of psychological distress. Certain specific techniques have been found to be particularly effective in reducing symptomology and are now being promoted as "evidence-based" or "best practices" therapy. Cognitive behavioral therapy, reality therapy, emotional focused therapy, rational-emotive therapy, *eye movement desensitization and reprocessing* (EMDR), desensitization, family systems, and strategic therapy are some of the most recognized and practiced "evidence-based" techniques associated with short-term, solution-focused therapy.

Short-term therapy is employed when a client has encountered a situation in which his problem solving abilities are insufficient to resolve the challenge. Thus, he remains stuck, and the symptomology (anxiety, tension, stress, etc.) resulting from being stuck begins to become intolerable. The symptoms created by those underlying problems become the motivating factor in the client seeking therapy.

The death of a loved one, the birth of a child, marriage, divorce, graduation, relocation, job trouble, and illness are types of situational stresses that can trigger a transitional crisis. The type of therapy generally recognized as most effective in treating these crises is categorized as "strategic." Strategic therapy is sometimes referred to as "brief" therapy because the therapy involves concentrated, short-term strategies to counter or resolve the situational stressors. This type of therapy differs from structural therapy in that although it requires a therapeutic alliance from the client(s), problem solving or structural realignment of the family, and not the transference, becomes the focus of the work. Resolution of the presenting problem, and not necessarily its underlying cause, is the primary goal of short-term therapy. The one significant exception to this is *strategic family therapy*, in which the short-term strategic correction of the family system addresses the family structural problem, not just the symptomology, and can produce long-term results.

The inherent limitation of problem solving therapy is that the presenting problem is often a symptom of an underlying personality problem or marital problem, and although resolving the presenting problem may help the transition phase challenge, it usually does not deal with the underlying issue, nor produce long-term results. As Jay Haley illustrated in his classic book on family therapy, *Leaving Home*, the teenager who is acting out is often the symptom of a family in crisis and a marriage in danger of failing. Treating the teenager without treating the family may temporarily relieve the acting-out of the identified patient, but rarely solves the deeper family challenges. As long as the clinician is aware of these limitations, short-term therapy has its place in the treatment hierarchy.

Short-term therapy is useful in symptom relief, problem solving, family relationship problems, and resolving transitional crises. It is particularly useful in assessing an underlying medical condition masquerading as a psychological or transition phase problem.

Most mental health practitioners are quite familiar with the affective disorders of manic depression and major depression, but we also need to be familiar with the physical disorders of the hormonal or neurological systems that often are disguised as emotional instability disorders. These conditions require medical attention, and in some cases, immediate hospitalization. In these situations, short-term therapy is simply supportive and the clinician should offer a referral to the appropriate medical professional.

LONG-TERM THERAPY

When personality is overly restrictive, it represses excessive amounts of emotional expression, thus producing a predictable symptom profile. Long-term therapy is required to activate and integrate the components of the psyche that are over-regulated and symptomatic. Thus, long-term therapy is designed to evolve the personality structure. Depending on the rigidity of the personality system and the severity of the client's trauma, therapy can last from two to four or more years (with the duration varying based on frequency of contact, motivation, situational stability, and physical health).

The first phase of long-term therapy is motivated by the intensity of suffering in the client's life. As s/he begins to express emotions that have been compromised for years there is a twofold positive effect: social stressors usually begin to subside and energy increases. This can actually happen fairly quickly (eight to ten sessions) and is often described as a "flight into health." The client usually feels better, and the social pressures are reduced because the client is no longer passively participating in toxic interactions. But this is really only a taste of health. It's as though the unconscious is presenting awareness with the experience of health, so that awareness knows what the final goal feels like. This burst of relief is the target goal of short-term therapy, but it does not provide a long-term solution to a restrictive personality. However, at this stage, there is often a marked rise in the client's energy and effectiveness in family and social interactions.

The immediate relief of the first phase of therapy is usually associated with the partial decontamination and improved expression of one or more neural-emotional complexes (sex, aggression, sadness, speech, thought). Long-term therapy systematically works with each and every complex (as they are triggered by environmental encounters) to improve perception and expression, thus significantly increasing accuracy of perception, immediacy of emotional expression, and overall energetic reserves.

The next phase of long-term therapy is the recovery and expression of the client's repressed psychological history in the form of emotions and memories; up to this point, these emotions have been producing symptoms. These emotions and memories are repressed due to historical trauma and the psychological rigidity associated with childhood discipline. When these emotions and memories become activated, the client's symptom profile also becomes activated. Social disapproval, in all forms (family, friends, co-workers), conspires to encourage the client to re-repress these emotional components and to further tolerate the symptoms associated with his or her repression.

Although the client begins to benefit from expressing himself more effectively, it triggers anticipatory anxiety concerning the negative consequences of past experiments with this emotional expression. The anxiety triggers an instinctual response to repress this new behavior and resist the therapeutic progress. Much of therapy deals with resolving this resistance. Our clients are working against their greater good out of fear of punishment, rejection, or isolation. In the end, insight, new behaviors, and the transformation of resistance into expressive emotion provide a much more flexible, expressive, and energetic personality system.

Since awareness is simply using personality to interact with the world, an excessively restrictive personality, although facilitating survival in childhood, confines awareness to an energetically, perceptually, and emotionally deficient prison. Long-term therapy provides the opportunity for the individual to do the difficult emotional, intellectual, memory, and expressive work required for a more functioning psychological system.

Ten Therapeutic Goals of Long-Term Therapy

1. *Develop the ability for neutral self-analysis:* A major aspect of mental health is the capacity to critique one's behavior without being hypercritical. This requires the formation of the neutral observer as a part of the psychological system. There is a significant difference between the criticism of a punitive personality and the healthy evaluation of an evolving psychological system.

2. *Resolve developmental issues:* Our childhoods are filled with blessings and curses. The strengths of our family are passed on to us through wisdom, modeling, creativity, humor, and joy, which support us throughout our lives. However, the punitive aspect of childhood, or the psychological blind-spots that our parents never corrected in themselves and passed on to us, are imbedded in our bodies; blocked emotions, faded memories, stress, anxiety, fear, prejudice, paranoia, and other equally destructive perspectives all lurk in our unconscious, waiting to be activated repeatedly as we live life. In the therapeutic process, we dedicate ourselves to clarity of vision, emotional equilibrium, and connectedness to the greater world around us.

3. *Spontaneously and fluidly express emotions in proportion to the moment:* This is as spectacularly difficult as it is spectacularly easy. Speak the truth, be genuine, be honest, don't hold back, and respect the right of others to have the same privileges. Emotion is energy and information. Emotion that is restricted by the personality in order to protect us against anticipated (and remembered) threats reduces the information and energy available to live full, creative lives.

4. *Accurately perceive the world:* Reality is reality; however, we see what we have been taught to see, selectively filtering out that which does not conform to our expectations. Since we are taught as children to perceive certain aspects of reality and to ignore other aspects, we become adults who create our own reality by ignoring huge amounts of information. What we experience in life is based on the information available to us, but due to our social and family psychological filters, we simply don't perceive all the information available. Perception is biased toward expectations. If you have been trained to expect fear and suffering, you will surely find it. The same goes with joy and happiness. Instead of narrowing the field of experience to fit the phenomena we have been trained and expect to encounter, we can be aided in opening our awareness to the vast brilliance of the universe.

5. *Respond to the world verbally with spontaneity:* This means simply to verbally express the emotions that arise in response to the world. The unconscious is a mirror that reflects the emotion, information, and energy of the moment. So, it automatically produces a response to any experience we encounter as we walk through life. The personality (which operates like a finishing school) is continuously in conflict with the unconscious. This conflict produces all the psychological symptoms that drive us crazy on a daily basis. The less we restrict our spontaneous response to the world, the greater our love of life and self. For an experiment, try allowing whatever you want to say to come out of your mouth. It immediately changes our perspective of the world; however, most people become nervous just considering doing this.

6. *Reduce self-destructive behaviors:* Self-destructive behaviors serve several purposes. They release repressed emotional energy, allow the individual to dissociate from psychological distress, numb the body to emotional frustration, and provide distraction from painful developmental history. Most self-destructive behaviors are the result of an overly restrictive personality combined with childhood neglect and abuse. Identifying those emotional wounds from the past and confronting those responsible will reduce the psycholog-

ical pressure that fuels acting out. Ultimately, it is the continuous expression of all of our emotions that provides the feelings of equilibrium and balance.

7. *Significantly improve physical health:* Since psychological health is directly related to physical health, long-term psychotherapy needs to inspire and incorporate a health regimen. During childhood, we adopt a variety of control strategies for our bodily functions that produce discomfort and stress. Psychological health seeks to align with these functions rather than oppose and control them. In adulthood, taking care of the body and aligning with the natural rhythms of the body are crucial to physical health. Since personality not only restricts the expression of the self, it restricts the expression of the body (as noted earlier, symptomology can easily translate into respiratory, digestive, and reproductive disorders); learning to cooperate with the rhythms of the body is fundamental to psychological health.

8. *Establish healthy adult relationships:* Most relationships are contaminated by our childhood developmental interruptions. It is very common to have distorted and unreasonable expectations of our partners and friends based on original family relationship styles. Curiously, our relationship with our selves is often a template for our relationship with others. We rarely treat others better than we treat ourselves, and much of therapy is learning to treat ourselves with respect and love.

9. *Find a meaningful sense of purpose in life:* The adult psyche naturally goes through a series of transformations based on age and accomplishment. From Maslow's point of view, as we successfully negotiate life's challenges, we naturally evolve to higher and higher levels of self-actualization. We begin to abandon the fear that life is random and chaotic, simply because we begin to understand how to live a life of purpose.

10. *Evolve a vital spiritual life:* With a sense of purpose comes a sense of interconnectedness, a growing feeling of common interest and relationship with other living creatures. Jung suggested that the human psyche is actually an extension of, and relates to, the collective consciousness of which all living creatures are a part. This perspective is the foundation for most religions and spiritual practices. A spiritual life involves serving principles greater than one's self, an understanding of one's responsibility to the world and its citizens, inclusiveness rather than exclusiveness, the ability to still or quiet one's mind, a respect for life, and the capacity to link with others through compassion and empathy.

The Eye of the Hurricane

During the course of therapy, the therapist is continually exposed to the psychological storm and the calm that the client is emotionally negotiating. If we are empathetic, we actually feel what the client feels. However, the therapist should be capable of stabilizing his or her own emotions so that they are appropriate to the situation, and ultimately, translate the feelings into information. Remember, feeling is ultimately information and energy. If the therapist resists the client's feelings during therapy, the therapist will finish the session exhausted and drained, not by the client's emotions, but by the therapist's resistance to his or her own emotional response. This is counter-transference and is predictably the source of most clinical burnout. Every emotion is potentially energetic for the client and the therapist. This means that even the strongest emotional events can be extraordinarily energetic. As long as the therapist is comfortable with his or her own feelings, energy is the result. To accomplish this, the therapist needs to establish his role in the therapy as the neutral observer, filled with curiosity and courage. I call it "sitting in the eye of the hurricane," to be *of* the storm, but not *in* the storm. This can be very difficult to sustain; just like real hurricanes, the eye of the storm is a continually moving location. The therapist must possess flexibility of perception and expression in order to sustain the calm center and still be able to engage and catalyze the therapeutic process. As soon as the therapist becomes rigid, s/he becomes compromised by the emotional storm.

During the natural course of therapy, clients are continually, and I mean continually, calling the therapist into the storm. In mythological terms, these emotional refugees of their family's battlefields call to the therapist to save them, fulfill their needs, bind their wounds, express their feelings, or do their thinking, luring the therapist toward the therapeutic rocks of the well-intentioned but misguided counselor. As soon as the therapist sees the client as a victim, all is lost.

By the time we reach adulthood, the life of the victim is an indirect but effective type of power and control. If we see our clients as victims, we have been compromised and/or manipulated. Wisdom is the knowledge that helplessness is a form of power and manipulation, and it is a wisdom that is hard to achieve. Sitting in the eye of the hurricane provides wisdom, energy, and a long life. Once this neutral observer is in place, therapy can proceed. The discipline of neutral self-observation will need to be revisited as awareness explores the various introjects of the psyche. Each introject will evoke harsh self-criticism as preliminary engagement occurs. Self-blame is a phenomenally successful defense against criticizing our family. The therapy will need to neutralize the harsh effects of dissociated emotions in order to permit integration of the information and energy.

TREATMENT: THE FUNDAMENTALS OF CLINICAL PSYCHOTHERAPY

Psychotherapy follows a fairly predictable path: (1) assessment, (2) diagnosis, (3) transference, (4) analysis, (5) strategy, (6) resistance, (7) progress, and (8) results.

ASSESSMENT

The initial contact with the client sets up the dynamics for the rest of therapy. Carl Jung believed that the first significant dream after initial contact is a comment by the unconscious as to the course the therapy will take. The assessment needs to be thorough in order to be accurate and effective. When beginning the course of treatment, it is important to get a client's medical, developmental, and emotional histories in order to determine the course of therapy. Although all clients are motivated by a set of symptoms, there are always several contributing variables that will predict both outcome and length of therapy. The emotional and situational material that the client is willing to present at the beginning of therapy, although significant, may actually vary considerably from the emotions, memories, and circumstances that eventually become the focus of the therapeutic work.

The initial therapeutic complaint, although very important, should be considered the "presenting problem" and is often a symptom of a much more complex problem concerning personality rigidity and self-expression.

As curious as it sounds, what the client *can* talk about and what the client *needs to* talk about are often different (but associated). For example, if I am unable to express anger, I may discuss feeling undervalued at work or at home without realizing the emotional connection between how I express my feelings and the conflicts in my life. In the beginning, the client is rarely expressing what is really bothering him or her. Instead, s/he is describing the symptoms of the problem. It is the job of the therapist, when developing a diagnosis and therapeutic strategy, to differentiate between the social triggers, the health issues, the developmental obstacles, and repressed self-expression.

To this end, there are four major areas of analysis that determine diagnosis and treatment strategy: environmental pressures, medical history, historical trauma, and repressed self-expression.

1. *Environmental pressures (transition phase failure):* Environmental pressures are situational forces associated with the current difficulties in your client's life. This category is best defined as transition phase stressors. The human psyche thrives on environmental stability, and any change to living patterns is experienced as an emotional stressor. This dynamic is clearly explained in Kenneth Pelletier's famous book on stress and health, *Mind as Healer, Mind as Slayer.* A complement to this theory is the *Holmes and Rahe Stress Scale,* which gives a numerical value to a variety of complex and challenging life-changing situations. The underlying theory is that health changes can be linked to stress levels.

   It is important to gather all of the data concerning the current stressors affecting the client's emotional welfare. The pressures from the environment combined with the repressed contents of the unconscious create the symptoms, but also provide motivation. Motivation will eventually determine how many of the therapeutic goals will be accomplished.

   Typically, there are very specific external motivating factors: marriage, employment, family, health, finances, or other transitional events. This motivation becomes the working energy of the therapy. There are two basic stages of motivation. Stage One is short-term therapy, externally driven, and motivated by desperation and the desire for relief. The goal of this type of therapy is to reduce suffering and symptomology, usually through problem solving, skill-set improvement, insight, and action/expression. The client simply wants to feel better but is not too concerned with, or aware of, the need for real psychological change. Thus, as the treatment moves forward and the client responds to the world in a more authentic manner, the contributing environmental pressures usually begin to subside, as does the client's motivation. In this first stage, desperation is the drive for relief, whereas in stage two, curiosity is the drive for transformation. Stage Two is long-term therapy, internally driven, and motivated by the desire to transform overall psychological functioning. This type of therapy requires the client to awaken and develop three critical psychological traits: curiosity, courage, and commitment. Most clients are comfortable with their life-long symptoms, so *curiosity* becomes the single most important psychological quality in moving long-term, transformative therapy forward. In addition, because the client (like all of us) has been trained to fear the consequences of self-activation and emotional expression, *courage* becomes the second quality required in long-term therapy. Therapy takes bravery. And finally, *commitment* is the final quality needed for the client to complete psychological evolution. Therapy is difficult, and commitment is required to overcome the various obstacles along the path. The final realization of long-term therapy is the recognition that psychological transformation is a life-long task and not just something to survive in order to feel better.

2. *Medical History, Disease, and Physical Health:* The client's medical history is a significant area of importance. Of concern are two elements: (1) the early medical traumas suffered as a child that can contribute to developmental interruption, regressive behavior, organ trauma, dissociative defenses, separation anxiety, and other trauma-based symptoms, and (2) current medical challenges. There are several major medical problems that mimic psychological problems. Affective disorders are typically multi-symptomatic: sleep problems, concentration problems, obsessive/compulsive features, post-traumatic stress disorder, ADD/ADHD features. Addiction issues, including sexually addictive behavior (affairs, impulsivity, pornography), gambling, alcohol, drugs, and prescription medications, are another problem. To further complicate this diagnostic criteria, issues concerning sleep patterns, hormone imbalances, thyroid, diabetes, hypertension, weight, eating patterns, and many other serious medical concerns are presented as contributing factors in the client's symptom profile.

The client's physical health will determine how much therapy can be accomplished, the amount of time that the therapeutic work takes, and the overall quality of the work. The energetic needs of the body directly compete or complement the energetic needs of the psyche. At a very fundamental level, insight requires energy. Additionally, any medications involved in treating any medical condition can drastically affect the client's ability to concentrate or even actively participate in the course of therapy. Medications for anxiety, pain, concentration, obsession, depression, or mania can either be helpful or completely undermine the client's functioning. Over the years of treating bi-polar clients, I have found four categories of drugs that can trigger mania or self-destructive behavior very quickly: anesthetics (commonly used in surgery and some dental work), alcohol in excess, opiate-based/mimic pain medications, and muscle relaxers (often prescribed for injured athletes and for some general muscle tension).

Inappropriate use of Benzodiazepines certainly falls into this category, with the exception of Clonazepam (Klonopin), which seems to have some long-term benefit when prescribed and taken responsibly. Here are three medically based challenges to therapy.

a. Drug Use: Obviously, if a client has a drug abuse problem, the therapy is almost always required to treat the chemical dependence first. Psychotherapy requires, at a very basic level, the activation and promotion of neural pathways that will be the bio-structural pathway for new behaviors and insights. The habitual use of any drugs that promote chemical dissociation undermine successful reprogramming of pathological neural pathways. Dr. Earnest Rossi suggested, in his lectures at the Milton Erickson Institute's Evolution of Psychotherapy Conference (the single largest continuing education conference in the world, occurring every four to five years, usually in Los Angeles), that the nervous system requires four weeks to activate a pattern, and sixteen weeks to secure the neural pattern that personality will use for new behavior and self-expression. Thus, with an active addict, the work never produces lasting change due to the continual neural compromise. Thus, every session with an active addict becomes the first session, over and over. The work never produces lasting change due to the neural compromise.

b. Pregnancy: Babies compete for all the energetic reserves of the mother. This is no big surprise. But it should inform the intensity and baseline functioning expectations of the therapy.

c. Post-traumatic Stress Disorder: PTSD is a specific form of neural trauma. Developmental interruptions have neurological consequences that lead to symptomatic patterned behavior, but PTSD is specific to a level of extreme shock to which the nervous system has been exposed. In most cases, this is life-threatening exposure, and in some cases, it is repeated life-threatening and extreme exposure: combat, disease, near-death illness or accident, or even, in some cases, adoption (severe bonding disruption). These neurological traumas simply require a great deal of energetic attention, treatment, and patience. The psychological challenge of this type of therapy is differentiating between the biological and psychological contributing features. Treatment becomes a question of priorities. A veteran, for example, may be dealing with PTSD, a DSM Axis 2 personality disorder, a marital conflict, an employment challenge, and a drug dependency issue, each contributing to the overall chaos in his or her life. Treatment may vary between a strategy of healing the neural trauma, working on this client's expressive dynamics, and simultaneously addressing the conflicted nature of the marriage. These are challenging therapies in that the body is simply competing for a limited amount of energy in the psychological system, and personal growth often takes a back seat to physical trauma.

I cannot stress enough the importance of medical, psychiatric, and chiropractic specialists, physical and massage therapists, exercise and nutrition experts, yoga, dance, and martial arts specialists, and whole health practitioners as allies in the diagnosis and treatment of your client. Know and create alliances with the professionals in your local health community. They will be invaluable in providing the comprehensive care your client deserves. (Know a few good attorneys and the local city/county prosecutor as well.)

3. *Historical Trauma (developmental phase interruption):* For any practitioner of long-term therapy, this is the area of significant importance. The client's developmental history will unfold over the course of therapy, particularly when they get to the phase of interviewing family members for stories, memories, family relocations, financial challenges, health crisis, separations, divorce, affairs, deaths, adoption, and other significant events that would have affected the emotional experiences of childhood. As explored earlier, developmental trauma includes both direct trauma (punishment/discipline, loss of a parent, health issues, abuse, abandonment, assault, abuse of or by siblings, etc.) and exposure trauma (family conflict, drug and alcoholism in the family, financial stress, marital fights, threats, rage, or threatening behavior, etc.). These two types of trauma will be part of the memories and emotions affecting function of the neural-emotional complexes. The developmental disruptions of childhood lead to the formation of dysfunctional personality structure and chaotic emotional expression patterns. Again, these developmental interruptions are what set both the threshold of perception and the threshold of expression, producing perceptual distortions and emotional symptomology.

4. *Repressed Self-Expression:* This part of the interview is the initial exploration of the expression and repression of each of the five neural-emotional complexes: thought, speech, sadness, anger, and sexuality. It is the function of these five complexes that regulate emotion, energy, information, and symptoms. This is ground zero of therapeutic work. The ability of the client to casually, or stressfully, discuss how he or she perceives the world

as well as express himself or herself in each of these five areas will reveal the work needing to be done.

Although there are certainly normal social inhibitions around casually discussing sexuality, for example, the client should be able to reveal his or her attitude towards sexual self-expression and the current interpersonal relationships in which this activity may exist. The significant information is contained in the underlying attitude that the client has about his or her sexuality, anger, or thinking ability. Improving emotional expressiveness is important in the therapeutic process, but changing one's attitude towards the expression is equally important. Overcoming one's expressive bias and the rational for that bias is a significant goal.

DIAGNOSIS

Diagnosis determines the course of therapy and the strategies that would be most effective. The success of therapy is directly dependent on accurate diagnosis. Diagnosis is one the great challenges facing today's practitioner. Although there is tacit agreement to use the DSM-V diagnostic system, it is, in fact, antiquated and essentially assembled by committee. It is literally a checklist collection of symptom-based personality profiles. Professionals are required to match the client's symptom profile with a checklist of possible symptoms and to diagnose personality disorders based upon the dominant symptoms.

The symptom diagnostic model has acquired some strong traction in the medical community, but is proving to be inaccurate and ineffective in treating personality disorders. Too many of the common psychological symptoms are shared by too many of the personality disorders, thus leading to confusion in diagnosis and failure in treatment. The single most egregious example of this is the DSM diagnosis of borderline personality disorder. The set of symptoms assigned to this treatment-resistant diagnosis is impossibly broad and results in contamination of the treatment. (See chapter 3, "Personality Structure," *The Borderline Diagnosis*.)

A transference-based diagnostic model, as proposed by Dr. James Masterson, is proving much more effective in identifying fundamental personality structures. This model, based on self-psychology and object relations theory, states simply that the quality, style, and expectations of personal relationships are a much more accurate indicator of personality structure.

While the transference-based diagnostic model works optimally in clinical treatment, it is the symptom model upon which the third party payment system is fundamentally based. Every psychological practitioner needs to be well versed in the DSM-V diagnostic system in order to be able to converse with other professionals in a common language and, ultimately, to be paid for services.

TRANSFERENCE

It is reported that Freud once asked Jung, "What is the alpha and omega of psychoanalysis?" to which Jung answered, "The transference!" Fundamentally, the term *transference* is the overall term used to describe specific styles of therapeutic relationships. Each personality structure obeys predictable rules of expectation, self-expression, and symptomology. As the client develops a transference with the therapist, the relationship begins to follow a predictable arc of interaction, usually with an activation of the client's unconscious psychological potentialities (sexuality, love, compassion, aggression, intellectual stimulation, fascination, infatuation) and an increase in psychological energy in the sessions. All transference relationships evolve during the course of the therapy. After the initial therapeutic agreement (*we can get along and work together*), and after the first positive rush of unconscious contents, the therapeutic relationship begins to activate emotional material that has been censored, perceptually and/or expressively, by the client's personality structure. At this juncture, there is an increase in anxiety and resistance to the process, and the transference becomes resistant and somewhat adversarial, due to a fear of expressive consequences. This unconscious fear must be identified emotionally and historically, which will then allow emotions to be differentiated from each other (sadness, anger, thought, sexuality) and also separated from their historical source and current trigger. This frees up the client to realign with the therapist and proceed to the next emotional obstacle. It really is like defusing a bomb that someone else placed in the client's unconscious that potentially, and occasionally, goes off in the therapist's face.

Transference-based therapy identifies the unconscious expectations of the client in relationship to the therapist and attempts to place them back into their historical context.

All therapies are ultimately transference dependent, due to the need for a therapeutic alliance in order for the client to trust the therapist, but *in short-term or strategic therapies*, there is little interest in processing the quality of the transference and instead, the therapies direct the client's motivation to expanding perceptual and expressive options. In long-term therapy, it is not unusual for the client to become strongly identified with the complexes of the unconscious, reliving failed hopes, punitive expectations, glorious and furious passions, and empowered self-realization. Short-term therapy tries to avoid these relationship complications by limiting the therapy to problem solving, reframing, and moderate insight work.

The therapeutic transference relationship is based on a combination of a rigid personality structure combined with the contents of the unconscious, both positive potentials and painful emotions. These two components shape the client's (everyone's) relationship style. This relationship style reveals the personality structure, which we diagnose, and is the core of the transference. A variety of types of transferences are described in psychological literature. The system that I prefer recognizes six basic transference types: merging, mirroring, idealizing, erotic, adversarial, and strategic. Except for the strategic transference (Asperger's), these types of transference are associated with the child's developmental stages, with each type of transference representing a step in the development of consciousness. In each developmental stage, awareness is mediated by a maturing nervous system, and the child's identity evolves from a non-differentiated, *merged* identity, to a more conscious *mirroring* of identity/behavior, to an even more conscious *idealizing* of external identity, to the clearly more complex, but not necessarily more stable, *erotic* transference. The erotic transference can be attached to mirroring or idealizing and thus provides an additional charge to the transference. The *adversarial* transference can occur at any stage of development or type of transference.

The *strategic* transference is associated with Asperger's and some forms of psychopathic operating systems. These clients often have an inventory of styles of relating, learned from mimicking significant people in their lives and applied with varying levels of success. These clients often come to therapy because their relationship strategies are no longer working.

Therapy will produce a variety of transferences during the course of treatment. Each of the neural-emotional sub-complexes (sub-personalities) is capable of its own unique transference capacity. For example, empathy may be highly differentiated and autonomous, while intellect may still be operating from a merging/shared function. Each of the five neural-emotional centers will have its own transference dynamic; thus, each complex in the client's unconscious wants to negotiate its own unique contract with the therapist.

Imagine a baby-sitter arriving at a home with five children. There may be a general agreement about how everyone should act, but the sitter will have to negotiate a behavioral contract with each of the children. Thus, the therapeutic strategy that worked effectively at one point in therapy becomes ineffective at another. Integration has occurred when there is simultaneous, mutual influence of all of the emotional functions: a shared voice. For example, empathy needs to be connected to thought, courage, speech, and passion. And sexuality needs to be connected to thought, love, courage, and speech. Ultimately, integration is the intercommunication of each of the five neural-emotional centers with each other.

Therapy begins with the initial transference that arises as the relationship builds momentum. Regardless of complexity, it is this initial transference that reveals specific personality structure and guides diagnosis and treatment strategy. Here are the six basic transferences:

1. *Merging* is strongly associated with the dependent personality in which the client, repressing most self-activation and autonomous behavior, passively cooperates with any dominant personality. In the therapy office, this client expects the therapist to direct therapy, presents a shallow motivation to examine psychological material, is passive, and becomes anxious when attempting to self-activate. The client will attempt to *merge* with the therapist's psychological functions (using the therapist's thoughts and communication in place of his or her own) and becomes frustrated and anxious, as the therapist requires the client to self-express. This is the dominant transference for the dependent-borderline personality.

2. *Mirroring* transference is represented by the client's mimicking of the therapists ideals, lifestyle, career choice, education, hobbies, etc., but in general is an attempt by the client to incorporate aspects of the therapist's psyche in order to raise his or her own psychological functioning. There is less differentiation with mirroring than idealizing. Children want to become mommy and daddy, not just be like them. Mirroring follows merging in that there is separation of function, but not an external separation of the idealized self.

3. *Idealizing* transference is hero worship. It is the process by which we identify qualities in others that are strongly appealing or even activating our own psychological potentials. Idealizing recognizes the separate "other" but seeks relationship in order to stimulate self-expression. We want to be like them.

4. *Erotic* transference is an idealized transference with a strong sexual component. One of the complex challenges of the erotic transference is the possessive nature of the attraction. It is often associated with the "completion fantasy" common to all

newly awakened lovers, in which the idealized other is all that is needed for psychological satisfaction. As with any awakened psychological function, the challenge for the client is to apply this feature in his or her daily life and not remain "stuck" in the clinical infatuation with an unobtainable object/subject. When the erotic transference is confronted, prepare for helplessness (merging) or anger (adversarial).

5. *Adversarial* transference has three significantly different presentations. The natural adversarial transference occurs when the client begins to test his or her dependency on and independence from the therapist. Part of the success of any therapy is manifested in the client's capacity to support him/herself internally and not need to submit habitually to the perceived authority of the therapist. During the adversarial transference, the client will begin to challenge the therapist in a variety of ways (usually attended by high anxiety at the risk of losing the relationship). The second type of adversarial transference occurs when the therapist "screws up," engaging a poorly timed confrontation or providing an insight that offends the client. The adversarial transference arises in natural response to a clumsy or insulting emotional interaction. These are the situations in which the therapist gets to model apologetic behavior and demonstrate relationship repair. The third type of adversarial transference is the anti-social transference. Since the anti-social personality anticipates being abused by those who demonstrate kindness or compassion, the adversarial transference is a defense mechanism designed to promote emotional distancing. The adversarial transference, in this case, is diagnostic, whereas in the previous two transference challenges, the adversarial transference is associated with process, not the basic personality structure.

6. *Strategic* transference is high functioning Asperger's. Without the neural mirroring function (a possible theory), these neural-diverse clients approach the therapeutic relationship from a strategic position, studying the therapist in order to develop a working relationship strategy. These types of transferences take time to develop, as the client's motivation and his/her strategic personality inventory, based on intelligence and experience, is experimented with during the therapeutic consultations. Insight therapy has limited effectiveness in a strategic transference. Cognitive behavioral therapy, reframing, direct information, and other more explorative problem solving techniques can be very effective. I am convinced that the typical high-functioning Asperger's client is actually quite common.

Once the transference and the personality structure have been diagnosed, a therapeutic strategy directs the therapy. The transference tells the therapist how to relate to the client in order to create a therapeutic alliance. In this way, the client allows the therapist to participate in his / her examination of the unconscious material.

The therapist is operating as an external function of the client's personality, providing a broader point of view, emotional and expressive modeling, and a combination of support and confrontation to keep the therapeutic process moving forward.

In the course of the therapy, the contents of the client's unconscious become active and shape the quality and arc of the relationship. The therapist's role is to identify the relationship dynamics and unconscious emotional material that create such chaos in the life of the client. Any emotion that has been repressed by the client will become active in the therapy, often in an energized form of intense emotional feelings toward and about the therapist. This is also true of any significant relationship in the client's life.

The therapist must remain emotionally neutral so that the entire contents of the relationship, and certainly the conflictual aspects, are identified as emotional remnants of the client's relationship history.

As a result of the therapist remaining essentially neutral, the client is eventually able to recognize how his unconscious expectations affect every aspect of his life, leaving him feeling passive, powerless, victimized, and resentful, or infatuated, full of longing and hope, obsessed, or possessed. The activation of any strong emotion is often the indication that the unconscious is shaping our perception of and reaction to certain situations and people in our environment. Our restricted perception of the world is charged with familiar relationships and emotional predictability, regardless of whether the relationships are helpful or the emotional expression is effective. We are expectantly experiencing a portion of reality: a portion of reality that is disappointingly predictable.

Reality unfolds and expands over the course of one's lifetime, partially limited by neurological capacity, but more certainly limited by personality structure. It is the personality structure that determines how much of reality we have been taught to perceive, how that perception is to be interpreted, the emotional response that is permitted, and the symptoms that will replace any emotions that are repressed.

Any information or experience that does not fit the rules of personality is repressed into the unconscious, creating pressure and symptoms. We don't create reality or falsify reality; rather, we condense reality from a nearly infinite amount of experiential data into a narrow bandwidth of expectations. Certain aspects of reality become super-charged by the contents of the unconscious, standing out in their attractive factor, whether pleasing or threatening. We are unconsciously attracted to people and situations that will activate the contents of the unconscious, providing yet another opportunity to psychologically evolve. We don't even realize that the reality we are aware of is filled predominantly with unconsciously charged objects. These charged contents attract our attention more than the rest of reality. The projected contents of the unconscious energize our attention toward certain people, objects, places, events, situations, books, movies, and music. These energized elements are attractive because they resonate with the contents of our unconscious and provide an opportunity to express and integrate repressed psychological material. As we become more adept at perceiving these energetic opportunities in the world, we begin to work with the emerging unconscious contents as they shape relationships and provide for creative self-expression. Initially, the contents of the unconscious are required to build up a significant charge before we become aware of their representation in the external world, but eventually, as we lower the energetic thresholds needed to perceive these attractors, we begin to identify even subtly charged unconscious material reflected in the mirror of reality.

The transference is essentially the energized attraction of and to the projected contents of the unconscious.

In medicine, the transference is the foundation of the placebo response. Common to all forms of sympathetic magic, if a person believes something will work, there is a higher incidence of success in achieving that goal. In an article in *American Indian Art*, a psychiatrist is reported to have asked a Navajo *Singer/Hataali* (shaman/healer) what he thought was the reason for his success with his patients. After a lengthy explanation of the healing process, the *Singer* looked at the psychiatrist and said, "If my patients believe in me, they get better."

This is the nature of transference. It will determine the diagnosis, therapeutic technique, therapeutic alliance, motivation, and psychological contents of long-term therapy. The transference is simply one of the symptoms of the repressed-dissociated contents of the unconscious. A strong transference indicates the quantity and intensity of the emotional content imprisoned in the unconscious. The therapeutic alliance will be tested with all the unconscious material. What starts out as an idealizing or "cooperative" merging transference inevitably becomes adversarial, as the resentment underlying the repressed contents comes to the surface. The transference will systematically reveal the contents and emotions of the unconscious that produce psychological symptoms. It is this very energy, produced by the repressed contents, in conflict with the client's psychological design potential, which presses the personality to adopt a more flexible, accepting, expressive, and stable structure, or suffer the consequences when resisted.

Resistance produces psychological suffering. Resistance is produced by fear, resulting from punitive behavioral training as a child or catastrophic trauma. As fear is transformed into curiosity and courage, the resistance to emotional activation is significantly reduced, releasing all the energies associated with emotional immediacy, perceptual accuracy, and creative expression. As the client's energy and expectations become grounded in reality rather than memory, the additional energies, previously powering the psychological defenses, migrate to the creative enterprises of the individual's psyche, thus motivating the client toward his or her creative destiny.

The chaos attending the transference is simply a lifetime of resisting psychological activation and suppressing emotional growth, unfolding in twenty-four months.

ANALYSIS

The analysis of the personality structure concerns the evaluation of the function of the client's five neural-emotional complexes in terms of his or her perceptual accuracy and emotional immediacy. Although symptom diagnosis is fundamentally flawed in determining personality structure, symptom analysis has significant purpose in a psychodynamic system that views symptoms as the tip of the iceberg, pointing to the underlying problem. Again, the symptom is not the problem; it is the solution to the problem. The symptom is the result of the indirect expression of the energy behind a blocked emotion.

Any blocked emotion or thought is capable of energizing any of the symptoms in the symptom profile. No experienced professional would state that anxiety is always the result of repressed sexuality or blocked aggression. We all know that anxiety can be produced by a wide variety of factors. However, in psychodynamics, as opposed to bio-dynamics, it is the overly restrictive personality structure that fuels the symptom profile. Thus, the analysis portion of treatment involves specific evaluation of the function of each of the five neural-emotional complexes to determine which complexes are energizing the symptoms.

As explored in chapter 4, each neural-emotional site has two specific functions: the threshold of perception and the threshold of expression. Analysis is the discerning of the type and location of perceptual distortion and emotional restriction.

STRATEGY AND TECHNIQUE

Chapter 9 is dedicated to this subject. Strategy and technique are the heart of the therapeutic work and need to be linked to the specific diagnosis.

RESISTANCE

One of the big questions in therapy is: Why would someone resist getting better? When we observe client behavior, there is clear evidence that the client is acting in ways that undermine his or her health, financial stability, relationships, and other central aspects of life. Even when given practical advice, the client sabotages the implementation of this advice. Resistance is the heart of psychotherapy, and it is governed by the Activation-Resistance Cycle (discussed later in this chapter).

What makes human beings therapeutically complicated is resistance to psychological repair and evolution. Resistance is the automatic psychological defense mechanism triggered when emotions and memories that have been internally prohibited are activated. The building of personality takes place over years of behavior modification at the hands of our environment. We learn to tolerate the anxieties and fears associated with emotional repression in order to protect ourselves from punitive social enforcement. We become experts at managing our environment through selective self-expression and "ignoring" the offensive or insensitive aspects of our family and world. Every time an emotion that was forbidden is triggered, the substitute symptom is activated instead. Instead of thought, speech, sadness, anger, or sexuality, we experience anxiety, tension, stress, guilt, shame, fear, resentment, worry, depression, somatization, or grief.

Emotion and perceptual information are directly related. As we limit our emotions, we limit the accuracy of our perception of the world. Every one of us lives life with part of reality blocked from awareness. Our bodies contain the missing information, but the personality structure restricts access to it, and instead, we only feel symptoms from the dissociated parts of the body holding the information. Any attempt by awareness to retrieve this inventory of information, emotion, events, and experiences immediately triggers our symptom profile. This is why therapy triggers resistance when simple questions about the family experience are explored. The client suddenly becomes quiet, stumbles in an attempt at description, becomes "fuzzy," claims a lack of memory, or simply says "I don't know." (The reframe I use when the client answers, "I don't know," too frequently, is to respond, "The phrase 'I don't know' is not allowed in therapy. However, you may use the phrase 'I'm not going to tell you' in its place.")

Our client will know that we are seeking information in this shadowy area of memory (personal unconscious) when he or she experiences anxiety, shame, guilt, or another symptom. If the client can overcome the fear of consequences, then the emotion, memory, and energy are spontaneously available. Suddenly the client "gets it," perceiving clearly the information that was once inaccessible. This is the moment of clarity and enlightenment, the *Aha!* experience. A bridge to the unconscious has been activated. Awareness has re-engaged with a part of the body from which it had been dissociated.

Dynamically, resistance is a fear-based response to the triggering of any restricted emotional response. The environment triggers an emotional response, and the personality immediately diverts that emotional expression into indirect forms of symptomatic expression. These symptoms are often viewed as emotions, which is not really accurate. We experience these symptoms as feelings, but feelings differ from emotion. Although these symptoms have a biochemical basis and are certainly "felt" or experienced, I cannot emphasize enough how important it is for the therapist and the client to know the difference between emotion, feeling, and symptom. As outlined in Chapter 1, a feeling is the result of any physical stimulation. Emotions are the specific expression of the five neural-emotional centers of awareness, and symptoms are the *sublimated, repressed, or dissociated* expressions of those emotions. Symptoms look like emotions, act like emotions, and are usually treated as emotions, but symptoms are the product of regulated emotions. There is a direct correlation between regulation of emotion and expression of symptom. *Both do not exist simultaneously.* The symptoms express the energy of the regulated emotion.

The client's symptom profile becomes his or her psychological "tell." Just as poker players observe the non-verbal behavior of their opponents to identify the subtle signals that give away their competitors' hidden cards, the psychotherapist identifies and explores the symptom profile of his or her clients to identify the underlying emotional blockage. Since symptoms are cyclical, surfacing, and disappearing, the therapist needs to identify the circumstances and emotional situations that trigger the client's symptoms. Identifying the external trigger, as well as the emotion(s) being blocked, will help with the diagnosis and treatment strategy.

The diagnostic analysis should include the following questions:
- What emotion would normally be appropriate to the situation?
- What circumstances/people trigger the block?
- What emotional expression increases perceptual accuracy?
- What emotional expression increases self-confidence?
- What emotional expression increases energy?

THE NEUTRAL OBSERVER

The neutral observer is crucial for the success of long-term therapy as well as most spiritual practices. Personality/ego is highly critical of the parts of self-expression that do not meet the perfectionistic goals set by the family and culture.

It is not uncommon that the main goal a client brings to therapy is the desire to change or even rid themselves of those "undesirable" parts of the psyche, whether those parts are physical or psychological. The ego/personality is a brutal master with little mercy or grace. A core value of this therapeutic system is the recognition of self-perfection and the acceptance of the wisdom of emotions and the body. To this end, awareness needs a platform from which to observe the function of the psyche, free from the critical evaluations that we learned in childhood. Thus, the neutral observer is the non-judgmental observer.

The Buddhists would claim that the neutral observer is a natural state of mind, resting in relaxed concentration, without any attachment to the phenomena of reality. This does require some effort, initially. The nervous system has been systematically programmed to translate reality and to react in familiar emotional patterns. This is simply behavior modification. Because the human body has a nearly infinite vibrational capacity, pattern behavior and pattern perception become the starting points for expanding and stabilizing our perception and response to the world. We are not trying to rid ourselves of any perspective or response; rather, we are seeking to expand our perceptual and expressive inventory to include all possibilities. To do this, one needs to be completely neutral about any particular perception or expression, thus allowing all behaviors to reside within one's psyche, without exclusion. This means that one begins to live in expectant anticipation of the creative potential of being human. And instead of forcing the world to fit a narrow set of expectations or to ruthlessly inhibit one's emotional responses, there is room for all phenomena and a variety of responses.

The neutral-observer is simply a "created" neural-emotional complex that provides personality-free perception, permitting self-observation and self-acceptance without inhibition or punishment. The activation and cultivation of the neutral-observer is critical to the success of any therapy. The neutral-observer establishes and resides in the eye of the collective psychic hurricane, which then allows participation in life without being swept away by the chaos of world.

Meditation is particularly helpful in solidifying the neutral observer. Since the repeating of any neural expression (practice makes perfect) lends itself to the creation and reinforcement of any new habit or talent, formal meditation is one of most effective methods of creating a new neutral core in the personality regulation system.

The early stages of long-term treatment should identify and track symptom expression. In spite of the client wanting immediate change, I do not recommend any attempt to correct the unwanted symptom at the beginning of therapy. The symptom plays an important role in releasing the energy of the blocked emotions. Any attempt to change the symptom will result in the creation of another symptom. Until the underlying blocked emotion is identified and expressed, *some* symptom will always be present. Furthermore, there is a fundamental unconscious resistance to change built into the structure of the personality. At the beginning of therapy, in spite of "good effort" by the client, most attempts to change behavior for the better bring eventual failure.

At the beginning of therapy, I strongly encourage my clients not to try to correct their behavior, but rather to observe it. This is a paradoxical approach to achieving mental health: to let the symptom of pathology exist in order to achieve the psychological goal.

The first step in symptom resolution is identifying the extent to which the symptom is being triggered. I use a particular technique I call "counting" (for obvious reasons). To help with the observation process, I have the client literally count how many times a particular symptom (psychological "tell") arises during the week between sessions. I'll use another layer of paradox on this assignment by suggesting that the symptom (self-accusation, negative self-talk, etc.) might show up as often as four or five times per day, to which the client universally exclaims, "Four or five times? How about forty or fifty times a day!?" Point made. This technique is both a paradoxical intervention and a conscious attempt to activate and energize the new neural pathways that become the foundation for the development in the client of the *neutral observer*.

Inappropriate and inaccurate self-criticism is a huge drain on energy, and it is always activated during insight work. The client will discover something significant about herself, and the critical inner voice will begin to pound, accusing the client of being stupid, of damaging her own children, or of wasting so much of her life, etc. The critical introject is a cruel and inaccurate inner commentator that ultimately needs to be repressed. We repress our creative potential; why not repress that nasty inner voice?

The intent of the strategic repression of negative self-talk helps the client gain mastery over his or her unconscious symptoms. One can apply will to most neurological function, even though we are ultimately attempting to free self-expression from the constraints of will. This transitional tactic of selective repression simply shows the client where the mental "brakes" are in his or her psychological architecture. Self-expression as a practiced discipline, and not just a spontaneous reaction, involves developing skill at "acceleration and braking." Although the final psychological product is akin to the T'ai Chi master who teaches "four ounces of pressure is all that it takes to move your opponent if you are pressing in the right place," the beginning stages of self-expression are more like learning to drive a stick-shift automobile: a lack of smoothness and a lot of concentration.

Healthy human beings exercise, engage in creative projects, expand the boundaries of their perception, think in fresh and innovative ways, practice compassion and love, pursue their passions and their sexual interests, feel comfortable with their competitive and courageous energies, and live a life that feeds them spiritually. Every one of these practices is a highly energetic experience. Since energy is the source of insight, creativity, truth, perceptual accuracy, and emotional expressiveness, overcoming the fundamental resistance to energetic experiences is the number one goal of therapy.

THE ACTIVATION-RESISTANCE CYCLE

This stage of therapy (resistance) focuses on working with the resistance to increase the client's energy. The biggest obstacle to increasing energy is that it triggers memory: memory of all the emotional losses, disappointments, heart-aches, childhood emotional wounds, and all of the un-expressed, unresolved emotional events of our lives. Every one of our emotional disappointments resides in our unconscious and is kept, in a manner, asleep (dissociated), by reducing the energy of the psyche to the point of depression. And when repression and dissociation begin to lose their powers to keep the sleeper unconscious, then we do drugs or create obsessive distractions to enforce staying "asleep."

When one's energy rises, the sleeper awakens. So, the client comes to therapy to wake up, but does everything possible to stay asleep, driven by fear of facing what was repressed, for good reason.

The underlying problem that fuels resistance is actually very simple. Every emotional wound that we have suffered in our lives, that we have not expressed or worked through, is stored in the body, producing symptoms as a byproduct of trapped emotional energy. The way we tolerate the symptoms of the repressed feelings is for awareness to dissociate from the parts of the body that contain the painful emotional experience. (See chapter 4, "Trauma Dynamics," *Dissociation*.) However, when we find ourselves energized by a new relationship or situation, our body is activated and many of the repressed emotions immediately begin to press awareness for release, right now! We experience the rush of these emotions initially as great joy (hope) or great anxiety (fear). Needless to say, we are drawn to the hope and try to avoid the fear. However, both sides of this experience emerge together: hope and fear, potential and memory.

The human psyche seeks environmental stability. A fixed point of view with predictable circumstances provides a constant and specific flow of energy for the personality to utilize for daily functioning. Any change to that routine signals an increase in energy (stimulation/response) to and from the unconscious, which will then be expressed as either a spontaneous emotion or as a psychological symptom. Thus, those events with terrific bursts of energy—love, sex, drugs, moving to a new home, divorce, death, marriage, and so on—trigger powerful energetic responses. These responses will either be creative/energetic or symptomatic/anxious/depressive. The initial burst of energy, often experienced as joy, love, acceptance, or spiritual awakening, is always followed, at some point, by anxiety, fear, concern, or disappointment.

Transition experiences increase energy because they challenge the emotional boundaries of expression by introducing unpredictable emotional triggers. This energetic surge triggers emotional responses that personality then inhibits and transforms into symptoms, which then collapses one's energy, creating a moderate depression. This cycle is repeated on a moment-to-moment basis, sometimes lasting only a few moments (mood shift), but often lasting for days, weeks, or months (mild to moderate depression: dysthymia), depending on the importance of the circumstances, people involved, or amount of unconscious material activated. Blocked emotions that are repeatedly triggered can produce significant symptoms, and in particular, anxiety and depression: the two most commonly reported psychological symptoms. Our overall psychological energy is directly dependent on how often our repressed emotional history is activated and our emotional response is compromised by a repressive personality. This process is the Activation-Resistance Cycle (ARC).

THE ACTIVATION-RESISTANCE CYCLE©

Stimulation	=	Environmental Trigger
activates		activates
The Body	=	Emotional Response
activates		activates
Memory & Emotion	=	Unexpressed Emotional History
activates		activates
Resistance	=	Personality
activates		activates
Symptoms	=	Emotion into Symptom
which		and then
Reduces Energy	=	Energy is Diverted into Symptom

The Activation-Resistance Cycle is the psychodynamic centerpiece of all long-term psychotherapy. Masterson viewed *self-activation* as the trigger for *abandonment depression (fear and resistance)*, but I would describe abandonment depression as the depression that results from fear of retaliation associated with self-activation. The Activation-Resistance Cycle examines the series of dynamics that occur behind Masterson's abbreviated description of this complex cycle.

Most people are attracted to some sort of high-energy experience: love, spirituality, athletics, adventure, danger, fright, sex, etc. These situations all share the quality of triggering strong feelings and excitement and make us feel particularly alive (which then triggers self-activation in response). On a practical level, this means that our world can trigger many varieties of emotional responses, and any emotions that are restricted from expression (family rules) manifest as symptoms, not emotions, or at least not the appropriate emotions (sadness instead of anger).

Many of life's challenges and adventures activate those parts of the psyche that are dissociated: the disconnected, disavowed, repressed, and controlled emotions. The psyche's initial response to any attractive experience is rising pleasure and joy (fascination); the secondary response is the stimulation of the dissociated emotions; the third response is resistance (fighting the emotions/history stored in the neural-emotional complex); the fourth response is the creation of symptoms (redirection of repressed emotional expression); and the final response is the reduction of available energy.

All relationships follow this activation-resistance cycle. This phenomenon is explored in depth in chapter 15. It is the most common cause for couples seeking relationship counseling. We give our partners credit for making us feel good, and we hold them accountable for making us feel bad. Of course, neither of these beliefs is entirely true. What truly makes us feel good (energized) is freely expressing ourselves in response to our partners, particularly during the courtship phase. Dropping all inhibition produces an ecstatic moment (that we credit to the object of our desire). But the energy of ecstasy triggers the remembered fear of previous disappointment and loss, which triggers caution, inhibition, and symptoms (to keep us safe).

There are three possibilities for fixing this problem: (1) abandon all fear and live with emotional freedom (rare), (2) develop curiosity and courage (this involves remembering our emotional history that is contaminating this moment, separating the emotions of the past from the present), or (3) create unconscious conflicts with our significant other (cyclical fighting) that provokes emotional distance and compromises the very intimacy triggering our fears. It is safe to say that most people prefer number three, the conflict/fighting solution.

Through conflict, we increase the amount of personal space around us by either isolating ourselves or driving the other person further away, reducing the energetic threat of intimacy.

The truly tragic aspect of human relationships is that too much intimacy will trigger our fears, but too much distance does the same. We need our loved ones close, but not too close, and not too far away, either. The intersection of two people's personal space is often a very narrow corridor in which intimacy, love, and peace take root. Anything more or less triggers the ARC, and chaos. Unfortunately, that emotional comfort zone, the eye of the hurricane (so to speak), that piece of relationship ground that is clear of the underlying emotional storm, is constantly moving. If either member of the relationship refuses to grow (keep moving), the storm eventually swallows them up.

When we speak of each person's need for personal space, we are euphe-mistically referring to the emotional and physical distance required to prevent triggering the ARC. It is the space needed to sustain our emotional comfort level. The ARC is triggered by both closeness and distance. Any experience that penetrates our personal space triggers the ARC, and withdrawing or loss does the same.

PROGRESS

One of the psychological rules that I use in therapy is that *truth has energy*. In the process of self-criticism or external evaluation of events, there are many possible interpretations of the world and self. In fact, cognitive behavioral therapy is founded on the principle that there are multiple points of view to be considered in resolving psychological conflict. I believe this to be true. However, reality is reality, and we are not just searching for some clever or seductive description of reality; we are searching for *reality*: accuracy of perception.

Malcolm Gladwell, in his brilliant book, *Blink*, describes the process by which awareness abandons its intuitive truth of reality and proceeds to embrace a distortion of reality, based on partial truths and filtered "facts." The result is chaos, confusion, and in some cases, catastrophe. Gladwell makes a strong case for our natural ability to instantaneously "know" the truth, thus perceiving reality clearly, only to have it over-whelmed by doubt and fear and replaced by a hallucination of the world. What I love about Gladwell's position is his conviction that we are designed to perceive the world accurately, and it happens in a flash, a blink.

If our point of view is distorted, and our emotional responses are blunted, we will be predictably depressed. When therapy is working effectively, the cli-ent will adopt a higher level of confidence in his or her perception of reality and begin to abandon the learned interpretations of reality that have failed to produce meaningful work, intimate relationships, or consistent health.

The question of how to measure progress in psychotherapy is widely debated. The early psychoanalysts understood that there is a sig-nificant difference between the symptoms of a psychological problem and the problem itself. As Freud so clearly stated, and I paraphrase, "If you successfully treat a symptom without addressing the underlying psychological conflict, the client will have to create another symptom to release the underlying energy of the psychological conflict." The symptom is not the problem: it is the solution to the problem. But, even as this fundamental truth celebrates over one hundred years of practice, most therapists simply do not understand this concept, nor do they apply it. We're still treating the symptoms. With pressure from insurance companies and other third party payers to provide quick solutions to the presenting psychological symptoms, we have adopted a "symptom relief" stance as proof of therapeutic progress. Evidence-based treatment has, unfortunately, become the code name for symptom-based treatment. And the shift in the therapeutic community from a psychodynamic foundation to an evidence-based foundation (symptom cessation) is disturbing to consider. So, I offer these quick assessments of progress in therapy (assuming physical health):

- A sustainable increase in the client's overall energy
- Spontaneous communication
- Less repressed emotion
- Accurate and proportional emotions
- Accurate perception of reality
- A faster learning curve in relationships
- Positive or encouraging dream images
- Reduction of symptomology

Increase in the client's energy: The true measure of therapeutic success is the amount of energy that the client is capable of achieving and sustaining. We all have our energetic moments, but the real breakthrough is in sustainable energy. Accuracy of perception and immediacy of expression, again, are the two contributors to the client's energy level. Either of these components can raise the energy level by itself, but not with any consistent results. You may perceive the world accurately, but an inhibition of response kills the energy. Or, you may be able to immediately respond to the world, but if that response is not in proportion to the moment or emotionally accurate, this also kills the energy. Both of these components, perception and expression, are required for sustainable energy levels.

Spontaneous Communication: During his word association experiments, Jung helped establish that a delay in response to a question or word indicates that repression is taking place. When repression is taking place, energy and information are being compromised. Thus, the ability to immediately and spontaneously respond to one's environment is a significant sign of progress. The phrase "I don't know" needs to be replaced with an honest assessment of one's emotional state or intellectual opinion. The lack of a perfect emotional response, or a brilliant intellectual comment, should not restrict immediate communication. Self-expression has a learning curve and requires a level of mastery comparable to any developed talent. In the same way that every musician starts as a novice by banging out a cacophony on an instrument, intellectual expression starts with the raw, clunky material of opinion and eventually finds logic, language, compassion, courage, and pleasure.

As therapists, it is not necessarily our job to improve the client's quality of response, as it is to improve the client's ability to respond.

Less repressed emotions: To achieve less repression of emotions, one either needs to be better at expressing oneself or to have retreated into social isolation where one's emotions are not continually being triggered. Obviously, therapy is aiming toward self-expression and not social isolation. Social isolation can produce its own unique psychological issues and should only be seriously considered in cases of severe PTSD, severe Asperger's, or psychosis, where limited stimulation is required for healing.

Self-expression is the underlying challenge in reducing emotional restriction. It actually takes energy to repress feelings and additional energy to keep those emotional responses locked up. In a sense, the individual suffers the same challenges as society. Are we going to have a prison culture or an education culture? At what point is our energy so compromised by the fascist aspects of personality that we finally begin to release our emotional prisoners, relieving the psychic system of its unending energetic debt?

Throughout therapy, our clients will practice expressing the emotions that they have repressed. If we have correctly diagnosed the neural-emotional complexes that are restricted, we should not be surprised when the client begins to fight with us, become sexually attracted to us, or have other transference reactions. These responses are the beginning of self-expression for the client. The sleeper has awakened—and they're not always happy about it.

The emotion that the client expresses effectively is of little consequence for the therapy and can actually be a distraction. Therapy does not require hours of crying if crying is easily emotionally available. It is the repressed emotional content with which we want to work. What is the emotion that the client does not express effectively?

Although most emotional expression and experimentation take place outside of the therapist's office, they eventually finds their way into our offices as part of the transference. The adversarial transference is often a difficult stage for many therapists. However, this phase is critical for the client's confidence in self-expression. The therapy room is the theater for practicing self-expression. Our clients will practice emotional expression on us and we should rejoice in, or at the very least, not interfere with, the process.

Accurate and proportional emotions: Is the client sad when feeling sad, angry when feeling angry, or are they crying when angry and raging when sad? Does sexuality trigger anxiety or fear? Does anger trigger passivity? Emotions need to be in proportion to the current moment, with no emotion used as a substitute for another. We are seeking no delay between emotional impact and emotional response—the spontaneous, immediate, and accurate emotional response to the world.

Accurate perception of reality: People don't have to be able to agree completely on reality, but we should be in the same neighborhood. Humanity is populated with descriptions of reality in which only portions of that description are accurate. The inaccurate parts of the description produce suffering and failed emotional experiments because we keep running into obstacles we can't or won't see. (There is a great character in the book *The Phantom Tollbooth* by Norton Juster who has the ability to see the tree behind the tree in front of him, but not the ability to see the first tree. The consequences are obvious, but he's great at finding lost baseballs.) It is one thing to be surprised by the world because we are trying something new or exploring new perceptual experiences. But it is something completely different to be repeatedly surprised by the world while running an experiment that we have conducted a dozen times. Perceptual blind spots continually undermine a healthy, happy life and create obstacles where there are none.

Faster learning curve: I measure therapeutic success predominantly through my client's confidence in experimentation and the acceleration of the client's learning curve. How fast does my client perceive a repeated pattern? When dating, does it take ten weeks, three weeks, or three hours to assess compatibility?

We are destined, by design, to repeat most social experiments. We cannot avoid being attracted to those who attract us. But we certainly can reduce the amount of time it takes us to know when the relationship is not working, and why. Initially, most people tolerate massive amounts of tension in inappropriate relationships. The time between realizing when this relationship is not working, and the actual act of breaking off the relationship, may actually be years and years. The perception is accurate, but the response is delayed. Or we may simply not have confidence in what we know, and so we wait patiently for a change in the perceptual data, a change that never occurs. "He'll change," we contend. Uh, no, he won't.

What we are attempting to accomplish in therapy is to abbreviate the amount of time between realization and action. We want to improve the learning curve. Many clients simply want to avoid the process, assuming that relationship suffering is normal and should be tolerated. It is not. We must learn to love with courage and recognize that many, if not most, relationships have a lifespan: some short, some long. Progress is realized in the learning curve.

Dreams: And then there is the problem of "false" reporting of progress by the client. At some stages of the therapy, the client may develop a strategy of trying to please the therapist. In these cases, the client will occasionally report doing better than he or she actually is. Through the use of dreams, the therapist can confirm or deny the client's self-report. Dreams are fairly transparent when it comes to progress or regress. If a client is dreaming of forest fires, he or she is in crisis. Severe weather, insect infestation, violence, death, illness, or monsters of any kind indicate suffering. However, food, sex, building construction, weddings, etc., all indicate growing confidence and more consistent energy. (See chapter 11, "Dream-Work.")

Reduction of symptomology: Psychological growth and progress should also be indicated in the successful execution of client goals: dating, mating, education, financial stability, health, and self-expression, to name a few. Although the client's goals and the therapeutic goals are not always the same, the needs and desires of the client should certainly inform the therapy and ultimately be successfully met. Since symptoms are the representation of psychological conflict, there is a reasonable expectation that the client's symptoms will recede as perception and expression improve. However, the fundamental neural pathways supporting symptomatic expression are still present, but not active. As the emotional energy is directly expressed, the pathological neural pathways will become dormant, except in situations of extreme stress. Like the canary in the coalmine, the reappearance of familiar fears and anxieties is the sign of major stress. As the stress level of the client exceeds even the new capacity for self-expression, the client's old symptom profile emerges, and once again, the client will report anxiety, tension, stress, and other difficulties.

We never rid ourselves of our capacity to produce stress symptoms, but we do reduce the amount of time the symptoms are present, the intensity of the symptoms, and the frequency of their activation.

THERAPEUTIC RESULTS

Regardless of the priorities set by training institutions, licensing boards, and insurance companies, as clinicians, we need to be clear about what it means to be a healthy human being. Here is a brief list of what I consider to be reasonable results of successful psychotherapy.

1. *Full Access to all Neural-Emotional Complexes*: There are five neural-emotional complexes that regulate information and expression: (1) thought/analysis, (2) speech/intent, (3) compassion/sadness, (4) courage/aggression, and (5) pleasure/sexuality. Each complex is located in a specific part of the body, and for awareness to have interactive access means that the emotional history stored at each location has been healed/expressed. As a result, the perceptual and expressive capacity at each physical location is not contaminated with repressed emotional history. Each of these complexes serves two specific functions (except for speech): perceptual information and emotional expression. Accurate perception leads to an accurate understanding of the world. Effective emotional expression leads to an energetic and creative life. Both capacities, at each neural-emotional site, are necessary to fulfill one's specific psychological design.

2. *Emotions are Available and in Proportion to the Moment*: Healthy emotions have two features: immediacy and proportion. Historical trauma, developmental or otherwise, leaves an emotional charge that contaminates emotional immediacy and proportion in the present. We know when emotions are unfairly intense or obsessive. We know when we have "over or under expressed." We feel the tension associated with self-restriction. To live energetically and emotionally in the moment means that the body is not carrying a strong emotional charge based on past experiences.

3. *Perceptual Accuracy*: To be able to perceive reality clearly and with confidence is a great psychological achievement. This is not the arrogance of conviction, but the experience of truth and accuracy. Since emotion is actually information and energy, emotional balance also implies perceptual accuracy. When we are experiencing emotions, we are accessing information about the world. When our psyche is clear, we know the source of emotional information. We know the difference between what we are emotionally generating and what we are receiving from the world. If one is capable of moving through life with emotional neutrality (lack of emotional historical charge), then nearly every emotional experience can be attributed to a charged signal from the world. At this stage of clarity, the phrase "It's not about you" is most accurate. It's really about our experience of the world.

4. *Spontaneous Expression*: This is my favorite goal. If psychological energy is in proportion to self-expression, and any delay between stimulus and response is an energy drain, then the capacity to immediately self-express under any conditions can lead to a consistency of energy on a moment-to-moment basis. Don't repress,

express! To consistently live in this manner takes curiosity and courage. One has to be brave in order to be free of self-constraint. We are taught at an early age to fear the consequences of certain forms of self-expression.

Once one has successfully lived in the moment for sufficient time, the nervous system quits alerting consciousness to the impending "doom" of self-expression, and instead, begins to reinforce keeping our tension and anxiety at a minimum.

We become familiar with and, in fact, expect to have a positive attitude and sufficient energy to live a creative life. Once personality is no longer in charge of self-expression, there is a greater likelihood of being inspired by one's own inner world and inner wisdom. We become continuously curious about what wants to be expressed. Every life encounter has its own element of inspiration and creative self-expression. No more boring or tedious thoughts or comments in our response to the world. Our response is being "created" in the moment, in proportion to the moment, based on the dynamic elements of the moment and our psyche.

5. *Self-Trust*: Perceptual accuracy combined with emotional expressiveness leads to self-acceptance. It takes time to develop confidence in one's ability to see reality accurately. It takes time to develop confidence in one's self-expression. Our developmental history is always challenging perceptual accuracy and emotional expression. One has to practice self-expression. One has to test perceptual accuracy. One has to train oneself to the energetic signature of truth. From the rush of the "Aha!" experience, to the subtle bursts of energy associated with living in the world in a mindful way, self-trust is the result of experiment and exploration.

6. *Becoming Fearless*: The courage to live life boldly needs to be cultivated. There is a difference between reckless abandon or adolescent impulsivity and spiritual courage. To walk the path of consciousness means to live in a world where we see our role in healing suffering and evolving humanity. To live fearlessly means that we abandon the childhood fantasy of being "taken care of" by someone else. It means that we understand that we are the caretakers. To live fearlessly means that we quit "dumbing down" in order to get approval. We quit responding passively to the predators of the world. We seek consciousness at every opportunity and do not despair at the gravitational pull

of the masses. We live in service to the betterment of humanity and all sentient beings: to boldly confront unconscious behavior both within us and outside of us, to effectively limit the bad behavior of those we encounter in the world, and to provide hope where it is lacking.

7. *Limited Symptomology*: Since symptoms are the products of repressed expression, it follows that successful therapy would significantly reduce psychological symptoms. Symptomology is simply poorly used energy, as well as "lost" information. Symptomology will be in inverse proportion to insight and self-expression.

8. *Family Shows Respect*: The popular idea that we can only change ourselves is pretty silly and weak. Part of true psychotherapeutic success is the transformation of those around us. This is a therapeutic outcome that is rarely discussed. I have a phrase that I use in therapy: "We get the relationships that we allow." Through our responses to others, we either positively or negatively reinforce how we are being treated. As we abandon passivity, we begin to renegotiate our relationship "narrative" with those in our lives.

Our ability to shift from unconscious responder into conscious strategist will determine the quality of our relationships with everyone, particularly our families.

There are no relationships in the world that are more significant in shaping our fundamental emotional function and self-image than our families of origin. We can practice honesty, truth, emotional freedom, and express our opinions with just about anyone in the world, and changing our expressive pattern with those in our lives can make a significant difference in our personality structure. But without a significant shift in the way we relate to our families, we have not neutralized those "relationship agreements" that have most influenced our negative self-expression. There are many reflections of our family dynamics appearing throughout our lives. We practice our family scripts with everyone we meet, and every relationship has the best and worst of our families directly connected through our love and fear. So much of our emotional contamination is associated with our family of origin, that without working through those original emotional histories, we will forever be repeating the very same dynamics with everyone we meet. As soon as we turn our attention to our family members and directly begin to release those self-expressive blocks, we begin to heal the emotions associated with them.

However, in those families with a history of bullying its family members, our effectiveness in challenging the culture of our family may be directly in proportion to our ability to physically defend ourselves. Without complete confidence that we can protect ourselves from the more aggressive members of our clan, it might be considered unwise to expose ourselves to those family members who are seriously aggressive or unstable.

We cannot over-estimate the violent potential of seriously dysfunctional families. Underlying paranoia, delusional disorder, manic-depressive disorder, aggressive Asperger's, PTSD victims, drug-addicted, and sexually abusive family members should be treated with extreme caution. No amount of good intention will bring about change. In these more extreme cases of family dysfunction, there are often serious neural-biological problems. Reason, love, and loyalty will have little effect, leaving only the option of being willing to renegotiate the relationship when those family members show a genuine desire for change. Avoidance may prove to be the best style of relating.

Keep in mind that no one in the family changes their fundamental functioning, but what these family members *are* changing is how they relate to us. If we allow bad behavior from our families, they will continue to use that bad behavior with us. Since everyone's psyche is constructed of loving aspects as well as controlling and mean aspects, why tolerate bad behavior when we know they are capable of better? Why passively permit our family members to express, to us, anything less than the best parts of their personalities? It's simply a matter of habit learned in childhood. We were taught to (and had no choice but to) tolerate the bullying. As adults, when we overcome our fear and passivity, we begin to insist that we be treated better. That's it. Through consistency and confrontation, the family members eventually shift how they see us and relate to us.

I am not saying that all the family members will get on board with this shift. But certainly, those in whom we are invested will change. But it requires that we become impeccable in limiting inappropriate emotional exchanges, or we might consider withdrawing until a time the family is ready for change.

Overcoming Being Stuck

There are many ways to get stuck during the course of treatment: the client loses motivation, the external motivating problem resolves, there is not a good match between the therapist and the client, there is too much unconscious material being activated all at once, the therapist mistimes a confrontation or avoids dealing with something significant in the client's life, the spouse/parent decides not to support the therapy, there is a financial crisis, and so forth. If the therapy does not terminate, but is simply bogged down and loses focus, there are a few practical steps to resolve this motivational blockage.

Revisit the originally agreed upon goals of the therapeutic contract. What brought the client to therapy and what were the original goals?

Revisit the initial diagnosis, including evaluating the current transference between the client and therapist. Was the original diagnosis correct? Why is the transference currently unproductive?

Revisit the therapeutic alliance. Agree to some new goals or discuss termination. Therapy is cyclical, and the client may need to come and go as he or she is motivated. Many clients finish their therapeutic work (for this cycle), but feel connected to the therapist and the habit of coming to therapy and even worry that terminating would be an insult to the therapist. After all, separation and individuation are critical parts of therapy and often not practiced until required by the circumstances. Do not be surprised when a client who has not been in therapy for years calls and wants to begin a new round of clinical work. The unconscious is often dormant for years until circumstances conspire to awaken "sleeping beauty," and suddenly, the second therapeutic cycle is launched.

Conclusion

During the course of therapy, the clinician will meet the varying parts of the client's psychological structure. We have to remember that people are structurally built as though having multiple personalities, and although there is often a "somewhat" seamless presentation of some of those components, it is just as likely that the more extremely repressed or dissociated complexes will manifest as highly resistant or even adversarial. Therapy will be challenged to build and rebuild the therapeutic alliance in order to proceed with the integrative work. Understanding the underlying expectations of the four major personality presentations will make diagnosis and treatment much more effective.

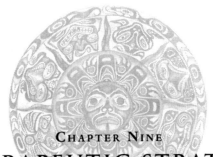

THERAPEUTIC STRATEGY AND TECHNIQUE

As therapists, it is not our job to solve problems for our clients; it is our job to expand their point of view so that they can solve their own problems.

STRATEGY AND TECHNIQUES

This is the T'ai Chi of psychotherapy. What follows are brief synopses of some of the psychotherapeutic techniques and treatment strategies that I have utilized over the years. Each is most effectively applied in association with accurate diagnosis and appropriate timing. Some of these techniques are excellent for developing a therapeutic alliance, and others are more aggressive forms of confronting pathological self-centeredness. This chapter is to be utilized when one has a working understanding of personality structure and energy dynamics.

Therapeutic strategy is one of the more contentious issues in the history of psychotherapeutic treatment. There are two approaches that lay on either side of this most significant divide: strategic therapy versus problem solving therapy. The strategic therapies are more associated with classical in-depth psychotherapy, in which diagnosis is associated with personality or group structural problems, and therapy requires a structural strategy to unlock the imprisoned potentialities of the psyche (the marriage of awareness and biology). Problem solving therapies, conversely, are based on symptom relief and seek to resolve the more transition-phase crises of the presenting problems.

Most schools of psychological thought agree that non-medical symptomology is produced by what could fittingly be called a "processing problem" in the client or a structural problem in the family. However, each school has its own thought about the nature, structure, and cause of that processing problem. There is some agreement on the evidence that social conditioning is at least part of the cause of the problem. And there is certainly strong evidence to link behavior with family dynamics, social stressors, and genetic influences. However, clinical therapeutic strategy is always based on the therapist's psychological super-system, which is usually directly associated with his/her training and adopted school of psychological thought.

In response to the medical community's emphasis on diagnosis, the early humanist movement within the psychotherapy community depicted diagnosis as de-humanizing, believing that diagnosis compressed the human potential into a set of symptoms, thus undermining the existential potential of client. The medical model argued back that if the presenting problems are not diagnosed, the therapist can not design a treatment strategy or measure success. The family systems school argued that the human being is a complex interplay of family, social, and biological identities that have become enmeshed in either a dysfunctional group system or dysfunctional communication system. Each of these perspectives brings a critical element of the whole truth. Diagnosis is critical, and the impact of family and social systems is undeniable. As a result of these competing schools of thought, *system dynamics* emerged from the fight. Whereas psychodynamics describes the structure and energy dynamics of the individual psyche, system dynamics seeks to codify the structure of group process, whether it is couple, family, or group. I would argue that modern practitioners should be trained in both psychodynamics and system dynamics in order to operate at the highest level of competency.

Evidence-Based Therapy

In the first decade of the 21st century, there reemerged pressure to emphasize symptom-based problem solving therapies rather than strategic-based treatment. As noted elsewhere in this book, cost containment was one of the principle forces behind this shift. Insurance companies, still entrenched in the medical model, fought to limit non-symptom-based treatments. For years, family and marriage counselors have been aware of the financial limitations that insurance companies have put on covering their specialty. In spite of years of outcome evidence of the success of these types of strategic treatment models, insurance companies continue to resist compensating licensed professionals for this type of therapy. As a result of this bias, we now see the growing emphasis of "evidence-based treatment."

Evidence-based therapies are treatment strategies and theories based predominantly on client symptom management.

The evidence used in the defense of this therapeutic orientation arises predominantly from research conducted by a variety of universities, psychotherapy and psychiatric training institutes, and studies funded by insurance companies. At a fundamental level, this research is conducted by measuring the prevalence and persistence of psychological symptoms and the effectiveness of particular therapeutic strategies in reducing/eliminating those particular symptoms. The logic of this approach is obvious. The client is complaining of particular symptoms, and the research is measuring the therapeutic effectiveness in reducing those symptoms.

However, a change in symptom may or may not be an accurate measure of treatment success.

In psychotherapy, symptom reduction should be placed in the same category that pain reduction occupies in medicine. In the medical model, we do not confuse pain relief with healing, and although there are certainly cases where pain relief is of predominant concern, particularly to the client, the conditions that have produced that pain are of particular importance when the pain appears to be a chronic expression of physical or psychological malfunction. In the same way, the reduction of a psychological symptom does not guarantee and may, in fact, deceive the client and the therapist, that the underlying emotional problem producing the symptom has been corrected.

Cognitive behavioral therapy (CBT) is probably the most well-known and widely practiced evidence-based therapy technique currently gaining traction in the therapeutic and insurance communities. There is nothing wrong with the concept of evidence-based treatment, but the question is always: "What are you measuring to determine treatment success?" We must ask ourselves what factors are actually the best indicators of treatment success. It is vital that we keep in mind that the symptom is usually not the problem, but rather the solution to the problem: the indirect release of the psychological energy associated with an emotional block. The symptom is the sign that there is a problem. But if the symptom is not the problem, what is?

The client's symptom profile is the "white rabbit" leading us to the structural problem in the unconscious (my apologies to Alice). Ultimately, all psychotherapeutic techniques share one goal: to help the client access the deeper wisdom of his or her psyche and express that wisdom with confidence, so that his or her perception of the world is more accurate and emotional expression is in proportion to the moment. In some psychological systems, this is done consciously, and with other systems, it is done strategically, not requiring the client's conscious participation. To this end, psychotherapy seeks to reframe reality and simultaneously train the nervous system to operate with a broader range of perceptual and emotionally expressive skills. However, at the beginning of therapy, every therapeutic strategy—as well as the techniques to be utilized—needs to be the direct result of the psychological diagnosis.

Narcissistic personalities and dependent personalities require significantly different treatment strategies. Narcissists require a more reflective engagement, whereas dependent personalities require confrontation. If you use confrontation with a narcissist too early in the treatment, they will terminate the therapy. If you use problem solving with a dependent, they will regress.

But these are the general rules to be used at the beginning of therapy in order to create a successful therapeutic alliance.

During the working-through phase of therapy, the interplay between client and therapist more resembles T'ai Chi combat, wherein the client brings to the therapy every avoidance and resistance skill set learned from family and gender training, combined with heightened and real anxiety about the consequences of breaking social rules of expression. Meanwhile, the therapist is attempting to counter every resistance with ferocity, comfort, kindness, ruthlessness, love, and general trickery, plus a battery of techniques learned from clinical experience.

TECHNIQUES

Clinicians choose from hundreds of therapeutic techniques in the course of therapy. Several years ago, I received a list of approximately two hundred techniques from my state board of examiners, requesting that I identify those techniques that I use in therapy. The list was extensive and thorough, including all of the most well-known therapeutic styles of the last fifty years: Gestalt, Eriksonian, reality, Jungian, behavioral, emotionally focused, psychodynamic, cognitive behavioral, dialectical behavioral, desensitization, exposure, Adlerian, strategic, Freudian, family systems, Rogerian, and hypnotic, to name a few. I found myself checking off about 150 of these techniques and marveling at the extensive list of "competing" therapeutic lineages represented on this list. When considering how these schools differ from each other in terms of theory, and simultaneously recognizing that all of these techniques could be very effective when used in a timely manner, I realized that there must be a common element that makes all of these techniques fundamentally effective. My conclusion:

Every psychological technique attempts to change the client's point of view, and in the very act of shifting one's point of view, psychological growth can occur.

Initially, this conclusion seems a bit simplistic, and yet a careful deconstruction of every technique will reveal its underlying goal: to shift perception and open possibility. To achieve the secondary goal of flexible emotional expression, the client is required to adopt either an accurate point of view, in which emotional expression is the natural outcome of the circumstances, or a courageous attitude, in which we bravely express ourselves in spite of our fears and anxieties of the moment. In either case, a shift in perception is required first. Remember, a shift in perception can be external or internal: *how I view others versus how I view self.*

A personality that is too rigid remains fixed in its view of the world and limited in its response to the world. However, the unconscious contains the compensatory attitude, the missing perceptual information, and energy needed to supplement the "tired" and failed point of view of the personality structure.

The overall goal of therapy is the creation of a more flexible relationship between awareness and one's unconscious and the potentialities contained within. To this end, any process that shifts one's point of view gives the unconscious opportunity to express its contents and reduce the symptomatology created by the perceptual and expressive regulation/suppression by the personality structure.

So what exactly is this unconscious of which we speak? As noted earlier in this book, Jung proposed that the unconscious was divided into two layers: the *personal unconscious* that represented the individual's blocked or inhibited personal emotional material and the *collective unconscious* that serves as the repository of all of the unknown elements and contents of the shared collective awareness. The Buddhists call the collective unconscious the *ocean of wisdom*. The important difference between these two types of unconscious is as follows.

The personal unconscious is predominantly pathological in effect, containing emotional and informational material that has been imprisoned by the censoring function of the individual's personality structure. The actual content of the personal unconscious contains both information and expression critical to the balanced functioning of the overall psyche. The contents and energy of the personal unconscious produces symptoms and psychological pressure. The collective unconscious is predominantly potential: creative capacities yet to unfold, spiritual symbol systems, higher and lower levels of consciousness, and emotional waves of collective group experience. The collective, however, is also responsible for those emotional viruses that can pervade a community based on the athletic victories or losses of the home team, the heightened anxiety of twenty thousand students in a small college town during finals, or the massive anxieties that accompany a terrorist attack. This is the unconscious tidal pull of collective fear.

The personal unconscious is the primary target of most psychotherapy. It contains the most immediately needed, and consistently repressed, aspects of psychological functions. The deeper adventures into the collective unconscious for spiritual, artistic, and intuitive rejuvenation are usually associated with spiritual transformation versus emotional functioning. Thus, the techniques used to access the personal unconscious would be directed at repressed memories and emotions, and the techniques used to access the collective unconscious might be viewed as more intuitive, artistic, spiritual, or even shamanic. For the most part, although there are certainly aspects of the theories in this book that bridge the personal and the collective unconscious, this book is more concerned with the personal unconscious and its reservoir of blocked memory, insight, and emotions. With the personal unconscious relatively free of historical contamination, awareness can naturally and spontaneously achieve less conflicted access to the deeper resources of the collective unconscious.

When therapy is working effectively, we see the decontamination of the personal unconscious and the development of a synergistic relationship between awareness, the collective unconscious, the biological body, and the material world. This synergy universally announces itself by an increase in psychological energy. Regardless of the therapeutic goal—whether symptom relief, better family functioning, marital intimacy, creativity and health, or simply better social and professional functioning—the increase and stabilization of energy is the psychological "cash" that purchases these results.

In measuring the effectiveness of any therapeutic technique, we are ultimately looking for an energetic response from the client, and hopefully, a sustainable energetic response. Truth, as I have argued, has energy. When a client's view of the world is distorted, that individual's energy is proportionally reduced. As perceptual clarity and emotional accuracy are achieved, there is a consistent rise in available energy.

At first, our energy is chaotic and fluctuates. But later, as awareness familiarizes itself with mastering emotional intensity and holding perceptual clarity, the energy available to the individual will remain, for the most part, stable, providing an inner sense of joy, purpose, and clarity.

As therapy progresses, there are several energetic resources that become immediately available. The first energetic stream is the therapeutic alliance and transference: *intimacy*. This fundamental relationship provides a sense of hope and positive potential missing from many clients' psychological perspectives. As a consequence, the transference creates a bridge between the energetic potential of the personal and, sometimes, collective unconscious and the client's awareness, in relationship with the therapist. The transference is a wildly unstable energy resource and cycles between merging, mirroring, idealizing, erotic, and adversarial relationship presentations. The second energetic stream is through accuracy of perception: *clarity*. Perceptual distortion restricts energy, so it follows that perceptual accuracy increases energy. The "Aha!" experience is a prime example of how insight (accuracy of perception) is associated with energy. It is a sudden "knowing" combined with a rush of energy. This type of knowing resonates at such a fundamental psychological level as to be felt as "remembering" a truth that one has always known but that has, until this moment, remained hidden. The second aspect of the accuracy of perception is a growing sense of the View: the integrated, interactive, and purposeful experience of reality. Energy provides a sense of spaciousness and purpose: The View.

The great "Aha!" is the wisdom of Remembering and The View.

The third energetic stream is through spontaneous self-expression: *immediacy.* Energy, again, manifests in proportion to self-expression. As the world engages us, even in the form of the slightest touch, the relative rapidity between stimulus and response determines the amount of energy available to the psyche in the moment. Although personality rigidly regulates response, it is possible to train oneself and assist clients to be spontaneous and not hold back, thus instantly freeing available energy. The immediacy of response is the most effective and efficient psychological method for raising psychological energy.

With these three governing principles—intimacy, clarity, and immediacy—in mind, let's examine some basic techniques.

PATIENCE

Although this seems obvious, patience is perhaps the therapist's most successfully used tool. However, patience can be overused and can subtly reinforce acting out, resistance, and unhealthy behavior. Clinicians want to give "space" to the client to sort out what needs to be said, what needs to be felt, and what needs to be emotionally expressed. Too much patience allows the client to fortify resistance. Sometimes patience is used when the clinician either lacks direction or is unsure of what is unfolding in the session. At this point, the therapist needs to reexamine the therapy goals, the therapeutic alliance, the diagnosis, and the transference. Returning to the diagnosis and overall therapeutic goals will, once again, move the therapy forward. Remember, as clinicians, the biggest obstacle we face is the client's resistance to psychological growth out of fear of the expressive consequences. Do not be distracted by the presentation of the client; attend to the diagnostic goal.

CONFRONTATION

At a fundamental level, all techniques are a form of confrontation. As clinicians, we are "assaulting" psychological defenses that have imprisoned our clients their whole lives. Confrontation has infinite aspects, from the subtle questioning of cognitive behavioral therapy to actually evicting clients from our office when they have crossed the line into inappropriate behavior (do not let your clients act crazy). Confrontation at the beginning of therapy is significantly different from the confrontation of the working-through phase. The gentle pushing, probing, and holding the client's feet to the fire of introspection are all fundamentally confronting. At every turn of therapy, we are confronting resistance and fear, while we simultaneously raise hope and increase relief.

In the working-through phase, confrontation is often stronger, more spontaneous, and more direct. It doesn't permit the client little excuses for indulgent and infantile behavior. Confrontation demands honesty, spontaneity, truth, mental stability, emotional availability, intellectual discipline, and energetic interplay. Confrontation should be in proportion to the strength of the transference and familiarity with the emotional material being worked on. Masterson suggests that in order for the confrontation to be effective, it has to be in proportion to the defense. As a general rule, confrontation is the therapeutic method of choice for working with dependent and anti-social personality disorders, both of which fall within what is broadly named the borderline personality disorder, discussed at length in chapter 3.

EMPATHY AND COMPASSION

Empathy is the emotional connection linking all living beings, and compassion is the state of curiosity that allows us to view the world from another living creature's point of view—in this case, from the point of view of our client. Empathy arises with the capacity to sympathetically resonate with, or mirror, the emotional states of other living creatures and perhaps even the Earth herself. Empathy is how awareness accesses the deeper resources of the collective unconscious and the information that exists in that reservoir of wisdom. Compassion is the curiosity and empathy is the connection. These are the fundamental psychological tools that allow us to experience, and thus accurately perceive, what our clients are feeling. It is the empathic connection that creates the bridge over which transference and counter-transference travel.

As clinicians, when we lack sufficient life experience or clinical experience, there are many emotions and feelings that we do not want to experience. Our natural reaction is to distance ourselves from certain types of emotional suffering. Clinical experience provides the therapist with a level of familiarity with complex emotions that only comes from standing in the hurricane of emotional chaos. Empathy and compassion become the source of wisdom, patience, courage, and energy.

ANALYSIS AND INSIGHT

Analysis leads to insight. In order to have strong analytic skills, the clinician must have a clearly defined understanding of personality structure and energy dynamics. If you do not understand why symptoms are the solution to the client's real problem, not the problem itself, it will be very difficult to illuminate to the client why he or she has a problem, why it is cyclical, how the symptoms relate directly to the problem, why the client resists change, and how the client can develop new behavior to resolve the underlying perceptual or expressive problem.

On a fundamental level, analysis and insight support the client's development of the neutral observer (See chapter 8, "Treatment.") The therapist needs to develop and model a fundamentally neutral and curious attitude toward the experiences and emotions the client is presenting. Analytic psychotherapy is strategically different from the assertive psychodynamic style, or the alliance/advocate style. Through the transference, the client begins to adopt a neutral observer neural complex that becomes the new center of judgment and aids in the integration of all of the neural-emotional complexes, without bias, repression, or dissociation.

This type of neutrality is sometimes considered a bit cold or uncaring. This style is designed less for comforting the client and more for an unbiased exploring of the client's perspective and response to reality. The therapist needs to differentiate between caring for the client and *taking care of* the client. Therapists, in their narcissistic need to feel they are doing something in the therapy, will often unconsciously operate as an adjunct of the client's personality, offering "helpful" solutions and suggestions, rather than truly helping the client examine the nature of any given psychological block. Helpful suggestions are often obvious suggestions that the clients would provide for themselves if they were not psychologically blocked. The neutral observer becomes a model for weathering the emotional chaos that occurs during therapy.

EMOTIONAL EXPRESSION

Emotions are the heart of psychotherapy. Emotions are the foundation of perceptual accuracy, energy, self-expression, insight, intimacy, self-image, self-worth, desire, stress relief, physical health, anxiety, tension, stress, guilt, shame, chaos, craziness, and biochemical imbalance. Emotional health is critical. But what does this mean? Psychoanalysis attempts to stabilize emotions through insight. Gestalt attempts to bring about psychological health through intense emotional "practice" and expression. Family therapy attempts to correct destructive emotional acting out by specific family members by correcting the family structure. I find it helpful to review a few rules about emotional function.

1. *What is not expressed as emotion or insight will be expressed as symptom.* This is a straightforward concept, one that I have expounded upon in earlier chapters. As I've argued, all emotion is ultimately information and energy. When emotion is repressed, the energetic charge produces a symptom instead that relieves, temporarily, the tension of the repressed emotion. The personality converts emotion into symptom. Diagnostically, the therapist needs to determine which blocked emotion is providing the energy that is driving the psychological symptoms of the client's symptom profile.

2. *Psychological symptoms are in proportion to repressed emotions.* Symptomatic intensity can vary from mild anxiety to a full-on conversion reaction in which extreme physical interruption is caused by psychological stress: body dysfunction, numbness, chronic pain, acute social phobia, or skin disorders, etc.

3. *Personality's job is to protect the individual from threat and punishment by repressing those emotions forbidden by the family.* Whenever a forbidden emotion is triggered by events in our world, the personality immediately represses or controls that emotion by transferring the energy behind the emotion into a predictable set of symptoms developed in childhood and adolescence. The intensity of the symptomology will be dictated by a combination of how rigid the personality is and how intense the triggering event is.

4. *The emotion the client can express is not the problem; it's the emotion the client cannot express that is the problem.* If emotional restriction is the source of psychological symptoms, then any emotion that is being expressed is usually not the source of psychological suffering.

5. *Any emotion can be a symptom for another emotion.* Emotions, for the most part, are cyclical. It is difficult to generate an intense emotion for several hours without relief, unless there is contamination by another emotion or interference resulting from a biological disorder. The body, as well as the psyche, is attempting to achieve a certain level of equanimity, including emotional equanimity. It is rare, indeed, except in extreme circumstances (such as death of a loved one), to sustain an emotional disruption for extended periods of time; thus, any emotion that seems out of balance to the moment or presents itself as intractable must be evaluated from the point of view of emotional contamination (multiple emotions posing as one) or being fueled by a biological component (which is often the problem in chronic emotional imbalance).

Most people are proficient at either anger or sadness, but rarely both. Gender roles often dictate which emotions we feel most comfortable in expressing. Women often cry when angry and men often get angry when they are sad. Sexual frustration can be transformed into anger, depression, sadness, anxiety, headaches, or perhaps an irritated mood. However, sexuality can also be used to express anger, sadness, or any number of other emotions. The manner in which emotions manifest depends on how one was raised, cultural standards, gender roles, and the need for approval. And indeed, emotional expression will reduce symptoms—unless the emotion being expressed is the "wrong" one. If you are sad, and you express your sadness, you will feel better. If you are angry and express your anger, you will feel better. However, just because you express an emotion well does not mean that every time you express that emotion, you are expressing the emotion that correctly aligns with the moment. Every moment has its own emotional accuracy: anger triggers anger, sadness triggers sadness, sexuality triggers sexuality. If sexuality triggers anger, sexuality is either being blocked and diverted into the anger complex or there is some angry historical material associated with one's sexual developmental history.

6. *Emotional regulation is as important as emotional expression.* Repression can be helpful, especially when correctly applied. In spite of all the positive benefits of emotional expression, there are certainly massive amounts of data that suggest that much of emotional expression is destructive, futile, threatening, manipulative, and crazy. Some people need to learn how to regulate their overcharged emotional expressions in order to learn how to express the other feelings in their psyche. If a person only expresses one or two emotions effectively, then those emotions will be overused,

too intense, or experienced by others as unfair and chaotic. Emotional health does not result from simply expressing any emotions; it emerges from expressing all emotions in proportion to the moment. For this to happen, present emotional reactions must be decontaminated from historical emotions that must be reconnected with their original history.

7. *Emotion expression should be in proportion to the moment.* A key aspect of emotional health, and one related to the issue of regulation, is the ability to express oneself in proportion to the moment. Emotions that are out of proportion to the events of the moment are contaminated/associated with historical events and relationships that have left an emotional charge (due to the holding back of emotion expression at the time of the original event) that is contaminating the present with the past. In therapy, it is not unusual that when the client begins to express emotions that have been restricted throughout his or her life, the newly surging emotions are associated with many historical experiences, even though the emotional trigger occurs in the present. When these emotions come to the surface, it is important for the client to remember as many events as possible that are associated with those emotions. For example, any sexual experience in the present has the capacity to remind us of all of our previous sexual experiences, both positive and negative. Thus, these historical emotions can contribute to the positive experience of the moment or suddenly undermine the current experience with anxiety, tension, stress, etc. Historical accuracy of emotion is fundamental to living in the moment, and not the past or future. Any heightened surge of emotion or fantasy is the potential of the personal unconscious, contaminated by previous experience, being activated in the moment. Awareness must first discipline itself to be suspicious of any highly charged negative or positive emotion. *In this way, we can differentiate between the internal energetic potential and the external object to which we give credit for the rush.*

PRACTICE AND ROLE PLAY

Two of Gestalt therapy's truly creative techniques are emotional practice and role play. Gestalt is designed to broaden self-expression, not only in intensity, but in style as well. The client tries out creative new behaviors both in session and in every life. At a basic level, most people are stuck in patterns of emotional self-expression that are simply too limiting, but have been reinforced for years and are now terribly bad habits. Gestalt proposes the simple solution of trying out new behaviors, and in particular, new emotional expression.

The most common phrase used by clients in therapy is: "I don't know." In reality, the client is simply "not allowed" to say what he or she knows; giving voice to some truths is forbidden by family rules. We all secretly know what we would like to say in every situation. We may lack experience, courage, flexibility, activation of the speech complex, or creative initiative, but the words are inside and sure as heck want out! Emotional practice is simply working on expressing any particular emotion during the course of therapy.

My first line of confrontation when the client is blocking immediate and authentic self-expression is to strongly encourage the client to say what they really want to say. Right here, right now. A sudden burst of emotion and attitude can really get a session going. If there is a resistance to spontaneity, a cognitive behavioral listing of possible responses will suffice. Inevitably, I ask the client to discuss their experience of their mutism, hesitation, and emotion self-restriction so that they, at minimum, have a cognitive perspective of their psychological "tells."

The classic Gestalt technique of the "empty chair" is another clever role-play strategy. I just point to an empty seat and require the client to say to the "person in the chair" what they need to say. Everyone is a little self-aware at first, and the dialogue is initially awkward. But with practice, and in particular when the therapist uses this method often enough that it doesn't seem weird or artificial, this technique is highly effective.

The rules of inhibition apply to an empty chair in the same way as if the person were present. Personality restricts the activation of the emotion expression, regardless of who is present or absent.

However, in the same way that the client projects a punitive response to genuine self-expression, they also fear the lack of support by the therapist and are immediately caught in a conundrum: do I displease my parents or my therapist? This is why the therapeutic alliance is so critical. I'm leveraging my client's need for my approval against my client's need to follow their family rules. And although it will certainly raise the client's anxiety to break ranks with the family rules and instead get the therapist's approval, there are several immediate benefits to the therapist's "approval": (1) an immediate surge of energy with the release of the emotion, (2) a reconnection between the client's awareness and their unconscious, and (3) the potential release of information and history waiting in the unconscious for discovery.

Role-play is simply another variation of practice. This is my favorite. I love to play the role of the client while they play the role of their mother, father, husband, wife, girl/boyfriend, etc. When a client has described the impenetrable conversations with any of those individuals, I know that the communication is locked-down due to my client refusing to be blunt and honest in the moment. During session I am continuously giving voice to the unexpressed aspects of the client's or my unconscious; I am temporarily voicing the unspoken unconscious, the locked-up inner voice suddenly released, the opinion not yet given, or the warrior responding to the not-so-subtle threats of those around us.

I also encourage my clients to learn how to growl like a bear: anything in the service of spontaneous self-expression and to relieve the emotional tension of the unconscious.

INTERRUPTION AND DISTRACTION

Too often in therapy, the client will start talking about something that has no therapeutic value. Blah, blah, blah. Depending on strength of the transference (this is not recommended early in the therapy), I simply change the subject, redirect to another issue, use a story to illustrate what the client is doing, or engage any number of interruptions or distractions. This is not without risk. A strong therapeutic alliance must be in place for the client to tolerate being interrupted. Often an adversarial (insult) or helpless (wounded) response will occur, which immediately provides therapeutic material. The real shift is moving away from the distracting object and reengaging in the transference as source material. In general, to allow a client to resist doing the therapeutic work is a ridiculous use of their time and yours. If you are bored during therapy, disrupt the process.

REFRAMING AND INTERPRETATION

Reframing and interpretation are two of the strongest tools in analytic and Gestalt therapies.

The technique of interpretation is based on the psychoanalytic theory that the client has a distorted belief system and that his or her interpretation of certain experiences is inaccurate, leading to repeated failures in the understanding of others, as well as ineffective or destructive self-expression. The therapist introduces a more accurate interpretation of experiences so that the client will adopt a more accurate point of view of reality. Interpretation attempts to reconnect emotional expression with the original historical experiences. Reconnecting history with emotion can explain to the client how and why they have developed certain psychological strategies.

Reframing, one of my most utilized tools, is simply providing the client with interpretive options. It can be used to introduce accuracy of perception and more effective self-expression, and it works well when the therapist needs to confront regressive behavior. In CBT, the client provides his or her own options of reality and ideally provides a more accurate perspective as one or more of the options; in reframing, it is the therapist who is introducing a different perspective. Reframing allows for a bit more flexibility in interrupting a distorted point of view or inappropriate or ineffective emotional response. Reframing can be confrontational, absurd, humorous, sarcastic, merciful, kind, relieving, loving, forgiving, and above all, healing.

When my clients avoid social experiences I often reframe that they might have particularly strong empathetic emotional radar and that it is overwhelming to experience the emotional chaos of those around us. This is, of course, predicated on a narcissistic personality that "personalizes" the painful emotions of others. When I treat women who are embarrassed by their sexual history, often with emotionally damaged men, I suggest that they are trying to save those partners through the giving of themselves and that their shame and guilt arise from the inability to save those damaged men. (There is a paradoxical element in this, in that the acts that provoked shame or guilt can now be viewed as acts of mercy and rescue. Sexuality can now be freed from the bonds of embarrassment.)

Reframing, at its best, provides mercy. One interpretation of sexual risk (assuming the person is not anti-social) is the willingness of the client to give anything and everything in order get approval or to be loved. This interpretation presents the client as weak, helpless, and with limited value, except where they allow themselves to be "used." To instead suggest the client is actually attempting, sexually, to save their partners, makes the client strong, generous, and kind. To freely give body and heart, even in dangerous or poisonous circumstances, can easily be viewed as heroic. The failure of the subject of affection to respond in a loving healthy manner is much more an issue of perceptual distortion, not compassionate intent. Which reframe is most effective in producing a courageous client: desperation or compassion?

A good therapist can suggest points of view that more accurately describe reality, as well as to offer a more honest emotional response to that reality. These types of reframes are attempts to shift the client's fixed point of view to a perspective that allows for "multiple points of view."

REFRAMING VIA PARADOX

Paradox is the art of disrupting or bypassing a client's psychological defense system in order to introduce a new behavior or point of view. All clients come to therapy because they are tired of suffering, and yet, their psychological defenses have every intention of resisting and undermining the therapeutic process. This presents a rich challenge for therapists: we must be at once trickier and safer than the client's parents.

As clinicians, we are essentially trying to get our clients to suspend their fear of the consequences of self-expression in order to explore the energetic potentials of healthy, creative, and spontaneous emotional expression.

The client needs to feel that the therapy is "safe" and that he or she will not be punished for speaking his or her mind in an honest manner. Usually, however, the client is terrified of speaking truth, even in therapy, due to the systematic discipline of childhood. Thus, the therapist has to be clever and protective.

The number one paradoxical intervention that I use throughout the course of therapy is that I verbally insist that my client is healthy and normal. I actually argue for my client's health. The more I promote my clients' fundamental health, the more my clients tell me exactly why they are not healthy or normal. They list, with detail, all the terrible things that they have done or that have been done to them. If I were to try to extract this information directly, I would get nothing. I could spend months mining for pathology and history with moderate success. By insisting that my client is normal and that there is nothing wrong with them, the client can't tell me fast enough all the psychological issues they have buried inside of them. Now, don't get me wrong; I still do diagnosis and treatment strategy. Throughout the process, I am evaluating which neural-emotional complexes are compromised and producing symptomology. But I hold to my view of the client's inherent health, lovability, normality, and creative brilliance. I know, for a fact, that they are doing the best they can with the emotional resources allowed them by their families. And when they discover a broader range of emotional expression, they will do much better. You might ask, "Doesn't the narcissist use this technique to feed his pathology?" Amazingly, no. Narcissists are so exhausted from the daily defending of how special they are that they welcome hearing it from someone who "gets them" and proceeds to describe all the emotional sufferings that they go through day after day. It's amazingly simple and brilliantly effective. Otherwise, the therapy would be blocked by the narcissist insisting that his childhood was wonderful and his mother was a saint. Praise is the key that frees the narcissist from suffering.

Paradox produces a type of confusion in the client while simultaneously disrupting entrenched defenses. Paradox can be presented in a seamless fashion so that the client is only subtly aware that the therapist has disrupted a defense. But it can also be pushy and obnoxious. I often suggest to my female clients who have embraced helplessness as a repeated defense that they should switch to fainting. And then I put my hand to my head and imitate falling into a faint. This nineteenth century culturally acceptable feminine social defense is so absurd that it perfectly illustrates the ineffective nature of helplessness. At the same time, it tends to inspire a bit of a courageous response by the client in her rejection of such an absurd suggestion.

Paradox, in simple terms, is a method of giving the client conflicting suggestions, so that the automatic resistance associated with self-activation is temporarily blunted and the unconscious is permitted expression. Paradox is a method of distracting the ego while the unconscious expresses itself in a less restricted manner. Paradox is strongly associated with the Milton Erickson school of therapy, although it is widely used by many schools. Although Erickson is known for his hypnotic technique, it is reported by the Erickson Training Institute that he only used formal hypnosis approximately fifteen percent of the time and that he considered paradox to be his most effective tool. What makes Erickson such an icon in the history of American psychotherapy is his ability to dismantle psychological defenses before they could derail the client from the therapeutic goal. Erickson anticipated the client's resistance to transformation and systematically laid a foundation of paradoxical interventions to bypass the resistance. Jay Haley's book on Erickson, *Uncommon Therapy*, provides a wonderful illustration of how creatively Erickson approached paradoxical psychotherapy. Erickson's boldness might have gotten him sued in today's litigious atmosphere, but the brilliance of his thinking and his commitment to his clients' welfare are absolutely indisputable. Erickson is unquestionably the greatest practitioner of paradoxical intervention in a pantheon of psychological trailblazers.

THE OUTRAGEOUS PARADOX

One form of paradox that I utilize regularly, I call "outrageous." It's actually a combination of paradox and reframing, because it frees the unconscious through paradox, but is fundamentally built on reframing the client's point of view. Clients fear their own fantasies, and why not? Because they repress their emotional expression due to fear of the consequences, the fantasies associated with those repressed feelings inevitably produce highly symptomatic responses. Since fantasy, as one of the five stages of perception, is a more primitive aspect of emotion, part of the therapist's job is to reframe the client's point of view so that the client feels more comfortable with his or her own fantasies.

What the "outrageous" reframe/paradox does is suggest something so outlandish that it minimizes the client's resistance to his or her own shameful "secret" fantasy. It produces a reaction in the client that suggests, "Wow, compared to that suggestion, my fantasy is kind of tame." This technique can be applied particularly well with repressed anger or repressed sexuality. Most clients who have repressed anger do so because they were exposed to brutal, crazy, or violent aggression in the family. Their perspective of anger is fundamentally corrupt. Attempting to de-guilt the client's repressed aggression is typically fruitless. But when the client is processing those events that clearly make him or her angry, and the therapist suggests a response that is so over the top it may seem downright silly, a paradox is created, wherein the client aligns with and expresses the repressed feeling in order to oppose the outrageous statement made by the therapist.

A classic outrageous paradox was used by the last psychoanalyst I trained with in the seventies. Let's call him Charles. During a group therapy session with six adults (I served as co-leader), this analyst, out of the blue, said, "If you can't imagine beating up both of your parents, you're too hung up!" (to no one in particular). There was some uncomfortable chuckling and some dismissing of the analyst as "Oh, that's just Charles." But the therapeutic effect was introduced. Even as we attempted to dismiss this outrageous statement, we raised the level of acceptance of our own repressed aggressive fantasies. How can you continue to condemn your own fearful fantasies when a respected analyst says something like this? This type of paradox is designed to reduce resistance and strategically encourage self-acceptance of one's fantasies associated with repressed emotion. This type of paradox requires the transference with your client to be very strong because this type of confrontation will, by design, immediately trigger an adversarial response.

The purpose and strategy of a paradox is to create a disruption of the self-imposed inhibition. I use a variation of this when I ask my clients to keep a dream journal. Many respond that they don't dream. I set up the paradox with a fact: everyone dreams every night. Then I list all the reasons my clients give to explain why keeping a dream journal is impossible. I call these resistances "the guardians at the gate of wisdom."

1. I don't remember my dreams.
2. I forgot to write the dream down.
3. The dream wasn't important enough to write down.
4. I went to the bathroom and lost the dream in those few minutes.
5. I can't read my own writing after recording the dream.
6. I left my dream journal at home.
7. The client asks me to read their written down dream, rather than the client reading the dream (this is the same a verbal inhibition where the client resists stating their emotional reactions).

Then, I complete the paradoxical strategy with the use of prediction: "I once had a client who, out of all my clients, was the worst at remembering dreams. It took a whole week before s/he remembered a dream." Or, I use praise: "You're so intuitive you might start remembering your dreams in forty-eight hours. It wouldn't surprise me at all."

SPONTANEOUS RESPONSE

This is the technique I use the most. It is the heart of my work with every client. My clients hate it; I love it. During the course of conversation, regardless of subject, I am tracking my client's hesitations, word substitutions, thought inhibition, or any other type of block in the flow of conversation. As Jung noted in his word association research, verbal hesitation is an act of psychological censorship. There are seven basic expressive cues or "tells" that I am alert for during therapy:

- The hesitant response
- Change of word of phrase
- Freudian slip
- Blocked words or thoughts
- Inhibition
- Reluctance to disclose
- Refusal to self-examine: the "I don't know" defense

These seven features are common forms of self-censorship. Since censorship is an act of self-protection, it is associated with a distorted view of reality combined with a fear of the consequences of psychological transparency. Verbal self-censoring behavior (speech inhibition or thought blockage) is obviously an unconscious act, and it takes time for the client to even be aware that he or she is self-censoring. I experience self-censoring as a break in the flow of conversational content.

In extreme cases of inhibition of self-activation (dependent personality), I actually have to cue the client that it is his or her turn to speak and contribute to the conversation. I am an interactive therapist, and although I am capable of providing a completely neutral and patient atmosphere for the client to find his or her voice and feeling, I have come to recognize that confrontation is the most effective treatment for passivity. It seems to me that we serve our clients better in helping them find their voices at lower anxiety levels rather than passively, by waiting and provoking them to cross their anxiety threshold and speak.

Regarding the psychodynamics of the delay in blocked communication, I offer seven findings from my clinical experience:

1. The delay is the result of dissociation (repression is a lesser drastic form of dissociation): In dissociation, awareness has withdrawn from traumatized parts of the body that contain information and/or feelings that are too painful to tolerate. When the answer to a question requires information contained at the site of trauma, there is an immediate conflict between the retrieval of the information (by awareness entering into the organ containing the information) and the simultaneous resistance to feeling the painful emotions stored at this physical site.

2. The delay is the influence of an unconscious complex at work: Inhibition is simply the reluctance to self-express. The influence of the family combined with a desire for social approval simply trains us to control/shape or block certain ideas and forms of self-expression. It is this internal training, in the form of blocked knowledge, attitude, or emotion, that presents itself as inhibition in our behavior. All self-expressive blocks are the influence of one or more unconscious complexes exerting a repressive, rather than expressive, influence. If one is repressing sexual expression, including sexual fantasy, the pressure from the complex increases as one is exposed to sexual stimuli in one's environment. If there is no sexual content in one's environment, the complex remains relatively dormant. However, living in the modern culture assures exposure to sexual ideas, displays, and general sexual content on a daily basis. Thus, the sexual neural complex exerts increasing pressure on awareness for acknowledgment and expression. It is this struggle between realization and repression that creates the block in self-expression. Eventually, the neural-emotional complex will gain sufficient strength, reaching a tipping-point, when suddenly the symptomology or fantasy will become more prevalent in the client's awareness. At this point, awareness is moderately or severely obsessed by the content of this complex: obsessions, compulsions, and extreme acting out are not uncommon.

3. The intensity of the delay predicts how much material is blocked: When emotional material is particularly painful, either by repeated trauma or extreme trauma, resistance to retrieval can be particularly strong. The therapist needs to be patient while the client is struggling with accessing the information, and there are several responses that can occur. A long wait may be required while the client attempts retrieval, the client may attempt to derail the therapeutic quest by changing the subject or denying knowing the answer, or there may be a sudden rush of surprising emotion. Sometimes, I will have the client place his or her hand on the part of the body where he or she is feeling the anxiety, in order to reconnect awareness with the physical site of the block.

4. The block indicates the possibility that too much material is rushing to the surface. Growing up in a family with anger problems, for example, produces many, many episodes of psychological wounding that are stored in the neural-emotional centers. Since these centers serve as the site of memory, history, emotion, and energy, when the client is attempting to respond to a question, he or she can experience a flood of possible answers. Each historical insult is uniquely energetically charged and is contributing its own symptom profile. When awareness initially engages with this material, it has to learn to differentiate the contributing pieces in order to sort out the relationship between the emotion, the information, and the history. As James Masterson has suggested, when trauma occurs, there appears to be a split between memory and emotion. Awareness will align with one or the other, relegating the complement into the unconscious. So one experiences memory but not emotion, or vice versa. We simply dissociate one aspect of our traumatic experience. The retrieval process floods awareness with either memory (information) or emotion. Learning to differentiate each of the contributing experiences of this wave of information/emotion is what causes the delay in the response to the therapeutic question.

5. The delay indicates that personality has found no "appropriate" answer: Personality filters self-expression based on threat assessment. If an emotional response has been repressed to keep from triggering a punitive response from the family or environment, the emotional material/expression is simply viewed as inappropriate and provokes anxiety when triggered, which happens all the time. In therapy, we are continually asking our clients to identify and express those emotionally repressed aspects of the psyche, and of course this triggers a lot of anxiety and resistance. As a result, when the therapeutic question is asked that requires expression

of these "inappropriate or dangerous" emotions, the personality's automatic protection mechanism (what I call "the guardian at the gate of wisdom") simply blocks access. It's almost as if the client doesn't have security clearance to access the forbidden material. In many cases, the client non-verbally illustrates an acute embarrassment about the answers that do break through, and therefore censors their vocal expression in the therapy session. The client shows all the signs of embarrassment, inhibition, shyness, or even reacting to an inside "joke." You might call these embarrassing admissions "the unspeakable."

6. The delay compromises information, emotion, and energy: Blocked communication, as a general rule, reflects the personality's attempt to filter/block/regulate information, emotion, and energy. When personality blocks perception and expression, self-expression becomes symptomatic. Hesitant communication is simply one of those symptoms. In clients who are grappling with inhibition, the verbal delay simply indicates that they are not allowed to know what they know or express what they feel. The consequence is the proportional reduction of both accuracy of perception and overall psychological energy. The stronger the block, the more perception is distorted, the less clients remember, the less they feel, and the less energy they have available.

7. The delay is replaced with a symptom: In this case, the client might immediately become sleepy, tired, distracted, or even "stupid." The "stupid" defense is curious in that the client feigns an inability to figure out the problem. This is an obvious passive-aggressive defense, and I will accuse a client, with whom I have a strong therapeutic alliance, that they have suddenly lost thirty IQ points. (This is a paradoxical strategy. Even if the client doesn't understand the IQ rating system, it is obvious that this comment is an insult that suggests that the client has superior intellect but is now acting lazy.)

REFLECTION AND CBT

This technique is the core for building the therapeutic neutral observer. Reflection is the ability to observe and examine the behaviors of self and others. Emotional regulation, learned through curiosity and reflection, provides access to both emotional courage and perceptual curiosity and increases the client's ability to integrate thought and feeling simultaneously. The cognitive behavioral therapy approach openly examines multiple options of interpreting experience and reality.

The single biggest psychological obstacle in our clients' lives is the fixed point of view: a perspective and interpretation of reality that is limited in scope, imagination, and options, and is, in many cases, inaccurate.

The CBT approach patiently asks the client to offer and examine multiple possible interpretations of reality, alternatives that the client himself will provide through the CBT technique. Our ability to consider multiple points of view provides the awareness with the possibility of a more accurate experience of reality, and as a result, to develop reasonable expectations of reality. Instead of the therapist trying to provide answers (as is done in some problem solving therapy), with CBT, the therapist provides a confrontational framework requiring the client to offer his own problem solving options, thus repairing the connection between awareness and the client's unconscious. The client is "taught" to open to his own self-generated answers, choosing from a list of possibilities he has provided from his own unconscious imagination. The actual solution is less important than the client trusting the process by which he arrived at a suitable answer.

Mirroring and Support

In working with narcissistic personalities, I find that providing support and praise can be an effective tool for triggering the underlying depression and anxiety. I use nurture, caring, sympathy, empathy, and positive regard to trigger the developmental suffering that is always just below the surface of a narcissist's grandiosity and insulated self-promotion. In severe cases, narcissists obsessively speak highly of themselves because, in reality, no one else will do it. They simply have either not received the narcissistic adoration so dearly needed in childhood or the praise they did receive was conditioned to please the parents in order to avoid criticism or punishment. Most narcissists are exhausted from propping up their battered sense of self-worth. They are weary from fending off what seems to be an endless stream of criticism from (their personalizing the emotional expression of) the people around them.

The therapeutic alliance is created by helping support the narcissistic shield. But instead of creating a self-absorbed monster, the client's relief at receiving some modicum of positive recognition almost always triggers the loneliness, isolation and frustration of these typically sensitive and intelligent individuals' childhoods. When I praise a narcissistic client, I'm honoring the components of his or her psyche that were blunted in childhood. I'm providing the positive mirroring that was either denied or too conditional. Obviously, this technique has a singularly opposite effect when applied to an anti-social personality. Unfortunately, many anti-social personalities, as well as Asperger's personalities, are diagnosed as narcissistic, and the failure of the therapy is inevitable.

EMBRACE THE DEFENSE

This is a Gestalt technique that is actually a paradoxical intervention in that the application of this technique produces the very effect the client is avoiding. Narcissistic clients can be particularly protective of their parents due to "shared" idealization: what criticizes the parent criticizes the client. The problem is that this is not an accurate view of the world or their childhood, and it produces some entrenched problems in interpersonal relationships.

The narcissist's need to be constantly affirmed is a result of his or her resisting the constant pressure of the dysthymia arising from the wounded self and the imprisoned unconscious.

As therapists, we are often at odds with our client's personality defenses, for the sake of the client's wounded self, and getting the client to fully examine his or her childhood suffering can be difficult. The Gestalt technique of embracing the defense is used when a client defends against the exploration of a painful childhood by insisting that the parent (and in particular, the mother) was ideal and wonderful, and it is clear that any direct confrontation against this point of view will undermine the therapeutic alliance. We are literally dealing with an enmeshed mother/son or mother/daughter imago: what criticizes the mother criticizes the client.

If one's self-worth is based on the parent's self-worth, criticism of the parent is experienced as criticism of oneself and will not be tolerated. Instead of exploring a critical review of the parenting, I simply have the client begin to list all of the positive traits of that parent until the client cannot resist throwing in some criticism.

We essentially agree to the view that the mother was wonderful and suggest that we discuss her positive traits. The client's unconscious, since it is not defending itself against criticism, will be unable to sustain this biased "positive" point of view for very long, until the natural critical aspect of the client's true childhood bursts forth with some spontaneous criticism of the parent. In some ways, this method is paradoxical. Embracing the positive triggers the wounded memories and emotions.

HYPNOTIC

Let me first state that I usually discourage standard hypnotic work. Since the whole point of psychotherapy is to become conscious, it strikes me as a bit ironic that we use methods predicated on the reduction of consciousness. With that said, however, the Milton Erickson Institute teaches forms of hypnosis that are particularly useful. I predominantly use sub-hypnotic techniques. When working with dreams or active imagination, I use a light hypnotic induction to provide simpler access to the unconscious components. Slight relaxation, breathing exercises, hand induction, systematic desensitization, distraction, and moving the client around the room (different chair, different perspective), are all part of my collection of hypnotic therapeutic tools.

Hypnotic skills are helpful in rethinking how to manage client resistance and psychological defenses in general. Hypnotic techniques can increase the creative impulse, improve expression of the unconscious, access fantasy more effectively, and provide a more relaxed experience in therapy.

METAPHOR

The use of metaphor is, at some level, hypnotic. The unconscious organizes repressed information, or for that matter, new and unfamiliar information, into mythic and symbolic structures. In psychotic states, these mythic organizational structures burst forth, seizing control of identity, often by imposing religious patterns on the individual and his world. But under normal circumstances, these underlying mythic structures only express their influence when excessive repressed emotional pressure builds up and emerges in dreams or fantasies. These unconscious mythic and symbolic structures, common to all people, hold our psychological potential. In the same way that children dream and fantasize (through play and make-believe) about what eventually becomes emotional wisdom, adults follow the same progression (from symptom to dream, fantasy, emotion, and finally, insight) with emotions that have been repressed or new situations that are unfamiliar to us. For therapy, this means that the client needs healthy images and metaphors for psychological growth and adult functioning. We need to set our sights on images and identities that we will become as we express and master the contents of our unconscious.

Metaphor speaks to the unconscious and presents images, role models, mythological themes, inspiration, hope, reframing, integrated emotional expression, and an endless supply of inspirational material representing evolved psychological states. The psyche needs models of human behavior that represent an evolved state of being and self-expression.

Although human potential, and certainly the higher states of self-expression, are built into the DNA and the unconscious of every person, our ability to conceive, access, and integrate that wisdom and emotional purpose is limited by the role models available to us in our culture. The unconscious is always seeking representations of our human potential in order to mirror or mimic those more evolved psychological capacities. Without heroes and heroines, without mythic battles, without the overcoming of evil, without the struggle for meaning and purpose and the passion and loyalty and brilliance of the human capacity for awakening, we are simply confused by our psychological potential and nature's evolutionary goals.

In therapy, the client is initially motivated by the hope of *relief from suffering*. The *quest for meaning* is a later stage of therapeutic accomplishment, and *soul purpose* is still further down the therapeutic road. As Abram Maslow proposed, there seems to be, underlying the human experience, an unfolding sequence of psychological and biological stages. He described a hierarchical progression through five categories of accomplishment: physiological needs, safety, longing/belonging, esteem, and finally, self-actualization. Maslow proposed a natural prioritizing of these life challenges, in which awareness would attend to the next level of accomplishment as each level before it was completed.

Clearly, the evolution of human culture has yet to be completed. Whether you embrace intelligent design or the science of evolution, it is apparent that human beings and their societies are rising to new levels of self-awareness and responsibility. Science and religion only argue over the source and name of the evolutionary pulse.

There is, within the psyche, both individual and collective, a drive to evolve. This drive is what puts pressure on the psyche when personality is too restrictive. This drive creates symptoms when emotions are suppressed. This drive, this energetic potential, requires illustration as its potential reaches a tipping point. Suddenly, we find ourselves attracted to certain situations, or people who have a particular, if mysterious, magnetic pull for us. This is our attraction to our evolving potential. We need symbols to hold the energetic appeal, and thus, represent the next step in our psychological evolution. We unconsciously seek and find those environmental images representing all the states of awareness. The individual is unconsciously drawn to those symbols, myths, and values that represent psychic potential that is not yet expressed.

Again, the psyche is not a passive system. It attempts to pressure awareness into the expression of all of the components of the unconscious. Our unconscious is naturally energetically attracted to the next level of self-expression and purpose (e.g., hero worship), and our attraction to anything in the world is predicated on our association with meaningful self-expression and self-representation.

Our ability to recognize and then pursue that which energizes us becomes the beginning of the next stage of our developmental adventure.

I always ask my clients (and recommend that they ask their dating partners) what their favorite movie is. This is often met with confusion and multiple answers. But most of the time there are a few movies that really represent their favorites. This is significant in that these films represent the "mythological" orientation of the person's psyche. The content and intent of these films usually matches the unconscious hopes and fears in the client's psyche. I also ask for my client's favorite fairy tale. Women are better able to answer this question than men. I believe this is because a great number of fairy tales are feminine in nature. Without going into detail, I believe that the oral tradition is the history of the matriarchy in culture and the written tradition is the history of the patriarchy. Fairy tales are, for the most part, the written records of the oral tradition of storytelling. The favorite fairy tale reveals the underlying hopes and fears of the client.

Dream-Work

See chapter 11 on dream analysis, dream interpretation, and dream content. If you are interested, my lecture on dream analysis (2004) can be found at my website: www.emotionalinsight.com.

Prayer, Meditation, and Spiritual Growth

It is rare that issues of prayer, meditation, or spiritual growth do not arise in long-term therapy. Part of spiritual practice is associated with the existential concerns of the purpose and meaning of life, as well as moral and ethical choices. Participating in a spiritual or religious practice will both expand and contract self-expression. It may initially give us our voice, a point of view different from our place of origin, and an enthusiasm to speak our newfound truth. However, this belief system may later confine and restrict our self-expression as we grow beyond the limits of its community structure. Too often, organized religion teaches self-restriction and self-criticism based on a philosophy that human nature is fundamentally damaged or corrupt and has to be corrected. I reject this point of view, but I do not reject spiritual practice and spiritual growth. There are aspects of all the world's religions that are worthy and inspiring. However, the first great psychological challenge for the "seeker" is to determine the difference between spiritual wisdom and institutional dogma. Faith must lead to wisdom to offer real and practical solace to the practitioner. Faith without wisdom is the result of an overly restrictive personality that undermines spiritual curiosity.

Spirituality is at its core the search for wisdom. In this manner, spiritual practice, spiritual discipline, or spiritual education lead to a bigger point of view. The bigger point of view is simply the result of the personality censor permitting new information into consciousness's inventory of experience. For this to occur, there needs to be both a psychological and neurological interface with the unconscious. Personality needs to develop an impartial complex that serves as the seat of awareness: the neutral observer (discussed earlier in this chapter). Meditation and prayer are particularly helpful in preparing and strengthening this component.

As the psyche examines its own nature, the personality makes subtle shifts in its structure to allow or restrict new information. In dreams, this evolution is often illustrated as construction taking place: a new building, a new floor on a building, or a newly discovered house. Each of these symbols is the result of awareness exploring, developing, or preparing new psychological structures and neurological pathways in order to access the wisdom of the unconscious.

Spiritual wisdom, at its highest function, provides a belief system or a set of disciplines that simply expands or prepares personality to evolve. Clinical psychotherapy follows a similar path, in that it works to expand perception and self-expression in order to increase wisdom and energy. Indeed, psychotherapy is widely and, I believe, appropriately viewed as the effort to help the individual become what he or she is designed to become.

When given the opportunity and safety to embrace one's true character (and psychological potential), the psyche has a natural affinity to expand past the limitations of family, culture, and religion. And although awareness seems to have limitless capacity to grow, personality still plays a role in regulating the speed in which this process happens. There are certainly joyous moments of expansion, but there are also terrifying moments of expansion. Thus, per-

sonality regulates expansion to prevent or limit the experience of being over-whelmed. To put it bluntly, we want growth and expansion to the point of joy, but not terror. Unfortunately, anxiety attends both growth and stagnation. This is why courage and curiosity are paramount.

The discipline of prayer is important because it develops focused intent. Several years ago, a book called *The Secret* became a runaway bestseller that promised to reveal the "secret" laws of attraction that lay untapped in the unconscious. It proposed that the mind, when directed with intent, was capable of attracting to the reader that which the reader desired: love, money, success, wisdom, spiritual truth, etc. Buddhist mental science suggests that this law of attraction is actually only one of four mental aspects. Dynamically, the mind has the ability to attract, repel, increase, or decrease the contents of the material world. Buddhist philosophy suggests that these can be competing intentions in the mind and that they can enhance or interfere with one's ability to produce one's intent in the world. Psychologists would say that if, for instance, the desire to have a life-mate is in conflict with the unconscious desire not to be emotionally hurt, no progress can be made in the dating department. The intent to attract intimacy is neutralized by the intent to avoid emotional hurt. As a result, the client moves through his or her daily life with a blind spot, unable to perceive potential partners.

In the spiritual practices of prayer and meditation, one is attempting to develop mastery of one's intent. There is no question that the psyche fights with itself. We are in direct conflict with our own best and worst interests. Prayer and meditation are, by design, methods of reducing internal conflict, producing directed, conflict-free intent (prayer), and creating the neutral observer, unattached to any of the four mental aspects: the powers of attraction, repulsion, increase, and decrease (meditation). One can see immediately how prayer and meditation can be of immense usefulness in therapy. To be able to hold one's concentration without random or chaotic emotional reactions would be extremely helpful in advancing emotional regulation and expression. To be able to hold one's intent without internal conflict undermining the results would significantly advance the client's ability to achieve life goals.

Homework

Homework should be practical, inspirational, expansive, and healthy. I have two requirements of all my clients: (1) keep a dream journal (as an inventory of emotional expression, and (2) exercise (obviously an energy generator). I also lend or assign certain books for my clients to read if they do not have something they have chosen themselves. I am particularly fond of the books by Alice Miller, and in particular *The Drama of the Gifted Child*. Her books on the psychological struggles of the child and family are very well received in my client population. I occasionally recommend Buddhist authors who address mindfulness or meditation. I regularly assign books on Meyers-Briggs typology (MBTI), especially with couples work: *Please Understand Me I* and *II* are particularly useful in differentiating pathology from personal style. The Meyers-Briggs type test is a self-evaluation tool that emphasizes psychological strengths and skills. We are all unique to our original psychological designs and abilities, and it usually helps to have some shortcuts in accepting those self-qualities that will energize our lives. And finally, I regularly assign movies to be watched: sometimes for romance, sometimes for hope, sometimes for heroic qualities, sometimes for mystical experiences, sometimes for insight, but mostly because film can speak truth to the unconscious and to personality in a manner that aids transformation. My top therapy films are *Whale Rider, The Secret of Roan Inish, Dangerous Beauty, Spirited Away, The Shipping News, Magnolia, Waking Life, What the Bleep Do We Know?, Illuminata, Moonstruck, Groundhog Day, Stewart Saves His Family, Sirens, Dark City, Don Juan DeMarco,* and *Wolf*. Each of these serves a different purpose, depending on where the client is in his or her therapeutic process. Regardless, the homework should reframe life's struggles, expand awareness, encourage emotional expression, develop a psychological discipline, or raise energy levels.

REPRESSION

Repression is most commonly thought of as "bad" in that repression kills energy, self-expression, and creativity. However, that's only true if you are repressing the direct expression of emotion. When one represses *symptomology*, the energy is forced to either create another, perhaps less offensive symptom (intermediate outcome) or reactivate the original emotional response (good outcome). Many families prefer symptoms like anxiety over anger or sexuality, and thus directly support the expression of such symptoms over honest emotion. We've been encouraged to express ourselves in this pathological manner and are threatened if we don't. So, we adopt symptomatic self-expression with the approval of our family and society.

The question we might want to ask ourselves is: "If we are capable of successfully repressing the good stuff (healthy emotions and opinions), then why wouldn't we be just as capable of repressing the bad stuff (symptoms or negative internal dialogue)?" The obvious answer is that we are absolutely capable of repressing that pathological stuff. The fact that therapists tolerate inappropriate behavior and acting out in their offices is amazing to me. The fact that the general population tolerates bad behavior in friends, family, and neighbors is equally amazing to me. Our passivity is a direct result of, and an illustration of, our own psychological blind-spot.

I expect my clients to be sane. I require my clients to be sane. They can act crazy anywhere else in their lives, but not in my office. I am asking them to be the master of their own emotional expression and expect them to conduct themselves in an adult manner. At a very basic level, we get the relationships we allow. As we become more conscious, we begin to actively shape the quality of the relationships in our lives. We abandon the fear that promotes passivity in relationship and begin to encourage the better qualities of our friends and families to emerge when they are with us.

Throughout this book, I've treated repression and dissociation as the prime examples of psychological wounding and have really only hinted that these behaviors might not have to be automatic, at all. In the same way that many of us unconsciously drive our automobiles, it is not impossible to be completely conscious while we are driving. During my thirties, my friends and I practiced "seamless" driving, during which we attempted to create a driving experience that produced no anxiety in the passengers or drew attention to the behavior of the car during transportation. We became the chauffeur for the Dalai Lama and drove as if His Holiness were our only concern. Those moments in the car illustrated the quality of driving that was possible when we prioritized the drive rather than the destination.

Our psyche is no different. With mindful application of will, combined with emotional skills and mental openness, our life path begins to take on a seamless quality, in which the passenger (awareness) relaxes and enjoys the experience in its fullness.

CONCLUSION

These techniques only represent those strategies and styles that I have found particularly useful over the years. There are many effective and wonderfully creative techniques that I have not mentioned in this list that I utilize and respect. And, of course, there are many techniques with which I am unfamiliar and, thus, can only encourage clinicians to be open to all the possibilities of human transformation. Ultimately, I believe that human beings, and human systems in general, seek to evolve to higher and more efficient functioning, that the unconscious urges us toward full expression of our design potential.

For any psychological technique to succeed, it must be able to shift one's point of view. Psychological pathology is marked by a fixed point of view that simply limits perception and restricts self-expression. When the individual's point of view is expanded, the unconscious has an opportunity to evolve the regulating system, whether it is the individual, family, or group structure. A shift in the point of view is finally what exposes us to a greater energy, information, and creativity. These elements enable us to make meaning from our experiences, find our purpose, and contribute profoundly to the communities and world in which we live. Plus, it gives us the ability to laugh at ourselves.

THERAPEUTIC STAGES
AND GOALS

IN THIS SECTION, I will attempt to condense the rather complex journey of the psychotherapeutic relationship into a set of stages and goals. The content of each therapy relationship will obviously vary depending on the client, but the structure and overall psychotherapeutic goals remain the same. In psychodynamic therapy, the goal is the overall health of the psyche, which then provides the necessary energy and information the client requires to resolve his or her life's challenges.

Be clear about the treatment options that you are offering the client and don't pretend that immediate help is the same as long-term transformation. It is the difference between pain relief and surgery.

STAGE 1: CLIENT INTRODUCTION: FIRST PHONE CALL AND FIRST SESSION

GOAL 1: GET AS MUCH INFORMATION AS POSSIBLE (A PRECISE HISTORY)

The Phone Interview: The client's first contact with the therapist's office is critical. We have a rule in my office: the person making the phone call is usually the one who really wants or needs therapy, even if he or she is calling for someone else.

It seems a bit obvious to say that motivation is everything in therapy, but there you have it, and motivation can occur in many forms. If the person is calling for an appointment for himself, the first challenge has been overcome: the courage to seek help. However, it is just as common to get a phone call inquiring about treatment for someone else. One major motivator in contacting a therapist is helping to fix someone else: "My son, wife, husband, daughter, mother, father, student, friend, mate, boss, etc. needs therapy. Can you help?" Of course, as a matter of professional protocol, the person needing therapy is required to make the appointment phone call, unless the potential client is a minor. However—*always, always, always*—the individual making the phone call is the one ready for therapy. That person is simply exhausted and has run out of options or patience with the identified patient.

In particular, when the caller is inquiring about therapy for a loved one, I find that a strategy session with the caller can help. It is important to identify the core problem and what might be done about it, and the strategy session provides some therapeutic relief for the concerned family member or friend. Occasionally, this can be done on the phone, but more often than not, the caller is more than willing to make an appointment and deal with the issues face to face. An in-person meeting will help create a therapeutic alliance. It will provide an opportunity for the motivated caller to work on the problem of enmeshment with the patient and to work with issues of guilt, helplessness, fury, shame, or simply practical worry about an at-risk individual in his or her life. Make no mistake, the subject of the phone call is probably in need of assistance, but the caller has shown motivation, initiated contact, and indicated a readiness to change how he or she is dealing with the presenting problem.

If the person making the therapy inquiry is the parent of the identified patient, and the therapist agrees to treat the child without attending to the parent's psychological distress, that parent will often disrupt

288

therapy with phone calls or requests for joint sessions, or even seek separate sessions, in pursuit of his or her own relief. The whole foundation of family therapy is that the entire family is in need of treatment, and each member is acting out through his or her role in the family. There are clearly many strategies for dealing with dysfunctional families; family therapy, marriage counseling, or even multiple individual therapies could potentially be successful. However, respect for the initial caller is paramount, and one could infer by the phone call that the initial caller is the most therapeutically motivated member of the family.

I highly recommend aligning with the person making the phone call in order to determine if that person needs to be immediately referred for support, or whether the subject of the phone call should be referred for therapy in favor of treating the caller. As professionals, we need an extended network of professionals that we can rely on to provide quality and effective psychological care.

This first phone call sets the stage for therapy. It illustrates the types of questions that will be asked, the level of honesty and truth that will be expected in the sessions, the therapist's style of relating, what the therapist is willing to do and what the therapist expects the client to do, the financial obligations of treatment, and the basic requirements for entering into psychotherapy.

A brief note about finances: highly motivated (essentially desperate) clients will often commit to financial obligations they simply cannot sustain over a long period of time. A realistic assessment of cost and capacity to pay must be a part of the initial therapeutic alliance so that the therapy doesn't collapse under the financial weight three months into the treatment.

I try to accomplish several things in the phone interview: empathy, problem solving, identified patient, motivated client, available social services, financial costs, the source of the referral, current medications, employment, and the marital and family situation. This information falls into three categories: situational, personal, and medical.

Do not confuse your need for information with the caller's attempt to process the problem over the phone. This is not a time for phone therapy. The first phone call must be directed by the therapist, or else the client will develop poor therapeutic habits and false expectations right from the start.

When we consider the phone interview, think "medical model": information, information, information. Clients will display amazing pathology on the first phone contact, demonstrating passivity, helplessness, rude behavior, super helpfulness, and reluctance, to name a few common attitudes.

The First Session: Once an agreement has been reached on the phone, the client is prepared for the first session in the office. There is a rather delicate interaction that occurs in the first face-to-face encounter. Both the therapist and the client are hoping that the other is not crazy. More specifically, the client is hoping beyond hope that the therapist is well trained and capable of helping, will be a good fit for his or her issues, and will not abuse the client's vulnerability. The therapist is, of course, hoping that the client has a problem he or she is familiar with and can successfully treat (something that should have been established in the phone interview), but also that the client is relatively stable with an extended support group (demonstrating the capacity and drive to bond with others and interpersonally interact), and not an unhinged psychopath trying to avoid jail. Each is trying to "read" the other to determine the likelihood of a successful alliance and positive outcome. The therapist, though, has two specific goals: to make a diagnosis and determine a treatment strategy.

Many therapists are challenged by the professional distance required to be effective in their work. For social workers, this can be particularly difficult. Social work training is strongly resource and solution-oriented, and the therapist can become a social service advocate rather than a clinical specialist. As psychotherapists, whether psychologist, counselor, or social worker, appropriate social distance is required to successfully work with the material in the unconscious. Sometimes thinking like an auto mechanic is helpful at this stage. In truth, it is not completely outrageous to compare a human psyche to an automobile. Both are designed to transfer energy into action, gather data about the environment, and provide a safe and successful journey through life. When some aspect of the car is not working properly, there are symptoms to express this malfunction. And at the beginning stages of automobile repair, we are less interested in being "friends" with the mechanic than we are in determining if he or she has the knowledge and ability to correct the problem. Later, with experience, we may develop an ongoing relationship with our mechanic and trust him or her with a variety of mechanical problems. Similarly, at the beginning, the therapist needs to gather information quickly and form a theory as to the psychological structural problem that is producing the suffering in our client. Even though the presenting problems and the symptoms are crystal clear, the core psychological problem that inhibits our client's ability to resolve those presenting problems is the real subject of the therapy. An accurate assessment of the contributing factors to our client's suffering will increase the possibility of the success of the treatment.

What follows is the interview structure that I use for diagnosis and treatment strategy. These areas will obviously overlap in their contribution to identifying the client's overall personality structure, emotional expression, self-image, and social functioning.

1. *Environmental Stressors:* These are often the most obvious issues in a client's life. But just as often, some contributing factors are hidden environmental stressors that the client is embarrassed about. We need to account for all of the situational stressors and determine which ones are acute and which are chronic. Employment, academic, financial, personal relationships, and legal, health, and transition problems (such as moving, graduation, death, marriage, birth, breakup/separation/divorce), are all examples of environmental stressors that may or may not be voluntarily revealed.

   Always keep in mind that our emotional reaction should be in proportion to the problem. Any emotions that are out of proportion to the reported stressors indicate the presence of an expressive disorder (over controlling personality structure and a history of blocked emotional expression).

   Environmental stressors are the most common "presenting problems" in therapy. In reality, these stressors are often the "straw that broke the camel's back": the tipping point that the client's personality structure was unable to manage. Under other circumstances, the client might have handled the problem without issue. In psychodynamic terms, the client's thresholds for perception and expression have been breached, and the emotional reaction (driven by repressed emotional material) has overloaded the psychological system, producing a wave of symptoms.

2. *Medical history:* In a culture with many mixed families or missing or avoidant parents, getting a complete family medical history is difficult. However, the possibility of the presence of an inherited affective disorder or learning disorder is common in this work. Chronic problems with concentration, grades, work performance, sexual performance, mood disorders, anxiety disorders, motivational issues, developmental disabilities, low energy, and a variety of neurological challenges are common contributing problems to the client's symptom profile.

   Within a twelve-month period, I had four college students suffering from dyscalculia (math processing problems). A feature they all shared was the inability to "read" an analogue clock. They couldn't quickly tell the time with a typical round clock with hands pointing at the numbers. They had each developed their own strategy for determining the time from an analogue clock, but their methods considerably delayed getting an answer to the question, "What time is it?" Some even wore analogue watches, but only as jewelry. Most used their digital clock on their phone to tell time. Another challenge that is linked with dyscalculia is the inability to make change if the cash register did not give them the specific amount to be returned. I began asking everyone who claimed math difficulties to tell me the time from my analogue wall clock, which provided a simple diagnostic clue.

Getting access to the family medical history can be very helpful in a differential diagnosis. In addition, the individual's personal medical history is often significant. Early childhood illnesses, medical emergencies, corrective procedures, hearing problems, word and math processing problems, speaking problems, mobility problems, digestive disorders, and other physiological issues can all affect psychological development. Remember, in the diagnostic stage, we are searching for the source of the symptoms, and developmental health traumas and / or biochemical predispositions can be significant in their influence on the client's personality structure and behavior.

3. *Developmental Trauma:* Of course, personal histories vary widely from client to client. Aggressive discipline, isolation, deaths, divorce, blended families, sexual abuse, parents with obsessions, compulsions, or phobias, a family that cyclically relocates (such as a military family), repeatedly broken bonds with schoolmates and friends through relocation, severe illnesses, operations and corrective surgeries, alcoholic or drug-dependent parents, family violence, and poverty are some of the more significant contributors to developmental trauma. As noted earlier in this book, these types of trauma can be divided into two categories: direct and exposure. (See chapter 4, "Trauma Dynamics," for a complete discussion of this topic.) Direct traumas are those that physically impact the child, causing high levels of distress, distorted self-image, rigid self-control, and destructive behaviors, while exposure traumas are those the child is repeatedly exposed to that create a chaotic, and even terrifying, environment and cause perceptual and emotional distortions.

Most, if not all, expressive inhibitions (personality disorders) that develop during the early developmental stages (up to seven years old) are associated with physical discipline and social isolation (separation). Although many clients will report little or no physical discipline, the severity of blocked self-expression is always in proportion to the threats of childhood. The more rigid the self-control, the more threatening the childhood trauma. Just because a child is able to avoid repeated physical discipline, this does not mean that he or she was not disciplined. It simply means that the child quickly compromised any behaviors necessary to avoid punishment. The threat or implementation of physical discipline is almost universally used to control children, regardless of culture. The consequence of this discipline is the inhibition of self-expression and a reduction of the child's quality of life. In this matter, the books by the analyst Alice Miller have been of particular help for both professionals and clients. I keep multiple copies of one of her most popular books, *The Drama of the Gifted Child*, in my office. There is a cycle to processing childhood discipline and punishment during therapy. As the client repeatedly encounters the anxiety associated with self-expression and self-activation, the rising emotional fear needs to be reconnected with its original punitive history. Emotion needs to be reconnected to the history that created the fear.

Never underestimate the use of physical discipline in childhood as the underlying threat behind many, if not most, blocked emotions.

For the clinician to truly understand the rigidity of the client's emotional expression, he or she needs to assess the extent of the underlying threat in the home. "I was only spanked a few times" is a common response when a client is asked to explore childhood discipline. Yet, those few incidents of physical discipline were sufficient enough to encourage the child to abandon the behavior linked to the spanking. Even if the child avoids repeated physical punishment, the fear of such consequences is sufficient to lead to the repression and dissociation associated with all personality disorders.

4. *Blocked Emotional Expression:* Sublimation, repression, and dissociation are the goldmine of psychotherapy. These defenses are what create perceptual distortion, emotional blockages, energy compromise, and poor self-image. However, if just identifying the repressed neural-emotional complex were sufficient to cure the client, therapy would last about two hours. Unfortunately, once the blocked emotions have been identified, overcoming developmental fears and generating new behaviors consistent with the client's quality of life takes many months, and more often, years.

The importance of self-expression is not difficult to understand. What can be surprising is the level of anxiety associated with the activation of a part of the psyche that was forbidden by the family.

"I never cry," "anger is destructive," "I know sex should be fun," "I'm a quiet person and don't say much," and "I'm not very

293

smart" are all common statements that reflect inhibited self-expression, and they are often spoken during the early sessions. Even without such comments, however, the assessment of repression is fairly straightforward.

I evaluate the functionality of each of the five major neural-emotional complexes: thought, speech, sadness, anger, and sexuality. (See chapter 2, "Structure of the Psyche.") Most people have access to, and express, a percentage of each of these emotions. However, in all of us, each of these emotions is compromised to some degree. It is not uncommon to encounter people who have highly evolved perceptual and expressive capacities in very specific areas of self-expression and simultaneously suffer from significantly restricted perception and expression with other emotions. The restricted emotional expression is what brings many people to therapy. The evaluation of these five centers of awareness will take place throughout therapy as a touchstone for growth and therapeutic improvement. We will return to these five neural-emotional complexes at several stages in this chapter.

So why do so many people have self-expressive issues? Part of the problem is that the unconscious, by design, immediately responds to every situation encountered, in proportion to the emotional requirements of the moment: sadness in, sadness out; thought in, thought out; anger in, anger out.

A general rule is that most people are good at either sadness or anger, but rarely both. The emotions that are easily expressed in the therapy session are the uninhibited emotions and are, for the most part, doing their job. If a client cries a lot during therapy, he or she probably does not really need to work on sadness; that client is already pretty good at expressing that emotion. The emotions that are restricted, repressed, and dissociated are the therapeutic problem areas.

Most presenting problems in therapy involve psychological blind spots that prevent the clients from solving their life crises on their own. The therapist's job is not to solve the problem for the client (shared functioning), but rather to help the client overcome the fear of accessing and expressing the emotions associated with the blind spot. So the fundamental questions are: can you think and have opinions, can you speak up for yourself, can you cry, can you get angry, and can you express your sexuality? Simple.

Motivating the client to overcome his or her fear of the consequences of self-activation and expression is the core of psychotherapy.

Stage 2: Build Therapeutic Alliance

Goal 2: Beginning of the Transference

The therapeutic alliance is of the highest significance. Without it, no therapy can take place. The therapeutic alliance is simply the emotional agreement to work together with minimum initial resistance. The therapeutic relationship is initially so artificial that suspicion and psychological defenses are alerted at the beginning of the treatment. The therapist only has a brief window of opportunity to assess compatibility, motivation, and psychological defenses and then to propose an alliance.

In many cases, an enduring therapeutic alliance may take a long time to accomplish, but in every case, an alliance is necessary for success. However, it is critical that the therapist discern the nature of a true alliance. Do not mistake hope and cooperation on the part of the client for a therapeutic alliance. Real trust only occurs when the client is satisfied that he or she is perceiving the therapist accurately. The client's willingness to trust a therapist is always initially based on a leap of faith (and sometimes a recommendation from a friend).

If I sense too much anxiety in the first session, I will suggest a five-session trial for the client to get a feel for the work and for me. I've found that any significant resistance to the therapy will surface at the third or fourth session. Obviously, missed sessions or chronic tardiness are negative indications for the success of the therapy. Some clients are simply not ready to do the deeper work that will provide the longest positive result. Changing symptoms is not difficult and can be accomplished quickly, but real psychological change requires effort, suffering, and a significant shift in self-perception and expression.

I always give two homework assignments at the first session: develop an exercise program and begin a dream journal. I am convinced that energy is the main missing component in a successful and enjoyable life. Most non-medical psychological challenges are directly associated with low energy, and I want to establish right from the start the importance of increasing one's energy level. The therapeutic alliance will evolve into the initial therapeutic transference, which is the beginning of an evolving perceptual and expressive transformation by the client. However, at the beginning stages of the therapeutic relationship, the client's style of relating will be shaped by the structure of his or her personality and the power of his or her unconscious contents. The transference is essentially the client's unconscious shaping of the therapeutic relationship, based on the rules and expectations of the client's personality.

As the transference arises, the client will begin an internal struggle for emotional expression versus re-repression and dissociation from those awakening memories and emotions. The potential threat of being psychologically re-injured presents itself as the anxiety and depression associated with self-activation (after all, the client is trying to differentiate between the therapeutic relationship and the punitive parental relationship). It is this relationship struggle—between client, the client's unconscious, and therapist—that provides the content and fuel for the therapy. ((See chapter 8, "Treatment," *Transference*.)

STAGE 3: BEGIN TREATMENT

GOAL 3: TRANSFERENCE DIAGNOSIS AND THERAPY STRATEGY

Keep in mind that Stage 2 and Stage 3 might happen within a couple of sessions. The therapeutic strategy is intimately linked to the therapeutic alliance. The alliance is simply the hesitant agreement between client and therapist that the relationship has potential and should be further pursued. Once the therapeutic alliance has been established, the client will begin to form a pattern of relating that will reveal the underlying personality structure, and when the personality structure is determined (the diagnosis), a therapy strategy will direct the beginning stages of treatment.

There are many methods of identifying "types" of transferences, but personality type has some predictable features: submissive, charming, adversarial, cooperative, chaotic, pleasing, strategic, and resistant are a few easily recognizable relationship characteristics. These features, combined with the Masterson diagnostic criteria (see chapter 3, "Personality Structure,") will provide a solid diagnosis.

There are specific therapeutic strategies for the treatment of each of the major personality structures. For narcissistic: supportive, empathetic, and reflective. For dependent-borderline: confrontive. For anti-social: confrontive. For Asperger's: informative, with intent to expand interactive skill set. Asperger's, due to its mimicking personality styles, can initially appear dependent, narcissistic, or anti-social. Asperger's and anti-social are the two most under-diagnosed categories. (See chapter 3, "Personality Structure.")

The passive-aggressive challenge: With a client who is particularly stubborn or passive aggressive, generating a therapeutic transference can be very challenging. Depending on what percentage of the client's personality is contaminated with this passive aggressive defense, there may be little clear personality with which to create an alliance. If the passive aggressive client has enough dependent traits, the client may come to therapy and, essentially, pretend to work without ever developing a sufficiently strong transference to actually provide the unconscious material to work with. In these cases the client makes little progress, the therapeutic goal (for the client) remains unclear, and the therapist should be able to feel the frustration with the lack of therapeutic traction. Continually challenging the client to address the questions "Why are we here?" and "What is your goal?" helps define the vision and confront the client's passive control of the therapy. The client's passivity is the undermining form of the adversarial transference: the hidden saboteur. These clients live in a world of moderate competence, with great potential and little to show for it. They pretend to be invested in their relationship goals when, in fact, they are subtly sabotaging every encounter. The passive aggressive feature in the transference simply holds the unconscious material and the psychological potential hostage, releasing just enough content to keep the therapy alive, but starving the process of real movement.

This is different from the subtle (and sometimes not so subtle) anti-social adversarial transference. In these cases, the client will do some problem solving to improve his or her quality of life, but as soon as the therapist attempts to establish more than a simple therapeutic alliance, because intimacy is perceived as a threat, the anti-social client will act out to provoke distance in the therapeutic relationship.

As I discuss throughout this book, when it comes to diagnosing and treating personality disorders, I find the DSM highly problematic. It is a symptom-based system that requires evidence of such extreme pathology that it interferes with accurate diagnosis and treatment in the less extreme population, the majority of clients seeking treatment. (One might suspect that the DSM committee makes sure the symptomatic "bar" for most diagnostic criteria is set higher than their own pathology.) The borderline diagnosis is the best example of the DSM's poor symptomatic criteria, poor treatment outcome, and blending of incompatible personality features. (See chapter 3, "Personality Structure," *The Borderline Diagnosis*.) How can one client have both extreme passivity combined with outrageous acting out? It is psychologically inconsistent. Only a committee could find agreement in putting these competing and conflicting features together in one category.

As clinicians, we need to be able to differentiate between the core personality structure and the other personality features. To review, the borderline diagnosis criteria are a blending of the dependent personality features with the anti-social personality features. It is my opinion that the borderline diagnosis is the hiding place for our society's anti-social population. Most research in psychopathic behavior is based on the superb work of Dr. Robert Hare, who outlined the biological aspects of psychopaths. He estimates a three percent saturation of the population by this biologically based psychopathic personality. However, I believe that the anti-social demographic is much higher: perhaps as much as fifteen to twenty percent of the total population, with the additional anti-social population emerging from developmental trauma.

The object relations diagnostic criteria of Dr. James Masterson is a more accurate diagnostic system. Masterson views narcissistic, dependent-borderline, and anti-social (non-biological psychopaths) as object relations personality structures arising predominantly out of the primary relationship with the mother or principle caregiver. It is a contract based on how the mother trains the child to relate to her and her world. In a bare-bones description of this process, the family trains the child by introducing and reinforcing:

- A cultural schema through which to perceive the world, insisting on adherence to this point of view;
- *Which* components of the child's psyche will be expressed or repressed;
- *How* these components will be expressed; and
- Which psychological symptoms will take the place of the repressed emotions (e.g., anxiety instead of sexuality).

This family / social training becomes the principal determiner of the child's personality structure.

It is the behavioral contract between family and child, expressed as personality style, that the client will use in therapy to relate to the therapist. The presenting symptoms are simply the expression of the components of the client's psyche that have been overly restricted.

I cannot emphasize this enough: psychological symptoms are not the problem; they are the presentation of, and chronic solution to, the problem. Symptoms release the psychological pressure caused by blocked self-expression.

Identifying the personality structure, developing a treatment strategy for increasing self-expression and accuracy of perception, and working through historical emotional wounds is true psychotherapy. Everything else is problem solving, shared functioning, or transition phase resolution: legitimate methods in short-term therapy but not long-term solutions to problems of a repressive psychological structure.

STAGE 4: SYMPTOM ANALYSIS

GOAL 4: IDENTIFY DOMINANT SYMPTOMS AND ACTING OUT BEHAVIOR

Stage 4 is the identification of the patient symptom profile. The client's presenting symptoms are usually directly in proportion to:

- the intensity of the current environmental stressors;
- the client's psychological ability to negotiate that environmental challenge;
- the client's overall physical health; and
- the rigidity of the personality structure: limited expressive options.

These four factors produce the client's symptom profile. The number, frequency, and intensity of the symptoms indicate how much of the client's self-expression is being repressed and begins to reveal the severity of the personality rigidity.

The more severe the psychological symptoms, the more difficult a true therapeutic alliance will be. The alliance will be in association with the healthier aspects of the personality (the true Self), and thus the severity of symptoms will indicate how much of the psyche the personality is controlling and how much natural function is left with which to develop an alliance.

Symptoms will vary even among those with similar personality diagnoses. Most symptoms are shared by all personality structures, and the symptoms that stand out from client to client are more of a comment about the client's family, culture, and gender role.

The client's symptom profile is directly associated with his or her repressed or dissociated emotions. If all emotions followed a 10-point scale, with 1 being a bit of emotion and 10 being fully empowered and unhesitant with emotion, most people have emotional blocks in the 4-8 range. For people with reasonable social skills, there is a comfortable window of emotional expression (1-3 range). Then, as environmental or interpersonal stress increases, the emotional tension crosses the expressive threshold, and the personality shuts the emotion down, triggering symptoms (4-7 range). Once the emotion reaches a critical mass and explodes, expression occurs again (8-10 range), allowing the person to feel and express virtually anything. That critical 4-7 range of emotional repression is what causes all the daily discomfort and produces most symptoms. This is the range associated with most inhibited self-expression. It is rare that any emotion is completely blocked, but this does happen.

For example, anger may be available when the client is mildly frustrated, but not when the client is angry or furious. At that point, the personality does its job and restricts self-expression out of fear of the social consequences. Immediately, symptoms replace the emotional expression, and the intensity of the symptom indicates the amount of emotion being controlled. Remember, if you have a healthy body, your emotional responses are naturally designed to reflect the intensity and emotion of the moment. If the emotional reaction is more or less than what is situationally proportional, either the client's emotional history is breaking out (too much emotion), another emotion is being sublimated through the over-amplified feeling (inaccurate emotion), or complete repression and dissociation is taking place, and the symptoms are the relief valve for the pressure generated by the emotions not being expressed.

All symptoms and acting out behaviors are attempts to bring energetic equilibrium to the psyche.

When the triggering events cease, the symptomology will eventually subside, the acting out will stop, and the person will operate within his or her normal personality style. When the triggering events are ongoing, the symptomology and acting out escalate in proportion to the level and longevity of the stressor.

As therapists, we only have the brief windows of symptomatic expression during which to identify the emotions that are being compromised and producing symptoms. I utilize the five neural-emotional centers approach—thought, speech, sadness, anger, and sexuality—as a way to reduce the distractions of the symptoms and to refocus the therapy to the actual underlying expressive psychological problem. I refer the reader to my psychosomatic scale. (See chapter 2, "Structure of the Psyche.")

Part of my interview and intervention process is to identify the one or two severely blocked emotional expressions that are the source of the symptomology and to orient the therapy around learning to express these emotions more directly and immediately. The resistance that arises from the attempt to self-activate (express forbidden feelings) leads to the deeper therapy of working through old emotional traumas (childhood history) and building the client's ability to safely and successfully defend against perceived and remembered threats to the client's physical, emotional, and spiritual safety.

Acting Out: There are six "acting out" criteria that affect the client's quality of life:

1. Psychological symptoms
2. Health issues
3. Alcohol, drugs, or prescription medications
4. Personal relationships
5. Financial issues
6. Self-destructive behaviors

Symptom identification is fairly simple. However, connecting the client's symptoms with their corresponding blocked emotions takes some effort and insight.

1. *Psychological Symptoms:* In my clinical work, I emphasize eleven major symptoms: anxiety, tension, stress, guilt, shame, fear, resentment, grief, worry, depression, and somatization. However, these symptoms are merely the distracting features of the client's repressive personality system. These symptoms are not the problem, merely *the evidence of a problem.* Once it becomes clear, for example, that the client's anxiety or guilt is associated with anger, the therapist has a shortcut to working on the expressive problem: the emotion of anger. When the client can express anger in an effective manner, symptoms will simply recede until the next wave of external stressors overwhelms the client's expressive ability and a new threshold of expression is breeched. For all of us, self-expression is an evolving goal in that we are continually learning to improve our ability to stabilize and express our emotional potential.

What initially starts as an expressive therapeutic goal eventually becomes the limiting threshold that we now wish to exceed in our pursuit of full emotional self-expression.

2. *Health Issues:* Health issues are often directly linked to:

- genetic predisposition to disease;
- traumatic developmental history; and
- blocked emotional expression.

There is often an intimate relationship between emotional expression and organ function. The following are possible links between psyche and soma:

- Headaches and obsessive tendencies
- Respiratory problems and sadness
- Digestive/elimination problems and anger
- Reproductive problems and sexual blocks

Disease is opportunistic. We don't give ourselves cancer or migraines, but we do provide the opportunity for disease to take advantage of the physical conditions created by stress. As our stress increases, the body's genetic vulnerabilities are revealed in illness and disease. Our emotional stress levels can directly contribute to the higher likelihood of physical health challenges.

Most clients have a target organ (a specific part of the body) that is the "smoke-alarm" of the client's stress levels. When the stress levels get too intense, that organ will start complaining first. Headaches, rash, STD activation, digestive disorders, illness susceptibility, and even being accident-prone are only a few of the physical manifestations of stress. Our first-to-react organs (back pain, headaches, etc.) are often our most susceptible to stress and provide useful information about our stress levels by producing symptoms. A good therapist will identify and then use the cycling symptomology of this organ to evaluate progress or regress in the therapy. In family systems, it is the identified patient who plays this role: the canary in the coalmine, the first to act out as the family stress level rises.

Integrative/holistic psychotherapy will use the physical symptoms of our clients as part of the overall treatment strategy. Chronic physical challenges limit the client's energy, ability to concentrate, and stamina and increase stress levels.

Two of the most widespread medical diagnoses often associated with psychotherapy are chronic fatigue and fibromyalgia. Each of these complicated syndromes contains psychological and physiological components. As psychotherapists, we must not underestimate the importance of poor health choices, developmental interruption, post-traumatic stress, affective disorders (depression or bi-polar spectrum), unresolved grief, highly toxic relationships, isolation, adoption, and other classic psychological stress producers, in the etiology of both of these physical disorders. Their near epidemic arrival during the 1990s and their stubborn resistance to any single type of treatment certainly requires the assembly of a treatment team that will work with the entire client: medical, psychological, and chiropractic practitioners; massage therapists, nutritionists, allergists; experts in environmental toxin evaluation, etc. Although no single treatment modality is likely to solve these complex syndromes, this multi-disciplined approach often provides a reduction in the illness cycle and longer-lasting relief, and it increases a client's ability to tolerate those painful cycles when they do occur.

3. Drugs or Prescription Medications: Anything that prevents the body from operating at its optimal level is to be considered a psychological issue. The body is the energy, emotion, and information resource system, and any limitation of its function undermines energy levels, emotional balance, and perceptual accuracy. So, of course we are concerned with our client's medications and "recreational" drug use. Narcotic use and alcoholism are seriously problematic in that drug dependency inhibits neural receptivity and emotional expression: therapy can only follow sobriety and any habitual use of drugs limits or undermines therapeutic success. There is a place for psychiatric medications, but this type of treatment needs to have a strategic place in the overall therapy.

A significant part of the medical doctor's healing arts as practiced in today's pharmaceutical culture is prescription medication. I am a holistic health practitioner, and I believe there is a place for medication in psychological treatment. And of course I believe in complementary healing methodologies, but I do not substitute conviction for wisdom. Too many alternative healing practitioners are in conflict with, rather than complementary to, healthy medical practices. Is medication over-prescribed? Absolutely. Anti-anxiety medications are probably the most widely substituted medication for psychotherapy. If you are taking anti-anxiety meds for extended periods of time without being diagnosed with an affective disorder (depression or bi-polar) or an anxiety disorder, a reassessment of your psychological needs is in order. For many people, however, medication is absolutely necessary and provides significant relief and correction of biological issues.

The placebo response is often viewed as fake healing, which is ridiculous. Belief is a powerful tool, and our conviction that we can and will be helped contributes greatly to the success of *any* healing process. Remember the Navajo healer mentioned in Chapter Eight "Treatment," *Transference*, who stated "If they [his patients] believe in me, they get better." This is the heart of all healing: faith in the healer. Medications, poultices, herbs, hypnosis, teas, and all forms of chemical and natural substances have purpose in the art of healing, but without confidence in the doctor/healer/shaman/therapist, the effectiveness of the medication, whatever its type, can be limited. The mind is a powerful source of cooperation or resistance, and the effect it has on the body is profound.

4. *Personal Relationships:* There are certainly enough people in the world for everyone to have the personal relationships they desire. One of the initial therapeutic tasks will be to reveal the perceptual blind spot that limits environmental options. The challenge with assembling friends and mates is *not* that there are insufficient people available to meet our needs, but that we have been trained psychologically to be attracted only to certain personality types (good or bad) and to ignore everyone else in our environment. Operating with a psychological blind-spot is not just a clever euphemism for another missed opportunity. Rather, the emotional signal of so many people falls below our threshold of perception so that we literally do not perceive these individuals in our environment. They are "flying under the radar," so to speak.

Relationships are certainly near the top of the list for what motivates clients into therapy. The client's relationship history is significant in diagnosing personality structure. The ability to create, stabilize, and grow within a variety of long-term relationships signifies a certain psychological maturity. A lack of extended family, peer relationships, or significant partnerships is ominous and a potential predictor for therapeutic chaos. The therapeutic relationship will follow a similar arc to the client's overall intimate relationship history, primarily because the individual's personality structure and relationship expectations are intimately related. How much of any relationship is intimacy and how much is dependency? There is certainly an obvious difference between appreciation and toleration. Are we in relationship to stimulate new and creative ideas or to engage in shared interests, or are we simply fulfilling our family contracts with substitute members? Pathology or reciprocity? The types and quality of relationships our clients report is significant in our understanding and diagnosis of their personality structure.

5. *Money Issues:* Freud is reported to have said, "If you don't pay your bill, you won't get better." Regardless of the historical truth of this statement, one certainly gets what one pays for. A psychiatric friend of mine said that he had two payment methods for his clients: at the beginning of the session or at the end of the session. It is not unusual that during the course of long-term therapy, finances become an issue. If the therapy debt increases, the client's motivation will unconsciously be reduced. I had one client who owed me a significant amount of money and anticipated complete payment due to a tax refund in the New Year (a contract we had negotiated). Upon paying off the debt by handing me a check, the client immediately began the session with "I'm much crazier than you think I am." The therapy, languishing for

months under the burden of the financial debt, suddenly soared with motivation. Money needs to be treated with the same care and dedication as an eating disorder, an obsessive-compulsive gambling disorder, or a history of relationship challenges.

6. *Self-Destructive Behaviors:* Poor eating habits, gambling, risk taking, affairs, indulgent drug and alcohol use, job conflicts, repeated physical injuries, impulsive/compulsive sexual risk, self-abuse, bad driving habits, confrontations with the law, academic failures: these are the well-known behaviors associated with clients in crisis. Whether chronic or acute, these behaviors are the signs of psychological or medical problems. If these are not a part of the client's presenting problems, they certainly need to be addressed if only in consideration of the diagnosis. Successful therapy is partially marked by a significant reduction in risk-taking behavior.

STAGE 5: NEURAL-EMOTIONAL COMPLEX ANALYSIS

GOAL 5: IDENTIFY THE PERCEPTUAL/EXPRESSIVE LEVELS OF FUNCTION OF THE FIVE NEURAL EMOTIONAL COMPLEXES

The neural-emotional assessment is simply an attempt to establish the functionality of each emotion in terms of input (perceptual accuracy) and output (proportional emotional expression). The clinician and the client are attempting to establish which centers of awareness (thought, voice, sadness, anger, sexuality) are actively expressed and which are being repressed and creating the psychological symptoms that have brought the client to therapy. Remember, neural complex (except speech) has two functions: perception and expression. Thus, we are evaluating how accurately the individual perceives the information provided by each neural-emotional center, as well as how each emotion is expressed in response.

Most people have at least partial access to each of the five expressive systems, but very few people have full and complete access to even one, much less all five. The body seems to have a nearly infinite capacity to resonate with phenomena, and awareness seems to be naturally driven (Maslow's hierarchy of needs) to grow and master our sensitivity and ability to emotionally tolerate, translate, and respond to all of the environmental information to which we are exposed. What modern human beings accept about their world as "obvious" would have been unthinkable to humanity even a few hundred years ago.

Part of the curious aspect of humanity's experience of the world is that we live with complete confidence about our perception of the world, while operating with perhaps as little as one percent of the information the world has to give us. This is conviction replacing wisdom. Since it is the duty of our neural-emotional centers to continually provide information to awareness, our capacity for emotional wisdom is, potentially, limitless. The more emotion we are capable of perceptually and expressively stabilizing, the more information we have at our disposal.

Just as a computer has faster and slower capacities of downloading information, the body's functioning varies in pace, with the personality structure dictating a download rate and exerting "parental controls" on forbidden content. The more rapid the download rate (reflecting minimal repression and dissociation) and the less restrictive the personality (with parental controls deactivated), the more energy, information, and emotional expression we have with which to experience and enjoy the world.

I've found that most clients have a fairly accurate assessment of their emotional abilities, although perceptual distortions can be very difficult to identify. This is why such distortions are referred to as "blind spots." They are not visible to the one who possesses them. Emotions are straightforward. You are either effectively expressing thought, speech, sadness, anger, and sexuality or you are not. Perceptual distortions are identified by the results they produce: cyclical and repeating dreams, failed relationships, inability to resolve interpersonal conflicts, trusting the wrong people, being taken advantage of, and a fundamental inability of the client to explain why he or she is unable to solve the problems leading him or her into therapy.

The client may have a very accurate perception of the world and simultaneously be extremely restricted in emotional response. Or, the client may have full expression of any of the emotions and lack perceptual accuracy. Thus, the client continuously runs failed experiments that lead to lots of emotion but produce no better results.

Therapeutic crises are almost always a combination of environmental and physical stressors overwhelming the person's expressive abilities. The world is demanding more of a response than the person feels comfortable expressing, creating tremendous internal pressure. The individual's threshold of expression is too restrictive for the current situation and the personality is producing symptoms instead of emotions or insights. For instance, too much sadness combined with too little crying produces symptomology.

One quick assessment tool is to determine whether the client can fantasize about the restricted emotion, the emotion that seems to be missing. Sexual fantasy, aggressive fantasy, sadness fantasy, and intellectual fantasy all illustrate the limits of perception and expression. Many clients feel very uncomfortable with their fantasy lives. Every once in a while, a fantasy sneaks into awareness, triggering familiar symptoms: guilt, shame, fear, etc. As clinicians, we can accomplish as much by deguilting fantasy as we can by supporting emotional expression, because fantasy is one of the steps leading up to emotional expression. The ability of awareness not only to tolerate fantasy but to enjoy the emotions associated with fantasy shows progress in psychological expression. Obviously, fantasy by itself is still limited self-expression, with some fantasies illustrating creative solutions for relieving emotional tension and other fantasies better left unfulfilled. But even the dangerous and dark fantasies at least illustrate blocked psychological content.

However, fantasy, just like emotion, has a pathological element when it becomes obsessive.

Fantasy is simply a key step in awareness moving toward consciousness, but is a transitional phase that should serve a temporary function on the road toward wisdom and response. Fantasy will always serve a purpose as new experiences are incorporated by awareness, but can become just as problematic as any emotion when held hostage without appropriate self-expression. To be stuck in a world of fantasy is just as debilitating as being stuck in any form of emotional depression: it does not allow for the full energetic potential of the psyche. It's merely a stage along the path to self-expression, integration, and wisdom.

Jung contended that there is no difference between energy and image, and the limits of fantasy were likewise the limits of psychological energy. Assessment needs to include not only the client's pathological expressions of thought, speech, sadness, aggression, and sexuality as a way of determining where the psyche is obstructed, but also where the individual has successfully integrated aspects of these emotional functions: insight, communication, love, courage, and intimacy as templates of successful psychological health. The client's ability to fantasize represents his or her growth potential, whereas his or her symptom profile reveals the more conflicted emotions.

Let's briefly examine an approach to assessing the five neural-emotional centers:

Thought: Obviously, everybody thinks, but clients are often not permitted to have opinions or to comment on what they think is going on with themselves—or to direct their own therapy. Asking about a favorite movie, book, piece of music, political opinion, or religious conviction will often quickly reveal the level of repression in the client's thinking. It is surprising how difficult it is for some clients to simply express an opinion or to spontaneously respond to simple questions. There is an aspect of intellectual inhibition in everyone, but in this assessment, we are attempting to determine the extent of the inhibition. The aim is to determine whether or not the client's intellectual process will be an ally or obstacle in the therapeutic process. It's not about intelligence, it's about the client's ability to express him/herself through the thinking function. Intellectual assessment, as far as expression goes, also includes the client's learning curve, how quickly the client absorbs complex or new ideas, and how much confidence the client has in his or her intuition. Sometimes, a simple question, asking clients how intelligent they consider themselves to be, can reveal potent material.

And then there are those clients who seem to have not taken advantage of their intellectual ability. They will be quick witted, possess a fast learning curve, and yet will be undereducated or underemployed. Why is their intellectual potential so compromised? The therapist needs to be willing to consider the likelihood of learning disorders in those clients whose intellect and vocation or education seem to be in conflict. I keep a dozen or so CD lectures on a variety of subjects ranging from dream analysis to art and physics, and I lend these to clients to assess curiosity and intellectual ability or to provide direction or modeling in therapy.

Speech: There is a difference between our ability to talk and our ability to express our emotions. The client's ability to connect speech to thought, sadness, anger, and sexuality is what completes the link in communicating who we are. Each neural-emotional complex has its own expressive and perceptual agenda, except for speech. Speech serves the other emotional centers. It is the voice of our psychological experience. Most people have been given selective permission about what is acceptable to speak of and what one should remain silent about. Often the emotional disconnect is *not* a matter of "I don't know what I feel," but rather, "I am not 'allowed' to express that feeling verbally." Discussing feelings for many people is a great challenge. Suggesting to couples that they talk to each other during sex is often received as embarrassing or provokes anxiety. Most people have one or two emotions they are unable to verbalize easily: opinions, sadness, anger, or sexuality.

The therapist's task is to determine which of these emotions can be discussed, described, or expressed and whether speech is successfully interconnected with these four neural-emotional complexes.

Sadness: Assessing emotional expression includes identifying where and when an emotion can be expressed. A client may say that he or she is capable of crying, but in reality, the client only cries when alone or isolated. Or, emotional expression may be available to the client, but solely under extreme circumstances. Ultimately, emotional health is the immediate experience and expression of feeling. Any delay will produce a corresponding reduction in energy and increase in symptoms. If a client can and will cry during a session and also reports that crying is not difficult, then using a lot of therapy time with the client crying is probably not helping much, except in cases of grief. As discussed earlier, allowing a client to substitute a safe emotion for a repressed emotion does not advance therapy. A habitual crier is no different than someone who constantly obsesses as a psychological symptom.

Allowing or supporting a client spending the entire session obsessing or crying or raging has no practical therapeutic value if the client is avoiding working on the emotion that is blocked. Psychological relief occurs only when the blocked emotion is expressed directly and not redirected through the familiar and developed emotions.

Anger: This assessment is the same as the assessment of sadness. Culturally, aggression seems to be polarized in American culture. Although we celebrate aggression in the media, sports, and military, it is difficult for many clients to perceive aggression as a positive emotion. Children are systematically exposed to parental aggression, which is not necessarily bad. However, if the adult aggression manifests in the threat or actuality of physical or emotional harm, the child either develops the parent's indulgent aggressive attitudes and actions or represses his or her own in submission to the threat. The client who develops aggression as a principle expression often sublimates sadness through anger, and in this case, it is the client's sadness that needs therapy. Conversely, the client who represses anger often develops a defensive attitude that anger is bad on a moral level and should be controlled due to its destructive nature. This is psychological prejudice.

Our inability to perceive the link between aggression and courage, or aggression and dynamism, leads to the continued repression of anger and the compromise of its energy and information.

What's curious about the human psyche is that it is attracted to the emotions that it represses. A passive person often finds him/herself dating an aggressive person. Or a sexually repressed individual dates a highly sexual person. It's not that we are attracted to our opposite; it's more likely that we are attracted to our complement, so that the couple's union represents the expression of all of the emotions.

In order to perceive the world accurately and respond in an emotionally appropriate manner, we need access to all of our emotions. To accurately perceive aggression in others, we need access to our own aggression. Ultimately, aggression, like all emotion (as Jung would suggest), is morally and ethically neutral. It is only our attitude toward our emotions, and the skill with which we express them, that charges them in any particular way.

Sexuality: Sexuality is a curious compass. Surely one of the most intimate of emotions, it serves as the ultimate expression of pleasure. When sexuality is severely repressed, our ability to pursue general healthy pleasure in our life is compromised, leading to various forms of compulsive behaviors in which pleasure becomes a sneaky process, fraught with guilt, indulgence, and deceit, with addictive overtones.

Pleasure is monumentally important in that it determines psychological, spiritual, and emotional preferences. We prefer one thing over another because of the pleasure or pain we experience with each. Without access to an internal pleasure compass, our dispassion rules our choices: any job will do, any academic major will do, or any friend will do. Without pleasure, there are no desires that move us through life with a satisfying arc of self-fulfillment. Everything is neutral. If our capacity to experience pleasure is healthy, as we walk through life, certain choices, people, and activities offer a subtle (and sometimes not so subtle) attraction that pulls us to that experience: something about the moment suggests this path or person over another. Without pleasure, our ability to quickly make any choice is delayed and compromised.

Sexuality is simply the most powerful expression of pleasure, and its repression affects the overall quality of our lives. Living a life of activated sexuality does not mean that you must be having regular sex with a partner, however. It simply means that you do not repress your sexual feelings. Sexual energy, like any emotional energy, can be used for a variety of activities, and although sublimation of an emotion is not as efficient as direct expression, one can effectively authorize a healthy redirection of sexual energy into many productive and creative tasks, with little symptomatic overtones. Gardening, music, and athletics, for example, can all serve as healthy redirections of not only sexuality, but of aggression and compassion as well. But this level of emotional mastery takes time and effort. Experimenting with one's own sexuality or aggression can be socially risky and certainly will challenge one's own emotional comfort level. Anxiety can be an indicator of repression, an indicator of extending beyond one's expressive limits, or an indicator of self-destructive behavior. Differentiating between these vastly different possibilities requires patience, emotional self-examination, and honesty. A personal journal, a dream journal, and trusted friends will be invaluable in this process.

Conclusion: Obviously, each emotion contributes its own wisdom to every choice that we make. Aggression protects and inspires us, pleasure soothes us, analysis assembles information, compassion connects us to the life force, and speech defines relationships. The over-control of one or more of these necessary and critical interfaces limits our success in life and certainly impairs our overall joy and energy.

Emotional integration is progressive. As children, we start with overwhelming input, limited mastery, little information, and a thirst for perceptual accuracy. As we master the translation of emotion into information, reality expands and energy increases in a never-ending process of mastery, expansion, and maturing.

STAGE 6: EMOTION ANALYSIS

GOAL 6: EMOTIONAL EXPRESSION, OBSTRUCTION, AND THRESHOLD

Once you've completed the overall assessment of emotional functioning, it should be fairly obvious which emotions function well and which ones do not. Remember, we are working on both perception and expression, as well as on the intensity thresholds required to activate or repress these two functions. These thresholds of perception and expression are the limits of our pathology (perceptual distortion and expressive imbalance). These thresholds determine how accurately we perceive the environment or whether our emotions are expressed or converted into symptoms. So, an emotion may be an emotion until a certain intensity is reached, and then it becomes a symptom, but later may become emotion again when the pressure becomes too much. The emotion remains an emotion as long as it stays below the intensity threshold that triggers sublimation, repression, or dissociation. Once the intensity of the emotion crosses that expressive barrier, personality immediately blocks and converts it into symptom: aggression becomes sadness, sadness becomes worry, sexuality becomes submission, etc. And then, once again, when the emotional pressure reaches the upper limit of toleration, it re-emerges in an explosion of affect, and suddenly the emotion has returned with an intensity often out of proportion to the moment, but sometimes perfectly in proportion to the moment. Remember: we repress our emotions and distort our perception to avoid the punishments we received growing up.

The perceptual threshold operates in a complementary way to the expressive threshold. We see reality, then we don't, and then we do. Perceptual accuracy is always a combination of knowledge, physical function, psychological interpretation, environmental pressure/threat/attraction, and the individual's perceptual threshold. A simple example would be an approaching storm. We may notice the gathering clouds, but in the going about of our daily business we ignore the building pressure of the environment until the storm breaks loose and we are suddenly re-aware of the intensity all around us. We see it, then we don't see it, and then we really see it. This type of perceptual filtering takes place continuously.

As therapists, we are trying to establish which emotions the client is aware of, what emotions the client can express, and how intense an experience has to be for perception and expression to take place. When we listen to a client describe highly stressful and even dangerous living conditions, we marvel at how the client both tolerates the abuse and resists changing the situation. We marvel because our, as therapists, our thresholds of perception and expression are (hopefully) set much lower and we perceive the problem more quickly and emotionally respond to the situation faster. The client either doesn't perceive the stress level yet or is insufficiently motivated to act.

Our childhood experiences set the thresholds through which we perceive and respond to the world. This is why childhood information is important: it tells us how much stress the client is capable of tolerating without taking action.

If we are incapable of perceiving the craziness of our childhood, the difficulties of our current situation are simply mystifying. Our toleration of our childhood traumas predicts our toleration of our chaotic adult circumstances, regardless of the suffering this produces. We only have our psychological and physical symptomology to alert us to the danger we perpetuate. Our bodies react to a situation regardless of whether the personality permits accurate perception or emotional expression, and the moment to moment emotional response from the body is immediate and in proportion to the experience. But the personality has been trained to turn our response into symptoms as a way of surviving our childhood experiences. Thus, our symptoms are the direct

result of the combination of our emotional history and our current circum-
stances. As therapists, our task is to help our clients develop enough courage to
activate their feelings, perceive the reality that they have co-created, and mas-
ter effective emotional communication in order to improve their quality of life.

It is highly possible that the emotion that works well at low levels
of stress, and even at high levels of stress, simply fails to function in the
middle range. The ability to operate emotionally with flexibility may
well be compromised at some range of emotional stressor. However,
everyone has that final threshold that, when crossed, permits the person
to communicate in a very dynamic or dramatic way. This is never more
clearly illustrated than in marriage/divorce counseling. Many divorce
fantasies are predicated on the belief that if the person were free of the
constraints of marriage, he or she could do and say whatever he or she
wanted, that it is the marriage that restricts his or her self-expression.
When couples actually begin to discuss divorce, and not just repair,
suddenly all the rules change and real progress can be made. "Now
I can be my true self. I don't *need* you anymore. I may *want* you, but
I don't *need* you." At this point, people simply start doing and saying
what they've really needed to do and say for years.

At a critical point in one couple's pre-marital therapy, I met with the
fiancée for an individual session to attempt to break through a strong
resentment toward her future husband that had built up over years. I
told her directly that the resentment she felt was due to all the compromises she had made in the relationship. I instructed her that she must
"from now on, only do what you want to do, and stop doing anything
you don't want to do." (Actually, I tell this to all my clients.) She then
looked at me and said, "You're crazy, no one can live that way," and she
never returned to therapy. We are amazingly committed to our own
continued suffering.

Relationships are not without compromise, but compromise is rarely with-
out penalty.

Certainly, it is hard to imagine a marriage without some compromise,
but compromise requires a repression of one's own needs, and with
every compromise there is a contribution to the overall pressure of
the unconscious. If there is limited or no reciprocity in the marital
compromise, the resentment begins to dictate and reduce the quality
of intimacy and affection. When self-expression is repeatedly insulted
by compromise, anger and resentment undermine the relationship. Of
course, everyone has reasons for compromise, and usually the reasoning
seems to make sense. But the type and intensity of the compromises we

are willing to make for our intimate relationships are usually founded on the exact same compromises we made as children to avoid punishment. This is not a good foundation for marriage, and ultimately, the ensuing resentment kills the relationship.

STAGE 7: THE NEUTRAL OBSERVER: OBSERVATION AND INTERVENTION

GOAL 7: REDUCE SELF-ATTACK THROUGH SELF-OBSERVATION

From the beginning, psychotherapy and analysis have been built upon the premise that clients can develop the capacity to observe and integrate new information or learn to express themselves in a manner that improves their psychological functioning, thus raising the quality of their lives. Central to this process is the therapist, whom we can also call the "witness." The role of the therapist varies from psychological school to psychological school. Some disciplines encourage complete neutrality (some would say passivity) combined with intellectual interpretations of client behavior. Other disciplines require a more dynamic interaction with the client, strategically dismantling dysfunctional relationships, or paradoxically bypassing client resistance as a way of activating unconscious material more rapidly than the passive method. However, even the more interactive disciplines are built upon the fundamental neutrality of the therapist. We are certainly allowed to care for our clients, and in some schools of thought, we build a bond that models emotional behavior previously unfamiliar to the client. But even in this more intimate model, the therapist retains a creative neutrality that advocates, not for the ego needs and pathological requirements our clients bring to session, but rather for the creative unfolding of the unconscious and the client's relationship to that dynamic internal resource that Jung called the Self. *To that end, the neutral observer is the single most important component of psychological growth._*

For therapy to succeed, the client needs to be able to observe his or her own behavior and emotional history without self-criticism or attack. This is the beginning of the client developing an internal neutral observer.

Thousands of years of meditation and contemplation have demonstrated the importance of the psychological skill of observation without attitude or attachment. Although Western psychology contributes significant wisdom to our understanding of suffering and liberation, I am convinced that without meditation or a contemplative discipline, full transformation from childhood conditioning will be limited. So much of personality is specifically designed to limit expression of the unconscious, that without the cultivation of a psychological complex (dedicated neural pathways) predicated on neutrality, curiosity, and self-observation without criticism, our psychological potential cannot flourish.

The development the neutral observer is one of the significant differences between the goals of short-term and long-term therapy. Both of these therapies certainly confront, and attempt to control, pathological self-criticism in our clients. Dynamically, automatic and unconscious self-criticism results in the constant short-circuiting of the energetic "budget" of our psyche. However, once self-criticism is contained or simply reduced, the energy previously dedicated to fueling negative thinking is suddenly available for psychological growth.

In short-term therapy, the therapist works to help the client replace some critical self-talk with strategies, reframing, and action plans. In long-term therapy, the neutral observer is mirrored by the therapist and then cultivated as a new habit by the client. This takes time, and the pathological ego is always competing for available psychological energy, so the therapeutic work must always be twofold: (1) interrupt pathological personality traits, and (2) reinforce the new psychological platform associated with the neutral observer.

One of the greatest challenges in psychotherapy is the time required to change years of neurological habits, activate new emotional pathways, and finally give birth to our deeper creative self. When you consider that the time needed for this work is also equated with suffering and financial cost, as professionals, we should be asking ourselves continually how we can abbreviate this process and still complete the deeper task of bringing about true psychological health and not just symptom management. I have seen that a contemplative discipline, like meditation, can be a critical component of thorough psychological transformation.

The ability to silence the mind and allow phenomena to drift by without attachment is a great psychological feat.

Positive imaging, positive self-talk, and all forms of positive psychological discipline and self-expression require energy and neural pathways to accomplish the greater goal of expanded consciousness. In order to access this type of consciousness, awareness has to unlink itself from the constant stream of thought occurring in all of us due, primarily, to our pre-programmed neural pathways. The challenge is not necessarily to stop thinking as much as it is to stop attaching to the thoughts. Silencing the mind is the first step in psychological neutrality.

We mistake thought for identity. We believe we are what we think. Certainly, our thinking can narrowly define our experience, but awareness will not be satisfied with the puny, impoverished prison of the personality structure. Awareness does not require thinking to function. In fact, there is a spontaneity to life when habitual thinking is abandoned. There is a built-in logic, compassion, creativity, strength, purpose, and spiritual depth in awareness that is free from compromise and control when it is not confined by the structures of thinking.

If the client abuses him or herself with every insight, the result would be battered and bruised clients by the end of any successful session. The therapist needs to interrupt the client's self-criticism and promote a model of curiosity and positive self-observation. This can take time and the client will need to be reminded how to engage in self-examination without the automatic punitive self-evaluation. Clearly, the strongest influence in the adoption of this behavior is the therapist's own neutrality and curiosity. Through the strength of the relationship and by mirroring the therapist's point of view, the client learns to incorporate a more patient and curious approach to his or her own psychological structure, "defects and all."

We are creatures seeking more efficient levels of functioning, and the mirror dance that occurs in therapy will be the subtle work that takes place. I am shaping my client's reflection in my side of the mirror with a more loving, appreciative, honest, and protective image/introject. As a result, there is a conflict between my reflection of the client and the client's habitual self-limiting perception. I am the mirror that corrects the psychological distortion. I will even ask clients, once I have established a therapeutic alliance and transference, what I would do in their situation. I am asking them to fantasize how I would represent their greater self, given their situation. Their answer helps me direct therapy in a couple of ways: It tells me how they perceive me, so it helps me shape the transference, and it reveals any distortions in their adoption of the transference material.

Through this mirroring, I am modeling behavior that is spontaneous, emotionally accurate, and in alignment with the direction and potential of the client's unconscious. Why shouldn't the therapist illustrate a variety of emotional responses consistent with healthy self-expression? Human beings mirror each other's behavior, gathering an emotional and behavioral inventory that can be drawn upon when needed. We practice expressing ourselves as a way of feeling more comfortable with new ways, or more effective ways, of dealing with problems. We unconsciously seek models of behavior that we can emulate, and through practice, integrate a more "desirable" personality.

There is a marvelous rock guitarist named Eric Johnson who recommends that guitar players seeking to improve their skills "steal" the styles and phrasing of their favorite guitarists. Through repeated practice of these stolen riffs, he argues, the natural and unique style of the student will eventually emerge. Simply through mirroring people and behaviors that we admire, we adopt those expressive features that lend meaning and purpose to our lives. The therapist can be one of those critical transitional and transformational models.

The danger that takes place in mirroring the behavior of others is that ego has a tendency to view the quest for perfection as a process of eliminating "bad behaviors" rather than incorporating and expanding new behaviors. Since birth, we have been taught to control certain aspects of the self, and as a result, we have developed the impulse to lean toward psychological subtraction rather than addition.

It is always healthier to add to one's self-expression than to repress one's perceived imperfections.

At this stage of building the neutral observer, the client will still be anxious to eliminate those "bad" behaviors that are actually only the symptoms of the deeper psychological block. Any attempt to correct these symptoms will simply lead to different or greater symptoms and perpetuate the inner self-conflict. The client needs to be able to observe these behaviors, without bias, in order to assess how often these symptoms are triggered.

The primary therapeutic technique that I use at this stage of therapy is counting. I have the client count how often a feeling, criticism, or behavior appears.

I want the client to be aware, consciously, of the frequency of their major symptomatic tells. I have actually encouraged some of my clients to purchase clickers (the small counters that are used to count attendance at social events) from an office supply store and simply count each time they notice the behavior we are attempting to isolate: guilt, anxiety, negative thoughts, shame. I have encouraged clients to carry small notebooks to keep track of the frequency of the symptoms. I know that this seems like such a small therapeutic technique, but out of small victories, great change can occur. What the client is actually doing is slightly dissociating awareness from the automatic symptomatic event enough to observe its trigger and results, but not dissociating so far as to feel only the pressure of the arising symptom. The main goal at this stage of therapy is to observe and slightly disengage from the habitual and systematic expression of one's psychological symptoms.

The client needs to resist trying to make corrections at this stage and instead marvel at the frequency of his or her symptoms. Any attempt to correct behavior at this stage will undermine the therapeutic process.

In most cases, the symptom manifests whenever the blocked emotion (fueling the symptom) is triggered. Thus, every time the client has sexuality, anger, sadness, or opinion triggered, the symptom shows up instead. In the case of anger, if it is strongly repressed, every little irritation could theoretically trigger a symptom such as guilt. The main rule to keep in mind at this stage is: The symptom is not the problem, it is the solution to the problem. We want to identify and observe the symptoms to eventually identify the blocked emotions.

One of the markers that the much-needed internal neutral observer is starting to affect perception is a rising sense of humor at the client's own pathology. The desperation that attends symptomatic suffering begins to give way as the client starts to experience some relief from the quest for perfection and acceptance of his or her humanity and imperfection.

STAGE 8: CURIOSITY

GOAL 8: RESEARCH: THE FUNDAMENTAL FEAR

Once the neutral observer begins to provide the client with some breathing room, we can begin to identify the core fears attending self-activation. For Masterson, it is the act of self-activation that triggers the symptom profile (what he called "abandonment depression"). When the client attempts to use the parts of his or her psyche that have been repressed or dissociated due to childhood trauma or discipline, but the function of which is critically necessary in resolving many of life's challenges, the attempt to access and express that emotion (self-activation) will immediately trigger anxiety and fear (or another common symptom). It is the behavioral response to developmental punishment. Even though that emotion could be the practical and accurate response to a particular situation, if it has been forbidden by the family, any attempt to activate it will trigger the client's symptoms.

Thanks to the neutral observer, we are now somewhat aware of how often the symptom gets triggered, but what exactly are we afraid of? What is this underlying fear that so paralyzes us and inhibits emotional expression? Here is a three-step process to conduct a self-analysis. (I teach this formula to every client and at every lecture on psychodynamics that I present.)

If you want to see the difference between how you were designed by nature, God, or the universe and how your family and society altered you for their own purposes:

1. Be yourself: be genuine, speak honestly, and don't hold back.
2. Observe your anxiety: when it goes up it means you are about to do something you have been taught not to do.
3. Identify your fear: whatever you fear will be the consequences of your self-expression, is the method used to control you as a child. (Masterson is to be credited for this bit of genius.)

So let's examine this formula a bit more closely. Step 1 is the courageous stage: *Be genuine all the time, be spontaneous, speak your mind, don't hold back.* It sounds so uncomplicated, and yet it's much like the old Steve Martin joke: "You can be a millionaire and never pay taxes. First, get a million dollars....next...." Easier said than done. Being genuine requires the greatest of all curiosity, courage, and commitment. We must be curious about what wants to come out of our mouths when it is not filtered by the desire for social approval, courageous in speaking our truth, and committed to the ongoing unfolding of self-expression.

True genuineness abandons the quest for approval and bows to no master other than the fulfillment of one's specific and unique design. In order to achieve this level of genuineness, we have to abandon two basic fears: that no one will love us and that we are secretly cruel human beings. These distortions are the social guardians that restrict the fullness of our self-expression. Add to this the personal fears that arise out of our family training and discipline. Then, the first steps toward becoming genuine are truly an act of courage and spiritual fearlessness. Remember, the psychopaths of the world are already operating without moral restriction, to the detriment of society. The kind and compassionate people are the ones who hold back their powerful nature out of fear of being cruel and, in doing so, allow the anti-socials to govern the world. We all have a role to perform as agents of evolution, but we inhibit our effectiveness when we doubt our true nature and inhibit our self-expression. We must develop the courage to do what's right and to protect those who are marginalized. But this is not a step to be taken lightly. Be genuine, be authentic, and be prepared to be confronted by the wolves disguised as sheep. Speak your mind with honesty and integrity. Truth is a powerful illuminator. When we speak our minds and hearts, honestly and openly, it is like turning on a brilliant light in a dark room that has not been cleaned for some time. It's a bit shocking. By speaking the truth, we discover very quickly that we have partially surrounded ourselves with people and circumstances that are toxic and that the only way these situations and people thrive in our presence is for us to repress our natural emotional expression to their behaviors and thoughts. When we begin to express authentically who we are, some people quickly terminate their relationship with us, and others slowly fade away. This cannot be helped. And everyone who stays and continues to relate to us begins to improve the quality of his/her interaction. When we become healthier, everyone around has to step up and become healthier or flee the scene.

Step 2 is the observational stage: *When our anxiety goes up, it means we are about to act on or express an emotion that we have been taught not to (repress).* Psychological anxiety is the product of childhood behavioral programming. I'm not speaking of the normal situational anxiety that arises when we don't have enough money or are facing a test in school. Psychological anxiety is the type that we are all familiar with that arises when we feel the pressure building up in us when we are facing a crazy boss or co-worker, feel that we have been treated unfairly, or are being picked on by some social bully. These are the restrictions of self-expression that have nothing to do with religious morality and have everything to do with how we were trained as children to be submissive to others and to block certain emotional expression. In these situations, anxiety is the byproduct of repressing an emotional response. At this step, awareness needs to be very curious about the nature and cause of the anxiety. What emotion is being blocked? What is happening in my world that it triggering this emotion/anxiety in me?

One of the major tasks in therapy is to identify the emotions underlying the symptoms so that we can assess the fear behind what is being blocked and eventually give voice to that restricted emotion. When anxiety goes up, we are facing our fear of the remembered consequences of our childhood.

Step 3 is the honesty stage: *Whatever you fear will be the consequences of your self-expression is what was used to control you as a child.* This final step is brilliant and somewhat complicated. People are rarely afraid of the unreasonable. As human beings, we all share fears of poverty, isolation, and being unloved, attacked, and humiliated. Each of these fears is predicated on experience. Although we may recognize those fears as common and understandable, we do not all carry the same core fears. Everyone has been taught to fear very specific consequences based on our childhood experiences.

We don't fear what we haven't experienced.

"But I fear lions and I've never been attacked by a lion. What about that?" Well, we've certainly seen enough lions in movies and on television to understand what a lion can do, so we actually have experienced, somewhat, the danger of a lion. But rarely have I found a client who blocks his or her anger, sadness, opinion, or sexuality based on the fear of being attacked by a lion. Everyone, deep down, knows what his or her core fears are. I'll even have clients, when I ask them what they are afraid will happen if they speak up, who will say, "You know," as if we secretly all know and share the same deep fear. And, of course, we do share some fears that relate to common styles of discipline. As creative as families can be in how they execute discipline, there are certain punishments we all respect and dread as children. Human beings, as animals, instinctively understand the threat posed by violence, for example. As children, none of us wants to incur physical wrath through our actions. But therapists can't know what specific fears lie under the surface until the client reveals them. For example, many people are strongly affected by the use of guilt, but in my family system, guilt was rarely used. As a result, I find the effectiveness of guilt to be fascinating, almost akin to magic. The ability of one person to manipulate another person almost exclusively by use of tone and verbal implication, the ability to evoke shame with a sentence, is a powerful weapon. On the face of it, guilt is really just one person suggesting that another person should be ashamed of himself or herself for some behavior, thought, or feeling. This does not seem like much of a threat. So why is guilt so universally effective? We might start with examining at what age guilt becomes effective. Babies are pretty immune to guilt. Can you imagine a mother trying to get an infant to eat his or her mashed carrots by saying, "What, suddenly my carrots aren't good enough for you? Now I can't make carrots, is that what you're saying?" This is an absurd scene. The baby would have no understanding of the underlying message. Guilt is only effective because the child has experienced what happens next if the guilt doesn't work. There is an Or-Else that is behind the use of guilt, and ninety-nine percent of the time, the Or-Else is physical discipline. So ultimately, the effective use of guilt, time-out, or simple submissive cooperation is predicated on the child attempting to avoid the physical consequences of upsetting the parents or other family members.

Never underestimate the common use of physical discipline as the core fear behind inhibited self-expression, no matter how the client downplays the frequency or ferocity. Guilt is insufficiently threatening to be effective in demanding cooperation from others; it is what happens next, if the guilt is resisted, that we want to avoid.

Our core fears are usually the threats that block self-expression. Even though repressing our self-expression has protected us in our families and at school, those imprisoned psychological components are critically necessary for a healthy, happy life.

Identifying our core fears is fundamental as we work towards dismantling the blocks, since ultimately, when we are prepared to protect ourselves in a direct manner, repression is no longer necessary. We are free to express ourselves because we are ready, willing, and able to defend ourselves from the monsters of the world. These acts of self-protection are no small feats.

Our ability to fend off verbal, emotional, and even physical threats are the skills that free our self-expression.

STAGE 9: MEMORY OR EMOTION

GOAL 9: BIND HISTORY AND EMOTION TOGETHER ACCURATELY

When trauma occurs (direct or exposure trauma) there is a split between memory and emotion, and awareness links with one and abandons or dissociates from the other. Every therapist has clients who arrive with strong emotions devoid of memory, or memories devoid of affect. I'm not sure which extreme is more disturbing: emotions with little regulation and missing sufficient history to explain the intensity of the emotion, or a very disciplined and honest assessment of how extreme discipline was applied in the family, with little or no emotional reaction to the assaults.

Each emotion, by association, is linked with our complete history of experiences associated with that particular emotion. Each experience reminds us, emotionally, of every other experience with the same emotion. My current sadness is associated with all of my previously under-expressed sad experiences. My current anger is associated with all of my previously under-expressed anger. My current sexual attraction is associated with all of my previous sexual attractions. These are memories connected to affect.

All of our psychological history is interlinked by the emotions associated with those experiences.

One of the most common experiences of this is when we accidentally refer to someone significant in our current life by the name of someone in our past—to use your mother's name when speaking of your wife, or to call your current boyfriend a previous boyfriend's name. The emotional connection can be positive or negative depending on the historical content associated with the moment.

This is the theory of association that Jung and his colleagues outlined in the early Twentieth Century.

Any past emotion that has not been fully expressed at the moment it occurred remains charged in the unconscious and contributes to the perceptual and expressive distortion of the present.

Remember, the unconscious, like a mirror, responds to every experience immediately in proportion to the intensity of the moment. Any regulation by personality to control the response will keep part of the emotional charge locked in the unconscious, exerting pressure on the psyche and producing symptoms to relieve the pressure. Any current emotional trigger has the capacity to release the entire unexpressed pool of emotion. Suddenly, the emotion being expressed is out of proportion to the intensity of the moment.

Psychologically, the problem is that repressed emotion seeks expression and will take advantage of any and all opportunities to be released. Thus, any situation that triggers a feeling may likely trigger all of those historical feelings as well, and suddenly our emotional reaction is more extreme than what warranted it in the moment. We've all done it, seen it, and felt it: "Whoa, that was way more emotion than the situation required."

Where does the extra emotion come from? It comes from *our repressed emotional history.* A healthy, integrated psyche expresses emotion at the level required by the moment. As a result, there is no leftover emotional charge relegated to the unconscious, waiting to contaminate future emotional experiences.

One of the great goals of therapy is to release the historical emotions stored in the unconscious, freeing awareness to be absolutely present and appropriate in the moment.

Gestalt therapy advocates the unrestricted expression of emotion as a method of stretching the boundaries of self-expression. The theory, which attempts to compensate for the limited emotional expression of psychoanalysis, is predicated on the belief that full emotional expression will free the client from the psychological pathology of repressed emotions: *Get your emotions out and feel better.* So clients rage and cry and scream themselves into an emotional frenzy and, without a doubt, many feel better. But the approach is hardly a universal cure. For some reason, a significant percentage of clients show no stable improvement. In the same way that analysis is intellectually biased, Gestalt is emotionally biased, and neither is a complete solution to the range of psychological challenges faced by human beings.

However, as far as creative therapeutic techniques are concerned, Gestalt is magnificent. In the same way that cognitive behavioral therapy has a limited theoretical structure but can be a highly effective approach with specific pathology, Gestalt therapy has an inventory of clinical strategies that are stunningly effective in facilitating the expression of emotional content and in practicing new and effective behaviors.

So why aren't Gestalt and cognitive behavioral therapies universally effective treatment strategies? There are hundreds of wonderful psychological techniques and workshops that are capable of temporarily raising the energy level of the client. This will provide the client with momentary heightened confidence and deeper insight, but there is no long-term change in the personality structure, and thus the energy and its effect are fleeting. Inevitably, this new energy activates memory, and the repressed emotions rise into consciousness either to be integrated or further repressed and acted out. This is the Activation-Resistance Cycle (see chapter 8, "Treatment,") and will be further discussed in Stage 11. The only way to sustain the energetic charge that we all desire and for which we are all designed is to reunite the constricted emotional content with their original memories, stored in the unconscious, freeing up our psychological energy to be available for creative responses, rather than activating our fears.

When we consider the split between memory and emotion, we are identifying the specific psychological material missing from consciousness.

As any emotion is triggered in the present moment, there is almost always a combination of current emotions and historical emotions. We are well aware of the triggering circumstances, but are usually unaware of the contamination of our historical emotional experiences, other than to recognize that our emotional expression is out of proportion to the moment.

Assessing our client's developmental history, family dynamics, childhood experiences, and importantly, the repeated traumas of family losses and discipline provides the therapist with a list of potentially charged emotional experiences that may become activated during therapy. Until these emotions are linked to their appropriate history, the client will continue to express emotional chaos in the present.

The added emotional intensity of the past is not just negatively experienced. The high-energy positive emotional experiences of finding kindred spirits, falling in love, or infatuation are charged with hope rather than fear, but they are still connected to underdeveloped aspects of our psyche. For example, why do we find ourselves attracted to people who are not attracted to us? Why is this such a common experience? Or, if they return the attraction, why does the relationship become conflictual? Any highly charged experience, positive or negative, is the result of accessing or activating a previously restricted part of the unconscious. (See chapter 15, "Love's Shadow.")

For trauma to be resolved, the memory and emotion of every situation must be linked. If awareness requires anything, it requires perceptual and expressive accuracy. We need to know that we are seeing the world as it truly is and not just as we hope or fear it is. We need to have confidence that our emotional response is reasonable. Ultimately, all emotion is information about the world. When we are experiencing emotional overload as a result of our repressed emotions surging forward at every opportunity, three possibilities arise: (1) we fear the consequences of this "forbidden" emotion/information, (2) we don't trust the emotional information arising within us because we can't tell past from present, or (3) we are possessed by an attitude of emotional bias (prejudice). The first possibility is simply being the negative behavioral conditioning of our childhood. The second is that we are unable to differentiate the truth of the moment from the gravity of the past. This problem obviously arises in all personal relationships in which we are trying to determine the honesty, integrity, and loyalty of those around us. We hope that what we are seeing is accurate, but our unconscious undermines that confidence in an attempt to protect us from past painful experiences. The third possibility is simple prejudice. Whether it is hopeful prejudice (infatuation) or fearful prejudice (dislike), we are possessed of an attitude that is inaccurate and overly emotionally charged. This third possibility might alternatively be labeled *conviction without wisdom*.

The power of historically repressed emotions and memories is significant. These experiences distort reality and relationships. To return to perceptual accuracy and emotional immediacy and proportion, history and its corresponding emotions need to be remembered, linked, and expressed. When my clients are drowning in emotion, I have them research their family history with relatives who are available. I have them journal their dreams (images of unexpressed emotion). I have them write down a list of all of the painful experiences that they can remember. I have them recall those marvelous historical moments of clarity, excitement, and connection. The therapeutic task at this point is to seek the memories connected to the emotions or else seek the missing emotions for the history that is remembered. Often, the memory is available, but the client has dismissed the effect the experience has on them.

We protect and defend our families by dismissing or rationalizing the effect of the punishment, isolation, being ignored, or bullying we experienced as children and, consequently, shift the emotional content from the past to the present where it undermines our current relationships.

As we reconnect emotion and memory, our present circumstances take on a quality of clarity. Free from the emotional bias of the past, we are able to experience the present moment in a lucid and stable way. People may still drive us crazy, but at least we remain perceptually accurate and can respond emotionally at a level that fits each situation. Thus, our psychological energy is consistent and available, moment-to-moment.

Stage 10: Begin New Behavior

Goal 10: Increase the Client's Energy Level

Milton Erikson remains one of the great psychological minds of the twentieth century. Jay Haley's book about Erikson, *Uncommon Therapy*, remains a "must read" for any serious clinician. It is one of several books that I recommend for all the therapists that I train. Erikson was a strategic genius. Because he anticipated resistance at all stages of therapeutic work, he designed his interventions to harness the energy of resistance.

Following Erikson's philosophy, I believe strongly that it is more effective to add behaviors than to subtract them. For example, when clients wish to deal with eating issues, I have them identify the types of food that contribute most to their compulsive eating behaviors. I then require them to identify and purchase the highest quality of that particular food. Instead of convenience store chocolate, I have them substitute Godiva. Instead of punishing the "eating symptom," I have them reward themselves with a food that will actually provide the "buzz" that the cheaper stuff simply does not provide. This sets up a paradox that begins to transform the self-destructive behavior:

1. It trains the client to pay attention to the act of acquiring the reward.
2. It refocuses awareness on to the act of eating, rather than unconsciously devouring the target food.

3. It begins to shift the process of eating into a reward rather than just relief.

4. A higher quality of satisfaction often requires a bit more effort; thus, paying the extra attention to the method and quality of collecting the rewards delays the satisfaction a bit longer in order to accomplish the task, while positively controlling the impulsivity associated with binge eating. The delay helps teach the client to stabilize the desire, if only for a bit.

5. The cost and effort increases the emotional value of the food, providing a more satisfying reward and creating a more satisfying ritual.

Indulgence is punitive when quantity replaces quality.

Every time we compromise our choices, we distance ourselves from the deeper satisfaction that we truly desire. We reinforce the self-compromise and increase our resentment level. The simple choice of making ourselves a priority and truly indulging the food reward, rather than consuming mediocre treats, begins to shift self-perception. This is simply a paradoxical intervention. It is a method of redirecting attention and evolving behavior.

The Top Energetic Strategies: The top strategies I use to increase energy both during the session and as clinical homework are: (1) spontaneous self-expression, (2) humor, (3) intimacy, (4) sex, (5) exercise, (6) diet, (7) physical rhythms (breathing, eating, elimination, and sleep), (8) social interaction, and (9) a dream journal.

1. *Spontaneous Self-Expression:* Spontaneous self-expression is the fastest route to dismantling pathological behaviors and evolving personality structure. I am constantly monitoring self-censoring verbal behavior in my clients. Any time a client remains silent, stops talking, interrupts himself or herself, verbally changes direction "midstream," or inhibits the free flow of conversation, I point it out. I ask, "What did you really want to say?" "What word were you about to say first?" I want my clients to express themselves immediately and directly with minimum inhibition. In Malcolm Gladwell's book *Blink*, he suggests that the initial response to any situation is often the most accurate and contains the best assessment of the information available. He further suggests that when that first thought is rejected or censored, the continued scanning for information to answer the question leads further and further away from accurate perception, from what the client knows to be the truth. As Jung found with his word-association experiments,

any delay in self-expression is the symptomatic marker of personal censoring, designed to inhibit any self-expression that might lead to threat. The markers of this censoring are often mid-sentence editing, redirection of content, silence, or just plain avoidance of directness. Inhibited self-expression, especially verbal self-expression, is left over from how we were raised. The anticipated attack, fueling the inhibition of expression, arises first from memory and second from situational dynamics. This means that the remembered fear is often stronger than our current perception of danger, so we block our expression out of fear of the remembered consequences and not necessarily the presence of the current danger.

When we inhibit our self-expression, we give opportunity for negative influences to gain traction in our lives, whether through illness or poisonous social encounters. In the same way that stress gives disease opportunity to compromise our physical health, repressed self-expression gives negative people opportunity to compromise our social health. So, the first strategy for raising energy is immediate self-expression. (See chapter 9, "Therapeutic Strategy and Technique.")

2. *Humor:* During session, I tell jokes, have clients tell jokes, and for the most part, use humor as a reframe. I compare our ridiculous situations to movies, fairly tales, mythology, songs, and media. There is always a risk at the beginning of therapy that my narcissistic patients will take offense and personalize the humor, but with reasonable timing we can help our clients regain a sense of humor about life and their lives. Chogyam Trungpa, a powerful Tibetan Buddhist teacher, wrote in his significant book, *Cutting Through Spiritual Materialism,* that there is no enlightenment without a sense of humor. Humor is fundamentally a technique that permits awareness to examine a rigid point of view with a bit of perspective. I often ask clients to tell me jokes, and if they don't have any, I assign them the task to find some jokes.

3. *Intimacy:* Isolation is common in those with high psychological stress. There is certainly a case to be made about the differences between introverted and extroverted social requirements; however, even introverts need to deal with the anxieties of social interaction in order to fully understand the contents of their unconscious. As part of the overall plan to raise the client's energy levels, social interaction and participation in social groups like church, service groups, dating, social media, etc. is a good energetic challenge. Without social interaction, we have a tendency to "lock" into limited self-perceptions and self-distortions. It is through the interaction with others that we practice new behaviors, gain new perspectives, and build some emotional "muscles."

Social interaction (dating, caring for others, joining a social network or church, and pursuing hobbies, sports, and other shared activities) is a valuable energetic resource. The client has to risk rejection to enjoy social intimacy, but isolation is one of the great curses of psychological suffering, and at some point in long-term therapy, clients must develop healthy, nourishing interpersonal relationships.

In the therapy session, energy can be raised by working with the client's transference perspective. Discussing the client's transference is a delicate process in that we do not want to compromise the energy assigned to this therapeutic relationship. When the transference is starting to positively affect self-image, but the client is still stuck in the critical self introject, I will ask clients, "How do you think I see you?" I can measure accuracy of perception and projected punitive or hopeful unconscious intent, and it removes the client from a pathological comfort zone. A fixed point of view is familiar, and even though it may cause great discomfort, at least it is familiar. Asking the client to project him/herself into my point of view always raises anxiety (energy) in the client but also provides me with the opportunity to respond, supporting those qualities that I genuinely like and admire in the client: intelligence, emotional sensitivity, physical looks, creative ability, and so forth. Never underestimate the power of commenting on the obvious; I praise my narcissistic clients for their gifts and sensitivities.

I teach and practice the following principle: the most powerful person in the room is the person who can give compliments. We are all longing for attention and confirmation. To be able to conduct oneself from the position of giving versus needing, changes one's complete social dynamic. I use my client's approval seeking to reinforce positive, healthy self-image (in this way I can support intellectual discipline, humor, emotional empathy, expressive courage) and to confront the client's need for approval. Since our clients seek our approval, the clinician should have a strategic plan in place for that transference feature.

4. *Sex:* As obvious as this might sound, the power of sex should never be underestimated. I have my clients discuss sexuality and sexual history right from the start in order to desensitize them to their anxiety about the subject and to ascertain how much trauma is associated with this aspect of their lives.

The sexual subject is tricky, however. Sexual knowledge ranges from self-exploration and self-satisfaction to full, unrestricted sexual participation with other people. Except in cases of long-term sexual abuse, sexual energy is usually available for creative self-expression. Sexuality, just like intellect, empathy, and courage, is a form of self-expression that can be improved upon, developed, and mastered.

Sexuality can certainly serve as an energy resource that aides psychological development.

Sexuality at the biological level is about reproduction and survival, but at the higher levels of psychological potential, it is about intimacy. This potent energy can be successfully sublimated into many practical, spiritual, and creative expressions, but the direct expression of sexuality is the most effective and efficient energetic release.

5. *Exercise:* I immediately establish two contracts with every client: keep a dream journal and develop an exercise program. Physical exercise is the most simple and achievable resource for health, vital for the body (as supported by the extensive research), possible to engage in anywhere, under any circumstances, and easy to increase or decrease based on physical needs, opportunity, and ability, and yet...*exercise is resisted most strongly.* Exploring the issue can be helpful to an extent, but on a certain level, the reasons for resisting exercise do not matter. This issue is similar, in my mind, to drug addiction: without sobriety, there is no therapy; without exercise, there is only limited therapy. The energetic reserve of the body is stunning. A poorly maintained body doesn't travel far and is a source of unending suffering, and a body that is not activated through movement restricts a person's ability to discover and express repressed material.

A regular exercise program is necessary for advanced psychological process. And to this, I would add: exercise your thinking, speaking, loving, courage, and pleasure, as well.

6. *Diet:* Eat healthy food. Enjoy what you eat. Most food has life force; respect that gift from the universe.

7. *Physical Rhythms:* The I Ching, the Chinese book of changes, is a wonderful ancient commentary on the rhythms of the universe to which we are subject. In somewhat obscure and poetic terms, it describes the varieties of elemental rhythmic influences—the forces of nature and humanity—that aid or interfere with our life journey. Imagine that instead of one common form of gravity, there are hundreds of gravitational influences that subtly and not so subtly affect how we walk the path of life. In the same way a sailor checks the weather in order to prepare for the environmental influences of his/her sea voyage, our ability to harness the rhythms of the universe currently shaping our world improves the outcome of our life's experiments.

The earth is a living, rhythmic organism, and the physical body replicates this same complex organic rhythm. The cycles of the body maintain its health, vitality, flexibility, and sensitivity. When the natural cycles of the body are restricted, blocked, and blunted through drugs, diet, and environmental toxins, we accelerate the breakdown of our physical integrity and suffer from disease and organ failure.

But we are certainly capable of doing simple maintenance on the body that will produce truly significant results. Three of the most significant rhythms that we can obey are breathing, digestion, and sleep. Air in, air out. Food in, food out. Go to sleep, wake up. Pretty simple rules.

Stress, for most of us, interferes with our natural breathing pattern, and when we pay attention, we will notice that we hold our breath, breathe in a shallow manner, or simply stop breathing for short periods of time. The same applies to digestion and elimination. I am forever struck by how many clients tell me that they are constipated or evacuate their bowels only a few times a week. Really? Yikes! Food in, food out, a natural rhythm. This should be a daily process: the natural rhythm of elimination. But again, one needs to pay attention to the feeling associated with elimination. On a very basic level, we are talking about being aware of all of the sensations that the body produces as a way of consciously participating in the natural rhythms of the body.

The body has natural rhythms that rise and fall based on physical function. The human will can, and does, resist obeying these physical rhythms, usually as a result of poor toilet training or an over-controlling or hostile childhood environment. In the same way surfers observe a wave pattern in order to "catch" the next swell, people can perceive the series of signals the body sends that indicate that the elimination wave is occurring. We either recognize and participate in that signal or we ignore or resist it.

Sleep is another of the most significant cyclical contributors to energy availability, concentration, and stress reduction. It seems ridiculous to make this argument, but go to sleep when you need to sleep, or suffer the consequences. If you fight your way through the first wave of sleep, you may find yourself having difficulty going to sleep later or will not receive enough sleep during that cycle.

The idea that we might try to arrange our lives in accordance with natural physical rhythms may seem inconvenient, but that is because we have personality structure that competes with the natural rhythms of the body. The use of will against natural rhythm—the undermining of the normal energetic systems of the body, the cycles of breath, elimination, and sleep—is the most common and subtle of neurotic behaviors. Helping our clients recognize that they are out of sync with their bodies' rhythmic cycles and supporting their correction of this malalignment assists in the reconfiguring of the personality. Welcoming and honoring our natural cycles is a way of syncing awareness with our organic wisdom and the clarity of perception that lives in our unconscious.

8. *A Dream Journal:* The dream journal serves to illustrate the inner dynamics of the client's personality. They reveal what emotion is rising, what emotion is subsiding, and what emotion or circumstances are in conflict. Since dream images are the illustrations of unexpressed emotions, and therapy is about the reclamation and expression of repressed emotion, dream journals are significantly helpful in the release of what is blocked. Clients offer a million excuses for resisting a dream journal, the most common one being "I don't dream." I tell them that everyone dreams and that dreaming is cyclical, and they will have accomplished a great step forward when they begin remembering their dreams. (See chapter 11, "Dream-Work.")

STAGE II: SELF-ACTIVATION

GOAL II: IDENTIFYING THE ACTIVATION-RESISTANCE CYCLE (ARC)

Self-activation is the simple act of spontaneously participating in the moment, without inhibition or reluctance. Our ability to interact with reality flexibly, creatively, and spontaneously offers an ongoing resource of information and energy. Restricted interaction limits information, produces symptomology, and reduces energy. So, *activation* is simply one's natural, emotional, creative, or intellectual response to encounters with the world. However, self-activation immediately increases the energy of the psyche, potentially triggering family and social rules of repression, inhibition, fear, and anxiety: the family/cultural/religious rules of engagement, so to speak.

Masterson describes a psychological phenomenon he calls "abandonment depression," which he associates with self-activation. As the environment places varying self-expressive challenges along our path, the attempted use of any behaviorally forbidden self-expression (anger, sadness, thought, speech, sexuality) triggers an immediate fearful censoring by the personality that results in a correspondingly immediate reduction in emotion, information, and energy, producing the depression identified by Masterson. An attempt by the individual to avoid this type of depression requires an avoidance of any self-expression, use of emotion, or activity that would trigger the blocked emotions that bring about the depressed state.

As noted earlier, most people have access to all of their emotions, but only within specific parameters of expression. Thus, at moderate levels, the expression of most emotions is available with little inhibition. But as emotional intensity grows, the stimulation crosses a neurological threshold that triggers the inhibiting function of the personality. When our emotional response crosses that emotional expressive threshold, our personality immediately converts the emotions into predictable and familiar symptoms (the client's symptom profile). However, if the emotional pressure continues to increase, there is a second threshold that is crossed in which the person, once again, begins to fully express his or her emotion, usually in a very intense manner. Exceeding the threshold is a kind of straw that broke the camel's back. The overall effect is a mixed emotional cycle: express, repress, express. This is the heart of a psychological expressive disorder and arises out of the Activation-Resistance Cycle.

Managing any particular external event may well be within our intellectual, physical, and emotional ability. But because we have been conditioned to limit our self-expression to meet family and social criteria, once the environmental demands extend beyond our expressive threshold, anxiety and symptomology replace action and expression in the personality. This is the Activation-Resistance Cycle.

The Activation-Resistance Cycle is simply a more complex outline of Masterson's abandonment depression and follows this series of steps: An environmental trigger activates the *body* (automatic emotional response) which then activates *memory* and *emotion* (unexpressed emotional history) which then activates *resistance* (personality censor) which then activates *symptoms* (converts emotion into symptom) which then limits overall energy.

THE ACTIVATION-RESISTANCE CYCLE©

Stimulation	=	Environmental Trigger
activates		activates
The Body	=	Emotional Response
activates		activates
Memory & Emotion	=	Unexpressed Emotional History
activates		activates
Resistance	=	Personality
activates		activates
Symptoms	=	Emotion into Symptom
which		and then
Limits Energy	=	Energy is Diverted into Symptom

This cycle can occur over several hours or in a flash of self-inhibition. An extremely mild and common form of this censorship is when someone is speaking and suddenly, mid-sentence, goes silent for a moment, grasping for a word or phrase. This is a mild form of the ARC: an obstruction in self-expression based on the subtle anxiety of being too "blunt" or too "hurtful" or too "crude" or too (fill in the blank) and searching for a word or phrase that will pass the internal censor.

A more significant and trauma-based example of the ARC occurs when someone who suffered sexual abuse as a child engages in intimacy as an adult. Often, abuse survivors find that as they activate sexual feelings, they suddenly become anxious and symptomatic. The intimacy activates their physical feelings, which in turn trigger trauma memory stored in that physical organ, which then activates resistance to the memory (dissociation or repression), which converts sexual feelings into symptoms (anxiety, tension, stress, guilt, shame, fear, resentment, worry, depression, grief, or somatization), which shift the energy from a high self-expressive state into the lower symptomatic state.

For each emotion, there is a threshold of intensity of stimulation that will trigger the ARC. A healthy psyche can experience large amounts of emotional stimulation before becoming symptomatic. Thus, what triggers one person may have little or no effect on someone else.

In our final analysis of the five centers of awareness (thought, speech, sadness, anger, and sexuality), we are assessing how much stimulation an individual can tolerate in each of these areas before becoming symptomatic (ARC). Each of these centers of awareness has its own unique threshold that turns feeling into symptoms. That threshold is determined by either family or social inhibition (threat) or by a lack of experience. Without previous sufficient exposure to new feelings or social situations, the anxiety threshold is set fairly low and thus can be triggered quickly. However, with practice and self-expression, we can master even the most complex emotional states or challenging situations.

STAGE 12: RESISTANCE

GOAL 12: BECOME AWARE OF HOW RESISTANCE ARISES AND CONTROLS ENERGY

Resistance rules the pace of therapy. All clients self-sabotage. As therapists, we have one major advantage: the client's unconscious is trying to help us. When you consider that personality is perhaps ten percent of consciousness, and the other ninety percent lays in the unconscious pressuring personality for release, any therapist that can achieve an alignment with the unconscious has real leverage to help the client toward self-actualization.

The therapeutic alliance is the conscious agreement between the client and the therapist. The therapeutic transference is the agreement between the therapist and the client's unconscious, and often, a variety of transferences occur during the course of therapy, so the contract is renegotiated again and again.

Resistance, as discussed in Stage 11, is a universal factor, but its presentation changes depending on the quality of the transference. The therapeutic interaction is defined by the transference, and the treatment technique should evolve flexibly to target the shifts in the client's unconscious response to the work.

Full self-expression is the most natural act of a human being. However, as I have argued throughout this book, our immediate emotional responses are systematically inhibited by a punitive environment that teaches us to symptomize or somaticize our responses to the world in order to fit into the family and cultural "script."

The great spiritual dilemma of being human is feeling crushed between the energetic joy of self-expression and the fear of the consequences.

So, therapy utilizes the client's strategized and familiar skills of self-expression as a foundation to help the client generate sufficient courage to face all real and remembered threats with an authentic and practiced voice. Freedom of expression occurs directly in proportion to one's confidence in protecting oneself (or complete ignorance of the punitive consequences, the infant's view of the world).

The therapeutic challenge for all clients at this stage is to resolve the Activation-Resistance Cycle and permit emotions and memory to lower the thresholds of inhibition. In doing this, the client will perceive reality more accurately, express emotion with greater immediacy, and experience increased energy. However, in order to avoid punishment or the fear of punishment, the client will automatically try to avoid the activation and expression of the forbidden components of his or her unconscious (self-activation). Since the dynamic energy of the unconscious is constantly challenging the expressive limits imposed by personality, the therapist is attempting to provide a structure that will encourage the expression of those unconscious components without the massive anxiety associated with the "punitive consequences" of self-activation. As Milton Erickson reportedly said, our job as therapists is not to help people feel better, but to help them feel stronger.

The therapist is conspiring with the unconscious (transference), while aligning with the personality (therapeutic alliance).

The therapist is requiring the client to do a series of things:

1. Self-activate (curiosity and courage)
2. Examine the rising anxiety (curiosity)
3. Resist shutting down self-expression (courage)
4. Examine multiple models of self-expression (curiosity)
5. Commit to practicing self-expression (commitment)
6. Prepare for possible "consequences" from the self-expression (courage)
7. Examine and analyze the results of the new self-expression (curiosity)
8. Practice self-expression to its most effective and efficient potential (courage and commitment)

One of the singular challenges of therapy is providing the client with a view of the therapeutic goal. Fundamentally, we are working to bring about two outcomes: an accurate perception of the world (to see the world "as it is"), and immediate emotional expressiveness in proportion to the moment (to mirror the moment).

All therapeutic techniques are fundamentally designed to neutralize our resistance to self-activation. All resistance is ruled by fear: fear of the remembered consequences of self-expression. Self-blame arises out of the fundamental fear of seeing the world as it is. Poor self-image and low energy are the results of blocked self-expression. These are not complicated psychological dynamics. Eventually, courage must replace fear. Self-expression must replace self-attack. Hamlet's brilliant line, "I could be bounded in a nutshell and count myself king of infinite space, were it not that I have bad dreams," describes the dilemma of humanity, perfectly.

Even a delusional mental state could be satisfying if not for the continued commentary from the unconscious to wake up! A highly restrictive personality will not stand without complaint from the soul.

Aggressive and Passive Resistances: The three major forms of aggressive resistance are: attack, withdraw (flee), act helpless. The fight defense is just that: yelling, assault, intimidation, threats, physical threatening, and any direct form of attack. The withdraw / flight form of defense occurs when a person simply leaves the conflictual situation: storms out of the room, runs away, or takes any other action that provides distance. The act helpless defense is the "wounded" defense: crying, moodiness, depression, disappointment, anxiety, self-pity, or any form of helplessness. Each of these aggressive forms of defensiveness signals that communication is *not* taking place. The challenge for any person seeking intimacy with family, friends, or partners is to persevere or confront his or her way through these defenses in order for intimacy to begin to take place.

The major forms of passive resistance are pleasing, seductive/charming, submissive, or helpful. These forms of behavior are not inherently pathological, but are often used pathologically to avoid possible attack. Sometimes our only clue that these behaviors are inappropriate is our sense that the intensity of the behavior is out of proportion to the moment. The behavior feels awkward, pushy, or compulsively helpful. Each of these styles of relating avoids being genuine and replaces authenticity with strategy, regardless of circumstances.

Psychological resistance will be unique at each of the neural-emotional sites. Each complex has its own personality, which means that it has its own relationship requirements and expressive style. The therapeutic alliance will vary depending on the dominant complex. Each emotional center has its own fears and hopes, and the therapist will have to negotiate a new relationship with each complex. With the activation of each complex, resistance and negotiation are repeated, and the therapeutic alliance and the transference will have to be renegotiated. Do not be surprised to have a long-term client come to therapy and suddenly present a completely new set of relationship requirements.

As humans, we seem to be more reflective than creative in our behaviors. We access new behaviors effectively if we have seen/felt/heard these behaviors in action. Without a broad expressive and perceptual database in our unconscious, we are limited in our options for emotional/expressive solutions. I operate from the theory that one should seek a variety of emotional experiences in order to provide the psyche with a spectrum of approaches for future expressive problems. The more extensive the array of strategies in the unconscious that can be activated when necessary, the more successful our interaction with the world.

Ultimately, we are trying to offer our clients versions of creative and skillful responses that can be adopted and mastered. The unconscious is always seeking to upgrade its operating system, to evolve human behavior in order to improve effective self-expression.

At the most fundamental level, the presenting personality is simply an outdated piece of software programmed to respond to the needs of our family and society, but lacking in flexibility and data processing to keep pace with the present circumstances. Instead of improving our operating system as the upgrades become available, we tolerate slow functioning, inadequate performance, a tedious and boring product, and anticipatory anxiety waiting for the system to crash when it is most needed to work.

STAGE 13: WORKING THROUGH

GOAL 13: REUNITING MEMORY AND EMOTION, REDUCING THE LEARNING CURVE

The working through stage begins after the therapeutic alliance has been established and the transference starts to shape the therapy dynamics. The client's awareness begins to explore the body systematically, testing the functions of each emotional site, attentive to the stress levels, memories, and emotions associated with each neurological complex. At this stage, the client will

1. methodically work on each of the neurological complexes, remembering and expressing the emotional history stored at each site;
2. work through repeated Activation-Resistance Cycle;
3. increase the immediacy and accuracy of emotional expression;
4. trust perceptual information without pathological defensiveness;
5. reduce tolerance for toxic circumstances and relationships; and
6. develop energetic resources through creative self-expression.

Since each neurological site has its own energetic charge based on emotional history and current emotional challenges, the therapy must have some flexibility as to the content of the work and the techniques being applied to the symptoms. The energetic charge that accelerates the work will rise and fall based on the amount of emotional history located at each site, how often that site is being triggered in the client's life, and the client's unconscious resistance to the emotional information and history stored at that site.

It is not unusual to spend months on a particular expressive block. Remember, identifying the symptom, and even the blocked emotion, is not that difficult. The challenge lies in helping the client develop sufficient courage to express him/herself despite fear of the consequences.

At some point, the client might feel that the outcome is not worth the effort and decide to live with the symptoms.

When the client is in the working-through phase, there is an active search for answers to chaotic feelings and foggy memories. Typically, the best place to answer many of these questions is through family members, and it is at this point that I often discuss such communication with clients. Family members will occasionally be surprisingly open about factors that impacted the client, such as traumatic experiences, crazy parental behavior, and significant illnesses. There are many stories that are repeatedly told in the family, but not all stories are shared equally with the family members.

Unfortunately, the client may have to deal with an alcoholic parent who has had significant blackouts or a parent who for any of a number of reasons simply denies that anything happened. These parents continue to be a problem by re-contributing to the pain of childhood with further insults in the present: the war on consciousness continues.

Contact with family members is critical during therapy. Family dynamics suggest that when any group is assembled, the members immediately assume the role they played in their family. When clients visit home, they can test their emotional strength and ability to self-activate, communicate, challenge oppressive family rules, ask for information, reconnect with lost relationships, become re-traumatized by abusive behavior, become desperate and depressed in response to their own repressed emotional material, or actually make some progress in evolving the family system.

Part of the drive of the unconscious is to successfully correct the failed childhood dynamics, and by doing so, gain access to and activate those long dormant psychological capacities of intimacy, love, success, opinion, courage, appreciation, loyalty, hope, joy, and wisdom. To this end, we often surround ourselves with friends and colleagues who operate similarly to our family members.

At this phase, clients will often confess the worry that their expression of feelings may wound another person. Clients fear that an open, direct expression of how they feel could be damaging to those with whom they are intimately associated. The evidence of this typically manifests in the emotional reaction others have to the clients' emerging honest expression of emotion. We have been trained by our families and communities that our actions can produce emotions in others. We suffer the same karma that we project onto others. We hold the people in our lives responsible for the positive and negative emotions that we experience with them. Therefore, it's not difficult to believe that our self-expression is capable of wounding others. Although it may be true that we experience a variety of emotions as we engage the world, our internal responses to the world are almost always predicated on how we were raised. Our narcissistic nature (carefully nurtured by our family) suggests that we have "caused" these wounds in others, when in fact what has happened is a collision of narcissistic defenses. The other acts as though we have caused him or her harm, and we believe we have that power. We treat each other as the cause of our suffering when in fact it is our own emotional response to our own unconscious material that produces the suffering.

339

Homework in the working-through phase differs slightly from earlier homework in that the client is attempting to strengthen the neutral observer, which further reduces the effect of the symptom profile. Homework should be designed to increase information, practice emotional flexibility, record emotional reactions to the therapeutic work, reduce neurotic stress, and identify the components of the personality currently influencing perception and expression. To this end, a dream journal, regular exercise, and spiritual curiosity are great therapeutic accelerators. Dream journals are significant in that the unconscious contains multiple psychological obstacles, and not each of these obstacles is equally charged; the energetic influence (charge) fluctuates depending on environmental stimuli and neurological maturation. The ongoing therapeutic challenge is to identify the emotional obstacles that are currently most troublesome. Dreams will often indicate which unconscious complex is currently influencing mood, attitude, emotion, and overall energy levels. (See chapter 11, "Dream-Work.")

As I have emphasized throughout this book, physical exercise is intimately related to increasing our overall energy and thus aids in the evolution of the psyche. A tired, overworked, out-of-shape body is an unconscious body with little to say other than "ouch." The body has to wake up in order to provide information leading to the transformation of unconscious behaviors and perceptions.

The discussion of religion and spiritual practice is quite appropriate in psychotherapy. Religious beliefs represent the symbolic superstructure of each person's psyche. The fears and hopes of faith are illustrations of the expectations of the individual. Religious beliefs provide the symbols that represent how the unconscious is ruled. Religious structure is psychological structure. The world is the mirror of our perceptual clarity and distortions and, as such, illustrates our own internal conflict. How one perceives the fate (heaven or hell, ecstasy or suffering) of the collective (humanity) reflects one's attitudes toward one's own personality components. How we judge others is how we judge ourselves. Thus, our religious and spiritual beliefs illustrate our attitude toward ourselves, which reveals personality structure.

Unfortunately, it is a very hard concept for those who suffer the distortions and paranoia of an unconscious and primitive mind to believe that it is not only possible, but necessary, that all people go to heaven.

Effective therapy will evolve our childhood superstitions into adult wisdom that calls us to higher functioning. One's psychological evolution will be extremely limited without a commitment to the wellbeing of others. To quote Jesus, "As you have done unto the least of these, you have done unto me." Nice.

STAGE 14: TERMINATION

GOAL 14: REDUCTION OF THERAPEUTIC CONTACT

Moving into the termination stage of therapy often triggers complexes that up to this moment have remained dormant. The real and imminent loss of the therapeutic ally can activate some very powerful emotions around loss that do not surface until a real loss occurs. Without a processing of the termination of therapy, there will be a missed opportunity to examine deeper unconscious separation fears, assess the strengths and insights gained in the course of therapy, or to introduce some challenges for the client transitioning out of regular contact. If therapy is the template for evolving our emotional expression and perceptual accuracy, separation and loss are issues that most people experience many times in life and thus need to address in therapy. The termination of therapy provides an opportunity to explore whether or not there are some left-over separation traumas heretofore unexplored. There are very few in-depth therapies that abruptly terminate, unless artificially limited by money, moving away, death, or illness. In my work, I typically meet with clients once per week during the working-through phase (although this can vary depending on the intensity of the emotional surge). When the therapy is moving toward termination, there is a natural winding down through reduction of contact to the point of complete termination. I reduce therapy to every other week, then once per month, and then even a six-month checkup. Even when this process goes smoothly, it is not unusual for clients to "check-in" periodically by phone or scheduled session. I tell clients that they do not have to have a crisis in order to meet with me. I don't like to unconsciously encourage a "crisis" if they only need a simple therapeutic check-up.

Post-therapeutic contact is a challenge in and of itself. I always ask my clients how they want me to recognize them when we cross paths socially: big hug, secret wave, avoid eye contact, complete stranger. These types of social contracts are important for the privacy and intimacy of the work that occurs in the office. I try and establish these greeting customs right from the start so that there are no embarrassing moments at a small party of an unknowing host. Some clients whom I've treated for months ask that when we cross paths in a social situation that I look them straight in the eye, shake their hand, and introduce myself, as if meeting for the very first time. I take my cue from the client in the moment of the encounter based upon our clinical agreement. I find that there are two kinds of clients. There are those who come to therapy pretending they are coming to visit the architect next door and those who wear a button on their chest that says, "Ask me about my therapy!" I try to respect the privacy wishes of my more formal clients as well as the boisterous enthusiasm of my enthusiastic "followers."

Termination can be lengthy or brief. Each client will have a different response based on emotional history and strength of the transference. I've had clients return to therapy after a separation of a few years. Some were just checking in after a difficult experience, and others were ready to deal with some personal history or emotional obstruction that was previously avoided. I have an open door policy and am available to any client I have ever treated (except the anti-socials).

CONCLUSION

Ultimately, the goal of successful therapy is that the client accesses, integrates, and expresses all components of the unconscious, giving awareness full range of perceptual accuracy and emotionally expressive honesty. The following are few of the major goals of in-depth therapy:

1. Accurate perception of the world
2. Spontaneous emotional response
3. Emotion in proportion to the moment
4. Capacity to self-activate
5. Capacity to self-soothe
6. Immediate access to the vibrant and creative world of the unconscious
7. A quick learning curve for examining and adopting new ideas and experiences
8. Trust and enjoyment of the inner dialogue
9. Capacity to apologize for our mistakes
10. Minimal psychological symptomology
11. Simultaneous arising of memory and emotion
12. Ability to enjoy and build intimacy
13. Ability to tolerate separation
14. Evolving sense of spirituality
15. A moral and ethical commitment to be in service to the greater good of humanity
16. A respect for other living beings
17. A religious or philosophical point of view that replaces superstition with wisdom
18. A sense of purpose and direction in life's larger matrix.

Personal growth is never finished. Nature has given us an evolving consciousness. As we master one aspect of our psychological, spiritual, and physical growth, we are confronted with the next challenge. There is no finished product. There is no completion. There is only wholeness and process.

Section Three:

QUICK READS:

DREAMS, ABUSE, GRIEF, SEX, AND ROMANCE

Dream-Work

Revisioning Treatment of Sexual Abuse

Sex Addiction

Anatomy and Treatment of Grief

Love's Shadow

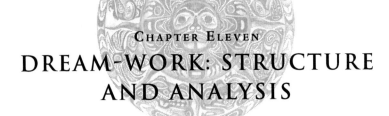

DREAM-WORK: STRUCTURE AND ANALYSIS

"I could be bounded in a nutshell and count myself a king of infinite space, were it not that I have bad dreams." Hamlet, William Shakespeare

INTRODUCTION

Our dream life is the autobiography of our unconscious. Each dream is a page in our book, and each dream cycle is a chapter in our book. Now, all we have to do is to translate the language of our own autobiography.

W E DREAM THE WORLD and the world dreams us. Both reality and the dream world are shaped by the same psychological bias, the *personality structure*. What is reality when we are awake is reality when we are asleep. What is fearful, symbolic, or symptomatic when we are awake is represented similarly when we are asleep. We perceive reality partially accurately, and we partially fill in the gaps in our knowledge with myth, metaphor, religion, superstition, magical thinking, and a variety of symptoms. Those portions of reality that we know, make sense. Those portions of reality that we do not know or misunderstand seem random, chaotic, mysterious, or fearful. Understanding the dream world follows the same premises as understanding reality: wisdom can arise from ignorance and superstition; curiosity, courage, and commitment are the keys.

Dream interpretation is often viewed as much more complex than it really needs to be. Let's start with a basic concept: all personality, structurally, is multiple personality. Once again, we have five major emotional centers: thought, speech, compassion, aggression, pleasure. Each center contributes to how we perceive reality and how we express emotions. As a result, each center also provides characters for our dreams. If our perception is distorted or inaccurate, that will be evident not only in our difficulties in real life, but in the drama that unfolds in our dreams. If our emotional expression is blunted or repressed, this will not only affect our impact in the world, but will be illustrated in the emotional intensity in dreams. How awareness relates to these very important neural-emotional centers is evident in the content and mood of our dreams.

Practical experience teaches each of us that all of our emotions are not always in agreement with each other and that our psyche presents multiple and competing points of view. Awareness has to learn to integrate these differing perspectives, which are offered in the forms of mixed emotions and a variety of dream images. When these emotional points of view are in conflict with each other (for example, safety versus intimacy) this inner emotional turmoil will be reflected in the dream's drama.

Dream life and family life share many qualities. Everyone's family has a certain amount of tension due to differing perspectives and personalities, and there is often an underlying script that each member seems to follow in playing his or her role in the family "movie." Simply studying the family for a day might give someone a taste of family life, but deeply comprehending how this family works and how its members relate to each other requires weeks and months of observation. The family is in transition, and the members are evolving, some for

345

the better and some for the worse. This fluid dynamic in a family is what gives it complexity and direction. Not surprisingly, dreams follow a similar fluid, evolving, unfolding expression.

Dream drama and dream characters are all in transition, evolving in appearance and role, their presentation shifting between polarities of conflict and resolution, dangerous circumstances or pleasant surroundings, strange animals or familiar people.

Each dream is part of a sequence of dreams, illustrating an overarching theme associated with our perception of the world and our emotional response to it. Each dream is one episode of an ongoing series that unfolds each night, commenting on how we are conducting our lives.

Our psychological challenges, perceptually and expressively, unfold from dream to dream like the frames of a film wherein the characters and circumstances are constantly in flux. Without examining multiple dreams, it is nearly impossible to accurately assess the overarching direction that consciousness is evolving in order to deal with a challenging world and constricted emotions. By working with the client's emotional expression and perceptual accuracy, therapy is attempting to edit the script as it is being dreamed. Psychotherapy is literally attempting to improve the function of the dream characters and dream circumstances.

At their basic level, dreams are the illustrations of unexpressed emotions and unrealized information. If we are in conflict with our emotions, we will be in conflict with the characters and situations representing those very same feelings in our dreams. The dream is the representation of the hidden parts of the unconscious, and our relationship with the unconscious is represented in the dream.

The drama of the dream is the illustration of the dreamer's experience of the world and his or her emotional response to that experience. Each emotional center (thought, speech, compassion, aggression, pleasure) has specific perceptual and emotional duties and will be represented in the dream by characters that personality has assigned the role to. If these duties are performed without restriction, the dream symbols and characters reflect healthy energetic activity. If these emotions are constricted or repressed by personality, the dream content is filled with tension and stress. Each emotion is represented by a character or characters in the dream, and these parts of the total self are literally in conflict or harmony with each other and play out this dramatic relationship within the dream.

The original script of the dreamer and the dream's contents is written by those who have taught us how to perceive the world and express ourselves as we are growing up, combined with the particular environmental pressures we are experiencing. At its essence, the dream content expresses how well we are relating to reality.

Jung suggested that the unconscious has two fundamental levels of information:

1. The personal unconscious, which encompasses the repressed emotional material that has been banished to the unconscious. This content of the personal unconscious is what produces symptomology. Anxiety, tension, stress, guilt, shame, fear, and resentment are all the agents of the personal unconscious, along with the dreams that illustrate this struggle with emotional reality.

2. The collective unconscious is one of the more brilliant and challenging structural components that Jung proposed. Very similar to the Buddhist "Ocean of Wisdom," it is our connection with our own potential and our intimate connection with all of the other living, conscious creatures. Jung suggested that the collective was our direct connection with the living universe. This second category also shows up in dreams as awakening potentials or environmental tidal waves. So, a dream of a forest fire may be a representation of repression (personal unconscious), or it may also be the sign of an awakening, deeper wisdom of the self: for example, the burning bush of Moses, or it may be a harbinger of a major social crisis, like WWII (collective unconscious). The collective unconscious, much like the ocean, has the capacity to generate great treasure and wisdom for those who can stabilize the waves of emotion. However, it can also produce a psychic undertow that drags humanity into the most primitive aspects of superstition and fear, resulting in war and collective insanity.

Our deeper psychological potential is held hostage by the parts of our psyche that are being repressed and clogging up self-expression. These intimate potentials, languishing in the unconscious, pressing awareness for release, appear in dreams as conflicted relationships and bizarre circumstances. As these potentials are expressed in real life, the dream shifts to a more positive illustration, indicating a better relationship to and resolution with that part of the unconscious.

Even though our emotional tension feels like it is being created by external forces, it is in fact our perception of the world and our response to that perception that create dream content/conflict/resolution.

Dream images often represent a struggle between how the world is pre-
senting itself and how the personality is interpreting that information and
expressing a response.

The world is always in transition from one state into another (like
dreaming). Thus, the world is often described as dreamlike. In this case,
the dream quality of the world means that where we lack knowledge
of or acceptance of reality, we fill in the gaps with superstition, fantasy,
religion, imagination, and anxiety. The more accurately we perceive
and respond to the world, the more anthropomorphic the dream
images become. The more constricted our perception and expression
are, the more theriomorphic or elemental the dream content.

Consider that the body and personality are struggling to decipher
information about the inner and outer worlds of experience. The body
is simply translating a variety of vibrations into coherent, recognizable
patterns that we call feelings and information, and personality determines what will be perceived and what will be expressed.

Since personality is given the task to regulate perception and expression,
dream images are shaped by the level of control that the personality exerts over
the phenomena we experience and to which we are responding.

New experiences are symbolized through archetypal cultural
images: weather, primitive animals, insects, etc. The feelings we have
that are familiar and comfortable are illustrated in dreams by people we
know and to whom we can easily assign specific meaning and descrip-
tors such as smart, sexy, competitive, and so on.

Myth Making

Consider the imaginary lives of children and it is easy to see how children populate their worlds with magical characters. These magical
associations represent all the new feelings they are experiencing as their
nervous systems wakes up. Remember, awareness follows a sequence
of interpreting reality that evolves from unknown phenomena to
known phenomena in the following five-step progression: symptom,
dream, fantasy, emotion, and finally, insight (emotional wisdom). (See
chapter 2, "Structure of the Psyche," *Reality and The Five Stages of Per-*
ception.) Imagination (dream and fantasy) is simply the middle part of
the process of the coming to consciousness. Since knowledge is, as far
as we know, infinite, there is always an aspect of reality that is rambling
through these five stages of awareness.

As we secure our experience of the specific known universe, the unknown or yet-to-be-known universe is interacting with the mythmaking apparatus of the psyche. There is always some new feeling, emotion, intuition, future insight, or song of reality being published by the unconscious in the form of myth, magic, or mystery.

Joseph Campbell, in his famous and profound book, *The Hero with a Thousand Faces*, describes how all world cultures tell stories of the hero's journey, and that this universally honored story is actually illustrating the path of evolving consciousness for every one of us. Each religion, each myth, each fairy tale describes the same pattern of transformation. The hero/heroine wakes up, faces the challenges that must be overcome in order to gain the treasure of great value, and either succeeds at the set of tasks and is transformed or fails and suffers. Although Campbell was describing the universal pattern of mythic literature, this same sequence applies to the dream world as well.

Dreams are the mythic universe of the dreamer. We are the hero and heroine of our dream world, and as such, are continually challenged to become more skillful in overcoming the psychological obstacles that we have inherited and invited into our life.

Mythology, religion, and fairy tales are the literature of how we dream the universe. That which we do not fully understand becomes the foundation for mythical or religious experience. Thus, fairy tales are the "dream journals" of earlier cultures and the mythic representations of the evolution of the consciousness of human beings. Although most fairy tales are not widely known, there are certain stories that have gained cross-cultural mythic proportion in American culture: *Snow White, Beauty and the Beast, Cinderella, Sleeping Beauty,* and *The Wizard of Oz,* to name a few. But even without fairy tales, mythology, or religion, people are drawn, without realizing it, to books, movies, television dramas, and, increasingly, online programming and even computer gaming that give meaning to the intra-psychic drama of their unconscious. Mythological patterns, and thus psychological truths, emerge from the shallowest of cultural content. Regardless of the skill or artistry evidenced in the work, there is something in drama that speaks to us at a deeper level.

Not only are we drawn to stories that capture the narratives of our unconscious selves, we are likewise hard-wired to generate these narratives from the beginning of our lives. One of the best examples of this type of spontaneous mythmaking and storytelling by children is reported in the book *The Boy Who Would Be a Helicopter* by Vivian Gussin

349

Paley, a Macarthur Genius Award recipient. This stunning text describes how pre-school children spontaneously tell stories that unconsciously shape and evolve the psychic needs of the children in their class. The creative stories that the children tell and portray in spontaneous plays, that Paley has the children enact as part of story-time, are stunning, and unconsciously scripted to address not only the emotional needs of the story-teller, but the emotional dramas of the children playing the various character roles. If you really want to understand how the unconscious organizes psychological drama and emotional challenges into "dream patterns," read this book.

The mythologies and tales that children invent are of the same source and structure as dream content. Each spontaneous imaginative story is a life correction by the unconscious of the author and the "actors," attending to the psychological imbalances of both the individual and community. The children heal each other, psychologically, through the ancient tradition of storytelling and theater.

One area of concern, however, is that television often helps define those mythic patterns adopted by children. Good television (positive models of social interaction, bravery, cleverness, reasoning, playfulness, creativity) can be very effective in exposing children to models of self-knowledge and self-expression in their struggle with new and potent feelings. However, television lacking in depth has the same power.

By narrowing the mythic content of television to the lowest common denominator of popular culture, we are unconsciously collapsing the psychological perceptual and expressive models we so desperately long for, leaving us with a shallow ocean in which there are no great fish, or for that matter, no great fish tales.

Movies have great potential to shape modern myths. The great success of the *Star Wars* series is partially due to the original three films' adherence to a mythological structure, thus producing a widely enthusiastic response from the world community. This mythological foundation was no lucky accident, as Joseph Campbell himself was a consultant on the first few films. In fact, the brilliant series of Bill Moyer interviews with Campbell before his death, titled *The Power of Myth* and broadcast on PBS, was filmed at *Star Wars* creator George Lucas's Skywalker Ranch.

The unconscious is constantly scanning the environment for those energetic patterns that represent evolving consciousness, and parents can certainly perform important roles in choosing or limiting the content of mass media that their children consume and mimic. As we mature, the psyche seems to be attracted to those patterns in our world that most clearly illustrate our psychic state and will naturally seek exposure to those forms of expression needed to bring balance to, and inspire, our lives.

The importance of the quality of content in our world is very simple; we mirror, or resonate, with the emotional dynamism that we are systematically exposed to. We become oriented to the emotions we practice; thus, exposure to violence tends to tune the psyche to a violent orientation. The same is true with sexuality, compassion, and intelligence.

The adult psyche follows the same structure of symbols as a child's psyche, and as a result, when an adult is exposed to new information, the symbol system in dreams is the same as the child's. Any experiential phenomenon that is not yet understood is organized into mythic patterns, and even when we do perceive the world accurately, there is still a mythic power to the natural world. I offer our response to "falling" stars, crop circles, and "ufo's" as evidence.

DREAM IMAGE

At a fundamental level, dreams are the images of unexpressed emotions. Like a library of our emotional history, the unconscious contains all of our unspoken emotional responses, organized by emotional category. Thus, all similar emotions are grouped together in a complex. This is why any current emotion can trigger any and all of the previously unexpressed emotions of the same type; current sadness triggers historical sadness, current anger triggers historical anger, and current lovers remind us of past lovers.

All of our seemingly isolated experiences are actually linked in our memories by their common emotional features. This is the nature of psychological association: the interconnection of our life experience tied together by emotion. These emotions, lingering in the unconscious, along with their corresponding memories and the personality structure that imprisoned them, are the subjects of therapy.

However, all complexes do not have an equal energetic charge all the time. This charge varies depending on circumstance and repressed emotional history; each complex rotates in and out of significant influence on the psyche. Some complexes have a stronger emotional charge and are producing symptoms and placing greater pressure on consciousness for expression. These are the emotional complexes that populate dreams. For each repressed emotion, there can be a representation in the dream that selectively appears depending on external triggers and internal pressure. And these images vary. The character or symbol that represents repressed sadness or anger in one dream may evolve or devolve in the next dream. As a result, the dream representation of a blocked emotion is highly changeable. For the more highly charged emotions of the moment, there is strong representation in the dream. And as such, dreams represent the emotions that have the highest potential to be understood and expressed by consciousness. The dream that is remembered usually contains emotions that are activated and ready for consciousness and expression.

The dream image does not create the emotion we awaken with, but rather, it is the unexpressed emotion, already active, that is creating the dream content. So, when we awaken in an anxious mood, the dream has not created that mood. That feeling was already present in our body and the dream images arise in concert with the feeling. Our attitude to the emotion behind the dream content (information or feeling) shapes the quality and character of the dream. The reason a dream seems to produce an anxious feeling is that we are already in conflict with the emotional information behind the dream image. Thus, the dream evokes the same emotion that created it.

Any aspect of reality that we feel uncomfortable with or is triggering forbidden emotions creates the characters and the dynamism of our dreams.

Since emotions are the biochemical/neurological descriptions of reality, if we are fighting reality, we are fighting our emotions. Perhaps the corollary is even more profound: if we are fighting our emotions, we are fighting reality. Those conflicted emotions, and thus our conflict with reality, appear as dream content. The dream is simply presenting, imaginatively, the part of reality we have yet to accept.

In dreamtime, we do not have the organizational convenience of waking life, in which we adopt magical thinking to disguise our ignorance.

Dream content is not so easily dismissed. The dream presents itself in an emotionally shocking and somewhat obscure manner simply because we are fighting our own natural, emotional response to the content represented in the dream. Thus, the dream usually illustrates the emotions and emotional history that need to be identified and expressed.

As the clinician helps the client identify the emotions that are fueling his or her psychological symptoms in waking life, any assistance in abbreviating this process is useful. Dreams perform that function. Dream content is a shortcut to the psychotherapeutic process because it helps identify the blocked emotions and emotional history that have been activated by circumstance. All of us carry a history of repressed emotions that are periodically triggered by events in our lives. When these emotions are triggered, they create both symptoms and dreams of our current emotional conflict.

It is helpful for the clinician to determine which emotional complexes in the unconscious are ready to be analyzed and not just wander around the psyche stumbling across this emotion or that. Just because something tragic occurred in our client's life does not necessarily mean that the client is ready or capable to work on that particular issue. When the dream presents emotional content and the dreamer remembers the dream, this is a signal that the three components (the client, the client's unconscious, and the therapist) are working together and there is a higher likelihood of therapeutic success. It is helpful to have the unconscious as an ally in the therapeutic process. In truth, without the cooperation of the unconscious, very little psychological growth can take place. By paying attention to and honoring our dreams, we develop an active and evolving alliance with the unconscious and its intentions.

The dream is a representation of the most active and available emotional complexes that awareness can tolerate. Otherwise, we wouldn't remember the dream and it would simply drop out of consciousness and emerge later. Sometimes an important emotional complex is insufficiently stimulated and needs an opportunity to awaken and announce its expressive intention through the dream material. Until that moment arises, working on an emotional complex, simply because the developmental history points to potential wounding, is unwise and ill timed. Waking up a complex can be tricky and fraught with peril.

Dreams also represent a significant feedback loop for the therapeutic process. Dream images illustrate whether the complex is moving toward conscious integration or being further repressed and dissociated. An emotion represented by a bear in one dream might be a human in the next if the dreamer is expressing the emotion creating the bear, or perhaps the bear morphs into a snake in the next dream if the emotion is further repressed. How do we know that the bear in one dream is a person or snake in the next? Grouping. If there are three people and a bear in one dream, and three people and a snake in the next dream, the grouping indicates that one character has transmogrified. If we are expressing our emotions more effectively, we feel better, so part of the "tell" is whether the client is feeling more or less energetic. If the client is energized, we expect the dream to reflect this mood, and the bear becomes human. If the client is still withholding emotions, the energy will be conflicted and the dream image will devolve, in our example, from bear to snake.

We treat the dream world with the same disrespect as we treat the real world: denial, superstition, repression, control, avoidance, and fear. As we learn to respect both the internal and external worlds, our sense of place in both of these worlds improves.

Dream images evolve as the dreamer fights with or learns to appreciate his or her varied emotions. Although one cannot say for certain that a particular image always illustrates a specific emotion, there is a greater likelihood that a bear or wolf, as opposed to a bird, will represent aggression, and a horse or a rabbit, a snake, or even a wasp might represent sexuality. Why would these symbols represent sexuality? A little knowledge of children's imagination and some familiarity with the literature of myth aids in our exploration of symbols. Little girls love to play with horses at the early genital stage of development (four to seven years old). Mythically, to catch a unicorn, you must use a virgin girl as bait. The centaur (half man, half horse) is the sexually underdeveloped masculine and the mermaid (half woman, half fish) is the sexually underdeveloped female. Rabbits are known to multiply quickly and are representatives of spring, the season of love. The snake is associated with Adam and Eve's sexual self-knowledge. The wasp is associated with Cupid, god of love, who is also called the "wasp-headed" god, due to his stinger/arrow. Familiarity with fairy tales and mythology is of great assistance in understanding the underlying meaning of a variety of symbols and their transformative nature in dreams. It is good to own a variety of symbol dictionaries if you want to do dream interpretation, as they will contribute a variety of cultural interpretations of a symbol (such as the Native American interpretation of the role of the bear, or the ancient Greek approach to the owl).

The exploration of these broader cultural symbols is helpful in expanding our search for the meaning of the content of our dreams. This expansive process helps trigger the imagination in a less threatening strategy than attempting the direct recovery of repressed emotional content through personal association. However, as the dreamer gains confidence in allowing memories and feelings to rise to the surface, the effectiveness of expanded cultural associations becomes limited. Cultural symbols, as part of dream work, serve the same purpose as the glass of water sitting besides the well that must be used to prime the pump in order to produce the deep water. We are certainly more interested in the water from the deep well. In those circumstances in which the dreamer resists providing personal associations, the examination of the broader historical and cultural meanings of dream symbols primes the personality to become curious about the material residing in the unconscious and makes a link between the collective and personal unconscious.

The personal unconscious, with its population of repressed emotions and perceptual corrections, initially produces the greatest number of dreams. It supplies the first great challenge to psychological growth and is the prime subject of psychotherapy. The recapitulation of the personal unconscious is the initial step in the journey of spiritual wisdom. Carlos Castaneda would often refer to this process as, *erasing personal history (Journey to Ixtlan)*. It is this clearing of the content of the personal unconscious that frees the deeper creativities and wisdoms of the collective to become available to awareness, free of the contamination of one's repressed emotional history.

The collective unconscious, the intimate connection with the entire life force, is a deep well of creativity, insight, wisdom, and chaos. As these potentialities are awakened and announce themselves to the individual psyche, dreams serve as the harbingers of this psychological wave.

Like the ocean, the collective unconscious brings great treasure and bounty to the stable mind and a host of erosive storms to those who are swept along by the tides of emotion.

However, as we mature, awareness must first orient itself in the biological body, adjusting to the neural-chemical cascade of perceptions and emotions arising from the maturing body in relationship to the ferocious dynamics of the material world. As the body awakens, awareness develops skill and stability when dealing with emotional intensity. As the five neural-emotional centers unfold, we evolve from a state of superstition and magic into wisdom and effectiveness in our interaction with the world.

THE WIZARD OF OZ

The contents of the unconscious are often presented in dreams and mythical stories as an unusual collection of humans, half-humans, strange allies and enemies, monsters, and animals. *The Wizard of Oz* and *Snow White* are stories from different generations, separated by hundreds of years, but share the same mythic structure and are populated by a similar cast of characters. Odd halflings, an evil queen, an absent or passive father, and questionably helpful allies populate the worlds of Snow White and Oz.

The story told in The Wizard of Oz (a novel published in 1900, adapted for the stage, and, of course, made famous as a movie in the 1939 musical) is a perfect example of how a dream populates its drama with characters representing psychological components. And remember, this adventure is actually Dorothy's dream, from which she awakens.

Knowing the developmental stage of the dreamer helps in our process of deciphering the characters in any dream. Because physical function is significant to dream content, knowing the age and stage of development of the dreamer is critical. The dream of a five-year-old is developmentally different than the dream of a twenty-five-year-old. Dorothy's age is unspecified in Frank Baum's books, but she is certainly presented consistently in book, on film, and on stage as a young adolescent. Dorothy is perhaps thirteen years old and only somewhat sexually aware (as might be expected in a story with a female protagonist published in the Victorian era). Her sexuality is still in transformation.

All of the characters in a dream represent the different emotional functions of the dreamer; thus, all of the characters in The Wizard of Oz represent Dorothy's psychological components. Some character functions are obvious, others less so. If every character in a dream has a function in the psyche, then each of the major characters in this story represents one of the five major neural-emotional centers: thought/insight, voice/speech, sadness/compassion, aggression/courage, and sexuality/pleasure. The Scarecrow is looking for a brain and, as such, represents Dorothy's growing confidence in her intellect. The Tin Man is looking for a heart, representing her search for love or compassion. The Lion is looking for courage, representing Dorothy's quest to develop confidence in her aggression. This leaves speech and sexuality to be divided between Dorothy herself and Toto. Toto doesn't speak and cannot represent the speech neural-center. Thus, Dorothy's character must represent speech, and Toto takes on the role of sexuality; but how can Toto, a pet dog, showing up in a dream, represent sexuality? No character appears in Dorothy's dream that has romantic potentialities. There's not even a suggestion of romance or sexuality in the film. If sexuality were to be represented in this tale, we would expect Prince Charming to appear, and to be sure, if this story were part of a sequence of dreams, and Dorothy was comfortable with her budding sexuality, Prince Charming would certainly eventually appear. The significant absence of romantic options suggests an underdeveloped sexual perspective on the part of the dreamer, and the more an emotional function is resisted by personality, the more primitive the symbol representing that function becomes. As we shall see, the Scarecrow, Tin Man, and the Lion all fall in the "monster" stage/category of dream symbols: half human, half other. Toto, however, is fully in the "animal" stage of dream symbols and, as such, represents a more primitive (repressive or unknown) attitude to the emotion he represents: sexuality.

Another dynamic that suggests that Toto represents Dorothy's awakening sexuality is how the neighbor, Elmira Gulch (who later appears as the Wicked Witch of the West in the movie) is trying to take Toto away and have him destroyed. Fairy tales are filled with witches and stepmothers competing with young girls in beauty and desirability. Indeed, Snow White doesn't become competition for the Queen until she becomes "of age" and the mirror reveals that Snow White is now the fairest in the land. This does not happen when the child is born. It is the sexual aspect of the young woman that sets the witch to her nefarious task: kill Snow White, kill Dorothy Gale.

When psychological components are repressed, a split is produced in which part of the division is threatening and part of the division is appealing. For example, we may repress our own sexuality but find ourselves attracted to sexually dynamic people in our lives. Good girls are attracted to bad boys. Passive men are attracted to dominating women. The result is that we become fascinated with these external representations of our own disowned psychological parts. We are drawn to what the Jungians call the "golden" (idealized) aspect of the shadow and are repulsed by the "corrupt" (distorted) side of the shadow. The irony is that our attraction to either the golden or corrupt sides of the shadow require us to deal with those disowned parts of our own psyche. If we repress our aggression, we will eventually find ourselves in the company of those who do not repress their aggression. If we repress our sexuality, we will find ourselves attracted to those who do not repress their sexuality. But as we build relationships with those individuals representing our shadow, we eventually fall into conflict, control, avoidance, and disappointment; we try to control them the same way we try to control our own shadow side. This is the power battle that all couples face in a long-term relationship; the attempt to subjugate the very qualities that attracted us to them.

Ultimately, all the components of the shadow are important for psychic wholeness, and thus the extreme variations of "good" or "bad" are simply distortions of self. As such, each extreme produces its counter-balancing opposite in the unconscious. However, evil is not all evil, and good is not all good, for within each of these components is a necessary aspect of the self. Psychodynamically, each polarity seeks reunification with its opposite.

This contaminated split in the idealized and distorted aspects of the shadow is wonderfully illustrated in *The Wizard of Oz* by Glenda the "Good" Witch and the (nameless) "Wicked" Witch of the West. For example, the Wicked Witch is just trying to retrieve the slippers that belonged to her sister, that are now on Dorothy's feet, thanks to Glenda the Good Witch. The Wicked Witch didn't start out to pick a fight with Dorothy, but thanks to the intervention of Glenda, Dorothy is eventually forced to battle the negative/devouring aspects of the feminine (as embodied by the Wicked Witch) that haunt her dreams. And Glenda also proves to be a real problem. She amplifies the conflict with the Wicked Witch, she doesn't tell Dorothy that the shoes will take her directly home, and she sends her to the Wizard, whom she knows is a charlatan. This type of catalytic behavior, which advances the story but usually creates obstacles to overcome and problems to be resolved, is the role of the Trickster: coyote, raven, Anansi the spider, Br'er Rabbit (Bugs Bunny), Loki, Puss in Boots, Pan, and now, Glenda.

Those shiny "golden" qualities that so strongly attract us to others serve both to advance our conflict with the shadow and to reveal the truth about the people in our world.

Another example of this splitting of the shadow into polar opposites is depicted by the Wizard, who first presents himself as a terrifying demi-god, complete with threats, demands, and intimidation, and later is revealed as a trickster and a coward. Unable or unwilling to fight the witch himself, he tricks Dorothy into fighting his battle for him. In the end, he offers Dorothy no relief in her quest and no helpful information about how to live life well and then abandons her, flying off uncontrollably in his balloon.

The corollary to this story, in real life, would be that teenage Dorothy would populate her circle of relationships with people who relate to her in these mythic roles: no Prince Charming in sight, and in fact most males seem boyish (underdeveloped half-men) at best; at least one very hostile female competing with Dorothy's rising sexual dynamism; and another female who needs to be the center of attention without really providing real friendship and who also seems to introduce Dorothy to bad friends. Dorothy would be working on trusting her intellect, while searching for love and needing to develop some courage to deal with the obstacles in her path. Her mother would be beautiful and dangerous and her father would be aggressively threatening, even terrifying, but secretly passive and weak (perhaps alcoholic), demanding that Dorothy fight with the mother because he doesn't have the courage to do it himself.

Ultimately, dreams, fairy tales, and mythological characters are representations of normal, everyday relationships—parents (giants), children (munchkins), mother/feminine (witch, fairy, siren, muse), father/masculine (wizard, king, devil, monster, hero)—and such reveal certain conflicts and potentialities in our psyche and the psyche of the culture. Each person's psychological struggle is predominantly concerned with the dynamics of his or her own psyche and not to the dynamics of the external world.

We are at war with ourselves, and our dreams illustrate that war through mythic patterns.

Our family and culture have helped place us into conflict with the fundamental design of our core self, and thus, the first great battle for psychological growth is learning to interact, respect, and express our own psychological potential, represented by the characters and environments of the dream world. We are tasked with embracing our authentic psychological design.

THE FIVE DREAM STAGES

There are common sense rules to working with dream images. Since most dreams are powered by the conflict between our personality, our emotions, and our world, dream characters morph as the external stimuli, and thus the conflicted emotional expression increases or decreases. Remember, emotions are a combination of information and energy, and dream characters are simply the representations of the conflicted emotions. The qualities of the characters in the dream are direct reflections of personality's attitude toward the information being thrust upon us by our emotional experience of reality. Our resistance to this information is either based on unfamiliarity or fear of the consequences of self-activation (prohibited emotion).

The reason dreams are mysterious is that the unconscious is essentially trying to sneak information into the domain of awareness while personality's effectiveness (threshold of perception) as a censor is reduced during sleep. There will always be something slightly threatening about the dream world (with the exception of those extraordinary dreams of spiritual awakening) because of (1) the threats and consequences we received when we explored these emotions initially as children, and (2) the powerful and transformative psychological tidal waves that wash over humanity through the collective unconscious. Either of these dream drivers will produce anxiety in the dreamer.

The contents of the dream follow an evolutionary order as consciousness wrestles with the emotional content fueling the dream images. The image appearing in the dream corresponds directly with the dreamer's resistance to that emotional information and expression. The higher the resistance to that emotion, the more primitive, evolutionarily, the representative image of that emotion is in the dream. As acceptance and expression of a restricted emotion improves, the dream images evolve to a higher evolutionary form.

There are five levels of symbols represented by dream images. Evolving from the most resisted feelings (most primitive) to the most accepted feelings (most evolved), the evolving symbols follow this arc, from most unfamiliar or feared to most familiar and embraced. The more comfortable we are with a feeling, the higher the evolutionary presentation, with the highest form being ourselves, our friends, or a spiritual teacher. Each level has its own hierarchy of positive and fearful presentation. There is a significant difference between rain and deluge, between a shark and a porpoise, between a bear and a mouse, or between a stranger and good friend. Working with dreams requires effectively experiencing the subtle differences in emotional impact, so that the dream images produce varying levels of comfort and discomfort. Our ability to distinguish subtle shifts in emotional response in our body permits quicker access to the information coded as emotion. After all, emotion is simply information.

The Five Major Evolutionary Categories of Dream Content:

1. Elemental (weather and other natural conditions, such as fires, floods, rain, storms, tornadoes)
2. Insect (bees, wasps, parasites, spiders, bity-stingy things)
3. Animal
   a. Lower order fish/amphibians/reptiles
   b. Higher order birds and mammals
4. Monster (half animal-half human, robot)
5. Human (different race, different gender, same race, same gender)

Each of these stages represents levels of recognition, acceptance, and integration, by awareness, of the feelings and information about reality represented in the dream images. The more theriomorphic or elemental a dream image is, the more likely that the emotion fueling the dream image is also expressed as a symptom (anxiety, tension, stress, etc.). The more anthropomorphic an image is, the more likely the information contained in the symbol is understood or recognized by awareness as specific emotion, intuition, or thought.

In a positively evolving sequence of dreams, stormy weather becomes biting insects, which then becomes a snake, which then becomes a bear, which then becomes a monster (half animal, half human), which then becomes an unknown human, which then becomes a known human. This is the course of dream images moving from fear and repression into acceptance and expression and can occur in as quickly as a few weeks or as long as several years. It is unlikely that this type of rapid evolution would take place within a few days because of the four-week rule of neurological change (see neural-plasticity in chapter 2). The nervous system needs time to adjust the chemical cascade associated with personality's interpretive and expressive habits.

In depth, the five levels of dream symbols can be broken down in the following way:

1. Environmental: This is when an emotion is represented by basic elemental components (fire, flood, rain, tornado, desert, river, lake, ocean, storm). These are the emotions that are either announcing their awakening or are being so strongly repressed that the image has no recognizable consciousness. The feelings associated with these symbols are of great dread, anxiety, fear, and anticipation. For the dreamer, these are large undifferentiated feelings in scope and effect. However, common sense can help identify the influencing emotion. Since we are operating from five basic neural-emotional complexes, it is a matter of associating a complex with the dream element. Two simple examples of this would be to interpret fire as anger and rain as sadness.

2. Insects: Insects often appear as burrowing, biting, stinging, or simply "bugging" characters in dreams. One might say that in the same sense that Cupid is known as the "wasp" of love, due to his arrow of awakening desire and the sting of love, insects play a similar role in dreams: to penetrate the surface of feeling and awaken the nervous system. Even though these creatures produce a rude feeling that punctures our psychological dullness, they nonetheless bring the nervous system to life. We certainly can feel their effect without knowing the meaning.

3. Animals: Throughout history, humans have identified with and imitated animals. In many cultures, we believe we are descended from animals and have inherited animal powers. There is a case to be made that certain animals exhibit the qualities of particular emotions, and exploring the history or legend of our dream animals certainly intrigues awareness and gives a certain honor to the animal "spirit" representing our emotions. However, the dream content changes so quickly, depending on a combination of the dreamer's comfort level with an emotion and the intensity of the environment in stimulating that emotion, that spending any considerable time analyzing the underlying nature of a particular animal symbol has limited use. Certainly, any dream or image that significantly repeats its appearance is worth the effort to decipher its meaning and message. Even within the animal category there are subsets of evolutionary images. From lowest to highest: fish, amphibians/reptiles, birds, and lower and higher order mammals. The symbol system represented in dreams is a combination of historical image, cultural image, and personal image. In the same way that the figures on a totem pole represent those animals more closely associated with a particular clan, each of us have personal associations with the images of our dreams, indicating the importance of each symbol. But in general there is much more value in tracking the evolution of the images to ascertain whether the therapeutic work associated with a particular feeling, for example, anger, is being more effectively expressed or more severely repressed.

If a sequence of dreams evolves from weather to animal or from animal to human, the therapeutic emotional work is progressing effectively and the client is becoming more accepting and expressive of the emotion. The devolution of an image obviously indicates repression and dissociation. If a client has a dream in which he or she is attacked by a pack of dogs, and then the next night, a dream in which he or she is attacked by a group of people, this would indicate, oddly enough, that the dreamer is becoming more accepting of the emotion behind the images. That's why the image has evolved from animal to human. The attacking nature of the dream content is still concerning, but we always feel attacked by the emotions we are fighting. At least the emotion is perceived as less primitive as the dreaming progresses (human versus animal). To have a series of dreams in which one is attacked first by people, then by animals, and finally by a storm, on the other hand, indicates strong and growing resistance to the emotions behind the images.

4. Monsters: The monster stage is a hybrid of the animal and human stages. It is one stage below the human stage, which signifies identification with and expression of a feeling (versus opposition or resistance to a feeling). The monster stage indicates that the emotion is nearly to a point of acceptance—it feels human—but still strikes the dreamer as a bit monstrous. The monstrous aspect is typically that the feeling is a bit super-charged and feels out of proportion to the moment, due to the historically repressed emotions bursting out at the same time.

The most common monster characters include: vampire, werewolf/ beast-person, ghost, zombie, demon, fairies, elves, trolls, Sasquatch, or other cultural symbols of the creatures of imagination, not animal, but also not quite human. Even though these characters evoke tremendous feeling in the dreamer, we must remember that the whole process of dreaming and consciousness is awakening to feelings in order to access the underlying energy and information. Again, the image does not create the feeling, but rather the feeling produces the illustration we call dreaming and fantasy.

5. Humans: The people who populate our dreams are the representations of the feelings we feel most comfortable with, and yet still repress slightly. When an emotion is represented by a human being/family/ friend, the indication is that the emotion is familiar, and for the most part is being expressed. Most emotions are at least partially expressed and not completely unconscious, except in the cases of extreme trauma producing massive dissociation. It is rare to find someone with a complete suppression of a major neural-emotional center. So, when we are discussing emotional repression, it is the intensity level of the emotion that is being regulated. Since personality regulates the intensity of emotion, it is possible that an emotion that is expressed at one level of intensity would be resisted at a more intense emotional level (See chapter 5, "Psychodynamics.") If you are feeling emotional rage, and this level of emotional intensity is unacceptable by family or social standards, you might well dream about a bear chasing you, or in extreme circumstances, about a great storm approaching or a tornado. These primitive dream images—bear, storm, tornado—simply indicate that the emotion is either a brand new emotional experience or the emotion is being severely repressed/dissociated and the energy of that emotion is being sidetracked into expressing itself though a variety of symptoms, including dreams. And whenever there is an internal illustration of psychic distress, there is a corresponding external distressing expression as well. On the inside, unruly dreams. On the outside, symptomatic expressions.

In the above example, we examined how blocked anger might be illustrated in a dream by animals or weather. These primitive symbols could just as easily represent repressed sexual feelings, great sadness, or even creative potential. The animal, like every symbol in a dream, is a transition symbol that is generated by the level of resistance to the expression of the emotions.

Although a particular dream symbol (such as a bear) will have some significance to both the dreamer and the culture of the dreamer, it is more significant to consider the direction in which the symbol is evolving from dream to dream. Is it becoming more human or more animalistic or more elemental? Is it working its way up the evolutionary scale, or retreating down the evolutionary scale?

All dream images are in transition, but in which direction? The direction of the symbol's evolution is directly associated with emotional expression versus repression. As the therapy proceeds and the client identifies which emotions are difficult to express and begins to express those feelings more bravely, the dream should illustrate improvement of the evolutionary level of the symbols from week to week. There are rarely massive shifts in dream images due to neurological habit/stability. However, even minute resistances are registered in the dream's human stage as indicated by symbols of race, gender, and familiarity.

There is an obvious and expected difference of comfort level in a dream of friends versus a dream of strangers, and in particular, strangers of a different race. Jung suggested that white Americans dream of Africans or Asians as representatives of the more repressed or shadow complexes. He discovered that the Swiss and Italians dream of each other the same way. The ethnicity illustrates our comfort level with an emotional perspective. For most people, there is a gradient of our comfort level with the various races and cultures of the planet, starting with the highest level of comfort being with our own race. Of course, these images can and do evolve as the person matures and becomes more self-accepting. You don't need a scapegoat if you are not resisting your own feelings. The stronger one resists one's emotional response to the world, the stronger the negative charge toward the representatives of those conflicted feelings. Overly strong reactions to common animals and situations (snakes, spiders, germs, heights, etc.) are the recipients of misdirected or symptomatic psychological energy. As mentioned in Chapter Two: "Structure of the Psyche": *Fear and Memory*, we rarely fear that which is not threatening. Our fears are reasonable, but overly charged or out of proportion for the moment or situation. As a result of the psychological prejudice of the shadow, one can begin to understand the roots of racism. People of other races, ethnicities, and countries of origin are the recipients of the usually negatively charged images of the unconscious. Family violence produces strong emotional repression, and repression creates negatively charged symbols of our suffering. The same fear and threat that we feel in our dreams we experience, and even perpetuate, in our daily lives. This fear thereby creates negatively and even violently charged attitudes toward those people who represent these repressed emotions in our own unconscious. The recipient of those projections of the family violence is often greeted with brutal prejudice. Thus, racism is directly linked to developmental family violence combined with cultural imprinting of race/ethnic/religious bias.

However, sometimes it is the "golden" charge that is projected, and we find ourselves enamored by people of other races and ethnicity. For example, the Tibetan people have come to represent a positive spiritual position in the American psyche. During the 70s, many Hindu teachers came to America and were enthusiastically received. Some of these teachers were quite spiritually advanced, but others proved to be charlatans and posers. The initial positive projection from the American psyche gave cover to the imposters until experience revealed them for their true nature, and then the teachers were separated from the predators. Prejudice is simply an inaccurate perception of reality.

SYMBOLS OF TRANSFORMATION

So, how do we measure psychological progress when working with dreams? There are specific types of dream themes that indicate progress is being made. These themes contain the symbols of transformation. In dreaming, there is a constantly illustrated stream of emotional conflict. Since personality keeps a fairly consistent grip on emotional expression, the characters and dynamics of dreaming do not change significantly unless there is a sudden awakening of the unconscious, often as a result of some transition in our lives. There are four significant catalysts, however, that do provoke change in dream content:

1. A sudden increase in our stress level generated by an environmental challenge: personal transition, loss, instability in work, love, or resources, or even positive changes that affect normal everyday patterns, such as a wedding, graduation, or birth.
2. The unfolding of latent potentials: the rhythms of the unconscious pushing new perceptual or emotional material to the surface of consciousness.
3. A strong psychological wave arising from the collective unconscious in response to a current occurrence (for example, a war, act of terror, natural disaster, or epidemic).
4. Undertaking a journey to become conscious: awareness seeking its original design by way of therapy, drugs, spiritual practice, or other routes.

These four catalysts will often be accompanied by dream content that indicates a significant shift in energy and information available to awareness, sometimes even assaulting it. The dream images that appear during these circumstances represent transformation. The energetic state of consciousness is going through a metamorphosis and the dream is illustrating this change.

Some of the more common positive transitional dream symbols (those that embody increased and expressed emotions) are finding a house, finding a new room in a house, construction on a building, attending a wedding, getting married, being pregnant, having or encountering a new-born baby, eating food, having sexual relations, or traveling in a vehicle that you are driving.

These symbols of transformation indicate that the client is expanding self-expression, and thus they are increasing energy.

Some of the more common negative transitional symbols (those that reflect repressed energy and emotion) are illness, death, dying, assault, imprisonment, torture, or being captured.

These symbols mean that the client is at war with some emotion or thought, and the psychological energy is being diminished. Not only that, it often means that the very emotion he or she is at war with is winning. A very important emotion (perhaps anger, sexuality, sadness) is so strongly charged that it is seizing control of the psyche and holding awareness captive against the client's will. In fairy tales, this is when the hero or heroine has been captured by the evil witch or wizard and is being held in a prison. Release will occur only if the emotion is expressed or the environmental trigger discontinues.

High energy is represented by wealth, opportunity, creativity, construction, and development. Low energy is represented by poverty, hunger, and loss.

An important part of dream interpretation is the use of common sense. Since high energy is the overarching goal of therapy, dreams reflecting high energy are most desirable. When a person dreams of war, poverty, or illness, the message is obviously that the psyche is in conflict with itself. One part of the psyche is attempting to suppress another important and energetic component of the psyche. The result of this intra-psychic conflict in the dream is some symbol of impoverishment, death, conflict, or illness. When a person dreams of wealth, food, exciting relationships, or generally positive and energetic circumstances, this is a positive transitional dream and represents an increase in psychological energy. Some dreams are of our impoverishment, some dreams are of our psychological synergy, and some dreams are about the journey between these two polarities, poverty and synergy.

Once we are successfully recording our dreams and have a sense of the direction of the dream cycle, how do we work with the dream content in order to access greater wisdom and energy? Two very convenient and available methods of working with dream images is through personal association and active imagination.

PERSONAL ASSOCIATIONS

Psychological associations are the way in which the psyche connects experiences, information, and emotions that are similar or related to each other in some manner. Associations allow us to make rapid assessments of our environment based on familiar patterns. Although the circumstances and situational details may vary considerably, the psyche uses an emotional "short-hand" to assume a sense of safety, familiarity, fear, and anxiety as a way of quickly interacting with the world. At a deeper level, however, associations are connected with significant emotional history.

We all know the embarrassment of referring to someone by someone else's name. Somehow, we have associated (connected) these two people together. How often does a situation or person remind us of someone else? This is the power and process of association. Sometimes it is obvious and easy to figure out the connection between the two people that causes an emotional overlap, but often it takes a bit of effort to "tease out" the emotional or historical connections that bond these people, circumstances, or locations together.

When working with dreams, patience and respect are required. The content of the dream is fundamentally emotionally uncomfortable; otherwise, we wouldn't need the dream to express that emotion. As such, there will be a natural resistance to seeking and encountering the history and associations behind the dream content. The information is in the unconscious and needs to be elevated to consciousness, but dream work is a bit like fishing, in which we explore the lake, searching for our prize to reveal itself.

Dream characters are the representations of feelings and memories of historical events and experiences that are being triggered in the present. It is through association that every character and place in a dream becomes significant. In a dream, you are experiencing your blocked up emotions and the memory connections with real events, past and present, presented as theater or movie. Dreams are literally illustrated emotional conflicts.

Mental and emotional associations, as a dynamic of the psyche, can be as simple as I say "dog" and you respond "cat." This is a simple association based on experience. This type of association could be offered by nearly everyone. However, if I say "dog" and you say "window," clearly you have an association with "dog" that is not widely shared and is connected to some experience in your life. This is a personal association. However, if you know the song, "How Much Is that Doggie in the Window?," a popular song of my childhood, which is my association with those two particular words and how they are linked together, then the association reveals something of your age or childhood, or even places the association to a particular time in your history. The more personal an association is, the more it aids in the search for charged contents in the unconscious, which might be creating symptoms, blind spots, and emotional inhibition.

The associations that are connected with emotional blocks are very personal and help us identify events, personal history, and emotional links to traumatic experiences. These associations help identify core emotional material of the unconscious. The dreamer starts with a dream symbol/character/component and begins to connect it to specific emotional experiences, people, places, and events. Our associations (memories of life experiences, literature, movies, television, music, etc.) with the dream characters/symbols help us understand the meaning of the character and the emotions fueling the character's role in the dream. Essentially, the dream plays the role of the white rabbit in *Alice in Wonderland*. It catches our attention and pulls us into a challenging adventure, exploring the unresolved emotional experiences of our childhood and the unfolding potentialities of our future.

Dream people, places, and events are all intimately associated with the dreamer specifically. As the therapist explores the dreamer's associations with the dream images, the more primitive dream images will prove more challenging in identifying the personal associations connected to the image. In these cases, the association process needs to include common social associations with the image: literature, film, religion/spiritual content, etc. In other words, we are including the historical and social associations (the social collective) with dream images and not necessarily just drawing personal connections with the material. Personal association collapses the dream image into specific emotional dynamics, whereas collective association expands the dream image into the greater ocean of humanity's cultural memory. If the dreamer is resistant to personal associations, then examining the dream symbol by including cultural associations can reduce resistance to exploring the meaning of the dream symbol.

Our emotional history is often represented in dreams by images of people, places, pets, houses, etc., that are directly associated with specific times and events in our lives. These memories contain a particular emotional charge that is seeking expression by announcing itself in the dream image. For example, one might dream of a dog that has the name of a pet the dreamer once cared for in seventh grade. Upon exploring that time period, the client may remember that it was in eighth grade that his or her parents divorced. The dream content essentially gets one near the point of the emotional trauma. It is up to the therapist and client to locate the emotional content of that time period. The dream is helpful in identifying those emotional events that are energetically potent enough to affect consciousness in the present. Even though a client may have reported a number of emotional events in the initial interview or during the course of therapy, our traumas lay dormant until there is sufficient stimulation to activate them. Jung referred to this as "constellating a complex." Any emotion that is affecting our mood or attitude will appear as an active component in our dreams. Any emotion that is not activated, regardless of trauma, remains inactive until triggered, and as a result, produces no representation in the dream world. Thus, the contents of the dream are usually those emotions and events that are ready to be worked on.

Active Imagination

The use of active imagination has found strong acceptance in the fields of competitive athletics, art, music, meditation, prayer, and healing. The use of the positive imaging of an action and its results, prior to the act, is used at almost every level of human performance: praying for someone's health, visualizing serving a tennis ball, practicing finger exercises in music, picturing the trajectory of the golf ball, shooting free throws in basketball, hitting a baseball, or even envisioning complex meditative mandalas. The visualizer is practicing concentration, shaping expectation, and perfecting quality of performance. The visualizer is attempting to achieve a number of things:

1. Build a bridge between consciousness and the unconscious
2. Allow unconscious material to enter into imagination/fantasy
3. Awaken new neural pathways to serve as expressive conduits for latent psychological abilities
4. Access old neural pathways associated with emotion, memory, and imagination
5. Train those neural pathways to function more energetically by imaginatively correcting dream conflicts
6. Stabilize concentration

Imagination is being utilized to accelerate the neurological and psychological learning curve of self-expression. On a practical daily-functioning level, active imagination is particularly helpful in correcting bad habits, limiting negative self-talk, increasing concentration, developing a positive attitude, and fundamentally training neural pathways to accomplish a specific goal.

Active imagination works the same way in dream therapy. In Gestalt dream therapy, one of the goals is for the client to directly identify with and express the energy and attitude of every one of the characters and objects in a dream, including the inanimate objects. In Fritz Perls' significant book, *Gestalt Therapy Verbatim*, there are approximately two hundred pages of transcriptions of Perls working live with an audience and volunteers. Perls has the volunteer dreamer "become" each character or object in the dream, imagining what each component feels and desires to express.

There is a cognitive behavioral feel to this imaginative process in that the dreamer must offer a variety of interpretations of the intent and content of the dream. Getting the dream correctly interpreted is not the goal. It is much more important that the dreamer access his or her unconscious in a more fluid and accepting manner. This allows the unconscious to inform awareness of the bigger picture of reality, offering broader emotions and complex information. It is the bridge between awareness and the unconscious that is important and not necessarily what emotion is crossing that bridge.

Jung, in his book *Dreams*, states that there is "no difference between image and energy." Thus, imaginatively identifying with the objects and agents in a dream provides awareness access to the energy and information contained within the dream symbol.

A wonderful variation of active imagination that I call "completing the dream" is to re-visualize the parts of the dream that are disturbing. Like a good editor or scriptwriter, through active imagination we can rewrite the aspect of the dream that is disturbing. The client is encouraged to take the central problem in the dream and to re-visualize the circumstances with a more positive result. It takes some discipline to get good at this technique, but with practice, one can develop some consistent skill with opening awareness to what might simply be called intuitive wisdom, producing an experience that is both energetic and informative.

A former client of mine once told me a dream in which she was a jailer. Her jail was filled with people hollering, "Let me out! Let us out!" and banging on the cell walls, shouting, and making noise. End of dream. So I asked her how she would prefer to have the dream end, imagining a new corrective dream ending. I've described this dream in dozens of training sessions and I always receive the same answer from the group of therapists: "Let the people out." This should be the obvious answer. Instead, my client said, "I want them all to shut up!" I sat back in my chair and thought to myself, "Well, this is going to take longer than I expected."

Curiously, the dream is not always cooperative with imaginative change. The dream content may actually resist the attempts by the active imagination to change the scenario. The dream characters are representatives of psychological components that have been repressed, in some cases for years, and some of these repressed emotions have built up quite an energetic charge. The stronger the repressed emotional charge, the more resilient the negative illustration will remain. However, the dynamics of expression support the eventual release of all of the contents of the unconscious, and with persistence and courage, active imagination can slowly but surely morph negative outcome into positive outcome. Think of that stubborn image as a rusty bolt that needs a bit more muscle to be broken free.

Our clients need to learn to interact positively with their unconscious in order to reduce symptoms, increase perceptual accuracy, raise energy levels, and express emotions in proportion to the moment. As positive as working with dreams can be, personality resists the contents of the unconscious because of painful associations. However, working with dream images is a direct engagement with the contents of the unconscious, and as a result, has a tendency to raise the level of anxiety. However, with a few relaxation exercises, breathing techniques, or very shallow hypnotic inductions (until the person feels comfortable working with his or her unconscious and these techniques are no longer necessary), the dreamer can very effectively interact with the contents of the unconscious and provide a much more satisfying resolution to the dream conflict. The goal is for the client to develop an active, stress-free interaction with his or her unconscious in order to access the wisdom and energy contained there.

However, being able to freely associate or fantasize about the components of a dream is a learned ability. Most people do not trust their unconscious and resist examining the spontaneous bursts of wisdom and emotional connection that emerge when summoned. The same filtering process that created the contents of the personal unconscious continues to restrict their availability to consciousness. Thus, even when one is requesting this repressed information to manifest, the personality censor is still at work limiting access. Curiosity, courage, and practice will produce easier and easier access to that unconscious wisdom. Eventually, the bridges between consciousness and unconsciousness will support a continuous flow of traffic, providing consciousness with the missing information about the world and the emotional expression of the moment. We train our nervous system, and thus our personality, to be less restrictive at the border between the conscious and unconscious and allow this traffic creative interplay with the waking mind.

FANTASY

The dream is the deeper, less accessible content of our psyche, whereas our fantasies are closer to the surface of consciousness (we have fantasies while we are awake) and can often be a great resource for unconscious material ready to be integrated. After all, even though fantasy is still a transitional state of awareness progressing from symptom to insight, our fantasies are simply a more conscious illustration of unexpressed emotional potential.

Fantasies are produced in inverse proportion to our self-expression and represent our energetic potential. That which is not expressed directly is expressed in fantasy. If you are expressing fifty percent of your aggression or fifty percent of your sexuality, the other fifty percent will be represented by fantasies. The fantasy always contains the emotion (and thus the energy) that is not being directly expressed. There is always a corresponding fantasy for every psychological symptom. The fantasy is simply a more evolved form of the blocked emotion creating the symptom. Remember, fantasy is the third level, out of five, of our perception of reality. Fantasy arises out of the tension between our total response to reality (conscious and unconscious) and the portion of that response that our personality is willing to express. That which is not expressed directly (emotion or insight) is expressed indirectly (symptom, dream, or fantasy).

The personality is what determines what is expressed as action and what is expressed as fantasy. When couples reach a level of comfort with each other, they often find that using fantasies in the sex life improves the energy and emotion of the encounter. This is because they are tapping their energetic/emotional potential. As we become proficient with expressing our fantasy life, we begin to access a larger worldview and raise our energy levels. Essentially, fantasy is reality that is being restricted by personality. The fantasy is the compensation for emotions and information that are not being directly expressed.

There is always tension between fantasy and morality because morality is the god of the ego. Culture first applies "corrections" to self-expressive behaviors of its citizens. When this creates psychological tension that expresses itself in symptomatic and self-destructive behaviors, culture then applies morality to suppress the acting out resulting from the initial "correction." Morality is learned and imposed on our natural self-expressive tendencies, with the excuse that without externally applied morality, the base character of the human being, self-indulgence, cruelty, and brutality would be uninhibitedly released on society. The problem in this thinking is that the basic nature of the human being is not corrupt. Society and families create the corruption they fear through the very methods used attempting to prevent it: discipline, guilt, shame, and fear. True morality is inherently energetic and therefore attractive. It is much easier to be kind to others than to be cruel. Cruelty takes effort. It is much easier to be merciful and forgiving than to be resentful. Resentment takes effort. Natural morality is associated with the evolution of consciousness and not necessarily social approval, thus the needs of society or family are often in competition with the needs of consciousness.

This tension between our soul design and our desire for social approval is what produces fantasy.

Once again, we return to the dilemma of self-perception: Are we inherently corrupt and in need of correction, or are we inherently "good" and attempting to correct the divine design? We must examine the possibility that the design of consciousness is good: not that we all achieve our moral or ethical potential, but that certainly we possess the drive to do so.

When to Avoid Dreams

In general, the stronger the feeling from a dream, the better the process, with several significant exceptions: PTSD, neural trauma, and psychosis each can evoke terrifying feelings and dreams illustrating damage to the body and the impairment of the psyche. These terrifying dreams are rarely helpful and are, in fact, often harmful. There is a significant difference between the two types of dreams: those sparked by environmental triggers and developing emotions and the traumatic and disturbing dreams induced by physical trauma that force terror onto consciousness and serve no purpose other than to alert the dreamer and therapist to the level of severe wounding the body is experiencing. In these cases, dream analysis and dream journals are rarely useful. What we are attempting to accomplish in this type of severe trauma (rehabilitation) therapy is to train concentration and consciousness to more effectively regulate, and in some cases, repress, the unconscious content. When will, alone, is insufficient to regulate these violent and disturbing dreams, medication is required to aid the process until such a time that bio-chemical equilibrium has been re-established and the client is capable of experiencing life in proportion to the "now" without having every moment contaminated by these significant historical traumas. Psychotic and pre-psychotic dreams are particularly disturbing. Dreams of rape, cannibalism, possession, disturbing animal mutations, or visitation by celestial beings or aliens should alert the therapist of a client that is acutely suffering and is no longer able to regulate his or her experience. When a client reports images that are significantly brutal, we need to make sure that there is not an underlying biochemical threat. Highly disturbing dreams, extreme anxiety, suicidal ideation, and sleep interruption are all features that should alert the therapist to the extreme possibility of imminent psychotic break. Immediate medical intervention is advised in these cases.

CONCLUSION

Part of the difficulty of dream work is learning to think of oneself as having multiple parts. We are so convinced of our individuality and isolation that the presentation of one consciousness having multiple containers (people, animals, weather) is simply shocking. However, as soon as one is capable of setting disbelief aside and embracing the fact that we are one, and the one is many, we stop feeling so lonely and begin to conduct our lives in the real world as though everyone we meet is an aspect of our self. The same applies to the dream world.

To understand dreams is to understand reality. Although we typically do not think of our perception of the world as "the current myth" to which we are committed, it is probably safe to say that the reality we cling to amounts to the smallest piccolo in the massive symphony that is the universe. An old neural-psychiatrist colleague and friend of mine once commented, "When we understood two percent of the nervous system, we thought we knew it all. And now that we understand four percent of the nervous system, we know that we don't know sh*t."

What we aren't aware of amounts to a psychic black hole, affecting our perception of the world by producing distortions in the field of awareness that, when studied, reveal hidden agents of great power and energy startling us into a wakefulness.

Our dream life is no different from the child's world, full of mystery, magic, danger, and dynamism yet to be deciphered. It may take us our whole lives to translate the emotional wisdom that we first encountered at five years old. And then again, we may be working our way up the ladder of consciousness, our dreams announcing the emerging abilities of a stable mind: gifts from the deep well of the collective unconscious.

REVISIONING THE TREATMENT
OF SEXUAL ABUSE

A SECOND LOOK AT FREUD

Since the 1970's, a significant amount of research has been done on the frequency of sexual abuse in America. To put it bluntly, the results are horrifying. We now know that both boys and girls are sexually abused at a rate that is alarming. However, before this research, there was an almost universal denial of how widespread child abuse is in America. Part of the problem was a fundamental tenet of psychoanalysis. Recent reexaminations of Freud's work indicate that his first conclusion concerning adult psychopathology, called the "seduction theory," asserted that much of the prevalent female neurosis was rooted in childhood sexual abuse. Before his now infamous theory of the "abuse fantasy" as a part of the oedipal phase of development, Freud essentially accused his community of abusing their children, resulting in acute suffering among adult survivors. There are many versions of what happened next, but there is evidence to suggest two primary reasons for the evolution of Freud's thoughts from identifying childhood sexual abuse as a significant source of adult psychopathology into the oedipal fantasy complex in which abuse was not real but imagined. It is suggested that he was at least partially motivated by the rejection (with extreme hostility) of his "seduction/ abuse" theory within the medical community. It is likewise argued that he was influenced to shift his views by his friendship with and loyalty to a sadistic surgeon who, in what seems a very strange proposition today, believed in a mystical connection between the structure of the nasal passage and sexual pathology (Jeffrey Masson, *Atlantic Monthly*, February 1984). Although Freud is often dismissed for his obsessively sexually biased theories, it is not difficult to make a case for his positive effect on psychotherapy with his biological stage theory. However:

> *Freud's abandonment of his original conviction of the prevalence of actual (not imagined) child abuse was one of the great cowardly acts in the history of psychology and created a pathologizing of children that has taken decades to begin to correct.*

Combined with widespread and very primitive religious notions concerning the importance of disciplining children to prevent their "corrupt" nature from dominating their character, Freud's reversal has led to a culture that still defends physical abuse, from spanking to more severe measures, as actions taken for the child's own good.

Every culture contains within its social fabric fundamental myths or core beliefs that describe the nature and purpose of humanity. These views permeate self-perception, whether or not one claims membership in any particular religious organization. America is a Christian nation, if only by the permeation of the Christian perspective that the human being is a fallen creature and that the physical body is sinful by nature. Although the teachings of Jesus Christ certainly repudiate much of the cultural bias of the Old Testament, there is no fundamental myth stronger than the concept that human beings have inherent and indulgent flaws that must be corrected. In the most extreme permutations of this myth, flaws are perceived to be evidence of a demonic force that attempts to control the soul.

Those who hold this view further contend that religious and physical discipline is needed to bring this sinister influence under control.

> *One may hear the argument that it is religious extremism that has driven many of the most brutal wars in human history, but the physical war on children occurs every day, in every nation, and in nearly every home.*

PATHOLOGIZING SEXUAL ABUSE

During my forty years of clinical work, Western culture has still not found its equilibrium concerning the prevalence and consequence of sexual and physical abuse. Our society pathologizes those who have experienced sexual abuse. The overall perception that these survivors of sexual abuse have been seriously, if not permanently, damaged often makes the experience of sexual abuse much, much worse. When clinicians observe and treat the PTSD associated with sexual abuse and assault, we often unconsciously fall in line with the notion that our clients are wounded and damaged. At a very subtle level, there is a conspiracy of therapy to reinforce the client's self-image of brokenness. I have seen no evidence that sexual abuse is significantly different from any highly traumatic physical abuse in its actual effect on the child. When I ask my clients to evaluate how their particular sexual abuse has affected them, it is most often the predatory nature of the perpetrator, rather than the actual sexual contact, that is the underlying source of the PTSD. The unexpressed rage at the physical insult of abuse is often the driving force of the anxiety, fear, and inhibition common to abuse victims. Sexual abuse survivors often have normal sex drives, are capable of achieving climax, and desire sexual intimacy. This would indicate organ resilience and function, thus relating minimum physical dissociation to the abuse. Let me be clear. I am not saying sexual abuse does not lead to sexual dissociation; it most certainly can and does. However, I am not convinced that the detachment from physical experience that occurs in sexual abuse survivors is particularly different from that associated with any other form of systematic or cruel physical abuse. Awareness will remove itself from any physical organ that is regularly under assault. Thus, I contend that the underlying psychodynamic in treating sexual abuse lies with the resolution of rage versus reversing sexual inhibition or improving poor self-image.

In a culture that pathologizes the woman's genital physiology at every stage of development from childhood to old age, it is sometimes difficult to determine whether inhibition of sexual expression is due to abuse or cultural bias and gender rules (which are, of course, a more subtle form of abuse). American culture seems to support the perception of women being "bitchy" more than it supports the idea of a woman being angry or furious. Social mores and cultural gender roles limit the self-expressive options for women concerning open expression of anger; thus, learned passivity and cooperation are often present in childhood sexual abuse. The psyche's survival mechanism in the face of danger resorts to a Stockholm syndrome dynamic; passivity and submission to the aggressor (it is not uncommon for an adolescent girl to actually continue to "date" someone who has been sexually assaultive). (See chapter 4: "Trauma Dynamics," *Stockholm Syndrome*.)

Due to the compensatory nature of the unconscious, any emotions to which we are exposed trigger a sympathetic emotional response within us, a "mirroring." As a result, abuse born out of the rage of the perpetrator triggers a simultaneous rage in the victim that is suppressed due to the great danger of the moment. This can produce more damage emotionally than it does physically, because it triggers in the victim a rage that is beyond any anger she has ever experienced.

Since personality regulates all surges of emotion, this rage is immediately transformed into symptoms—symptoms that may remain for a lifetime if not expressively released. Books and homework designed to improve self-image are useless against the tsunami of fury buried in the unconscious and controlled by the victim's desire for social approval and safety, a combination of social training and the Stockholm effect. To begin to reduce the traumatic emotional pressure, the victim needs to learn effective self-expression. This begins with overcoming the need for approval. We seek approval at the expense of autonomy, creative self-expression, and self-defense. The submission response is our attempt to secure approval in threatening situations. Courage, curiosity, and a commitment to developing the ability to protect oneself must replace fear and submission as a survival strategy.

GENDER ROLES

With so much sexual abuse being driven by angry, resentful, and rageful assailants, a sexually abused woman is doubly harmed by both the assault and the cultural gender rules concerning expression of rage. Family and society seem more comfortable with the broken girl rather than the rageful girl. The willingness of the family/culture to promote depression, moodiness, self-criticism, and a damaged self-image— rather than address the furious offense the survivor is actually feeling— becomes a brutal, self-reinforcing cycle. Little boys are expected to recover fully from being severely physically disciplined; this is a reverse form of gender bias and promotes secrecy and denial among male abuse survivors. But girls carry a view of themselves as damaged goods. The boys are encouraged to deny the effect of their abuse, and the girls are encouraged to embrace victimization. This punitive self-image is fueled by repressed rage. Remember, the strength of self-image is in proportion to self-expression. When a client presents as having poor self-image and reports a history of sexual abuse, be assured, there is rage that needs release. Most people recover from the physical abuse of sexual assault but are impaired by the anger that arises in response to the experience. However, significantly improving a client's self-image cannot be achieved without addressing the repressed emotions that promote that distorted self-perception. Supportive comments, empathy, self-improvement books, and homework are strategic ways of building a relationship with the client and lay a solid groundwork for the deeper work of emotional expression. Building a nurturing relationship and providing role models with high self-esteem can help the client envision the therapeutic goals, but the client's personality structure, which limits positive self-image by limiting self-expression, needs to evolve in order to provide the energy and expression associated with that positive sense of self. Without the client's releasing the repressed emotions, her personality structure remains fixed in a negative cycle. The therapeutic alliance, built upon the foundation of support, care, nurture, empathy, and patience, along with reframing the trauma through homework, journaling, reading resources, and support groups, eventually leads to the deeper emotional release that evolves self-expression and self-image.

The psychodynamics and treatment of sexual abuse are not significantly different from any other form of abuse; the repressed emotional response to abuse fuels the symptomatic profile and poor perception of self.

To correct distorted self-image, relieve the emotional pressure, and reduce the symptomatic profile, the client is required to identify the blocked emotions, reconnect those emotions with their historical events, develop active imagination scenarios of expression and confrontation, practice emotional expression in therapy and with those "safer" friends, and eventually express those emotions directly in the moment, often confronting those involved in the original emotional insults.

TREATMENT DYNAMICS

How long does this take? A long time. Why? Therapy does not simply deal with the harm caused by a single event. The restriction of self-expression, although potentially triggered by a single event, is created by the systematic compromise of self-expression throughout life. Therapy does not only address the moment, but the individual's emotional history that manifests in the form of a restrictive personality structure. The regulation of emotional expression learned in our families and through social norms may work reasonably well until one suffers a life-changing emotional experience, and the personality structure is unable to handle the increased emotional pressure of that triggering event. The levees of New Orleans provide an excellent parallel with the human nervous system. The levees worked just fine until they were confronted with Hurricane Katrina, and suddenly, the city suffered catastrophic damage as the levee system failed to handle the storm surge. Just as when the city suffered storm damage and the citizens moved elsewhere, awareness dissociates from the physical sites of abuse. On a personal scale, sexual abuse is no less damaging than Hurricane Katrina. Too much, too much, too much.

There is one other significant dynamic in correcting the damage associated with physical and sexual abuse: the fear that arises when we believe (often accurately) that we are unable to defend ourselves physically. In the psychotherapy and healing communities there is a philosophy of "letting things go," often through forgiveness. Although I've never fully understood the psychodynamics of "letting something go" or "moving on," I certainly understand the concept of forgiveness. In most religions, forgiveness is directly connected with confession, through which the conscious acknowledgment by the abuser of his transgressions against others is fully understood, stated, and corrected.

Forgiveness, in this sense, is partially an acknowledgment by the wounded that she is no longer afraid of the behavior of the other and is willing to receive the offender back into her community. Without a genuine confession, though, how can she feel safe or offer forgiveness?

Forgiveness can be a powerful spiritual path when practiced consistently throughout life. The application of forgiveness as an element of compassion has certainly been proven to free one from the brutal nature of the world that feels so personal. Forgiveness can be a spiritual path unto itself, a spiritual technique designed to expand one's sense of caring for all living beings while simultaneously requiring the individual to dismantle the narcissistic perception that takes everything so personally.

Forgiveness can provide an energetic boost when wisdom replaces resentment.

However, our memory of childhood vulnerability and inconsistent or abusive authority figures makes us forever vigilant about the consequences of self-expression. Forgiving the abusive acts of others does not fundamentally change our awareness of being in danger, with one significant exception. There are abuses we suffer as children that are the result of parental inexperience and ignorance. And then there are abuses that we suffer as children that are the indulgences of the cruel intent of others. Forgiving ignorance is significantly different from forgiving cruelty.

Truly understanding the difference between parental foolishness and indulgent malice does provide an opportunity to forgive. However, this differentiation also clearly defines the actions of malevolent intent. The willingness of a very large person to physically threaten and wound a smaller and weaker person is not born out of ignorance; it is born out of cruelty. The threats and the consequences experienced by the child are real, not fantasy. Our willingness as adults to suffer the symptoms associated with repression and dissociation is directly in proportion to that childhood threat. In these cases, forgiveness has limited traction.

For most people, the fear of punitive consequences is at the heart of all emotional inhibition and poor self-image.

Self-Defense

So, what is the solution to this persistent fear of the consequences of self-expression? The answer is simple: effective self-defense. The psyche knows when it is safe and when it is vulnerable. The unconscious immediately provides the energy needed to defend oneself, but is limited by the *ability of the body* to physically defend itself. Without practical training or defensive weapons, the body is limited in its ability to protect itself against predators. Let's face it: if you are being hunted by a lion, your positive self-image and a willingness to forgive the lion's pointy teeth and razor sharp claws will not protect you. Passively permitting ourselves to be hunted is the result of socialization. I often ask clients this question: "If you knew someone was stalking you with harmful intent, what would you do?" The answer is usually some form of passivity or denial. The act of self-defense often remains suppressed.

Active Imagination

Therapeutically, there are some basic steps to developing an effective, accurate, and reasonable self-protection system. First, we start with imagination. The limits of your imagination become the limits of your actions. Fantasy precedes action. If you block your fantasies, you block the self-expressive options available to you. If you cannot fantasize about aggression (or sex, athletic ability, or good grades) your behavior will be similarly limited. Remember, personality is an information/emotion/energy-regulating system. Your personality's inventory of expressive options is limited to your developmental training. Developing new strategies for self-expression requires you to develop the capacity to fantasize about those strategies first.

The ability to fantasize and to trust its symbolic power can feel dangerous. Active imagination is a psychological skill that is no different from any forbidden form of self-expression; it is simply occurring in the imaginary state rather than the expressive state. The same inhibitions and self-restrictions that inhibit action inhibit fantasy.

At first, fantasy operates in proportion to the amount of historical emotion repressed in the unconscious, and as a result, the initial fantasies can be particularly powerful or scary. This is akin to the fantasies we have about food after being on a diet for several weeks or months. So, consider how powerful the fantasies are when you've been on an emotional diet for *decades*. Needless to say, these fantasies, and sometimes the emotions, may be out of proportion to the moment. Thus, our concern about how reasonable our behavior would be if we really cut loose is somewhat warranted. But eventually, as the emotional pressure is reduced by expressing those repressed feelings more openly, honestly, and immediately, our emotional fantasies and actions become proportional to the moment.

We do not consider the imagination of childhood to be forbidden. A child's imagination is the imagery that feeling produces before the child is capable of identifying emotions. As the child's nervous system matures, imagery and fantasy precede activity and self-knowledge. A child's world is filled with active make-believe characters who communicate and comment on the child's behavior and experience. The child practices behavior through imagination.

One of the most significant psychological rules is that imagination is compensatory to self-expression. Imagination represents that which is not expressed, yet.

Feeling is either imagined or expressed, or it is turned into psychological symptoms. As the child matures, fantasy evolves into emotions and, ultimately, wisdom. However, what is not expressed emotionally remains fantasy or symptom. This means that any emotional reaction that a child has is either directly expressed in the moment or indirectly expressed and remains in the realms of imaginary play, uncomfortable dreams, or psychological symptoms like anxiety or stress. For children and adults alike, imagery is the symbol of emotional potential. For example, when you are given a speeding ticket unfairly, your emotional expression is usually in proportion to your sense of consequences. You repress what you would really like to say. Fear of the consequences prohibits much of your emotional expression. Thus, as you drive away, you begin to say all the things you would have liked to have said, or you fantasize about them. The fantasy contains the unexpressed emotional charge.

This type of psychological repression occurs throughout the day, every day of our life. This is why we feel stress, anxiety, depression, etc. These are the daily symptoms of restricted self-expression. To reduce these symptoms, we need to begin to express the material that has been repressed for days, weeks, months, and years. It is a major step in therapy for a client to allow fantasy to replace symptomology. This is also why dream journals are so effective. Through the experiencing, remembering, recording, and reciting of dreams, one begins to convert emotion from symptom into fantasy and, eventually, into direct expression.

From Fantasy to Action

It is still a long way from fantasy to action, but at least the personality's prime directive to manipulate the world through approval or submission has been challenged, and one's self-expression options have expanded. After a client sorts out the intensity of her own fantasies and begins to express her feelings more directly, she is capable of perceiving the world more accurately. However, she is still left with the challenge of how she can protect herself when she feels threatened. On a very basic level, self-confidence and self-security come down to her ability to physically defend herself. At some point in therapy, depending on the type of intimidation used in the family or due to a history of physical assault, I recommend that the client study martial arts or weapons training. I have an arrangement with a local martial arts master who understands the need to teach self-defense in non-threatening steps so that the client is not re-traumatized by the intensity of the physical contact, until she is prepared and willing. For some clients, the gentle martial art of T'ai Chi is a wonderful form of energy and movement training. For others, I recommend the more ferocious Krav Maga Israeli commando training. In some cases,

I recommend carrying pepper spray, mace, and even occasionally, a weapon. Each person needs to be able to determine what form of self-protection produces his or her energetic satisfaction. One young woman I worked with could only sleep well if she had a knife under her pillow. While the knife was a tangible tool for self-defense, the simple act of confronting her fear by taking action provided the relief. The knife was simply the symbol of that action.

Each person needs to assess his or her safety needs and to approach self-defense in a manner tailored to those needs. How we navigate through life is partially determined by the way in which we present ourselves. Predators recognize prey, and our willingness and prepared-ness to protect ourselves often shapes the types of experiences that manifest in our lives. Thus, we often see women who have been abused as children encounter predators to a disproportionate degree as they move through adulthood. The first step is to transform symptomology (repressed feelings) into imagination. The second step is to practice the activity of the imagination physically until ability is achieved. Over-coming inhibition is fundamental in gaining mastery over one's life.

INTEGRATION

One of the more significant challenges in healing sexual abuse is the survivor's ability to overcome the dissociation associated with the abuse and reintegrate awareness with the body. There are many won-derful and sensitive styles of bodywork that can expedite this process: yoga, massage, T'ai Chi, to name a few, as well as most cardio-work-outs designed to get the body in shape. The great challenge of healing and evolving is how to encourage one's awareness to literally explore, feel, and express the entire dynamism of the body. Reluctance, fear, and anxiety tend to discourage spontaneous healing, so one needs to strate-gically plan how to begin and support one's own healing process. One must involve one's physical, mental, emotional, and spiritual capacities in the quest for healing self-expression and self-image.

CONCLUSION

Sexual abuse, its treatment, and the process of healing is a spectacularly complex subject. In this small chapter, I have attempted to explore what I perceive to be an ongoing social pathologizing of women with rage and address an under-recognized aspect of treatment: the crucial role of claiming physical self-protection in the present. Healing from any form of physical abuse, much less the significantly personal experience of sexual abuse, requires courage, curiosity, and commitment.

While many elements are important to the transformation of the sexual abuse survivor's negative self-perception and learned helplessness, taking the reins with effective self-defense, both imaginary and real, is critical. Without this step, power remains in the hands of the perpetrator and in the grasp of a society that wishes to see women's agency suppressed.

CHAPTER THIRTEEN

SEX ADDICTION AND COMPULSIVE SEXUAL DYNAMICS

SEPARATING THE DANGEROUS FROM THE IMPAIRED

Recently, I was preparing a lecture on sexual compulsivity versus sexual predatory behavior and the importance of accurate diagnosis in order for the treatment strategy to be effective. With sexual predatory behavior, we are dealing with a person who is unable to share an emotional link with other living beings. These human predators are either biological psychopaths who suffer from a neurological processing problem that prevents them from sharing in the intimacy of the human experience, or developmental anti-social personalities who suffer from brutal child abuse and neglect and view the world and the people in it simply as resources. These disorders are incapable of emotionally identifying with the experience of the "other," which means that inflicting suffering has no inhibiting effect. The nearly impossible treatment of these predators is not discussed in this chapter. (See chapter 3, "Personality Structure," *The Borderline Diagnosis*.)

SEXUAL COMPULSION

Sexual compulsion, by contrast, can be the result of several unique and treatable problems:

1. A biochemical "impairment" (manic depressive, bipolar disorder) in which a biochemical imbalance triggers an insatiable sexual appetite and drives compulsive sexual behavior.
2. A psychological expressive disorder:
   a. The compulsion of sexual freedom
   b. Early developmental stage sexual activation (abuse/trauma)
   c. Sublimation of other feelings through sexual expression

BIOCHEMICAL IMPAIRMENT

The more extreme form of manic depression/bipolar affective disorder is usually attended by extraordinarily high sexual appetites. Even when these individuals are successfully medically treated, their libidos are usually significantly higher than the general population and sexual tension with their mates is a predictable issue in counseling. The therapeutic strategy for these individuals is the acceptance of a lovemaking schedule that the partner will honor and the redirection/sublimation of the additional libido into creative and competitive activities, shifting the burden of sexual satisfaction from the exhausted partner to a fundamental lifestyle shift—regular exercise, for example.

Although the DSM recognizes three variations of this bipolar biochemistry; manic depression, cyclothymia, and hypomania, the diagnostic requirements fail to cover a great many people who express, biologically, the symptoms and drives that are associated with the manic-depression spectrum—in particular, impulsive libido and high sex drive. These individuals are often frustrated that their romantic relationships fail, in the long-term, to meet their libidinal requirements.

In many, if not most, romantic relationships, the initial courtship behavior includes frequent sexual engagement. The fascination and release of sexual energy carries the relationship forward to the more difficult emotional compatibility stage in which sexual behavior returns to an expressive level much more consistent with each individual's typical sexual appetite. The partner with the significantly higher libido often finds himself or herself frustrated by the infrequency of sexual contact and begins to seek release of sexual tension through a variety of behaviors, including sexually specific behaviors such as pornography. This is sometimes inaccurately diagnosed as sex addiction, when in fact it is a biochemically driven behavior that will be a lifelong issue. In these cases, pornography probably needs to be addressed in a manner similar to how a diabetic approaches sugar: a lot is simply not a good idea, and there are higher quality life experiences available to those with that "extra" energy. It is simply a matter of evolving one's lifestyle to include creative activity challenges that require more energy than the typical person.

PSYCHOLOGICAL EXPRESSIVE DISORDER

The foundation of this book rests on the idea that all non-medically based psychological symptoms are the result of an "expressive disorder." This means that the manner in which one's personality regulates self-expression either supports perceiving the world accurately and responding emotionally in proportion to the moment or perceiving a distortion of reality and expressing a variety of symptoms in place of genuine emotions.

In the personality structure of sexual obsession and compulsion, the neural-emotional centers of sadness, aggression, and thought are all sublimated (re-routed) through the reproductive center, triggering sexual obsession and/or compulsion when any other emotional site is activated. In this structure, there is an extreme sublimation problem. Awareness is expressively connected only with sexual expression, and the other four complexes (anger, sadness, thought, speech) are all sublimated through sexual expression. This means that every time this person gets angry or sad, he or she experiences sexual impulses. Until the sexually obsessed person further develops emotional and thinking abilities, the person will remain sexually compulsive. In addition, speech is only linked with sexual perception and expression; thus, verbal content will have a highly sexualized content.

THE COMPULSION OF SEXUAL FREEDOM

Sexuality and sexual expression are highly charged social targets. Religious institutions, family systems, gender roles, and moral and ethical rules abound, leaving no one unscathed by the inhibitory or expressive requirements of our social contracts. In some cases, family systems will so consistently avoid the subject of sexuality that the child can grow up in a sexually inhibited family and yet, suffer little inhibition of sexual expression as an adult. The family simply avoided the subject so thoroughly that there is very little learned inhibition. In these cases, when awareness expresses itself sexually, there is a sense of uninhibited freedom and self-expression.

The desire to test the limits of emotional and, in this case, sexual freedom is commonly experienced in the courtship phase of personal relationships. Falling in love, or infatuation, is attended by a freedom of emotional expression that is rarely so completely socially accepted in any other form. As a society, particularly in America, we kind of expect people to act "crazy" and to "yadda, yadda" about the subject of their love infatuation. The television sitcom industry is founded on these types of relationships.

If sexual expression is the only place that a person "feels good" about himself or herself, then that person will naturally return to this behavior again and again. This can appear to be a pathological expression of sexuality, and because (in this example) it is the only aspect of self-expression that is uninhibited, it will be compulsively or obsessively used to provide relief for all the other restricted emotional material through sublimation. However, any emotion can play this role. What therapy and personal growth are attempting to accomplish is universal freedom of expression of all of the emotions. Thus, we can use the experience of sexual freedom as a template for the potential freedom of expression of all of our emotions. In this way, sexual expression becomes only one of several energetic resources, taking its place in a pantheon of self-expression, and is expressed within a balanced and anxiety-free psychological system.

When treating sexual compulsion that is not anti-social or solely neurological (manic phase bipolar), we are presented with a personality structural problem: sexual expression has evolved into one of the dominant symptoms in the personality symptom profile.

Sexual compulsion or obsession is symptomatically no different from any mental obsession, such as grief, resentment, or romantic infatuation. The sexual content of the symptom simply identifies the area of the body that is being used by the personality structure to discharge the overall emotional tension of the psyche.

Through sublimation, the emotional distress of any blocked feeling is being rerouted through sexual expression, manifesting as an obsession or compulsion when the other feelings are being repressed. Thus, anger is expressed sexually, sadness is expressed sexually, and so forth. To truly understand sexual compulsion, we have to think of the sexual act as a mechanism to relieve anxiety. Pornography "addiction" is commonly reported in dysfunctional couples, isolated individuals, and adolescents. In these cases, pornography is not the problem; it is actually the solution to an overly restrictive personality structure. Sexuality becomes compulsive or obsessive in proportion to the underlying emotional pressure. If sexual release becomes a significant anxiety relief mechanism, and the individual has not developed any other stress relief behaviors (exercise, sports, music, socializing, gardening, or hobbies) then we can expect that the individual will repeatedly return to sexual expression in order to reduce stress level.

Any psychological compulsion could certainly be both biological and psychological. When diagnosing sexual compulsion, first rule out bipolar genetics. A person may not have full-blown mania, but may certainly be in the bipolar spectrum. Be sure to inquire about sleep patterns, spending patterns, eccentric family behavior, gambling, affairs, and relatives on medication. This type of differential diagnosis should be utilized with all addictive behaviors.

EARLY SEXUAL ACTIVATION (ABUSE / TRAUMA)

Most children are curious about sexual differences long before they feel sexual information transmitted by their genitals. When the genitals "wake-up" around three-and-a-half to four years old, boys and girls both begin to notice and become curious about sexual information in the world, sexual identity, and stimulation. This also includes natural curiosity about gender differences. Sexual feelings are present in young children without them having any knowledge of what they are feeling or what their bodies are telling them. As a result of emotional longing without understanding, children mythologize sexual feelings into fantasy play, "dress-up," creating "families," pretending to marry daddy or mommy, and in many cases, "playing doctor" with other children. This is all natural curiosity.

For the child, every part of the body is a wonder that "speaks" of its purpose. Children experiment with all the different feelings of the body, thus gaining an inventory of experience and information about the world and our emotional response to it. Ideally for the child's development, most of these exploratory experiences are pleasantly informative if not outright pleasurable, for pleasure is integrative while pain is dissociative.

Children have little mastery over the intensity of feeling that the human body can produce. What is fundamentally true about all trauma is that it is an experience that overwhelms the nervous system. As a result, what might be pleasurable for an adult can be frightening and produce dissociation in a child. This is particularly true with sexual experience. When children of the same age play doctor, it is usually mysteriously exciting and rarely harmful to the child. Neither child should have the knowledge or experience to neurologically overwhelm the other with their sexual "ability."

However, predatory adults, older children, or children who have been abused have the capacity, and often the intent, to overwhelm the inexperienced child. This is the brutal, rather than the natural, awakening of sexual knowledge and experience. If one could theoretically transfer the sexual mastery of a twenty-five-year-old adult directly into the nervous system of a five-year-old child, that child's awareness would simply leap (dissociate) out of his or her body, attempting to flee the overwhelming neural tsunami.

This is trauma: the overstimulation of the nervous system beyond the regulatory capacity of the child.

As a result of sexual trauma, the child suddenly becomes hyper-aware of overwhelming and mixed sexual feelings. He or she will become preoccupied with the traumatically echoing (obsessive/compulsive) sexual feelings/pressure and will attempt to act-out or express the underlying tension and emotional pressure the trauma has produced. The child is attempting to gain control over very difficult and complex emotions.

Typically, emotional practice is how we all get better at expressing emotions. This is also true about sexual feelings. There is a drive to understand, modify, control, and express those sexual emotional tensions in order to calm what has become a raging nervous system. As a result, many traumatized children practice and practice sexual behavior, often with other children. The extreme danger occurs when this behavior becomes compulsive, not necessarily with cruel intent, but certainly with potentially traumatic results for the other children.

The tragedy of sexually abused children is that somewhere an adult has started this chain reaction.

These victims of early sexual activation typically deal with the experience in one of two ways: hyper-focus acting out or dissociation. The sexually hyper-focused individual presents as a "sexual-compulsive." Although there appears to be a potential predatory aspect to this type of sexual compulsivity, the child is attempting to learn to regulate overwhelming feelings.

*As in all trauma, individuals are seeking expressive remedies to the emo-
tional pressure created by those hostile individuals and events in their lives.*

If the impulsive behavior continues into adolescence, it often presents as self-destructive, compulsive, or predatory. The predatory aspect
is more likely to occur in cases in which the sexually abused child also
suffers from a personality disorder or developmental disability where
impulse control is lacking. Since the unconscious often mirrors the
behaviors we have been systematically exposed to, the abused child
potentially adopts some of the strategies, behaviors, and techniques of
the predator, without actually being psychopathic. Curiously, this is due
to the corruption of the aggressive drives, and sexuality serves as the
weapon. The child mirrors and practices the aggressive intent of the
predator who is simply using sexuality as an expression of aggression.
It is not unusual that the emotional challenge resulting from sexual
abuse is more about the trauma created by the intent of the predator—
fear, anxiety, domination, threat, and deceit—than about the specific
sexual contact.

There is a type of lesser sexual trauma that is a result of passive/
exposure dynamics in the family. I call this the "California Family" in
which nudity is common, and everyone bathes and sleeps together.
Like puppies. Until a child reaches the genital activation stage, around
four years old, this is not a problem. Children perceive sexual differences with moderate curiosity, but simply lack the neural stimulation
to respond to the adult sexual cues. However, after the age of four, the
child begins to react emotionally and physically to the presence of sexually mature adults in the family. When parents expose their children
to nudity and naked intimacy (everyone sleeping together), the child
eventually becomes overwhelmed by the sexual stimulation and begins
acting out his or her stress. A parent who casually and consistently sexually stimulates a child by wearing provocative or revealing attire will
produce a highly anxious or seductive child who might over-bond with
the seductive parent, alter their gender identity role, or act out sexual
frustration with anyone available. This is exposure trauma.

Now to be clear, there are many situations in which children seek
comfort in the parent's bed from fear, anxiety, bad dreams, illness, and
separation anxiety. The parent needs not fear that they are harming
their children by providing this comfort. The sexual anxiety is always
in proportion to the exposure. Many parents in their thirties are still
working out their own sexual dynamics and are unaware that their
child is also responding to those adult sexual cues. It is normal for
children to identify mature sexuality in the adults or older children in
the family. And it is certainly okay for mothers and fathers to express

their romantic attraction to each other in a healthy and open manner. Healthy expression of affection is important to model to children. Our ability to give physical affection to each other is an important aspect of human health. As we discovered in the '50s, children need to be held in order to thrive, and as the great therapist Virginia Satir stated in the '70s, and I paraphrase, "Human beings need four hugs a day for survival, eight hugs a day for maintenance, and twelve hugs a day for growth." Children require illustrations of adult behavior as part of their social inventory. This is normal and natural.

COMPULSIVE SEXUAL EXPRESSION THROUGH EMOTIONAL SUBLIMATION

Emotions that are being systematically expressed are typically not the core problem causing psychological symptoms. Someone with anger problems may in fact have a problem expressing any other emotion, so anger becomes the outlet for all feelings. Emotional sublimation means that the expressed emotion is potentially a symptomatic expression of another, separate, blocked emotion. Any emotion can be a symptom for another emotion. As noted in Chapter Five, "Psychodynamics," *Sublimation*, through sublimation, any of the neural-emotional centers can discharge (less effectively) the emotional tension produced by a repressed or dissociated emotion. The therapeutic challenge is to identify the emotions that are *not* being expressed but that are flooding the emotion that *is* being expressed—in this case, sexuality.

When emotions, such as anger or sadness, are repressed, but sexual expression is not restricted, all emotions potentially lead to sexual release. Sexual compulsion may not actually be the problem. Rather, the compulsion is much more likely the solution to the problem: sexual expression relieves the pressure of the other restricted emotions. This is no different from the people who cry when they are angry or get angry when they are sad. In this case, the sublimation is the expression of restricted emotion through sexual behavior. The compulsive behavior manifests in proportion to how often the blocked emotions are triggered and need to be relieved. Alexander Lowen, in his book on *Narcissism*, called these people "phallic narcissists": those who use sexuality to break out of their emotional inhibition through sexual contact. Sexual compulsivity is simply the repeated transfer of the energy from a blocked emotion through an emotion that is being expressed—in this case, sexuality.

The therapeutic challenge with this client is to not focus on repressing the sexual expression, and thus force the creation of another symptom, although this is often what occurs in therapy. Rather, the aim is for the client to learn to feel and express those non-sexual emotions that are rigidly controlled by the personality structure and being relieved by sexual behavior.

Part of changing or evolving self-destructive behavior is the eventual repression of the behavior that serves as the psychological symptom. But this is not the starting point. When changing the direction of a river, one digs the alternative route first before damming up the river and flooding the community. Once the alternate channel has been established, then the river is ready to be successfully diverted. Otherwise, the dammed-up river simply creates its own alternate route—a new symptom.

Most people have some inhibition in the expression of each of their emotions. Families train their members to avoid certain emotional states (and the information contained therein) and to bias their self-expression to those emotions and symptoms preferred by the family, even when those symptoms become self-destructive or destructive to others. Sexual compulsion is only one of many substitute expressions for blocked emotions.

CONCLUSION

Because sexuality has a certain volatile quality in western culture, it is easy for the clinician to be just as fascinated as the client with the details of sexual obsession/compulsion and miss the underlying psychodynamics. There is a high likelihood that one or more of the client's emotions is severely blocked and fueling the sexual behavior. The diagnosis of "sexual addiction," a symptom-based diagnosis, is convenient, but does not actually describe the psychodynamics that lead to compulsive sexual behavior. Sexual "addiction" can be more accurately described as a syndrome: a combination of developmental, situational, biological, and traumatic elements. The therapy will need to deconstruct the influencing psychological components in order for the client to begin emotional expression in a more direct and effective manner. The overarching problem, however, is that the nervous system often has years of practice of this particular behavior, which will undermine the new behavior. As long as one is reinforcing a neurological pattern, that pattern will have momentum and a gravitational pull. This is, of course, true of any habit, helpful or not.

THE ANATOMY
AND TREATMENT OF GRIEF

GRIEF

Grief is an unavoidable human experience, and there is certainly evidence that the behavior of grief even exists among certain animal species. The expression of grief is culturally embedded; collectively, we recognize the need to grieve and attempt to socially accommodate the varying expressions of this most intimate feeling. The bonds that link humans not only to each other but, in some cases, to special animal and plant partners are so significant that we sometimes do not survive their loss. Viktor Frankl, in his book *Man's Search for Meaning* (a memoir of his experience in the Nazi concentration camps of Auschwitz and Dachau), reports that his fellow prisoners could tolerate monstrous physical and emotional suffering as long as their sense of purpose in association with their family (often imprisoned elsewhere) remained hopeful for reunification. At the moment when that purposeful connection was lost, usually due to the death of family members, it was not uncommon for that prisoner to die soon afterward. The very link to life is associated with significant relationships, and grief is our response to that loss. There are also moving stories of everyday loving couples who die within days or weeks of each other, as if they shared one mind, or one soul, divided between two bodies. We are energetically connected in ways both mundane and mysterious. In spite of our obvious physical isolation from each other, there is a psychological link between us that is often clearly revealed in those more extraordinary human circumstances.

In grief, our quality of life and ability to function becomes impaired for an unpredictable period of time. And perhaps it is this timetable of loss and suffering that is the most complex, uncontrollable, and devastating aspect of grief. If we knew for certain that in four months, ten months, or two years we would feel normal again, we would struggle through the grief period, expecting and receiving relief at the appointed time. But grief is not so convenient. Some people barely suffer loss, and others are devastated by it. It may be the seemingly unending quality of grief that is so punishing. When we are in any heightened emotional state, there is a time-stands-still quality to it, but through experience, we know that all emotion is transitional, and unless one suffers from a medical disorder that drives extended and unbalanced emotional expression, every emotion eventually achieves equilibrium, usually within a short time span. Grief does not act in this predictable manner. There is something about grief that can endure for months and years. Most people report that their initial experience of loss is emotionally brutal and constant, but then the grief transitions into a cycle that is nearly as intense but with less frequency.

STAGES OF GRIEF AND TRANSITION

One significant cultural break-through in the study of grief was Elisabeth Kubler-Ross's landmark book, *On Death and Dying*, in which she outlined five psychological stages in the process of dying: denial, anger, bargaining, depression, and acceptance. The psychological community almost immediately recognized that Dr. Kubler-Ross had outlined the archetypal emotional structure associated with any loss, and these five stages became a widely accepted template for many emotional transitional experiences, including divorce, social, financial, or health traumas, relocation, or loss of intimate relationship. The five stages are at play in every major transition phase in our lives.

Dr. Kubler-Ross's work has been discussed now for over four decades, and although some find her work somewhat simplistic in describing the grief cycle, her work remains significant in that it gives a reasonable outline for a very complex process. The adoption of her ideas, both professionally and culturally, illustrate our need to understand emotional transition, and if nothing else, Dr. Kubler-Ross provides a starting point and framework for understanding this wave of emotion associated with loss, grief, and transition.

Transitions can be terrifying. Thus human beings require ritual to mollify the anxiety associated with the unknown. Our ability, as a culture and as therapists, to provide some structure to this difficult process is usually experienced as merciful. To be able to identify even broad parameters of a seemingly endless ocean provides sailors with some hope of returning to shore intact.

The long-term ongoing unresolved symptoms of grief can be described as the failure to transition from grief to resolution. Resolution does not mean that one no longer grieves, but it does mean that grief has purpose. But what does this mean? How much grief is enough? What does the resolution look like? As a culture, because we treat grief as normal and healthy, there is flexibility in how we support those who have suffered losses. There is something natural about the suffering associated with loss. But even in this ancient emotional expression, we, as the support group, know when someone becomes stuck in this grief stage. For some people, society will encourage the individual to show more grief, and for others, society will encourage him or her to move on with life, rebuilding or giving meaning to what has been lost. The collective wisdom recognizes that unexpressed grief can be psychologically damaging in many ways: loss of health, loss of hope, loss of meaning, loss of spiritual direction, and loss of social contribution. And yet, too much grief can be damaging in exactly the same ways. Intuitively, we recognize that someone should not remain critically stuck, even after catastrophic loss. So again, how much grief is enough? When does grief become worrisome instead of therapeutic?

The emotional bonds of long-term adult relationship can be as strong as those significant childhood relationship bonds that build personality and define reality for the rest of our lives. Through the repetition of interaction and emotional expectation, long-term relationships establish powerful crucial neurological, emotional, and energetic patterns. One might say that these relationships are critical parts of our self-mythology; they determine how we view ourselves, define ourselves, and perceive our place in the world. The energetic and neurological commitment to a particular relationship will often dictate the intensity and quality of the grief we suffer when those relationships are severed. Although it may seem somewhat "cold" to examine grief from a psychological structural point of view, for a clinician to effectively help a client resolve his or her grief, it is important to understand the energetic, neurological, and psychological components that power grief. As in all things psychological, there is a science to self-expression, energy dynamics, mental health, love and loss, spiritual consciousness, and yes, grief.

THE ANATOMY OF GRIEF

Although grief is often treated as an emotion unto itself, it appears that grief is actually a combination of blocked emotions. There are some straightforward emotional investments that we have made with each other, and the more important a person is in our life, the more emotional energy will be invested in that relationship. To be clear, except for the significance of the birth mother, whose importance cannot be overestimated, the level of importance a loved one has in our life is directly associated with the amount of time, energy, and emotional interaction that occurs with that loved one on a regular basis. Loss and grief are in direct proportion to time and emotion invested in the relationship. Our level of loss can be linked directly to the significance of that relationship.

The content of grief is complex and varying. Besides the obvious losses of a loving, intellectual, competitive, or sexual relationship, there can be a sense of lost opportunity: the lost hope for an improved relationship, the lost effort in the creation of the current relationship, certain feelings—both positive and critical—that went unspoken, the sense of abandonment and loneliness, and the even more complex roles of shared-functioning.

SHARED FUNCTIONING

In shared-functioning, a couple (any significant pairing) completes certain personality "blind spots" in each other. We might view these as the psychological skill sets and emotional abilities that each person brings to the relationship that actually complete the functioning of the loved one. One partner may bring the passion, one may bring the patience, one may bring intellect, one may bring financial capabilities, one may bring a sense of adventure, and one may bring good communication skills. Regardless, it is rare to find any person who has completed his or her psychological growth, and thus it is very common that couples seek out completion with each other. In the cases of shared functioning, the loss is not only personal, but also practical. The person who remains faces not only the absence of the loved one but of the functioning role that the loved one played in the relationship. In those relationships where the surviving member doesn't deal with financial matters, can't drive, or is in some other way significantly dependent on the mate, the loss can be especially devastating.

RESOLVING GRIEF

There are several psychodynamic elements that affect the resolution of the symptoms of grief. Psychological habit and loyalty are two of the most significant. The neurological system prioritizes all habits, and the relationships that have years of history are psychologically highly prioritized so that emotions associated with loved ones command great respect both energetically and biologically. The human psyche is a complex blend of the habits of neural pathways, self-expression, expectation, and shared functioning.

There is momentum to our expectations of constancy and it carries us through a spectacularly complex reality with a sense of confidence or dread. We expect the world to repeat itself and we live as though it does. One description would be to say that the world works (or doesn't) because we expect it to, and we perceive those features of reality that reinforce our expectation and deny those features of reality that challenge our expectations. We live with the expectation of constancy and "scan" the environment for confirmation of our beliefs.

The profound Hindu spiritual text, *The Mahabharata*, states that the greatest marvel is, "Every day death strikes, and yet we live as though we are immortal." The sense of security in our lives is founded on habit, and any transition triggers anxiety. Any unfamiliar experience activates the unconscious, calling upon parts of our psyche that have been inhibited or are underdeveloped.

If we were capable of resolving our life issues with just our personality skills, there would be no need for awareness to return to the unconscious for a missing insight or ability. But personality has its limitations, and the parts of the psyche that are capable of dealing with new and challenging situations are often locked in the unconscious.

When a relationship is absent for any reason, memory and fantasy are activated to contain the feelings we are unable to express directly.

When permanent loss occurs, we experience not only the significant immediate change in our emotional interplay with the other, but also a rush from the unconscious of all the painful and joyful memories that we have accumulated through the years.

We don't just grieve this moment: we grieve every moment.

The experience of grief is directly in proportion to the amount of energy associated with the loss, which can be significant. The ultimate goal of therapy is to address the emotional needs arising from the loss of the significant other and then, ultimately, to help the client reinvest that energy in other relationships, activities, or new psychological skills.

Without the reinvestment of that emotional energy, the symptoms of grief will be ongoing. Grief is fueled by the energy assigned to the lost relationship, which now has nowhere to go, so it is being expressed as symptoms.

The energetic challenge of personality is to distribute the energy available to the psyche into activities and relationships on a daily basis. Psychological equilibrium is achieved when the amount of energy available to the psyche is equivalent to the amount of energy being expressed. If more energy is available than is expressed, symptomology is the result: the extra energy becomes symptoms instead of emotional expression. This is the great challenge of grief: the sudden abundance of energy, previously associated with the significant relationship, now has no place to go. But getting the client to transition from grief and loss to reinvestment in others or other activities is complex.

EMOTIONAL REPRESSION SCALE

Even the symptoms of grief have healthier and less healthy aspects. In the cases of significant loss or transition, one should expect significant physical and emotional symptoms to arise quickly. The emotional repression scale is a progressive list of symptoms occurring in order of severity of repression, beginning with the actual emotion and regressing to actual physical illness. The four levels of this scale are emotion, anxiety, depression, and somatization. When we initially resist expressing an emotion, the first sign is the familiar *symptom* profile: anxiety, tension, stress, guilt, shame, fear, worry, and resentment. If the emotion is further repressed, *depression* occurs. If the emotion is even more severely repressed, *somatization* takes place; the physical body breaks down through marked physical dysfunction, including illness and disease. Our concern as therapists should be to transition the client through the lower level manifestation of somatization, through the depressive phase, into the symptomatic phase, and eventually into direct expression of emotions.

There are additional complexities at the emotional stage of grief. Each of our neural-emotional complexes—thought, speech, sadness, anger, and sexuality—will produce its own particular sensation of grief and expression of loss. As awareness attempts to insulate itself from suffering by dissociating from those parts of the body that are grieving the loss of self-expression, we begin to feel fragmented and disconnected from self and others. Grief is probably more accurately described as the loss of parts of our self. It is only through the process of expressing our emotions that we sustain our continuity of self.

Initially, grief does not differentiate between loss of love, loss of sexual intimacy, loss of communication or competition, loss of intel-lectual stimulation, loss of verbal intimacy, or even loss of completion. All these losses combine into a wave of suffering, undifferentiated and immediate. Each neural-emotional complex contributes to a part of our overall suffering, and our successful negotiating of the grief pro-cess requires the eventual satisfaction of all of these emotional needs. Grief is driving us to emotionally reinvest in the world, verbally, intel-lectually, lovingly, courageously, and sexually.

LOYALTY

At this stage of reinvestment, the issues of loyalty influence the amount of time needed for working through loss and grief. There is an aspect of the human bond that is sacred: the uniqueness of the individual, family member, or intimate relationship feels simply irreplaceable. And this is true. The relationship is irreplaceable. The history of the rela-tionship, the shared psychological and biological experiences, are sim-ply not interchangeable with another relationship. It is extremely rare for any person to fill the loss of a partner of twenty years. And there are some losses that are never going to be replaced, ever. In those rela-tionships, the psyche will simply always prioritize a part of its energy to honor the memory of that person. When you've related intimately to a person for decades, or even more tragically, given birth to a child who is lost, the impact is devastating, and the greatest hope for healing is giving purpose to that loss: to find a way to continue to celebrate that person's life and mourn the loss.

However, there are many occasions where grief is sustained by our loyalty to the loved one. When loyalty is a cherished aspect of a signif-icant relationship, that loyalty is carried forward after the relationship has ceased. In those cases, the individual stays in grief until the loyalty issue is resolved and the individual feel permitted to reinvest in another relationship. Consider this: almost all relationships are built upon the same qualities of the relationship we have with our mothers. Developmentally, the mother serves as the most significant relationship in the first five years of our life, and as such, our loyalty to her is our template for our emotional availability to anyone. Thus, the transition between significant relationships is always influenced by our sense of loyalty. Previous relationships constantly compete with current relationships.

Our sense of emotional safety and vulnerability is strongly affected by the mother template. Our sense of intimacy, and the portability of that emotional capacity, is directly linked to the pattern of emotional closeness and reliability, or lack there-of, learned from mother.

As a consequence, much of the challenge of transferring psychological intimacy from one significant relationship to another requires us to wrestle with the rules established in that foundational relationship with mother. We are not only working through the transition phase of loss of intimacy, comfort, and caring with the lost relationship; we are renegotiating our contract with our mother.

Why can't we just walk away from bad relationships? Pattern loyalty. We feel the connection to our history and it interferes with our flexibility in the moment. Even when we know we need to "walk away," we are torn by the needs of, and loyalty to, our emotional history. This is why almost every therapist wants to talk about your mother!

Anyone who has been involved with a partner who is still tied to his or her mother knows the difficulty of creating a loyal, intimate relationship that is free of the influence of the mother. And there are many mothers who simply challenge the notion of independence from mother. After all, who loves you more than your mother? Well, maybe lots of people. Loyalty to mother affects every relationship, regardless of whether that original maternal relationship was healthy, loving, dangerous, or engulfing.

Becoming conscious of the rules of relationship established by one's family permits relationship transition with less suffering and delay. Ultimately, a healthy psyche obeys its own internal rules and strives to fulfill its creative and expressive destiny. And to do this, we must abandon the great need for approval, no matter from whom. Thus, loyalty to the historical relationship directly affects the transition through grief.

THE MYTH OF THE LOVED ONE

Part of the grieving process involves the mythologizing of the lost person. Even in cases where the person was particularly difficult to deal with, upon their loss, the psyche has a tendency to re-assemble parts of the relationship to represent the whole of the relationship. In the film *Cannery Row*, Debra Winger tells Nick Nolte, "I really like you a lot when you're not around." This is the mythologizing of the person, the selective perception of those significant relationships in order to sustain a positive psychological fantasy.

When my mother died six years ago, the family sat in her hospice room with her body, and within literally minutes of her passing, we were telling stories about our experiences with her. We were creating the *Myth of Mom*. This mythmaking was primarily directed by loyal stories that raised up her accomplishments and avoided those experiences that were associated with frustration, disappointment, and conflict. There was little place for analysis, anger, or disappointment. That would come later.

The complete inventory of any relationship only occurs if we are capable of accessing all of our experiences with a person, through all of our emotions: thought, speech, sadness, aggression, and sexuality. Each emotion contributes a piece of the overall information describing the relationship. When awareness avoids those neurological centers that contain emotional suffering, our view of reality becomes incomplete, and in some ways, distorted. We are unable to perceive and relate to the whole person or the whole situation. We fragment our perceptual data and emotional response, and although the information and emotional response are available, awareness simply avoids the physical sites where those painful experiences are registered. The resolution of grief simply requires us to acknowledge and account for the whole person and not just some fragmented bias.

THE COMPLEXITY OF GRIEF

Grief represents two specific and complicated dynamics: emotional commitment and neurological patterns. Our neurophysiology has the ability to abbreviate recognition patterns in order to provide awareness with a sense of continuity in the world. Neurological patterning reduces the time needed to perform remembered experiences and associated history. As a result, we recreate our world, and our relationships with it, on a moment-to-moment basis with near seamlessness.

The familiarity of the world and our place in it depends upon this ever-present capacity for the instantaneous reproduction of reality. In fact, awareness depends on this continuity, without which we would remain in a highly alert and anxious state. In order to produce this familiar universe, the body neurologically prioritizes, over time, the recognition and response to those activities and people with whom we are in regular relationship. Any event that disrupts this familiar pattern triggers our symptom profile.

Close personal relationships are particularly shaped in this manner. When emotional energy becomes committed to the people in our lives, the nervous system simply develops a pattern of responding that creates a recognition/memory shortcut. This patterning produces the emotional charge we associate with familiar people, places, and events.

When we recognize someone, we feel a cascade of emotions and memories associated with that person, which produces a feeling (positive or negative) of connection and history. Thus, we don't have to build relationships over and over from the start each time we meet. We experience the history and feelings associated with each person in the moment we are with or remember the person. An emotionally significant person does not need to be present for us to feel his or her effect on our lives. Our emotional memory and nervous system supply the relationship. This is the psychodynamic of association, and it rules our experience of reality.

A relationship is essentially a combination of time and emotion invested in a person or place. If forty percent of our time and emotion is dedicated to caring for or loving someone, this represents a huge investment, energetically and neurologically. Our entire psychic system has prioritized massive amounts of energy to sustaining this particular relationship. As a result, in grief, the healing period often occurs in direct proportion to the amount of time, emotion, and energy that has been invested in that person.

Grief follows the same psychological truth as all feelings: The more often any feeling is experienced but remains unexpressed, the stronger the symptoms and the more powerful the cumulative effect. This means that any grief experiences that have occurred throughout our lives and have not been completely expressed contribute to the total amount of grief we are experiencing in this current grief cycle.

Here are the factors that determine how long the healing process will take.

1. The reinvestment factor: Healing requires the reinvestment of the energy, emotion, and time previously dedicated to the lost relationship(s). This means that without reinvestment of the energy and emotion, the grief could potentially last forever. As long as the energy is bound to the past relationship, it will generate symptoms until reinvested. Other options might include rededicating this energy and emotion to other activities, causes, service, or spiritual practice.

2. The intensity factor: The intensity of the grief will be in proportion to the importance, time spent with, and energy invested in that relationship, combined with any grief/losses we have experienced throughout our life. All activities and relationships that require significant psychological investment can produce grief symptoms when the relationship is lost. This applies to pets, work, people, and any significant, ongoing, psychological commitment. A mother is particularly vulnerable to grief when children leave home because her role in the family has changed. The energy previously dedicated to caring for the family has no place to go and can result in grief symptoms (of course this can be true of fathers, as well). What makes grief different from the much more common transition-phase symptoms of anxiety or stress is that there is considerably more energy, emotion, and personal investment in the person, place, or relationship that give rise to grief.

3. The loyalty factor: The amount of loyalty that one associates with the lost relationship will contribute to the length of time needed to resolve the grief. Often, feeling disloyal to a lost loved one prevents us from developing the relationships with others that would help resolve the grief. It might feel disrespectful or disloyal to turn our attention to a new person. Our commitment to the memory of the loved one trumps the relief we would feel in reinvesting the energy. In significant relationships, there is always some grief, regardless of the reinvestment in another. It is impossible to recreate, in a short period of time, the effort, energy, and emotion of a thirty-year relationship. Inevitably, the person grieving will have memories and emotions arise periodically in response to people, places, and significant annual events. Grief is an ongoing working through (expressing emotion) and reinvestment process, and our level of loyalty to the missing person makes a significant difference.

4. The guilt factor: After a prolonged illness or suffering by the loved one that has created significant stress on the caretakers and family members, there is often anger or even relief at the passing of the loved one. The survivors are left with the task of repairing their lives. The burden of the loss weighs heavily and affects almost every task. The psyche has to fight to create a psychological space that is not inundated with memories and emotional chaos. Financial strains, emotionally wounded family members (especially children), and a host of daily obstacles require our attention and call for a return to normalcy. Yet, there is no normalcy. These challenges often trigger frustration, anger, and resentment.

Anger is common in these situations. It is part of the psyche's attempt to push back against the ongoing stress, feelings of abandonment, or loneliness that arise day after day following a loved one's death. Accepting and appropriately expressing one's anger can become a formidable task, and therapy is often the place where permission is given to express emotions that seem unfair or inappropriate. In the way that the dying person struggled with the stages of death and dying, the survivors must struggle with the same stages in response to the catastrophic changes in their lives: denial, anger, bargaining, depression, and finally, acceptance. Anger is an essential part of the transformation and reparative process.

The second part of the guilt factor is relief. The emotional feeling of relief when the separation or dying process is complete can produce a variety of conflicted emotions. The simple removal of the daily pressures of caring for and witnessing the disintegrating health of a loved one produces relief, if for not any other reason, as a result of the significant reduction of stress related to those demands. The people who remain after the loved one has departed will often show signs of PTSD: interrupted sleep, painful dreams, and cyclical anxiety, to name a few. Letting go of the stress of the daily requirements of care naturally produces grief, but rarely without guilt. Whether by therapist, clergy, or friends, this relief needs to be affirmed as normal and needed.

5. *The replacement factor:* When a child loses a pet, it often helps, after appropriate respect is paid to the emotional history with the original pet, to replace the pet with a new one. This allows the child/family to reinvest the energy dedicated to the previous pet in the new one. Grief is always in proportion to the blocked emotional expression, so once a new emotional investment is made, the symptom of grief is reduced. But what we learn with pets is not so easily applied to human relationships. With human relationships, establishing a new relationship that has the energetic potential of someone who has been near and dear to us for years, if not decades, is extraordinarily difficult. We simply lack sufficient history with a new person to produce the energetic response required to reassign the energy available. Thus, some grief can be very difficult to overcome without a dedication to love again, a commitment to the process, or a relationship with an emotionally compatible person.

6. *The unfinished business factor:* Rarely are personal relationships free of emotional conflicts, failed expectations, unexpressed emotions, disappointments, and unrealized hopes. As a result, when a person is lost, these unfinished aspects remain both energized and blocked. "What I needed to say," or "What I needed to get from him or her" or "What I needed to give him or her" are only a few of the dilemmas that pervade grief work. Being able to share these struggles with others verbally, journal one's feelings, giving or asking for forgiveness in one's heart, or engaging in prayer or meditation can be of great help. A cognitive behavioral approach to examining and cataloguing creative solutions to unfinished business can also be very useful. The client's ability to access the resources of his or her unconscious is doubly important in grief. So much emotional energy is stored in the unconscious when a significant relationship is lost that any opportunity to help the client build a bridge to the unconscious can be of profound service. Helpful suggestions are needed only when the client lacks imagination or is simply unfamiliar with common expressive tools. Activities such as journaling, dream work, letter writing, engaging in active imagination, building a shrine, helping improve the lives of others, creating a memorial gift, sharing grief with others, and sifting through photographs and home movies can be offered as possibilities.

7. *The biological factor:* Since emotional expression is regulated by the nervous system, biochemical problems such as depression or anxiety often become aggressively activated at times of great loss.

Neurological disorders mimic emotional expression and, in fact, can look and feel identical to emotional grief. But these biological conditions are not grief. They are the dysfunctional nervous system producing emotion-like symptoms.

When grief is triggered by emotional loss, the intensity of the symptoms varies, hour-to-hour, day-to-day, and week-to-week. Emotional symptoms are cyclical and are triggered when one has experiences that remind one of the missing relationship. So, places, people, events, and anniversary dates (birthdays, holidays, etc.) re-trigger the feelings of grief. In time, the intensity of these memories usually changes, but can still produce strong grief occasionally.

With biological/neurological problems, the symptoms are often severe, constant, unrelenting, and can trigger a hopelessness that interferes with mood, sleeping, eating, hygiene, and increases emotional agitation. This is a medical condition that needs to be treated by a medical specialist. An untreated biological depression can create the illusion that one is working through the emotions of the lost relationship, when in fact one is simply suffering from physical depression. It is important to know the difference.

8. *The medical factor:* The medical profession can sometimes diagnose emotional problems as physical problems and then attempt to treat them with medication. Medication is often given to grieving individuals in order to control crying, anxiety, sleep interruption, and other symptoms. In cases of catastrophic loss, the health of the body can be severely compromised, especially in the beginning of the grief process where the person is still strongly reacting to the tragedy. One of the greatest concerns of the clinician is when the client's sleep cycle is repeatedly interrupted. Sleep is critical for concentration, judgment, energetic rejuvenation, emotional balance, and the capacity to think clearly. When the client is not sleeping, a crisis is imminent and medical intervention is required immediately.

If the grieving individual does not have an affective disorder or other medical challenge, medication will do little to resolve the emotional conflicts associated with grief. However, a physical depression/anxiety disorder, left untreated, can lead to self-destructive behavior and hopelessness. It is important to know the difference.

CONCLUSION

Grief work must be approached with great respect and patience. The complexity of emotion due to the mixing of the current loss with a history of love and disappointment creates a psychological landscape that is at one moment joyous, and at another, crushingly depressive. But the rules of psychodynamics still apply: without full expression of all of our emotions, there will be an overload evident in the emotions that are being expressed. When the energy and work of our five major emotions (thought, speech, anger, sadness, and sexuality) is expressively collapsed into one or two emotions, the expression of those emotions will be out of balance. Mental obsession, verbal muteness, sexual compulsion, the obsessive/compulsive features of grief, or deep-seated resentment: each of these represents the overloading of one emotional expression and the constricting of our worldview. Until we increase our awareness and the expression of our full emotional spectrum and bring thinking, speaking, crying, anger, and pleasure to the process of grief, there is a high probability that we will remain locked in the single emotion that we are expressing, and we will continue to repress, sublimate, or symptomize the unexpressed emotions.

The most direct method of developing psychological balance and significantly reducing symptomology is by the expression of all of our emotions. This means feeling pleasurable feelings, feeling anger, feeling sadness, accepting one's thoughts, and speaking up for ourselves. At first, this sounds incredibly simple. And the unconscious is continually pressuring personality to do just this. But once again, fear binds us to our current suffering.

We would rather endure the inconvenient but familiar suffering of this moment than remember, name, and defeat the ferocious demons of our past.

Emotion seeks the truth of its own history, and without that truth, awareness believes that all of the emotion triggered in this moment is a result of this moment. This is only partially true. The emotion is certainly being triggered in this moment, but it is often out of proportion to this moment. Our unexpressed childhood experiences of painful regret and disappointment contribute to the intensity of the current moment. These are the emotions that rise up in grief and become so tenacious and difficult to resolve.

CHAPTER FIFTEEN
LOVE'S SHADOW

"MIRROR, MIRROR, ON THE WALL..."

Depending on how enthusiastically one falls in love, the experience can vary between mild infatuation to full blown *folie a deux* (shared madness.)

Illumination produces shadows and love is no exception.

The rush of love will transform even the most socially conservative people into the obsessive and blithering revelers of Dionysus. But eventually, sobriety returns, and we are face to face with the real world and real relationship challenges. In spite of the return of brutal clarity, we know from whence we have come, and the memory of love and infatuation now serves as a bitter reminder of what has been "lost" and what is desired. We want that feeling back.

The problem is how to sustain the joy. Literature is filled with stories, sacred and profane, that illustrate this human challenge. Religious ecstasy follows the same arc as love when soaring to the heights only to suffer the fall. The entire theological canon of the world's religions is dedicated to this problem. And yet we suffer.

In the simplest of terms, to find fulfillment in another, even temporarily, requires that some potential become activated in the lovers' psyches, something mutual. It's as though some sort of completion has taken place, and the only way that we can describe this completion is through the language of feeling. "I feel whole." "I feel as if I am one with this person." "When we are separated, I do not feel complete." Psychodynamically, this may actually be a true statement, in that each of the partners offers some unique expressive aspect to the relationship unavailable to the other before this encounter. Thus, each person suddenly experiences the expressive relief of his or her partner's emotional abilities.

What if the potentials of our deeper psyche are activated and expressed only when we are with a special person, and otherwise these psychological components are mute and the energy is not immediately available? These potentials, these complexes, these sub-personalities all reside in the part of the psyche that the Jungians refer to as the Shadow. And when these aspects of the Shadow are activated, they bring both the joy of release and memories of the past. Jungian structural theory proposes two levels of the unconscious: the personal unconscious and the collective unconscious. For the subject of love, we are concerned with the personal unconscious, which is predominantly populated with repressed psychological material: those parts of our natural being that have been punished and suppressed, those memories that are associated with disappointment, those components of the psyche that complete our design and birth the deeper potentials of the collective unconscious.

The unconscious, personal and collective, contains our complete psychological inventory, ready and waiting for activation. Children begin life by expressing absolutely everything that arises within them. The family, though, systematically teaches the child to restrict the expression of certain parts of the child's psyche that are in conflict with the family values. As we grow up and become cognizant of the dictates of the world around us, we further repress our authentic responses to avoid social ostracism. The result is an ongoing inner struggle between expression and repression. If we are at war with parts of our own psychological potential, then our self-image is wounded. Self-image is distorted because part of it is repressed, not missing, which means that the solution is within grasp. Self-image is repaired by awareness accessing the unconscious and expressing those parts of the unconscious that have been repressed. The task is to give awareness access to the complete Self, unregulated by the rules of family and society. The psyche then begins to operate as an energetic "economy" powered by clarity of perception and immediacy of expression, versus the depressive "economy" of the quest for approval. First, the psyche must be activated, and then the shadow work begins in earnest. The activation of a psychic component is what produces either the joy or the suffering, depending on how the personality structure permits perception and expression in the moment: expression equals energy, repression equals symptoms.

Self-expression determines our available psychological energy. When we restrict self-expression, we feel the energetic consequences. The more we restrict ourselves, the less energy is available. Depression and anxiety are the two most common symptoms reported in clients seeking therapy. These appear along with tension, stress, guilt, shame, fear, resentment, obsession, and grief, to make up the complete list of the symptoms associated with emotional repression. The personality structure/ego has diverted emotional expression into symptomatic expression, and the energy is no longer available. Much of our comfort-seeking behavior—compulsive eating, drug use, sex, shopping, and television, for instance—are attempts to increase energy and soothe the chronic presence of psychological symptoms. However, the underlying problem is never addressed. Attempting to treat our suffering with these compulsive efforts is like trying to fill a bucket with a hole in the bottom.

So, let's examine one of the most common high-energy experiences of the human mythology: falling in love. If falling in love is so transformative, why does the intensity inevitably fall away, leaving us to return to our common complaints of feeling unloved or unappreciated?

FALLING IN LOVE AND SURVIVING THE SUDDEN STOP

I always remind myself that the couple that comes for therapy, ready to kill each other, were at one time madly in love with each other. Conflicts of all sorts, from fighting, arguing, and control battles to money, sex, and intimacy issues abound. It is safe to assume that when these two individuals discovered each other, they found each other fascinating, and in fact felt better together than apart. Unique qualities were appreciated, physical chemistry flowered, and the anticipation of seeing the loved one made the day last forever. What is usually reported by couples in that state of love is that uninhibited communication goes on for hours: witty banter, shared stories, common interests, family histories, and a generally unrestricted interaction of love and joy. This level of intense attraction can last from a few hours to a few weeks, and in those fortunate few, a few months, but it eventually cools down to a more familiar level of intensity.

Psychiatrist and author M. Scott Peck once commented, "Falling in love is like falling in a hole." This is widely appreciated as a humorous interpretation of love. But as British humorist Douglas Adams is sometimes quoted, "It's not the fall that kills you; it's the sudden stop!" So why do the feelings stop? We find that no matter how much we love someone, the intensity and idealization will eventually level out and the significant other will inevitably reveal irritating qualities, stubborn attitudes, and manipulative tendencies. It is as though the love has worn thin and we are left with someone we frankly don't like some of the time. Was our loved one always this way? Did we miss something? Or worse, was it something we did?

Peck, in his now-famous book, *The Road Less Traveled*, suggests that love is a trick of nature designed to keep us interested in each other long enough to conceive children, thus promoting the survival of the species. If this is true, then what takes the place of all that energy that we call love after we lose the positive infatuation with the other? In most relationships, what replaces infatuation is months and years of trying to change our partner to better serve our needs or obey our family of origin's rules. The energy of love becomes the energy of power struggle. But why? We've had a taste of joy, love, appreciation, affection, and acceptance. Why would we choose an ongoing power struggle over intimacy? And we know that this happens. We know that love will give way to struggle.

The initial infatuation state produces little inhibition from either partner. The openness and responsiveness directly put each partner into a positive relationship with his or her own unconscious. Although we tend to give the other person the credit for triggering or creating this magnificent experience, the fact is that the individuals themselves, being spontaneous and *not* withholding, produce the energetic fantasy. Theoretically, this energy is possible to experience with anyone, and although it is difficult for us to imagine having this special response with just anyone, it is not difficult for us to conceive of the possibility that almost everyone has experienced a version of this phenomenon with someone. At minimum, we have all held those secret, taboo crushes that thrill us even if never revealed. In this last case, the fantasy is the illustration of the unexpressed energy available for intimacy, but constrained by the lack of opportunity or fear of the consequences. Obviously, the fantasy is rarely as powerful as the real relationship.

What collapses the energetic intensity of love is the activation of memories associated with past relationship difficulties, including the fundamental relationships with the family of origin.

Each memory of loss, betrayal, frustration, control, abuse, or strong conflict is emotionally charged in order to remind and warn us of the dangers of intimacy. These emotional memories serve as guardians, protecting us from another possible painful experience. Although much of the negative effect that is eventually triggered during the early stages of a relationship is associated with the past, the psyche treats each of the emotional memories as though it is occurring in this very moment. Even though it is true that the current situation is triggering or activating these emotions, the emotional reaction is often out of proportion to this moment, contaminating the current experience with unresolved and unexpressed fears from the past.

These fears, our childhood's painful emotional experiences combined with our damaged adult relationships, are literally activated by the energy of becoming intimate and vulnerable to someone. This means that the very act of falling in love will eventually remind us of and wake up all of the feelings associated with the previous relationships that wounded us. The result is that we become wary, cautious, critical, distant, sexually cool, depressed, or anxious and, in general, suspicious of our loved one.

When emotional experiences become too painful, awareness abandons the site where the memories are stored. Awareness simply adopts strategies for ignoring our painful emotional experiences instead of expressing them. Thus, these memories and feelings are relegated to the unconscious. Masterson takes this idea one step further and argues that memory and emotion split during trauma and awareness only holds on to one or the other of these components. So as adults, we either have the memories of our experiences but lack the emotions or we have the emotions but no memories of the events. It's not that the memories or emotions are missing from the psyche; it's that they are not joined to each other. It's like we're sitting in front of a movie and we either have picture or sound, but not both.

Except in cases of universal trauma—war, adoption, significant early childhood separation, catastrophic illness, or PTSD—where the entire nervous system has been wounded, emotions and memories are organ/site specific. As discussed earlier, sexual feelings arise from the reproductive system. Anger is located in the digestive system. Sadness is located in the respiratory system. Obsession is located in the brain. In a sense, the body knows what it has been through. Through repeated exposure to offensive experiences, our responses become more and more compromised and awareness begins to retreat further and further from the parts of the body that are reporting the trauma. If we repress our anger consistently over time, eventually awareness does not want to know what the digestive system is experiencing or storing. Awareness avoids, through dissociation, experiencing of all of the pent-up resentment located at that site. If our experiences become significantly painful, awareness will completely abandon those physical organs, and we begin to see a disease process emerging as a reaction to the emotions stored there.

What we don't know, we feel; what we don't feel, we experience as symptoms. Unexpressed symptoms become depression, and unexpressed depression becomes physical illness.

WAKING SLEEPING BEAUTY

Repressed emotions and memories remain "asleep" (dissociated) until external conditions reawaken that physical/psychological function, and suddenly, the specific memories, emotions, or symptoms are jolted awake. For example, memories and emotions associated with sexual abuse suffered as a child might remain "asleep" or symptomatic, until the child is grown and is involved with an adult sexual relationship, at which point the memories/emotions/symptoms are abruptly triggered. Until there is enough external energy to trigger the emotions and memories back to consciousness, they simply lack sufficient stimuli and thus remain dormant. Since these newly activated memories contain so many uncomfortable, and sometimes painful, experiences, many people simply adopt lives of isolation to prevent the possibility of being triggered.

People will separate, avoid dating, or move away from places and people who repeatedly trigger painful memories to reduce the cycle of these emotions. In working with great loss and grief, the therapist must consider the psychological value of eliminating an emotional trigger. Working through the emotions has great psychological value, but there is certainly a case to be made that the geographic/relocation cure helps many people interrupt very painful emotional cycles associated with specific people and places. Sometimes you really just need to leave the problem behind or at least leave the trigger. Many sufferers of PTSD chose the path of isolation and insulation to reduce the triggering of anxiety.

However, if psychotherapy is to be successful, these dormant memories and emotions must be located, awakened, expressed, and not avoided, if possible. The client is required to become aware of the significant events and relationships that formed his personality and shape his perceptions of the world. When one is raised by a competitive mother or a passive father, it has psychological consequences. A number of fairy tales point out this dynamic directly. Snow White is a powerful example. The daughter of the king is ruthlessly assaulted by a stepmother who obsessively competes with her and is jealous of the young girl's beauty. The Queen eventually succeeds in poisoning the young girl into unconsciousness until circumstances intervene and awaken her. What the fairy tale does not illustrate is the effect of this dangerous mother figure upon this girl after she wakes up. For Snow White, her father, the King, is completely absent or passive, allowing the ruthless stepmother to compulsively compete with the daughter. The stepmother's hostilities eventually force the girl to run away and take up residence with a bunch of odd men. The stepmother then tracks the girl down and attempts three times to kill her, with the last attempt leaving the girl unconscious. These are the memories to which Snow White must awaken. These are the memories of Snow White's childhood and family dynamics.

PSYCHOLOGICAL COMPLEXES

Analysts call these collections of forgotten memories a complex and usually assign a name to them, signifying the source of the pain. Thus, a mother complex denotes memories associated with mother. Snow White portrays a ruthless mother complex and a passive father complex. It is the hostile, manipulative, and competitive mother who requires the daughter to abandon aspects of her self-expression in order to stay safe. Individuals who struggle with these complexes are typically raised by mothers who act like older sisters, often because they also were raised by older siblings rather than parents, so their reference for parenting is a sibling model. Snow White also illustrates a passive father complex in that the father gives no confidence to his daughter that men can be, well, manly, to protect and nurture. The dwarf-men that Snow White lives with illustrate her perception of men as developmentally stunted or unfinished. Mythically, the dwarf walks between the world of the unconscious and consciousness. In *The Wizard of Oz*, a mythical variation of *Snow White*, Dorothy finds herself in the exact same predicament as Snow White: pursued by a witch, surrounded by dwarves, and abandoned by a passive father figure, the wizard.

A problematic father complex is illustrated in *Beauty and the Beast*. In the story, Beauty's mother has died, and her father, upon returning from a trip to town, has offended the neighboring Beast and must pay compensation for the offense by becoming the Beast's servant. Beauty offers to take the father's place, and the father agrees. The father, in his weakness and cowardice, sacrifices his daughter to the Beast. Beauty must wake up to the consequences of the death of her mother, her dependency on her father, his willingness to let her pay his debt, and her conviction that the Beast can be saved. Beauty's biggest blind spot is caused by projecting her own beastliness (shadow) onto the men around her and then compulsively being attracted to those same men. Until she loves and transforms her own distorted self-perception, she will find herself in disappointing relationships. The psychological pressure to always seek approval, be charming, or be compulsively nice requires repression of those protective aggressive components of the psyche. The more we restrict these natural guardians, the more ferocious and threatening they become, appearing in dreams as threatening characters or manifesting as nagging dysphoric moods. It is learning to love those forbidden aspects of self-expression and the acceptance of those repressed components that frees us from their distorted influence and allows them to transform us.

Psychological complexes are named in order to define the relationship that is the source of the repressed feelings. Long-term relationships with mother or father, or in some cases with siblings, create relationship expectations that will be followed in every situation outside of the family, regardless of whether these rules of relating actually work. Due to the impact of these significant developmental relationships, complexes become scripts that prescribe how to relate to others and what to expect in specific types of relationships. Complexes produce predictable styles of relationships and relationship expectations. The experiences that form specific complexes teach us what to expect from future relationships, collapsing our actual potential into mere hopes of intimacy and fears of rejection.

Those early and significant relationships of childhood serve as a template for all of our expectations, against which all future relationships are measured.

When we are adults, if a loved one hurts our feelings, we have the option to change how we relate or simply leave the relationship. But as children, we are dependent on our parents and can't leave the relationship. We need them to be strong, protective, nurturing, and safe. In order to maintain that image of our parents, we repress the truth about their poor behavior, and our primary way of doing this is to blame ourselves for the failures of our parents. "Oh," we say, "I must be a bad child, and that's why mommy and daddy are angry (or depressed, crazy, or drunk)." Unfortunately, it is often the people we love and depend on most who hurt us most, and after a number of years of inconsistent love or harsh treatment, we develop a pool of resentment, restricted self-expression, poor self-image, guilt, and anxiety, all arising out of the pain of our childhood experiences.

To be fair, we also receive great blessings from our parents. Although they vary from child to child, gifts like intellect, love, loyalty, creativity, intuition, curiosity, manners, faith, as well as passion for and skills involved in work, music, art, sports, nature, and hobbies may be among the positives of our family. But the nurturing gifts that we receive from our parents are what make the losses and wounds all the more obvious. Our parents' psychological blind spots become our psychological blind spots. Those who raise us can't teach us to see something they are unable to see. In order to achieve our potential in affectionate and intimate adult relationships, we need to discover and heal the impaired emotions created in childhood and activated in our adult relationships.

PARENTING CHALLENGES

Parents often create psychological problems in their children with the best of intentions, and even with deep love for the child. What the child needs psychologically, and how the parents believe they have to act in order to be good parents, are often in direct opposition to each other. Parents will actively restrict any expression in their children that fails to meet cultural, religious, or social approval.

The child's psyche is regularly sacrificed on the altar of social approval.

The biggest parenting problem that can be avoided starts with the use of physical discipline. Although current statistics indicate that up to ninety percent of Americans have experienced physical discipline during childhood, few of my clients would ever say that they were physically abused. They acknowledge that as children, they were spanked, slapped, or hit with a belt, but typically they deny any negative effects. In fact, there are many, many people who claim that they would not be the healthy, disciplined people that they are today without that physical discipline from their parents. The fact that we have learned to make the best of the discipline we received as children does not mean that all discipline was positive. The child figures out how to avoid physical discipline by "correcting" the behavior that triggers the punitive response in the parent. We simply compromise our self-expression to avoid punishment. At one level, this seems obvious. Don't we all try to avoid punishment? Of course. In those families where punishment was used regularly, the child is constantly compromising self-expression in an attempt to negotiate the family rules safely. And there are those families in which nothing the child does is effective in avoiding punishment. In those families, it's as though the parents are at war with the children. These are the families that can produce sociopathic tendencies.

But there are reasons for inconsistent and punitive parenting. People do not treat others better than they treat themselves. Parents offer their children the same level of love and respect they offer themselves, which is often highly critical. Additionally, the person who raised you is your model for future parenting. So, the obvious applies here as well, in that loving parents produce loving parents and punitive parents produce punitive parents. But there is one family dynamic that always creates serious problems in future parenting skills: children raised predominantly by their siblings. Although there may be adults in the home, younger children are often principally cared for by older siblings. And sibling rules apply. The broad use of intimidation, threat, physical consequences, and intellectual, emotional, or physical competition is common. As older siblings go out of their way to exercise a hierarchy of power and order in the family, smaller or younger children who are exposed to this type of domination for years at a time, without any significant protection by the parents, can develop a variety of self-expressive problems and often become seriously problematic parents. This sibling domination often produces the next generation of parents who operate using these sibling rules with their own children.

And finally, drugs and alcohol directly interfere with positive parenting. Much has been written about this, so I will simply say that drugs and alcohol undermine a parent's judgment, increase emotional volatility, increase the possibility for physical conflict, and produce disturbing and sometimes horrifying emotional experiences for the children. There is a distinct possibility that the offender will not remember destructive behavior due to blackouts. As a result of these parenting challenges, the child's inventory of emotional experiences contains a fair amount of disappointment, loss, longing, fear, anxiety, and curiously, hope. The hope of fulfillment in the future.

LOVE'S LIMITS

The simplest way to keep from feeling emotional pain is to reduce the amount of energy in our lives to the point where those emotions are not activated. We begin to numb our feelings by numbing our bodies with compulsive behaviors. The consequence of these choices is depression. This is why depression is the number one symptom that individuals describe when they start therapy. We are unconsciously choosing to be depressed rather than fully experience the sadness and emotional penalties of our childhood.

We all long for love, and when the miraculous opportunity arrives, we are gravitationally pulled into its caress, completely oblivious to the emotional sufferings that will be awakened by our lover's kiss.

When we fall in love, we experience reality without filters, almost as if ego has let go of its protective grip and we are suddenly, spontaneously, living in the moment without holding back. We are fully emotionally exposed and expressed. The hope of fulfillment and completion is nearly irresistible. There is a marvelous scene in the movie *A Bug's Life* in which two moths are hovering outside of the bright purple light of a bug zapper. One moth is saying in a drunken tone, "It's so pretty!" and the other is repeating in a panic, "Don't go into the light! Don't go into the light!" Whereupon there is a bright flash and a loud zap, as the one moth can't resist the glow. First the infatuation, later the "zap" (memory).

The great pull of love is the hope for completion and fulfillment. The memories of danger come later. The brilliance of love and the energetic surge that comes with liberated self-expression commit us to a relationship that will eventually bring all of our fears to the surface as well. There is no love without emotional history being activated. Remember, energy activates memory, and the new abundance of energy activated by romantic love eventually reactivates those parts of the body containing emotional memories that have been asleep in the unconscious. As those emotions/memories awaken, personality, whose job is to protect us from our painful past, begins shutting down this newfound open expression of emotion, and suddenly, we find we are experiencing symptoms instead of love and affection. Anxiety, tension, stress, guilt, shame, fear, and resentment take the place of joy, love, and infatuation.

One of the curious features of emotional memory is that awareness perceives all emotion as occurring in the present. Even though the loved one is attractive beyond all reasonable expectation, or the amount of rage bubbling to the surface is well out of proportion to the moment, awareness is fully convinced that these emotions are in fact the result of this moment, this person, or these circumstances. Even though a later assessment of these current experiences is often sobering, we will nonetheless be swept up in the next emotional wave with the same level of conviction, in spite of what we have learned from the last infatuation or resentment.

The emotion (infatuation or resentment) may be being triggered in the moment, but a large portion of our emotional reaction to what is occurring in the present is often made up of leftover emotions from past experiences in which the emotions were repressed. All those memories of being hurt, neglected, or abandoned by our past loved ones suddenly begin influencing our perception of our current loved one. And of course, since our loved one is not perfect, there are usually ample opportunities to find fault with the object of our affection. Our partner arrives late or carries a bit too much weight, doesn't listen well, ignores our complaints, refuses to change for us, wants more or less sex. Regardless, the energy of falling in love has now reminded us of our vulnerability, based on past experience and charged up on past painful emotion. So, in order to protect ourselves, we begin to create distance, either by generating animosity, withdrawing, or behaving as though we are helpless. These actions of sabotage have one goal: to create emotional distance in the relationship and thereby reduce the energy that is activating the painful memories. The phrase "Distance makes the heart grow fonder" can certainly be applied here. Within the "walls" of one's "personal space" resides a history of emotions and memories. When that invisible barrier is breached, those historical emotions use the romantic attraction to find release. The affection gives way to anxiety and the infatuation cannot be regained until the boundaries of one's personal space are reestablished. It is as though we all desire and can experience short bursts of intense affection, love, and adoration, but after a time period that is different for each person, the old feelings of longing, depression, or frustration gain strength, and we begin to contaminate the moment.

It's as though we kill the passion in order to survive the relationship.

Sometimes it is literally the physical closeness of the person that sets off the emotional trigger. Every person has his or her own "personal space" requirements: that magical distance that provides some form of intimacy with minimal threat. In the early 1970s, when I was beginning my training, the church fellowship group in which I was a youth leader did some group exercises. We gave everyone masking tape and asked them to create a circle or box around themselves, defining the amount of space required for them to feel comfortable. The differences were stunning. Some needed only a few inches around their feet to declare their personal space. Others created circles ten feet in diameter. And what was additionally interesting was how people reacted to this very clear declaration of distance. Some were respectful of the tape, and others ignored it completely, invading the boundaries clearly delineated in the exercise. Some people can tolerate and even appreciate close physical contact, while others respond to this closeness with anxiety. And still for others, too much space triggers anxiety. Even the people we love the most are subject to changing space requirements. If one member of a couple enjoys or even requires close contact, and the other member only enjoys close contact occasionally, there will always be the tension of longing in the first member and anxiety in the second as they work out their personal space requirements. Often one member of the couple will fight with the other upon feeling his or her personal space has been invaded. Then, as the distance between the two grows, the more reluctant partner will suddenly feel more comfortable and may begin to pursue the other person with greater vigor, only to find anxiety rising as the more eager partner closes in to satisfy a need for intimacy. Rarely do both members of a couple enjoy the same personal space requirements, producing a continuing tension between invasion and yearning.

The three strongest fears that people in relationship experience with each other are fear of abandonment, fear of being dominated or controlled (which includes shame, guilt, and humiliation), and fear of being ignored. As a result of these fears, we try to manipulate every relationship into the level of intimacy with which we feel comfort. If the adjusted level of closeness matches the intimacy needs of those in our lives, there is little problem with the emotional interactions. However, most people have subtle differences in the intensity of intimacy they desire or can tolerate. As a result, once someone wants more closeness than the other can abide, the power struggle begins. The power struggle is really an indication that we are fearful of each other and that we are now trying to control our fear by controlling the behavior of our significant other.

CONCLUSION

Ultimately, our relationship with the world is a mirror of our relationship with our own unconscious and body. How we treat others is the mirror for how we treat ourselves, so whatever method we use to control our loved one is also the way in which we control ourselves. And typically, when we over-control or habitually control ourselves, our physical health may be affected. What we don't want to see, hear, say, feel, or express actually starts to affect those physical organs associated with that function, and resulting problems with eyesight, hearing, respiration, stomach and intestines, and sexual organs are very, very common. For this reason, experienced therapists pay close attention to the physical complaints of their clients as a way of determining what avenues of psychological expression are blocked. Learning to express the feelings that are associated with those malfunctioning organs begins to heal the body as well as the mind.

How we treat ourselves is the model for how we treat others, and the healing of our relationships begins with the healing of ourselves. An old preacher friend of mine once delivered a sermon on the Golden Rule, *treat others as you treat yourself.* After twenty-five years, I still remember his comment to the congregation: "I've seen how you treat yourselves. Please don't treat me that way. Learn to treat yourselves better!"

CHAPTER SIXTEEN
CONCLUSION

Is it possible that the world, and I mean the whole of the universe and nature, actually interacts with us in a personal and intimate way? For millennia, we have believed that God and the gods spoke to at least some of us, if not all of us, and gave instruction or inspiration or meted out punishment. And it was personal. As civilization has matured, we have come to view these influencing agents more as functions of physics, biology, and psychology and less as the workings of the divine.

The gods and goddesses of history have become the archetypes of science and psychology. Our superstitious anthropomorphizing of the patterns of nature has now evolved into a respect for the majesty, rhythm, and fractal designs of the cosmos, which are no less thrilling and terrifying, but perhaps a bit less personal.

But what about consciousness in this evolving human theology? How does our sense of consciousness inform our place in, and expectations of, the world? Let's face it, we do take the world personally. When the world appears to be working well, or to our advantage, we feel lucky or blessed. Those synchronous moments where we feel we are "in the zone" are sufficiently rare as to evoke a sense of magical good fortune to this seeming randomness of life. But something else seems to happen as we begin to embrace reality rather than fear it. We start to believe it has intention and purpose. Luck evolves into expectation and even predictability. Our hopes, perceptions, and actions begin to operate together, and we become less surprised when what we've wanted works out than when it doesn't. When the psyche is conflict-free, spirituality is much less magical and much more scientific. When the psyche is willing to allow all information about reality to reach awareness, our interactions with the world become consistent with the way the world actually *is*.

Let's suspend the moral and ethical aspects of the theory of karma and simply accept the idea of cause and effect. Let's look at Newton's third law of motion—for every action, there is an equal and opposite reaction—as a description of the dynamic mirror that reality affords awareness. As we begin to recognize the results of our own actions and attitudes, we can harness the mirror-like immediacy and symmetry of reality and benefit from grace and mercy rather than remain fixed in a battle with obstacle and suffering.

To every child the world is a chaotic, unpredictable, and mythic mess. But as we gain experience, wisdom, and mastery, we learn that the universe has both beautiful and harsh rules. However, the more we operate within the parameters of reality as it is, the better life works. Gravity and hard surfaces must be respected. The strengths and limitations of the human form must be respected. Everything that is alive is not your friend. We are not the victims of life, but we certainly are the subjects of life.

The I Ching describes the rhythmic patterns of life and how potentialities wax and wane; it is the wise and successful person who respects and harnesses the ebb and flow of reality's potentialities. These rhythms arise out of the quantum field as it interacts with consciousness, and we are specifically designed to intimately interface with these patterns.

The world is rhythmic and our bodies are the receivers.

Any discussion about the relationship of the individual with the nature of the universe inevitably leads to the philosophical/theological question of free will. If personality is pathological and predictable by design, biology dictates drives and instincts beyond our limited control, and the physics of relativity and quantum nature describe the patterned nature of the cosmos, free will, alas, seems to be an illusion. It's as though we are all caught in the current of the river of life, and because we are capable of swimming futilely against the current, we call this resistance "free will." All this struggle and strain to exert our "choice" lacks humor and perspective. Cultural instruction encourages us to divide our identity into our higher and baser selves, and urges us to control our baser selves for the good of humanity and for the good of our own spiritual growth. However, it appears that the very restriction of our natural self is what causes the corruptions and suffering of humanity.

The only people who seem to be true to their nature are the anti-social personalities, so we hold up their uninhibited actions as an example of what will happen if we express ourselves without inhibition, as though we are all psychopaths under the thin veneer of civilization.

It is time to stop using the worst of us to represent basic human nature. It makes us all afraid of ourselves.

Our basic spirit is playful, experimental, curious, sensitive, kind, loving, and compassionate. We abhor suffering that has no purpose, and we cheer for the good guys to defeat the evildoers. We root for the underdogs and pray for those who need help. This is the foundation of compassion, and the evolved human psyche has no need to restrict the expression of our higher self out of fear of being disapproved of or rejected.

So what does the integrated and evolved psyche look like? Here is a list that addresses a few of those qualities. The integrated mind:

- Is curious above all
- Is capable of accessing multiple points of view
- Values wisdom over control
- Possesses a healthy sense of humor devoid of cruelty
- Utilizes emotion as information
- Holds genuineness and authenticity as social goals
- Derives energy from truth and allows it to illuminate our path
- Appreciates both the complexity and the simplicity of the world
- Is committed to social justice
- Is committed to service
- Is committed to the cessation of suffering of all living beings
- Recognizes the greater consciousness of which we are all a part
- Is a catalyst for evolving humanity to a higher level of functioning and self-realization

To experience reality with accuracy, we must release the blocked aspects of ourselves, express the emotions they hold, and allow the information they contain to become part of our consciousness. This work involves pain. It requires us to face the unknown over and over again. It also involves the delight that comes with discovery. And it is the path through which we can liberate tremendous—indeed, infinite—stores of energy held hostage by our familial and societal training.

What once was a point of view that collapsed the majesty of life into the anticipated events we had been trained to see as children, commences to unfold into a stunningly ferocious and beautiful world filled with living beings who have forgotten who they are.

The interconnectedness of the life force is mostly ignored in science and anthropomorphized by the ultra religious, each side describing an aspect of the world, but incomplete in and of itself. For me, the world has intent: it pushes awareness, driving evolution and consciousness to reduce conflict and increase the stability of culture. As each stage of human development is fulfilled, consciousness is drawn into the next stage of mastery and unfolding. The stability of one stage leads to the exploration of the next stage.

Although we know that an acorn produces an oak tree, we have no clear outline for the end product of the human seed. We hold great teachers, like His Holiness the XIV Dalai Lama, as examples of evolutionary maturity, and yet he would hardly claim to be the final product of human evolution. What marvelous unfolding awaits us?

WILLIAM FINLEY SYMES, JR.

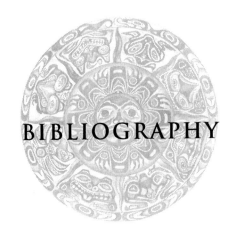

BIBLIOGRAPHY

Adler, G. (1967). *Studies in analytical psychology.* New York: Putnam for the C.G. Jung Foundation for Analytical Psychology.

Benson, G. (1972). *Then joy breaks through.* New York: Seabury Press.

Bosnak, R. (1988). *A little course in dreams.* Boston: Shambhala;

Cahalan, S. (2012). *Brain on fire: My month of madness.* New York: Free Press.

Campbell, J. (1972). *The hero with a thousand faces* (2d ed.). Princeton, N.J.: Princeton University Press.

Campbell, J. (1982). *Oriental mythology* (Reprinted. ed.). Harmondsworth [u.a.: Penguin Books.

Campbell, J. (1988). *Historical Atlas of World Mythology Vol. II: The Way of the Seeded Earth, Part 1: The Sacrifice.* New York: Harper & Row.

Campbell, J. (1988). *Historical Atlas of World Mythology, Vol. 1: The Way of the Animal Powers, Part 1, Mythologies of the Primitive Hunters and Gatherers.* New York: Perennial Library.

Campbell, J. (1989). *Historical atlas of world mythology Vol II: Way of the Seeded Earth, Part 2: Mythologies of the Primitive Planters - The Northern Americas.* New York: Harper & Row.

Campbell, J. (1989). *Historical atlas of world mythology. Volume II, the way of the seeded earth. Part 3, Mythologies of the primitive planters: The Middle and Southern Americas.* New York: Perennial Library.

Campbell, J. (1991). *Creative mythology.* New York: Arkana.

Campbell, J. (1991). *Historical Atlas of World Mythology, Vol. I: The Way of the Animal Powers, Part 2: Mythologies of the Great Hunt.* New York, NY: HarperCollins.

Campbell, J. (1991). *Occidental mythology.* Harmondsworth: Penguin Books.

Campbell, J. (1991). *Primitive mythology.* Harmondsworth: Penguin Books.

Campbell, J., & Abadie, M. (1974). *The mythic image.* Princeton, N.J.: Princeton University Press.

Campbell, J., & Moyers, B. (1988). *The power of myth.* New York: Doubleday.

Cashdan, S. (1999). *The witch must die: The hidden meaning of fairy tales.* New York: Basic Books.

Castaneda, C. (1968). *The teachings of Don Juan; a Yaqui way of knowledge.* Berkeley: University of California Press.

Castaneda, C. (1971). *A separate reality: Further conversations with Don Juan.* New York: Simon and Schuster.

Castaneda, C. (1972). *Journey to Ixtlan: The lessons of Don Juan.* New York: Simon and Schuster.

Castaneda, C. (1974). *Tales of power.* New York: Simon and Schuster.

Castaneda, C. (1977). *The second ring of power.* New York: Simon and Schuster.

Castaneda, C. (1981). *The eagle's gift.* New York: Simon and Schuster.

Castaneda, C. (1984). *The fire from within.* New York: Simon and Schuster.

Castaneda, C. (1987). *The power of silence: Further lessons of Don Juan.* New York: Simon and Schuster.

Castaneda, C. (1993). *The art of dreaming.* New York, NY: HarperCollins Pub.

Conze, E. (1973). *The perfection of wisdom in eight thousand lines and its verse summary.* Bolinas: Four Seasons Foundation.

Dhargyey, N., & Wallace, A. (1985). *A commentary on the Kalachakra Tantra.* Dharamsala: Library of Tibetan Works & Archives.

Erickson, M., & Haley, J. (1985). *Changing individuals.* New York, N.Y.: Triangle Press:.

Erickson, M., & Haley, J. (1985). *Changing couples.* New York, N.Y.: Triangle Press :.

Erikson, E. (1964). *Childhood and society* (2d ed.). New York: Norton.

Estes, C. (1992). *Women who run with the wolves: Myths and stories of the wild woman archetype.* New York: Ballantine Books.

Frankl, V. (1965). *The doctor and the soul, from psychotherapy to logotherapy,* (2d expanded ed.). New York: A. A. Knopf.

Frankl, V. (2006). *Man's search for meaning.* Boston: Beacon Press.

Franz, M. (1977). *Individuation in fairy tales.* Zürich: Spring Publications.

Franz, M. (1986). *On dreams and death: A Jungian interpretation.* Boston: Shambhala.

Franz, M. (1993). *The feminine in fairy tales* (Rev. ed., 1st Shambhala ed.). Boston: Shambhala.

Franz, M. (1995). *Shadow and evil in fairy tales* (Rev. ed.). Boston: Shambhala.

Franz, M., & Franz, M. (1996). *The interpretation of fairy tales* (Rev. ed.). Boston: Shambhala.

Franz, M., & Hillman, J. (1986). *Lectures on Jung's typology: The inferior function: The feeling function.* Dallas: Spring publications.

Freud, S. (1952). *Totem and taboo; some points of agreement between the mental lives of savages and neurotics.* New York: Norton.

Freud, S., & Crick, J. (1999). *The interpretation of dreams.* Oxford: Oxford University Press.

Freud, S., & Riviere, J. (1935). *A general introduction to psycho-analysis: A course of twenty-eight lectures delivered at the University of Vienna.* New York: Liveright Pub.

Gladwell, M. (2000). *The tipping point: How little things can make a big difference.* Boston: Little, Brown.

Gladwell, M. (2005). *Blink: The power of thinking without thinking.* New York: Little, Brown and.

Gladwell, M. (n.d.). *David and Goliath: Underdogs, misfits, and the art of battling giants.*

Gladwell, M. (n.d.). *Outliers: The story of success.*

Gorman, P. (1985). *How can I help?: Stories and reflections on service.* New York: Knopf.

Grimm, J., & Grimm, W. (1972). *The complete Grimm's fairy tales.* New York: Pantheon.

Guenther, H. (1959). *Jewel ornament of liberation.* London: Rider.

Guenther, H. (1975). *Kindly bent to ease us: From the Trilogy of finding comfort and ease = Ngal-gso skor-gsum.* Emeryville, Calif.: Dharma Pub.

Gyatso, G. (1992). *Clear light of bliss: A commentary to the practice of Mahamudra in Vajrayana Buddhism* (2nd ed.). London: Tharpa Publications.

Gyatso, G. (2001). *Heart of wisdom: A commentary to the Heart Sutra* (4th ed.). Ulverston: Tharpa.

Haley, J. (1973). *Uncommon therapy; the psychiatric techniques of Milton H. Erickson, M.D.* New York: Norton.

Haley, J. (1980). *Leaving home: The therapy of disturbed young people.* New York: McGraw-Hill.

Harding, M. (1965). *The "I" and the "not-I"; a study in the development of consciousness.* New York: [Bollingen Foundation; distributed by] Pantheon Books.

Hare, R. (1999). *Without conscience: The disturbing world of the psychopaths among us.* New York: Guilford Press.

Hillman, J. (1964). *Suicide and the soul.* New York: Harper & Row.

Hillman, J. (1975). *Re-visioning psychology.* New York: Harper & Row.

Hopkins, J. (1984). *Kindness, clarity, and insight.* Ithaca, N.Y., USA: Snow Lion Publications.

Hopkins, J. (1985). *The Klachakra tantra: Rite of initiation for the stage of generation : A commentary on the text of Kay-drup-ge-lek-b l-sang-b .* London: Wisdom Publications.

James, W. (2008). *The varieties of religious experience a study in human nature.* Waiheke Island: Floating Press.

Jaynes, J. (1976). *The origin of consciousness in the breakdown of the bicameral mind.* Boston: Houghton Mifflin.

Jung, C. (1933). *Modern man in search of a soul.* New York: Harcourt, Brace & World.

Jung, C. (1938). *Psychology and religion,.* New Haven: Yale University Press;.

Jung, C. (1959). *Aion: Researches into the phenomenology of the self* (2d ed.). Princeton. N.J.: Princeton University Press.

Jung, C. (1961). *Freud and psychoanalysis.* Princeton, N.J.: Princeton University Press.

Jung, C. (1968). *Psychology and alchemy* (2nd ed.). Princeton, N.J.: Princeton University Press.

Jung, C. (1969). *Psychology and religion: West and East* (2d ed.). Princeton, N.J.: Princeton University Press.

Jung, C. (1969). *The structure and dynamics of the psyche* (2d ed.). Princeton, N.J.: Princeton University Press.

Jung, C. (1970). *Civilization in transition* (2nd ed.). Princeton, N.J.: Princeton University Press.

Jung, C. (1970). *Psychiatric studies* (2d ed.). Princeton, N.J.: Princeton Univ. Press.

Jung, C. (1971). *The spirit in man, art, and literature*. Princeton, N.J.: Princeton University Press.

Jung, C. (1973). *Experimental researches*. Princeton, N.J.: Princeton University Press.

Jung, C. (1975). *The practice of psychotherapy: Essays on the psychology of the transference and other subjects* (2nd ed.). Princeton, N.J.: Princeton University Press.

Jung, C. (1976). *Psychological types* (A revision / ed.). Princeton, N.J.: Princeton University Press.

Jung, C. (1976). *Symbols of transformation: An analysis of the prelude to a case of schizophrenia* (2d ed.). Princeton, N.J.: Princeton University Press.

Jung, C. (1976). *The symbolic life: Miscellaneous writings*. Princeton, N.J.: Princeton University Press.

Jung, C. (1977). *Mysterium coniunctionis: An inquiry into the separation and synthesis of psychic opposites in alchemy* (2d ed.). Princeton, N.J.: Princeton University Press.

Jung, C. (1983). *Alchemical studies*. Princeton, N.J.: Princeton University Press.

Jung, C., & Campbell, J. (1976). *The portable Jung*. New York: Penguin Books.

Jung, C., & Franz, M. (1964). *Man and his symbols*. Garden City, N.Y.: Doubleday.

Jung, C., & Hull, R. (1966). *Two essays on analytical psychology* (2nd ed.). Princeton, N.J.: Princeton University Press.

Jung, C., & Hull, R. (1980). *The archetypes and the collective unconscious* (2nd ed.). Princeton, N.J.: Princeton University Press.

Jung, C., & Hull, R. (1981). *The development of personality*. Princeton, N.J.: Princeton University Press.

Jung, C., & Hull, R. (1982). *The psychogenesis of mental disease*. Princeton, N.J.: Princeton University Press.

Jung, C., & Shamdasani, S. (2009). *The red book = Liber novus*. New York: W.W. Norton &.

Jung, E., & Jung, E. (1985). *Animus and Anima*. Dallas, Tex.: Spring Publications.

Katz, M. (1992). *Dream yoga and the practice of natural light*. Ithaca, N.Y.: Snow Lion Publications.

Keirsey, D., & Bates, M. (1984). *Please understand me: Character and temperament types* (5th ed.). Del Mar, CA: Distributed by Prometheus Nemesis Book.

Keirsey, D., & Keirsey, D. (1998). *Please understand me II: Temperament, character, intelligence*. Del Mar, CA: Prometheus Nemesis.

Kolbert, E. (n.d.). *The sixth extinction: An unnatural history*.

Laing, R. (1967). *The politics of experience*. New York: Pantheon Books.

Latner, J. (1973). *The Gestalt therapy book; a holistic guide to the theory, principles, and techniques of Gestalt therapy developed by Frederick S. Perls and others*. New York: Julian Press.

Levine, S. (1977). *Grist for the mill*. Santa Cruz, Calif.: Unity Press.

Levitt, S., & Dubner, S. (2005). *Freakonomics: A rogue economist explores the hidden side of everything*. New York: William Morrow.

Lhalungpa, L. (1986). *Mah mudr : The quintessence of mind and meditation*. Boston: Shambhala.

Maslow, A. (1999). *Towards a psychology of being* (3.rd ed.). New York: John Wiley and Sons.

Masterson, J. (1972). *Treatment of the borderline adolescent; a developmental approach*. New York: Wiley-Interscience.

Masterson, J. (1976). *Psychotherapy of the borderline adult: A developmental approach*. New York: Brunner/Mazel.

Masterson, J. (1981). *The narcissistic and borderline disorders: An integrated developmental approach*. New York: Brunner/Mazel.

Masterson, J. (1983). *Countertransference and psychotherapeutic technique: Teaching seminars on psychotherapy of the borderline adult*. New York: Brunner/Mazel.

Masterson, J. (1988). *The search for the real self: Unmasking the personality disorders of our age*. New York: Free Press.

Masterson, J. (1989). *Psychotherapy of the disorders of the self: The Masterson approach*. New York: Brunner/Mazel.

Masterson, J. (2000). *The personality disorders: A new look at the developmental self and object relations approach : Theory, diagnosis, treatment*. Phoenix, Ariz.: Zeig, Tucker.

Masterson, J. (2004). *A therapist's guide to the personality disorders: The Masterson approach: A handbook and workbook*. Phoenix, AZ: Zeig, Tucker & Theisen.

Masterson, J. (2005). *The personality disorders through the lens of attachment theory and the neurobiologic development of the self: A clinical integration*. Phoenix, Ariz.: Zeig, Tucker & Theisen.

Masterson, J., & Costello, J. (1980). *From borderline adolescent to functioning adult: The test of time : A follow-up report of psychoanalytic psychotherapy of the borderline adolescent and family*. New York: Brunner/Mazel.

Matthews, W. (1997). *The mountain chant a Navajo ceremony*. Salt Lake City: University of Utah Press.

Miller, A. (1983). *For your own good: Hidden cruelty in child-rearing and the roots of violence*. New York: Farrar, Straus, Giroux.

Miller, A. (1984). *Thou shalt not be aware: Society's betrayal of the child* (American ed.). New York: Farrar, Straus, Giroux.

Miller, A. (1990). *The untouched key: Tracing childhood trauma in creativity and destructiveness*. New York: Doubleday.

Miller, A., & Ward, R. (1997). *The drama of the gifted child: The search for the true self* (Completely rev. & updated / ed.). New York: BasicBooks.

Miyamoto, M., & Harris, V. (1974). *A book of five rings*. New York: Overlook Press.

Moody, R. (1975). *Life after life: And Reflections on Life after life*. Carmel, N.Y.: Guideposts.

Moon, B. (1991). *An encyclopedia of archetypal symbolism*. Boston: Shambhala.

Myers, I., & Myers, P. (1980). *Gifts differing*. Palo Alto, CA: Consulting Psychologists Press.

Neumann, E. (1955). *The great mother; an analysis of the archetype*. New York: Pantheon Books.

Neumann, E. (1969). *Depth psychology and a new ethic*. New York: Published by G.P. Putnam's Sons for the C.G. Jung Foundation for Analytical Psychology.

Neumann, E. (1988). *The child structure and dynamics of the nascent personality*. London: Maresfield.

Newcomb, F., & Reichard, G. (1975). *Sandpaintings of the Navajo shooting chant*. New York: Dover Publications.

Niebuhr, H. (1941). *The meaning of revelation*. New York: Macmillan.

Niebuhr, H. (1960). *Radical monotheism and Western civilization*. Lincoln: University of Nebraska.

Paley, V. (1990). *The boy who would be a helicopter*. Cambridge, Mass.: Harvard University Press.

Peck, M. (1978). *The road less traveled: A new psychology of love, traditional values, and spiritual growth*. New York: Simon and Schuster.

Perls, F. (1973). *The gestalt approach and eyewitness to therapy: Fritz Perls*. Palo Alto, Calif.: Science and Behaviour Books.

Perls, F. (1975). *Gestalt is: A collection of articles about Gestalt therapy and living*. Moab, Utah: Real People press.

Perls, F., & Perls, F. (1973). *The gestalt approach & Eye witness to therapy*. Ben Lomond, Calif.: Science & Behavior Books.

Perls, F., & Stevens, J. (1971). *Gestalt therapy verbatim*. Toronto [etc.: Bantam Books.

Polster, E., & Polster, M. (1973). *Gestalt therapy integrated; contours of theory and practice,*. New York: Brunner/Mazel.

Progoff, I. (1975). *At a journal workshop: The basic text and guide for using the Intensive Journal*. New York: Dialogue House Library.

Rabjampa, L. (1979). *The four-themed precious garland: An introduction to Dzogchen, the great completeness*. Dharamsala: Library of Tibetan Works & Archives.

Reich, W. (1972). *Character analysis* (3d, enl. ed.). New York: Farrar, Straus and Giroux.

Reynolds, J. (1987). *The cycle of day and night: Where one proceeds along the path of the primordial yoga : An essential Tibetan text on the practice of Dzogchen* (2nd ed.). Barrytown, N.Y.: Station Hill Press.

Rhoton, J. (1995). *The three levels of spiritual perception: An oral commentary on The three visions (nang sum) of Ngorchen Konchog Lhundrub*. Boston: Wisdom Publication.

Ronson, J. (2011). *The psychopath test: A journey through the madness industry*. New York: Riverhead Books.

Ross, E. (1975). *Death: The final stage of growth*. Englewood Cliffs, N.J.: Prentice-Hall.

Ruiz, M. (1997). *The four agreements: A practical guide to personal freedom*. San Rafael, Calif.: Amber-Allen Pub.

S, C., & Chang, C. (1961). *Esoteric teachings of the Tibetan Tantra*. Lausanne, Switzerland: Falcon's Wing Press.

Sacks, O. (1985). *The man who mistook his wife for a hat and other clinical tales*. New York: Summit Books.

Sacks, O. (2007). *Musicophilia: Tales of music and the brain*. New York: Alfred A. Knopf.

Sahn, S. (1976). *Dropping ashes on the Buddha: The teaching of Zen master Seung Sahn*. New York: Grove Press: distributed by Random House.

Sahn, S. (2007). *Ten gates: The kong-an teaching of Zen master Seung Sahn* (Rev. and updated ed.). Boston: Shambhala.

Sakya Trizin. (1991). *The beautiful ornament of the three visions*. Ithaca, N.Y., USA: Snow Lion.

Shane, J. (1986). *The crystal and the way of light: Sutra, tantra, and dzogchen: The teachings of Namkhai Norbu*. New York: Routledge & Kegan Paul.

Shimano, E., & Levine, J. (1979). *Golden wind: Zen talks*. Tokyo, Japan: Japan Publications.

Simonton, O., & Simonton, S. (1978). *Getting well again: A step-by-step, self-help guide to overcoming cancer for patients and their families*. Los Angeles: J.P. Tarcher.

Singer, J. (1972). *Boundaries of the soul; the practice of Jung's psychology*. Garden City, N.Y.: Doubleday.

Singer, J. (1976). *Androgyny: Toward a new theory of sexuality*. Garden City, N.Y.: Anchor Press.

Slusser, G. (1986). *From Jung to Jesus: Myth and consciousness in the New Testament*. Atlanta, Ga.: J. Knox Press.

Smith, H. (1958). *The religions of man*. New York: Harper & Row.

Stevens, B. (1970). *Don't push the river (it flows by itself)*. Lafayette, Calif.: [Real People Press].

Stout, M. (2005). *The sociopath next door: The ruthless versus the rest of us*. New York: Broadway Books.

Tarthang-tulku. (1977). *Gesture of balance: A guide to awareness, self-healing, and meditation*. Emeryville, Calif.: Dharma Pub.

Tarthang-tulku. (1977). *Time, space, and knowledge: A new vision of reality*. Emeryville, Calif.: Dharma Pub.

Tendzin, O., & Holm, D. (1982). *Buddha in the palm of your hand*. Boulder: Shambhala.

Tharchin, L. (1987). *A commentary on guru yoga and offering of the mandala*. Ithaca, N.Y., USA: Snow Lion Publications.

Thathang Tulku. (1978). *Skillful means*. Berkeley, Calif.: Dharma Pub.

Thathang Tulku. (1981). *Hidden mind of freedom*. Berkeley, Calif.: Dharma Pub.

Tieger, P., & Tieger, B. (2007). *Do what you are: Discover the perfect career for you through the secrets of personality type* (4th ed.). New York: Little, Brown and.

Trungpa, C. (1970). *Meditation in action*. Berkeley: Shambala.

Trungpa, C. (1985). *Journey without goal: The tantric wisdom of the Buddha*. Boston: Shambhala.

Trungpa, C., & Baker, J. (1973). *Cutting through spiritual materialism,*. Berkeley: Shambhala.

Trungpa, C., & Baker, J. (1976). *The myth of freedom and the way of meditation.* Berkeley: Shambhala.

Trungpa, C., & Gimian, C. (1984). *Shambhala: The sacred path of the warrior.* Boulder, Colo.: Shambhala.

Walker, B. (1986). *The women's encyclopedia of myths and secrets.*

Waters, F. (1950). *Masked gods: Navaho and Pueblo ceremonialism.* Albuquerque, N.M.: University of New Mexico Press.

Watkins, M. (1976). *Waking dreams.* New York: Gordon and Breach.

Watts, A. (1957). *The way of Zen.* New York: Pantheon.

Watts, A. (1962). *The joyous cosmology; adventures in the chemistry of consciousness.* New York: Pantheon Books.

Weil, A. (1972). *The natural mind: A new way of looking at drugs and the higher consciousness.* Boston: Houghton Mifflin.

Weiss, B. (1988). *Many lives, many masters.* New York: Simon & Schuster.

Wilhelm, R. (1967). *The I ching; or, Book of changes.* ([3d ed.). Princeton, N.J.: Princeton University Press.

Zukav, G. (1979). *The dancing wu li masters: An overview of the new physics.* New York: Morrow.

CPSIA information can be obtained at www.ICGtesting.com
Printed in the USA
LVOW07s2316181215

467205LV00003B/3/P